ALSO BY RONALD C. WHITE, JR.

Lincoln's Greatest Speech:
The Second Inaugural

Liberty and Justice for All:
Racial Reform and the Social Gospel

An Unsettled Arena:
Religion and the Bill of Rights
editor, with Albright G. Zimmerman

Partners in Peace and Education
editor, with Eugene J. Fisher

American Christianity:
A Case Approach
with Garth Rosell and Louis B. Weeks

The Social Gospel:
Religion and Reform in Changing America
with C. Howard Hopkins

THE ELOQUENT PRESIDENT

RANDOM HOUSE
NEW YORK

THE ELOQUENT PRESIDENT

A PORTRAIT OF LINCOLN THROUGH HIS WORDS

Ronald C. White, Jr.

Published in the United States by Random House, an imprint of The Random House Publishing Group, a division of Random House, Inc., New York.

Random House and colophon are registered trademarks of Random House, Inc.

ISBN 0-7394-5668-7

Printed in the United States of America

Book design by Gretchen Achilles

For

JIM McPHERSON

teacher, historian, tennis partner,

friend

CONTENTS

CHRONOLOGY

1809	FEBRUARY 12	Born near Hodgenville, Kentucky
1816	DECEMBER	Family moves near Pigeon Creek, Indiana
1828	APRIL	Flatboat trip to New Orleans, Louisiana
1830	MARCH 15	Family moves near Decatur, Illinois, on Sangamon River
1831	MARCH	Leaves home and settles in New Salem, Illinois
1832	APRIL 21	Elected captain in Black Hawk War
1832	AUGUST 6	First attempt—unsuccessful—at political office in state legislature
1834	AUGUST	Elected to Illinois House of Representatives in Vandalia
1837	APRIL 15	Moves to Springfield; becomes law partner with John Stuart
1838	JANUARY 27	Address before the Young Men's Lyceum in Springfield
1842	NOVEMBER 4	Marries Mary Todd
1847	DECEMBER 6	Begins term in House of Representatives, in Washington, D.C.
1850	FEBRUARY 1	Son Edward, not quite four, dies of pulmonary tuberculosis
1854	OCTOBER 16	Speech at Peoria criticizing the Kansas-Nebraska Act revives political career
1856	FEBRUARY	Participates in forming Republican Party in Illinois
1858	JUNE 16	"House Divided" speech in Springfield

1858	AUGUST–OCTOBER	Debates Stephen A. Douglas in contest for U.S. Senate
1860	FEBRUARY 27	Delivers Cooper Union address in New York City
1860	MAY 18	Selected as Republican candidate for president
1860	NOVEMBER 6	Elected president of the United States
1861	FEBRUARY 11	Farewell Address at Springfield
1861	FEBRUARY 11–23	Speeches on the journey from Springfield to Washington
1861	FEBRUARY 18	Jefferson Davis inaugurated as provisional president of the Confederate States of America
1861	MARCH 4	Inaugurated as sixteenth president; First Inaugural Address
1861	APRIL 12–13	Fort Sumter attacked and surrenders
1861	APRIL 15	President Lincoln calls for seventy-five thousand volunteers to serve three months
1861	JULY 4	Message to Congress in Special Session
1861	JULY 21	Union defeat at the Battle of Bull Run
1862	FEBRUARY 20	Willie Lincoln, age eleven, dies at White House of typhoid fever
1862	AUGUST 22	Reply to Horace Greeley
1862	SEPTEMBER 2(?)	Meditation on the Divine Will
1862	SEPTEMBER 22	Lincoln announces preliminary emancipation proclamation
1862	DECEMBER 1	Annual message to Congress
1863	JANUARY 1	Emancipation Proclamation
1863	JULY 1–3	Battle at Gettysburg
1863	JULY 4	Victory at Vicksburg
1863	SEPTEMBER 3	Letter to the rally at Springfield
1863	NOVEMBER 19	Gettysburg Address
1864	APRIL 4	"Little Speech" to Albert G. Hodges

1864	JUNE 8	Nominated by the Republican (National Union) Party for second term
1864	SEPTEMBER 2	Gen. William Tecumseh Sherman captures Atlanta
1864	NOVEMBER 8	Wins second term as president by defeating George B. McClellan
1865	JANUARY 31	Thirteenth Amendment, abolishing slavery, proposed to the states
1865	MARCH 4	Second Inaugural Address
1865	APRIL 9	Robert E. Lee surrenders to Ulysses S. Grant at Appomattox
1865	APRIL 11	Last public speech
1865	APRIL 14–15	Shot by John Wilkes Booth at Ford's Theatre; dies at 7:22 A.M.

INDEX TO LINCOLN SPEECHES AND TEXTS

PROLOGUE

FROM ACROSS THE UNITED STATES—indeed, from around the world—people come day after day to see and to read Abraham Lincoln's words, carved on Indiana limestone, in the templed space of the Lincoln Memorial. I have asked persons in different parts of the nation to recall their feelings as they read the words of the Gettysburg Address and the Second Inaugural Address in their visit to the Lincoln Memorial, whether the visit was six months or ten years ago. Their responses have ranged from "deeply emotional" to "surprise" to "reverence." The reply I have heard most often: "awe."

But awe is not the same thing as understanding. This book is a journey of understanding into the development of Abraham Lincoln's eloquence during the four years he served as president in a nation transformed by the tragedy of civil war. His character was tested and displayed in purpose, suffering, resolve, and ultimately compassion in his speeches, annual messages to Congress, and public letters. Most historians and biographers have noted his rhetorical skills, but this has been more a grace note than a great contrapuntal theme.

The movement from awe to understanding is not a simple journey. In attempting to understand Lincoln's eloquence I found myself confronting a puzzle with many pieces. How did Lincoln, a person with so little formal education, become our most eloquent president? Why did he often stumble when attempting to speak extemporaneously? How are we to understand the lingering mystery of his long silences as president? What were his habits and methods of writing speeches? In an era of presidential speechwriters we need to ask, were these Lincoln speeches, or did others contribute? What was the place of religion in the form and content of his presidential rhetoric? How were Lincoln's speeches understood in his day? How did Lincoln's rhetoric undergird his political leadership as president?

Often we fail to remember how Lincoln regarded himself. We raise him up to the status of a literary figure and give less weight to his role as a speaker. To do so is to pay no attention to either his career or the political culture of his times. Lincoln's private secretaries, John G. Nicolay and John M. Hay, declared, "Nothing would have amazed him while he lived than to hear himself called a man of letters." If today's politicians are glued to their teleprompters because their speeches are written by others and meant to be read, Lincoln was attentive to the real audience crowded before him as he delivered speeches written by himself that were meant to be heard.[1]

IT MAY SURPRISE modern readers, many of whom have been instilled from childhood with the aura of the Lincoln myth, that Lincoln's artistry with words was not fully appreciated at the beginning of his presidency. J. G. Randall, the first academic historian to turn his full attention to Lincoln, observed, "For Americans of a later day it is interesting to note that Lincoln was not then regarded as a master of style."[2] Stump speaking, so people said, was not the same thing as the kind of communication Lincoln would be asked to do as president. Debates lasting more than three hours with Douglas, however popular they may have been in Illinois, did not prepare him for the kind of debates that would take place in Washington. His little speeches on the train trip from Springfield to Washington in February 1861 had not inspired but rather diminished expectations of Lincoln as a speaker.

How did Lincoln develop his rhetorical skills? Lincoln, the active politician, said little about his development as a speaker. I believe he did leave some rough drafts of a map, however, with some roads and intersections sketched in, which we will attempt to follow. Friends and colleagues have also left their observations tucked away in letters and diaries. To get at this question is to spend time with the private Lincoln who shut himself away to write and rewrite his most important speeches.

ACROSS THE YEARS Aristotle's *Treatise on Rhetoric* has continued to define the elements of excellent speaking. The ancient Greek philosopher characterized rhetoric as the art of persuasion: "A faculty of considering all the possible means of persuasion on every subject." He goes on to describe three modes of persuasion "furnished by the spoken word." First, "persuasion is achieved by means of moral character, when the speech shall have been spoken in such a way as to render the speaker worthy of confidence." Aristotle argued that *ethos* (ηθος), or credibility, was the most powerful means of persuasion. Personal character and the spoken word are inseparable. Second, "persuasion may come through the hearers, when they have been brought to a state of excitement under the influence of the speech." Aristotle, in his explanation of this principle, points to the effective speaker's ability to understand the thoughts and feelings of the audience to whom he is speaking. Third, "persuasion is effected through the speech itself when we have proved a truth or an apparent truth by means of persuasive arguments suitable to the case in question." This last principle focuses on the kinds of arguments the speaker brings to his speech.[3]

I do not think that Lincoln read Aristotle, but I have come to believe that Lincoln's rhetoric embodies the principles of the ancient Greek philosopher. I have found Aristotle's definitions helpful in analyzing Lincoln's rhetorical artistry. The narrative of Lincoln's eloquence is the stirring story of his increasing ability to employ "all the possible means of persuasion on every subject."

Each chapter in this book is a story of Lincoln's response to challenges and opportunities to state his political vision for a nation in the midst of Civil War. Some of Lincoln's statements are set pieces—two inaugural addresses, two messages to Congress. One is a hastily written public letter to Horace Greeley, quixotic New York newspaper editor, who challenged Lincoln's leadership on the war and the evils of slavery. Another is a speech Lincoln wanted to give in person to a huge Republican rally in his hometown of Springfield but that he sent instead to a close friend with an accompanying telegram: "Read it slowly." I have included a private musing, written for his eyes only, which was found only after his death but is a key to his last and greatest speech.

EVERY GENERATION has produced new editions of anthologies of Lincoln's speeches and writings. I have used several Lincoln anthologies in teaching Lincoln and the Civil War. These collections are valuable, but because of the brief introductions to the various speeches and letters, I found myself taking time in class to place the particular Lincoln speech in a broader historical context that would help students understand Lincoln's intentions more fully.

This portrait of Lincoln focuses on an even more fundamental but overlooked question: what are the relationships among Lincoln's speeches? Biographers and historians have asked about Lincoln's sources—Theodore Parker, Daniel Webster, Henry Clay—but by and large have not asked about Lincoln on Lincoln. In tracking Lincoln's rhetorical journey, I have discovered how closely interconnected his speeches are.

These speeches are like a string of pearls, each with its own size and coloration. Some are well-known gems. Other speeches, known in their own day, have receded from memory in our day, and are presented and interpreted here as important signposts both of Lincoln's political vision and of his rhetorical artistry. The contention that underlies this book is that Lincoln's speeches can be appreciated best not in splendid isolation from one another, but when they are seen together in all their shimmering beauty.

LINCOLN WROTE for the ear. Most politicians and academics write for the eye. Lincoln often spoke or whispered out loud before putting his Faber pencil to paper. He was fascinated by the sound of words. I contend that even his written communications, such as the conclusions of his annual messages to Congress, even when he knew they were to be read by clerks, contained the marks of his best oratory.

Lincoln's pattern was to speak or read his addresses slowly. The average person speaks at about 150 or 160 words per minute. Lincoln spoke 105 to 110 words per minute.[4] His slower speed was an aid to hearers, especially in an outdoor environment without the aid of the technology of loudspeakers.

Before starting this journey, may I suggest taking the time to hear the selection of Lincoln's words from each speech at the beginning of each chapter. Speak them aloud. Do so slowly, as Lincoln would have done. This simple exercise will be helpful preparation to enter more fully into a portrait of Lincoln's eloquence.

THE ELOQUENT PRESIDENT

This is the last photograph of Lincoln in Springfield. The photograph, by C. S. German, was taken on February 9, 1861, just two days before his departure for Washington. The new, heavy beard made the features of his face softer.

LIBRARY OF CONGRESS

CHAPTER ONE

"WITH A TASK BEFORE ME GREATER THAN . . . WASHINGTON"

FAREWELL ADDRESS AT SPRINGFIELD
FEBRUARY 11, 1861

My friends.

No one, not in my situation, can appreciate my feeling of sadness at this parting. To this place, and the kindness of these people, I owe every thing. Here I have been a quarter of a century, and have passed from a young to an old man. Here my children have been born, and one is buried. I now leave, not knowing when, or whether ever, I may return, with a task before me greater than that which rested upon Washington. Without the assistance of that Divine Being, who ever attended him, I cannot succeed. With that assistance I cannot fail. Trusting in Him, who can go with me, and remain with you and be every where for good, let us confidently hope that all will yet be well. To His care commending you, as I hope in your prayers you will commend me, I bid you an affectionate farewell.

ABRAHAM LINCOLN ARRIVED at the small brick Great Western Railway station in Springfield on February 11, 1861, prepared to travel to Washington and his inauguration as the sixteenth president of the United States. The day dawned cold and miserable, with intermittent rain dripping from the low-hanging clouds. Parked at the station was the Presidential Special, a train consisting of only two cars, an ordinary passenger coach and a baggage car, standing by to receive the president and his party. Both cars were painted a bright yellow. The grand locomotive—the L. M. Wiley, brasswork gleaming, with its huge balloon stack—hissed at the ready.

Lincoln had decided beforehand that he would offer no remarks, and the press had been so informed. After the many farewells of recent days, Lincoln believed there was no need for any more words. Newspaperman Henry Villard, a twenty-five-year-old German immigrant posted to Springfield in November by the *New York Herald* to report on Lincoln's daily activities after his election as president, captured a remarkable scene. "The President elect took his station in the waiting-room, and allowed his friends to pass by him and take his hand for the last time." Villard observed that Lincoln's "face was pale, and quivered with emotion so deep as to render him almost unable to utter a single word."[1]

The ringing of the engine bell alerted Lincoln that it was time to board the train. Mary Lincoln and the two younger boys, Willie and Tad, had originally planned not to depart for several days. However, Gen. Winfield Scott, general-in-chief of the U.S. Army, had suggested to Lincoln that Mary and the boys leave that evening and meet Lincoln in Indianapolis. General Scott, concerned for the president-elect's security, thought it would be safer for Lincoln if he was surrounded by his family. Robert, the Lincolns' oldest son, would travel with his father from Springfield.

As Lincoln stepped out onto the platform, he found himself surrounded by a crowd of about one thousand of his fellow citizens. Friends and neighbors crowded the platform and each side of the festively decorated train. These friends and fellow townspeople had come to say their good-byes. Despite his publicly announced intention not to speak, the crowd thronging around the rear platform encouraged their neighbor to offer some remarks.

Responding to these requests, Lincoln, after entering the second of the two cars, appeared on the rear platform of the train. He removed his beaver hat and asked for silence. He paused, struggling to contain his feelings, gathering himself to give a speech he had not intended to give.

BEFORE LEAVING SPRINGFIELD, Abraham Lincoln had already resolved to confine his speaking as president to a few major occasions

Lincoln arrived at the Great Western Railway station on February 11, 1861. Met by a crowd of one thousand Springfield residents, Lincoln offered farewell remarks.

ABRAHAM LINCOLN PRESIDENTIAL LIBRARY

when he would have adequate time to prepare. In the three months since his election, as the storm clouds of war darkened, he had excused himself again and again from speaking about any of his positions or future policies. He did not want to say something that could be misinterpreted by foe or friend.

But how could he keep silent on this morning? Caught off guard, Lincoln spoke briefly in an uncharacteristically personal manner to friends and neighbors. Some who were present had known him for twenty years or more. Lincoln would speak only 152 words, but his words touched his audience in Springfield profoundly. In the poignancy of this moment—leaving the place where he had lived for half his life—Lincoln bared his spirit in deeply emotive language.

His farewell words at Springfield did not remain in Springfield. His remarks were printed in newspapers the next day and in *Harper's*

Weekly Magazine. Citizens in Albany, Fort Wayne, Dover, Trenton, Providence, and countless small cities and towns were eager to know more about this gangly rail splitter from the West who was about to become their president.

ABRAHAM LINCOLN had been saying his farewells to family and friends over the past weeks. As the time for their departure drew nearer, Mary Lincoln invited groups of friends to their home. These gatherings included a children's party. She wrote out the invitations to the children, cards that would be cherished by their recipients well into the twentieth century.[2]

On January 30, Lincoln slipped away from the persistent stream of reporters and office seekers to offer a special good-bye. He traveled by train and by horse and buggy to Farmington, a small remote community in Coles County, in southern Illinois. He wanted to see his aging stepmother, Sarah Bush Lincoln.

Lincoln's mother, Nancy Hanks Lincoln, had died in 1818. Sarah, a widow, had come from Kentucky as Thomas Lincoln's new wife. Her great gift was to bring nurture and order to the whole family. She gave to young Abraham, a boy of ten, love and encouragement. Sarah, now seventy-three, when hearing of her stepson's nomination, feared that if he was elected, something awful would happen to him.[3]

As he retraced his route to Springfield, Lincoln's stepmother traveled with him as far as Charleston. (In March 1830, a young Lincoln had driven a yoke of oxen pulling one of the wagons in the family move from Spencer County, Indiana, to this area of Illinois.) At an evening reception on January 31, everyone was eager to hear Lincoln speak, but he declined the invitation. Lincoln did join in with reminiscence and stories of his simpler days with folk who had known him since he was barely twenty-one.

RETURNING TO SPRINGFIELD, Lincoln requested privacy. A notice appeared each day that week in the *Illinois State Journal:* "The present week being the last that Mr. Lincoln remains at Springfield, and it being indispensable that he should have a portion of time to himself, he will see visitors only at his office, No. 4, Johnson building, from 3½ to 5 o'clock, P.M., each day."[4]

Lincoln had to conclude many personal and family matters. He had rented the family home at the northeast corner of Eighth and Jackson Streets to Lucian Tilton, the retired owner of the Wabash Railroad, for $350 a year. The Lincolns sold much of their furniture. They gave their dog, Fido, to a neighbor. Mary burned heaps of old letters and papers in the rear alley.

A MAJOR TASK was the preparation of his inaugural address. Gov. John Wood had offered Lincoln offices on the second floor in the Illinois State House, in the center of the public square. The governor did not need the offices, as the Illinois state legislature was not in session. Lincoln accepted gladly. He set up an office in the State House and established John G. Nicolay, a former journalist and clerk to the Illinois secretary of state, as his secretary and one-man transition committee. Lincoln knew his dingy law offices would not do as a place to work on his address or to greet visitors.

Lincoln began his research for his inaugural address shortly after his election. He wanted plenty of time for research, writing, and rewriting. On November 13, only one week to the day after his election, Lincoln borrowed from the Illinois State Library the *Statesman's Manual of the Constitution of the United States,* volumes I and II. Lincoln refreshed his memory about the nullification controversy of 1832 and President Andrew Jackson's proclamation against nullification. Lincoln was looking for precedents or patterns. He returned the books on December 29.[5]

Late in December, with the impending convening of the Illinois state legislature on January 7, it became necessary to give up the second-floor space on the southeast corner of the State House. Joel Johnson, owner of an office building, offered Lincoln two offices on the second floor of Johnson's Building, across the street from the Chenery House.

By January the torrent of old friends, advisers, newspaper reporters, and office seekers pouring into Springfield became relentless. Lincoln could discover no privacy by day or night.

He next accepted an offer from Clark Moulton Smith, his brother-in-law, to use a room on the third floor of his store as his writing space. Lincoln found the privacy he was seeking, as the room could be entered only through the private office of Smith, in the rear of his storeroom. Here Lincoln closeted himself for the serious work of writing. Day after day he wrote and revised at an old merchant's desk with a slanting front and plenty of pigeonholes.[6]

Later in January, Lincoln asked William H. Herndon, his law partner, to supply him with copies of two speeches he much admired. Lincoln had first read Daniel Webster's "Reply to Robert Hayne" when he was a young man living in New Salem. In 1830, after Senator Hayne of South Carolina had defended the right of nullification on the floor of the Senate, Senator Webster of Massachusetts replied to him, closing with the memorable words "Liberty and Union, now and forever, one and inseparable." Lincoln also asked for a copy of Sen. Henry Clay's speech in support of the Compromise of 1850, an affirmation at the end of Clay's life of his love of the Union. Clay of Kentucky was, in the words of Lincoln's eulogy of "the Great Compromiser," delivered on July 6, 1852, "my beau ideal of a statesman." Lincoln said that "Mr. Clay's eloquence" proceeded "from great sincerity and a thorough conviction, in the speaker of the justice and importance of his cause." The man from Springfield could have been describing his own eloquence nearly ten years later.[7]

A FOURTH VENUE for writing developed as an unexpected consequence of the arrival of a visiting artist. Sculptor Thomas D. Jones arrived in Springfield from Cincinnati on Christmas Day at 6 P.M. Jones, having already executed busts of Henry Clay, Gen. Zachary Taylor, and Gen. Winfield Scott, came with letters of commendation from two of his most recent subjects, Salmon P. Chase and Thomas Ewing. On December 26, Lincoln met Jones at 9 A.M. and agreed to pose for a bust.

Within a couple of days Jones set up his modeling stand and clay in a temporary studio on the top floor of the St. Nicholas Hotel. Jones was seeking a place with the best light and as far removed as possible from the increasing noise of the comings and goings of preinaugural Springfield. Lincoln agreed to come each morning for a series of one-hour sittings.[8]

Lincoln used this time to read his growing daily mail and to write the speeches for his journey to Washington. Jones described Lincoln as writing while sitting with his legs crossed, "using one knee as a writing table." Lincoln wrote with a small portfolio and ample amounts of writing paper. Jones delighted in sharpening Lincoln's Fabers, an excellent brand of pencil that Lincoln used for his writing and rewriting. Jones observed that Lincoln always had copies of his own published speeches next to him for ready reference. From time to time Lincoln would ask the sculptor if he could read the latest version to him. Lincoln said he believed he could edit best by both hearing and reading a speech. He was intensely interested in the sound of the words.

Jones, who would remain in Springfield until the summer to complete his work, thought the emerging bust a great achievement. Lincoln joked that Jones was producing his "mud head." Jones believed that photographs of Lincoln always failed to portray "the ideas of the *man.*" As the day for Lincoln's departure approached, Jones asked his subject for "the kindness to tell what you think of the result thus far." Lincoln laid down his writing materials, examined the bust for a considerable time, and finally replied, "I think it looks very much like the critter."[9]

ON WEDNESDAY, February 6, the Lincolns said farewell in a formal levee, or reception, in the first-floor parlors of their home. An invitation was printed in the *Illinois State Journal* on Tuesday and Wednesday, stating, "Mr. Lincoln will be pleased to receive his friends on Wednesday evening, at his residence."[10] Lincoln did not restrict the reception to special associates or political allies, but extended an open invitation to "his friends." Over seven hundred guests, many of them waiting twenty to thirty minutes to get to the front door, joined an evening of mixed merriment and sadness that lasted until midnight.

Anna Ridgely, a nineteen-year-old girl who attended the reception, recorded her varied reactions to Lincoln in her diary. She was the daughter of Nicholas H. Ridgely, a prominent banker and one of the wealthiest persons in Springfield. Ridgely was a former Whig who became a Democrat. He did not vote for Lincoln in the presidential election. After Lincoln's election, Anna confided to her diary, "We were disappointed, for we had hoped that such a man as he, without the great knowledge of state affairs, without any polish of manners, would not be sent to be the representative of this great nation."[11]

Now, three months later, she and her family came to the Lincoln home for the farewell reception. Having earlier expressed her displeasure with Lincoln's election, she now wrote in her diary her impressions of Lincoln. "Mr. L really looked handsome to me his whiskers are a great improvement and he has such a pleasant smile I could not but admire him."[12]

ON HIS FINAL DAY in Springfield, Sunday, February 10, Abraham Lincoln wandered down to his law office, at 105 South Fifth Street, to meet Herndon. Entering their second-floor office, Lincoln threw himself down on the old sofa one last time. After reminiscing about old times and talking about how to complete unfinished legal business, Lincoln made a request that the signboard that swung on rusty hinges at the foot of the stairway should stay. He said to Billy, "Let it hang there undisturbed." Lincoln added, "If I live I'm coming back some time, and then we'll go right on practicing law as if nothing had ever happened."[13]

Lincoln and Herndon went out into the narrow hallway and down the stairs. Lincoln lingered for a last look at the old quarters. Then, as Herndon related it, Lincoln told him that "the sorrow of parting from his old associations was deeper than most persons would imagine." He told his law partner that he was experiencing of late a "feeling which had become irrepressible that he would never return alive."[14]

ON SUNDAY EVENING Lincoln roped the family trunks at the Chenery House, on the northeast corner of Fourth and Washington. He took some Chenery House cards, turned them over, and wrote, A. LINCOLN, EXECUTIVE MANSION, WASHINGTON. The luggage was now ready for transportation to the train station the next morning, to be placed on the special train for the trip to Washington.

Lincoln had asked his friend William H. Bailhache, one of the owners of the *Illinois State Journal*, to print copies secretly of his inaugural address. This first draft, upon which Lincoln wrote "First Edition" at the top of the first page, numbered eight pages. Lincoln had multiple copies printed because he had decided to seek the criticism and suggestions of some old friends and a new colleague. He placed the copies of his inaugural address, plus the speeches he intended to give on the trip to Washington, in a black oilcloth handbag. He gave the bag to his son Robert, entrusting the speeches to his son's safekeeping on the train and during visits to the various cities in the days ahead.

Rising early the next morning, Lincoln left the Chenery House at 7:30 A.M. Abraham, Mary, and their three boys traveled the few blocks by carriage to the Great Western station located at Tenth and Monroe Streets.

ABRAHAM LINCOLN began his farewell by giving voice to his feelings:

> *My friends—No one, not in my situation, can appreciate my feeling of sadness at this parting.*

Lincoln, whose personality usually prompted him to conceal rather than to reveal his emotions, now spoke openly of his feelings as he prepared to leave this place and these people. The sadness etched in his face was now voiced in his words. In thirteen succinct words, Lincoln offered heartfelt appreciation to a city and to his neighbors and friends.

> *To this place, and the kindness of these people, I owe every thing.*

Lincoln had lived and worked for twenty-four years in Springfield. Some in the crowd surely reflected on the contrast between Lincoln's arrival in the spring of 1837 and his departure now in the winter of 1861. It would not be surprising if Lincoln remembered his coming, even as he spoke of his going.

IN THE WINTER of 1837, a joint session of the state legislature had voted to relocate the state capital from the southern Illinois town of Vandalia to the more central location of Springfield. Lincoln had been part of the campaign for that change. He intended to make the new capital his home.

Lincoln hardly looked the part of a conquering hero when he arrived in Springfield on a borrowed horse on April 15, 1837. He was barely twenty-eight when he entered the general store of A. Y. Ellis & Company on the town square. Inquiring of one of the proprietors, Joshua Speed, about the cost of a mattress and bedding, Lincoln confessed that he did not have the money for the purchase. Speed offered to share his bed with Lincoln in the upstairs bedroom. Lincoln brought in all his worldly possessions, which were contained in two saddlebags. As he came back down the winding stairs, Lincoln announced, "Well, Speed, I'm moved."[15]

Springfield in 1837 was an unprepossessing town of twelve or thirteen hundred inhabitants. Most people lived in small frame houses. There was an occasional commanding new house, just as there remained a plain cabin here and there built by early settlers. Small stores lined the central square.

The day that Lincoln arrived, the *Illinois State Journal* announced that "J. T. Stuart and A. Lincoln, Attorneys and Counsellors at Law, will practice, conjointly, in the Courts of this Judicial Circuit. Office No. 4 Hoffman's Row, upstairs."[16] The young lawyer, from the beginning, was fortunate to be associated with Stuart, one of the most successful lawyers in Springfield. From day one Lincoln was the beneficiary of a full practice.

LINCOLN ELABORATED BRIEFLY on what he meant by *every thing.* He had lived in Springfield *a quarter of a century.* This was half a lifetime in the middle of the nineteenth century. Although one day shy of fifty-two, in what we would call middle age, Lincoln described himself as one who had

> *passed from a young to an old man*

He recognized his family by invoking the images of birth and death.

> *Here my children have been born, and one is buried.*

He did not name the members of his family. Eleven years earlier, he and Mary had buried their son Edward. He had traveled a long way in terms of family and friends from the awkward bachelor who rode into town in 1837.

Lincoln moved from past to present with the words *I now leave.* He added to an already emotion-laden moment heartfelt words that spoke to the immensity of the task that lay ahead.

> *not knowing when, or whether ever, I may return*

Why did Lincoln offer these words? What do they mean? After Lincoln's assassination, people would look back on these words and ask whether Lincoln had a premonition of his own death. Since his election he had been receiving death threats. The words do seem sad, if not morose. He had expressed something of the same sentiment to Herndon.

> *with a task before me greater than that which rested upon Washington*

This phrase leapt out of Lincoln's remarks. So far he had steadfastly refrained from speaking about the task that lay ahead. He had determined to speak about those responsibilities only after he had delivered his inaugural address in Washington. Now, in the midst of spontaneous remarks about community and family, he inserted what could sound like an overconfident comment about his own understanding of his task.

Lincoln, as a young boy, had developed a reverence for George Washington, encouraged by reading Parson Weems's *Life of George Washington.* Now he compared his task to that of the renowned Father of His Country. The audience may have wanted to hear more. But Lincoln left his comparison to Washington right there.

WE CANNOT LEAVE it there. In contemplating Lincoln's last speech in Springfield, we are compelled to return to Abraham Lincoln's first speech in Springfield. We do so to sense the full impact of Lincoln's claim,

> *with a task before me greater than that which rested upon Washington*

As Lincoln was settling into his new hometown in the summer and fall of 1837, he was invited to speak to the Young Men's Lyceum in Springfield in January 1838. The Young Men's Lyceum was organized in 1833, and by 1836 had become a prominent cultural presence in the community. A central opportunity offered by the Young Men's Lyceum was for young men to exhibit their rhetorical skills.

Lincoln rose to the occasion with grand but sometimes long-winded oratory. The twenty-eight-year-old Lincoln, in an address called "The Perpetuation of Our Political Institutions," offered his best thoughts and rhetoric on the past, present, and future of the experiment in republican government. This address has been endlessly interpreted for clues about Lincoln's understanding of himself as an aspiring young leader.[17] In the light of the farewell remarks in February 1861, we do well to listen to parts of the speech delivered twenty-three years earlier.

Lincoln began by praising the Founders with rhetorical flourish. He evoked the heritage handed down to his generation.

> *We find ourselves under the government of a system of political institutions, conducing more essentially to the ends of civil and religious liberty, than any of which the history of former times tells us. We, when mounting the stage of existence, found ourselves the legal inheritors of these fundamental blessings. We toiled not in the acquirement or establishment of them—they are a legacy bequeathed to us, by a once hardy, brave, and patriotic, but now lamented and departed race of ancestors.*[18]

If we hear the idealism of the young Lincoln, his soaring rhetoric often contained more words than were necessary. Thus, *than any of which the history of former times tells us.* Instead of the spare, clean, one-syllable words that became a hallmark of the mature Lincoln, in the address to his fellow young men of the Lyceum, he offered: *We, when mounting the stage of existence.*

Lincoln's point in sketching the establishment of the nation's political institutions was to emphasize the contrast between the quite different tasks separating the founding generation from the present generation, who were the heirs of the noble work and sacrifice of Washington and Jefferson and their cohorts.

> *Their's was the task (and nobly they performed it) to possess themselves, and through themselves us, of this goodly land; and to uprear upon its hills and its valleys, a political edifice of liberty and equal rights.*[19]

If a major theme was all praise to the Founders, an accompanying idea was the role of Lincoln and his generation just now coming into their maturity. Their task was much more limited compared to the Founders'.

> *. . . 'tis ours only, to transmit these, the former, unprofaned by the foot of the invader; the latter, undecayed by the lapse of time, and untorn by usurpation—to the latest generation that fate shall permit the world to know.*[20]

Tucked away inside Lincoln's soaring language we can hear a plaintive sadness. Speaking in 1838, fifty years after the election of George Washington as the first president of the new nation, Lincoln believed that nearly all of the great work of nation building had already been accomplished. Rather than builders, Lincoln and his generation were given the subsidiary role of transmitters.

Lincoln did recognize that there remained the task of defending these hard-won liberties. An immediate context for Lincoln's remarks was an outbreak of mob violence that had *pervaded the country, from New England to Louisiana.* Thus the danger, Lincoln said, would not come from *some transatlantic military giant,* but rather from foes and forces that *must spring up amongst us.* In words that have been remembered down through the years, Lincoln exclaimed, *If destruction be our lot, we must ourselves be its author and finisher. As a nation of freemen, we must live through all time, or die by suicide.*[21]

Lincoln concluded with melancholy and hope. His fascination with both history and memory taught him that *nearly every adult male had been a participator in some of* the scenes of the American Revolution. Consequently, in the first decades of the nineteenth century a *living history was to be found in every family.* Now, by 1838, Lincoln observed, *those histories are gone.* Employing the figure that those courageous forebears were *a fortress of strength,* Lincoln declared that *what invading foemen could* never do, *the silent artillery of time* has done; *the leveling of its walls.*[22]

The recollection of Lincoln's first address in Springfield helps place his last words in Springfield in broader context. At twenty-eight, Lincoln had spoken of the lesser role of his own generation in relation to the giants of the revolutionary generation, of whom George Washington stood in the lead. As a young man he knew he was standing at the end of the revolutionary generation now being carried away by *the silent artillery of time.* Now, by his own reckoning an *old man* as he offered his farewell remarks at Springfield in 1861, by some unsearchable fate or providence he was being summoned to *a task . . . greater than . . . Washington.* We can now see that these words were not boastful or audacious. Lincoln offered them with a sense of an appointment with destiny.

EVEN THOUGH LINCOLN was speaking extemporaneously, he organized his thoughts in sentences with parallel structures.

To this place,	*and the kindness of these people . . .*
Here I have been a quarter of a century,	*and have passed from a young to an old man.*
Here my children have been born,	*and one is buried.*
To His care commending you,	*as I hope in your prayers you will commend me . . .*

For Lincoln the speaker, parallel sentences became a way that he arranged his ideas. For the audience, they provided a structure both to hear and to remember. But their purpose was far more than functional. In Lincoln's hands and voice they became a pattern that was coupled with an almost metered cadence. They were a mostly invisible symmetry that provided a musical rhythm to Lincoln's words.

LINCOLN CONCLUDED his remarks by invoking the ubiquity of God.

> *Without the assistance of that Divine Being, who ever attended him, I cannot succeed. With that assistance I cannot fail. Trusting in Him, who can go with me, and remain with you and be every where for good, let us confidently hope that all will yet be well. To His care commending you, as I hope in your prayers you will commend me . . .*

He devoted 63 of his 152 words to sketching in the omnipresence of God.

Many politicians, especially those on a national stage, quickly adapt to the roles they must play in a fast-paced political life. Central to their roles are the numerous speeches and remarks they are asked to give. Today it has become commonplace for politicians across the political spectrum to invoke religion by concluding addresses with "God bless America." Many commentators have noted Lincoln's religious language, but have usually accounted for it by assigning it to the role of a politician speaking in an era when Christian faith was pervasive. Religious sensibilities were central to the Whig tradition and party, in which Lincoln grew to political manhood. Any carefully prepared speech often tapped into those sensibilities in an attempt to connect with a largely Protestant audience.

But this speech was not prepared. This fact heightens our curiosity about the prominent place Lincoln gives both to the presence of God and the practice of prayer. Even in these brief remarks Lincoln goes deeper and broader than any invocation of "God bless America" at the end of a modern speech.

The God that Lincoln appealed to was a God who acts in history. This God, who *attended* George Washington in the past, is able to *go* with Abraham Lincoln to Washington in the present, and can *remain* with Lincoln's friends in Springfield in the future. This God was more than the creative force invoked by Thomas Jefferson.

If God was present in history, Lincoln affirmed all these interactions through the practice of prayer.

> *To His care commending you, as I hope in your prayers you will commend me . . .*

In terms of style, this marvelous phrase was an example of Lincoln's penchant for parallel structures. Lincoln reached for prayer as the invisible connective tissue that would bind him to those he was about to leave. His words about prayer were not passive platitudes but instead a call to action in his time of need.

LINCOLN'S REMARKABLE ABILITY to bond with his audience was captured in their response. Villard, in his description, reported,

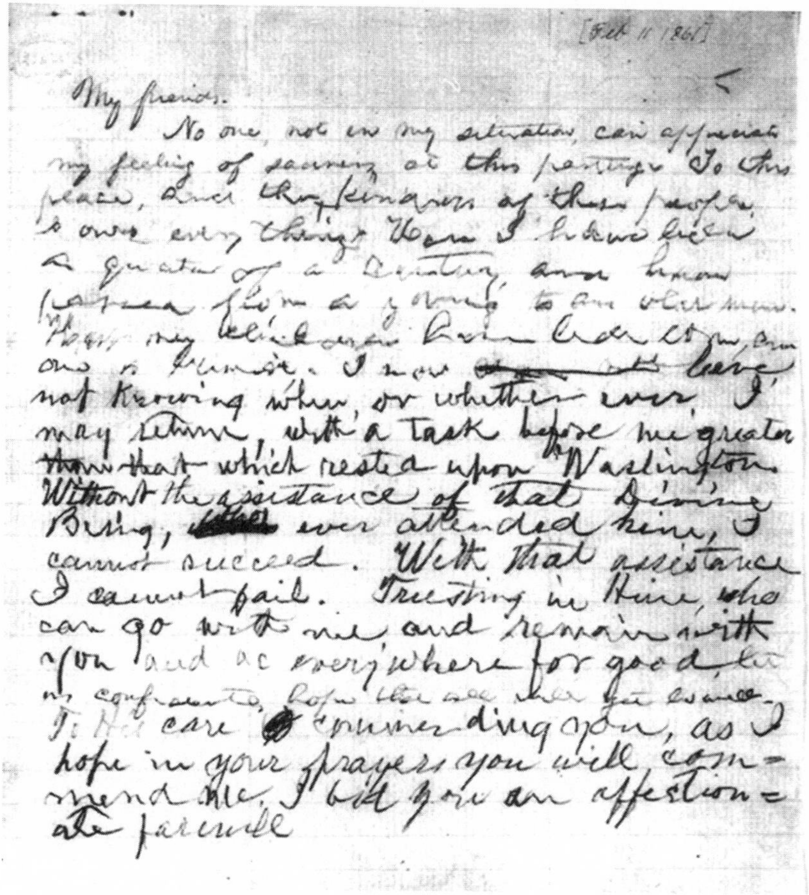

[Feb 11 1861]

My friends.

No one, not in my situation, can appreciate my feeling of sadness at this parting. To this place, and the kindness of these people, I owe every thing. Here I have lived a quarter of a century, and have passed from a young to an old man. Here my children have been born, and one is buried. I now leave, not knowing when, or whether ever, I may return, with a task before me greater than that which rested upon Washington. Without the assistance of that Divine Being, who ever attended him, I cannot succeed. With that assistance I cannot fail. Trusting in Him, who can go with me, and remain with you and be every where for good, let us confidently hope that all will yet be well. To His care commending you, as I hope in your prayers you will commend me, I bid you an affectionate farewell

Shortly after Lincoln's departure from Springfield, he began to write out his farewell remarks. Struggling to write on a moving train, at the beginning of the fifth sentence Lincoln handed the paper to his secretary, John G. Nicolay, and dictated the rest of his address.

LIBRARY OF CONGRESS

"Towards the conclusion of his remarks himself and the audience were moved to tears." His exhortation to pray elicited choked exclamations of "We will do it, we will do it." As Lincoln turned to reenter the cars, three cheers were given, and a few seconds afterward the train moved slowly out of sight of the silent gathering.[23]

AS LINCOLN TOOK his seat in the flat-roofed passenger car, he was beset immediately by newspaper correspondents—Villard; Edward L. Baker, editor and co-owner of the *Illinois State Journal* in Springfield; and Henry M. Smith of the *Chicago Tribune*—who wanted to ask him questions about the speech, which had come as a complete surprise to all three. In response, Lincoln sat down in a coach seat and attempted to write down what he had said. The effects of a moving train, and perhaps a hand swollen by countless handshakes, made the task difficult. His handwriting became less legible as the train picked up speed. At the beginning of the fifth sentence, immediately after the words *I now*, Lincoln handed the paper to his young secretary, Nicolay, who took up the task of writing. Lincoln dictated what he remembered saying.

Meanwhile, unbeknownst to Lincoln, a reporter for the *Illinois State Journal*, not expecting a speech, had hurriedly written down his words of farewell. This version was printed the next day, February 12, 1861.[24] (See Appendix 1.)

Villard, the only Eastern correspondent on the train as it departed Springfield, said that he "prevailed on Mr. Lincoln, immediately after starting to write it out for me on a 'pad.' " The newspaper correspondent sent this version "over the wires from the first telegraph station." Though he was employed by the *New York Herald* (whose editor, James Gordon Bennett, was antagonistic to Lincoln), Villard's stories about Lincoln, by prior agreement, would be circulated by the Associated Press to many newspapers throughout the country.

Villard did not publish until 1904 his account of his conversation with Lincoln and how he came to get the transcript of the address. It seems unlikely that Lincoln would have written down the address a second time. Villard said that he once had the penciled version of the address in his possession but lost it during the Civil War.[25]

AS HE SAID good-bye, Lincoln combined sad reminiscence with confident hope. He built on a rhetorical structure of parallelisms that came to life in moving, metered cadence. The rational lawyer here revealed rather than concealed a fuller range of his emotions as he spoke

The backdrop for the statue that honors Abraham Lincoln in the Washington National Cathedral is the complete text of his Farewell Address at Springfield.

DONOVAN MARKS/WASHINGTON NATIONAL CATHEDRAL

of family and community. The onetime skeptic here spontaneously invoked the omnipresence of God in language that would foreshadow Lincoln's deepening religious faith as president.

Lincoln's neighbor and good friend James C. Conkling captured some of the feeling of the audience's response to Lincoln's farewell remarks. The next day Conkling wrote to his son Clinton, a good friend of Robert Lincoln. Conkling described the emotions both of "Mr. Lincoln" and of the crowd. Of the crowd, the elder Conkling wrote, "Many eyes were filled to overflowing." Of Mr. Lincoln, his "breast heaved with emotion and he could scarcely command his feelings sufficiently to commence."[26]

The *Illinois State Journal,* a supporter of Lincoln through the years, wrote of the special quality of Lincoln's remarks. Edward Baker, editor of the *Journal,* was a personal and political friend of Lincoln who was invited to accompany the president-elect on the presidential train. In the next day's issue, the *Journal* opined, "We have known Mr. Lincoln for many years; we have heard him speak upon a hundred different occasions; but we never saw him so profoundly affected, nor did he ever utter an address which seemed to us so full of simple and touching eloquence."[27]

ABRAHAM LINCOLN'S FAREWELL ADDRESS at Springfield prefigures his developing and expanding eloquence as president. Delivered extemporaneously, these words reveal Lincoln's power with words at a pivotal, transitional moment in his life. Lincoln's impromptu words while still president-elect are the first signpost of a journey pointing to an expanding eloquence that would serve to advance Lincoln's leadership in his presidency.

Lincoln's eloquence was quickly to be tested in the twelve-day journey from Springfield to Washington. He had spoken to friends in Springfield; he would be speaking to strangers in Indianapolis and Pittsburgh and New York and Philadelphia. In the days that lay ahead eager eyes and ears would be anxious to take the measure of the president-elect. What would he say about the impending crisis of civil war and his vision for America? And how would he say it?

CHAPTER TWO

"THIS, HIS ALMOST CHOSEN PEOPLE"

SPEECHES AND REMARKS
TRAIN TRIP FROM SPRINGFIELD TO WASHINGTON
FEBRUARY 11–23, 1861

I do not expect, upon this occasion, or on any occasion, till after I get to Washington, to attempt any lengthy speech.

ADDRESS AT INDIANAPOLIS, FEBRUARY 11, 1861

I shall be most happy indeed if I shall be an humble instrument in the hands of the Almighty, and of this, his almost chosen people . . .

ADDRESS TO THE NEW JERSEY SENATE, FEBRUARY 21, 1861

I have never had a feeling politically that did not spring from the sentiments embodied in the Declaration of Independence. . . . I have often inquired of myself, what great principle or idea it was that kept this Confederacy so long together. It was not the mere matter of the separation of the colonies from the mother land; but something in that Declaration giving liberty, not alone to the people of this country, but hope to the world for all future time. It was that which gave promise that in due time the weights should be lifted from the shoulders of all men, and that all should have an equal chance.

SPEECH IN INDEPENDENCE HALL, PHILADELPHIA, FEBRUARY 22, 1861

ABRAHAM LINCOLN'S JOURNEY from Springfield to Washington would be his first opportunity to speak to the American people since his nomination in May 1860. In the twelve days and nights that lay ahead he would see and be seen by more people in more places than any American president before him. Lincoln's speeches became the subject of close scrutiny by politicians, press, and people as the clue to his ability to lead the nation into an impending war. After his prolonged silence in Springfield, everyone along the way was curious to hear what Lincoln would say.

Lincoln's speeches and whistle-stop remarks on his journey from Springfield to Washington have usually been either overlooked or undervalued. The journey began with high expectations and ended in controversy. Upon a closer look, his speeches and responses reveal dimensions of both the struggles and the strengths of Lincoln as he was about to be inaugurated as the sixteenth president of the United States.

AT EVERY MAJOR STOP on the journey to Washington, the expectation was that Lincoln would make a speech—or two or three. He spoke, now from the platform of the train, then from his hotel balcony, and again from the steps of a statehouse. Even at the small towns, where the train stopped only briefly, the crowds expected Lincoln to speak. In the next twelve days Lincoln would make nearly one hundred speeches, some of them very brief, or responses to speeches, speaking twelve times on one exhausting day.

The speeches presented at least two problems for Lincoln. First, he had decided months before that he did not want to speak about his policies before he took up the reins of the presidency on March 4. Second, he was wary of impromptu speaking, recognizing his past misstatements when not fully prepared. He did not want to say anything inadvertently that could be misinterpreted in the North or could ignite the explosive situation in the South. But how could he respond to a reception in his honor, offered by his fellow citizens, without offering some kind of speech?

THE ITINERARY CALLED for a circuitous rail journey from the prairies of Illinois, not yet a generation removed from the frontier, through the center of Indiana and Ohio, down to the boundary of the South at Cincinnati, on the Ohio River. In eastern Ohio at Cleveland,

and in western Pennsylvania at Pittsburgh, Lincoln would meet people living on the western border of the urban-industrial frontier of a rapidly expanding America. He would enter New York State in a region settled by New England Yankees and travel down through the center of the state to New York City, where he had received only 35 percent of the vote. Lincoln was looking forward to his visit to Independence Hall in Philadelphia, the birthplace of the nation. Overnight stops were scheduled in Indianapolis, Cincinnati, Columbus, Pittsburgh, Cleveland, Buffalo, Albany, New York City, Philadelphia, and Harrisburg. The trip was scheduled to last twelve days, between February 11 and 23. The journey of 1,904 miles would go over the tracks of eighteen separate railroads. The train traveled slowly, usually no more than thirty miles an hour. Lincoln was scheduled to arrive in the nation's capital late on Saturday afternoon, February 23.[1]

Besides the crowds he encountered, millions more would read Lincoln's words. Henry Villard and a whole flock of reporters who would join the trip along the way would send their reports instantaneously by the miracle of the magnetic telegraph. Reporters and politicians would offer their report card on every Lincoln step and misstep.

The events of the next twelve days would combine the festive moods of a carnival, a political rally, and a religious revival. Between the major cities the train would make numerous stops at smaller towns. All along the way crowds gathered by the side of the tracks to cheer and wave even when they knew that Lincoln would not be stopping. The villages and towns were decorated with American flags. People came to the stations on horseback, in wagons and buggies, and on foot.

Lincoln's preinaugural trip was planned in response to numerous invitations from governors and mayors as well as state and local committees. No one need consult a map to see that Lincoln subjected himself to a long zigzag route. From Pittsburgh the Presidential Special would travel back west and then north to Cleveland. From Philadelphia the Lincoln train traveled west again to Harrisburg before heading south and east through Baltimore to Washington. An invitation from the governor of Massachusetts was declined because it would have added too much zag to the trip.

Lincoln's journey from Springfield to Washington is depicted on has been superimposed on this period map.

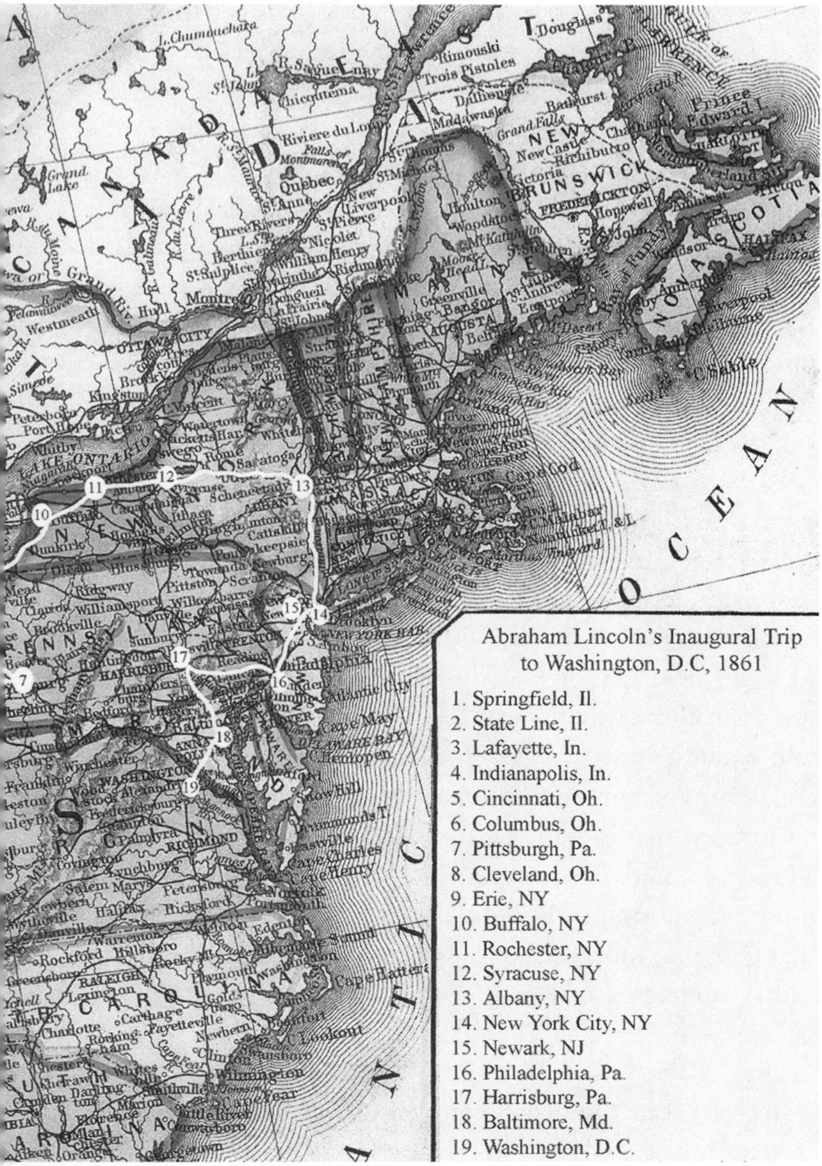

a map that highlights nineteen stops. The circuitous rail route

ADAPTED FROM AN 1860 RAILROAD MAP BY KAREN NEEDLES

DESPITE WHAT MANY BELIEVED to be the mounting danger to Lincoln, there was no official military escort on the train, because Lincoln insisted he was traveling as a private citizen. William S. Wood, a former railroad official, became superintendent of arrangements. Wood had made an inspection tour of the entire route the train would travel. All along the route precautions were taken to prevent sabotage. Flagmen were stationed at every road crossing, and in some places every half mile. As the train passed by, the American flag was displayed as a signal of "all right."[2]

Four military officers did volunteer to serve as escorts. Two came aboard at the Illinois-Indiana state line, and two more at Indianapolis, acceding to Lincoln's instructions. Serving as Lincoln's personal bodyguard was Ward Hill Lamon, Lincoln's lawyer friend from the days of traveling the Eighth Judicial Circuit together in central Illinois. Lamon, barrel-chested and walrus-mustachioed, cut quite a figure in his personally designed military uniform. He went about his duties protecting his friend Lincoln with two pistols and a bowie knife wedged in his belt. Lamon ended up being the only person to accompany Lincoln all the way to Washington.

As Lincoln would enunciate again and again, the celebrations en route were not about a person but about an office and a nation. In that spirit Lincoln insisted that the guest list should not be partisan but should include representatives of all political parties. Lincoln invited to ride with him, in addition to Republicans, persons who had supported Stephen Douglas, John Breckenridge, and John Bell, the other three presidential candidates in 1860.

WILLIAM H. SEWARD, Lincoln's chief competitor for the Republican nomination for president, and now his choice for secretary of state, urged Lincoln to make such a trip. What better way to make known this relatively unknown Western politician than to parade him through some of the most populous states? Seward believed the trip could introduce Lincoln to the people and at the same time consolidate the local machinery of the Republican Party in each state.

Anxiety about both Lincoln's abilities and his policies had been building. Lincoln, acceding to nineteenth-century custom, did not speak during the campaign for the presidency in the summer and fall of 1860. He believed it would have been immodest and unseemly to do so. Other Republican leaders did speak across the country on Lincoln's behalf.

His hometown champion, the *Illinois State Journal*, supported his decision. "The American people have always believed it would be in exceedingly bad taste and censurable in a candidate for the high office of President to . . . electioneer by making political speeches." Some, including Henry Clay, Winfield Scott, and James Buchanan, had defied the tradition. Stephen A. Douglas, one of Lincoln's opponents in the 1860 election, had spoken for his own candidacy, but was disparaged for doing so. The *State Journal* spoke for most Americans when it said that the presidency was "an office no man should seek by direct means."[3] One of those means was political rhetoric.

At a Republican rally in Springfield on the evening of August 8, Lincoln told the assembled crowd, "It has been my purpose, since I have been placed in my present position, to make no speeches."[4] During this period he had continually reminded the press and people that his views were well known through his many speeches of recent years. Lincoln's prolonged silence, both during the campaign and after his election, only served to heighten the expectations for this train trip.

Lincoln's decision to be silent muted his greatest strength. Prior to his nomination in May 1860, Lincoln had always been eager to speak. He accepted invitations to speak at political rallies and community events of all kinds. He built his reputation as a superb stump speaker because of his remarkable ability to enter into a give-and-take with the audience. Stephen A. Douglas, on the eve of his debates with Lincoln in the summer of 1858, acknowledged that Lincoln was "the strong man of his party—full of wit, facts, dates, and the best stump-speaker with droll-ways and dry jokes in the west."[5] This long train trip, after Lincoln was elected but before he was inaugurated, could be the occasion for speaking that Lincoln had forgone for eight months.

WHATEVER MAY HAVE BEEN the original impulses for such a trip, by the time of the departure from Springfield, the trip had become controversial. Seward had long ago changed his mind about the wisdom of the journey. He wrote to Lincoln on December 29, 1860, informing the president-elect of a plot to seize the capital on or before March 4. Seward stated, "I am not giving you opinions and rumors. Believe that I know what I write." Seward suggested that Lincoln abandon plans for an extensive train trip, saying, "I therefore renew my suggestion of your coming earlier than you otherwise would—and coming in by surprise—without announcement."[6] Lincoln did not take Seward's advice and proceeded with plans for his extended preinaugural trip.

For the next two weeks Lincoln's life consisted of processions, receptions, military parades, bonfires, and all manner of civic celebrations. Lincoln's young secretary, John Nicolay, and his younger assistant, John Hay, would write later of this trip that Lincoln "had no fondness for public display" but well understood "the importance of personal confidence and live sympathy" between a leader and his constituents, both leaders and ordinary people.[7]

AS IF THE LINCOLN TRAIN were not drama enough, in what today we would consign to the stuff of a movie script, there were actually two trains and two presidents-elect departing on the same day, February 11, and bound for an inauguration. Only one week before Lincoln's departure, on February 4, delegates from six Southern states gathered in Montgomery, Alabama, to begin the task of creating a new nation. Four days later, on February 8, this Confederate convention adopted a provisional constitution. The next day they unanimously elected a provisional president, Jefferson Davis, and a provisional vice president, Alexander H. Stephens. A chief concern throughout the North in the weeks before Lincoln's inauguration was to prevent the other Southern states from joining this secessionist nation.

Starting on February 11, all eyes across the nation were fixed not on one but on two trains. Abraham Lincoln, departing from Springfield, was moving slowly east through Indianapolis, Columbus, and Pittsburgh toward Washington. Jefferson Davis, leaving his plantation, Brierfield, in Mississippi, and carried by boat to Vicksburg, then traveled by train in a roundabout route through Jackson, Chattanooga, and Atlanta toward Montgomery. The trains along both routes stopped frequently in order for Lincoln and Davis to speak and crowds to cheer. The fascination with these two journeys to two capitals was captured in the *New York Times* for February 11, 1861. The *Times* reported on these dual actions in two columns placed side by side:

"The New Administration" "The New Confederacy."[8]

THE LINCOLN TRAIN arrived at the first overnight stop, Indianapolis, right on schedule, at 5 P.M. on February 11. Gov. Oliver P. Morton, Indiana's first native-born governor, welcomed Lincoln, standing to speak in an open carriage drawn by four white horses. Lincoln, speaking from the rear of the train, responded. This was the first of many occasions he had to reply extemporaneously to welcoming words by a local politician.

Early in his impromptu remarks Lincoln offered what would become an oft-repeated demur:

> *I do not expect, upon this occasion, or on any occasion, till after I get to Washington, to attempt any lengthy speech.*

Lincoln would repeat this apology for not speaking again and again during the trip to Washington—even as he continued to feel obliged to speak.[9]

Energized by the enthusiasm of the crowd in Indianapolis, Lincoln spoke of his determination to preserve the Union, declaring,

> *When the people rise in masses in behalf of the Union and the liberties of their country, truly may it be said, "The gates of hell shall not prevail against them."*

Speaking in the atmosphere of a political rally, Lincoln employed religious imagery familiar to his audience. First, Lincoln said that the present crisis was about nothing less than the *salvation* of the nation. Second, to strengthen his point about resolve, Lincoln resorted to a figure from the Bible where Jesus declared to Peter that his mission was to build his church, and "the gates of hell will not prevail against it."[10] Lincoln used this figure of *the gates of hell* to underscore the gravity of opposition, but even more to point to the perpetuity of the nation.

Governor Morton, an antislavery Democrat who had become a Republican, emphasized the need of the people to yield to the authority of the elected government. Lincoln changed if not challenged the governor's approach by building his response rather around an ennobled role of the people, not the government, as the primary actors in the struggle that lay ahead.

> *In all the trying positions in which I shall be placed, and doubtless I shall be placed in many trying ones, my reliance will be placed upon you and the people of the United States—and I wish you to remember now and forever, that it is your business, and not mine; that if the union of these States, and the liberties of this people, shall be lost, it is but little to any one man of fifty-two years of age, but a great deal to the thirty millions of people who inhabit these United States, and to their posterity in all coming time.*[11]

Lincoln shifted the focus from himself to the people standing before him.

In his closing appeal Lincoln referred to himself as an *accidental instrument.* He would work with this figure in various ways in the days ahead. Lincoln described his responsibility as president by saying his role was *temporary* and *for a limited time.* His goal was to increase the expectations ordinary citizens must have of one another.

The remarks in Indianapolis underscored Lincoln's deep faith in the people. He stated that the ultimate questions now resided not with politicians but with citizens. As a skilled speaker, Lincoln concluded his speech with the question each person in his audience must answer:

> *Shall the Union and shall the liberties of this country be preserved to the latest generation?*[12]

In these words Lincoln gave voice to the two major themes that would run consistently through his speeches and remarks—union and liberty. The audience erupted in loud and prolonged applause.

AFTER AN ARRAY of speakers, the presidential parade traveled through Indianapolis, down Washington Street to Pennsylvania Street, and finally to the Bates House. At the train station, and along the way, Lincoln bowed continuously to the crowd. Future president Rutherford B. Hayes was in the crowd that day in Indianapolis. In a letter to a friend, Hayes shared his delight if not amusement at Lincoln's efforts. Hayes wrote, "His chin rises—his body breaks in two at the hips—there is bend of the knees at a queer angle."[13]

When Lincoln emerged from a carriage at the Bates House he was almost swallowed up in a milling mass of people. Shortly he appeared on a balcony to deliver his prepared speech. Lincoln held in his left hand a paper marked simply "For Indianapolis."

Lincoln constructed his remarks around a series of questions. He began by pressing the questions

> *What, then, is "coercion"?*

and

> *What is "invasion"?*

President James Buchanan, in his final message to Congress on December 3, 1860, had denied to the states in the South the right of secession, but stated that the federal government had no power to coerce a state to stay within the Union. Buchanan, in the four months that was then the rule between election and inauguration, struggled and sputtered in Washington while everything around him deteriorated. Buchanan's inaction only increased the pressure on Lincoln for action.

Sounding now like a prosecuting attorney, Lincoln asked his questions.

> *Would the marching of an army into South Carolina, for instance, without the consent of her people, and in hostility against them, be coercion or invasion?*[14]

He answered his own question before asking more questions.

> *I very frankly say, I think it would be invasion, and it would be coercion too, if the people of that country were forced to submit. But if the Government, for instance, but simply insists upon holding its own forts, or retaking those forts which belong to it, or the enforcement of the laws of the United States in the collection of duties upon foreign importations, or even the withdrawal of the mails from those portions of the country where the mails themselves are habitually violated; would any or all of these things be coercion?*[15]

As Lincoln asked his questions, the newspaper correspondents present reported, the audience applauded and cheered. By now the audience had caught on that Lincoln's questions were really a recapitulation of arguments being voiced daily by the seceding states. Lincoln's strategy was to deride the South's elevation of the rights of individual states and their consequent demeaning of the rights of the Union. With this tactic Lincoln had the crowd cheering continually. In speaking of the seceding states, he offered an analogy.

> *In their view, the Union, as a family relation, would not be anything like a regular marriage at all, but only as a sort of free-love arrangement,—[laughter,]—to be maintained on what that sect calls passionate attraction. [Continued laughter.]*[16]

The comments in brackets were supplied by local reporters.

Lincoln put the finishing touches on his rhetorical thrust by asking, *What is the particular sacredness of a State?* After again holding up to derision the secessionists' determination to place the state above the Union, Lincoln drew his lawyerly logic to a derisive conclusion:

> *I am speaking of that assumed right of a State, as a primary principle, that the Constitution should rule all that is less than itself, and ruin all that is bigger than itself.*[17]

At this sentence, and for the remainder of the brief speech, the reporter for the *Indianapolis Daily Sentinel* reported laughter, and more laughter, culminating in rousing cheering at the end of the address.

WHILE WAITING to be served dinner, Lincoln was besieged by autograph hunters, local officials, and office seekers. During a reception in his suite for members of the Indiana legislature, Lincoln grew impatient as he asked for his speeches, which he had entrusted to his son. Robert, who was being dubbed the Prince of Rails, son of the Rail Splitter, was being entertained by some young Republicans. The boy and the bag containing the speeches were missing.

When Robert finally arrived, he explained that he had left the oilcloth bag with the hotel clerk. Lincoln was irritated as his long legs carried him quickly down the stairs to the hotel lobby. Digging through the pile of luggage, Lincoln opened the first bag that seemed to be his. The bag yielded up a dirty shirt, playing cards, and a half-empty whiskey bottle. Lincoln quickly found his bag. The copies of the inaugural address plus the other speeches now in hand, the whole incident was good for a laugh at the end of an exhausting day.[18]

A long-lost scrapbook kept by his young assistant private secretary, John M. Hay, contains newspaper accounts pasted carefully to preserve the record of that journey. At the top of the clipping "Mr. Lincoln's Speeches at Indianapolis" is a preface stating, "The following are the speeches delivered by Mr. Lincoln in Indianapolis as revised by himself for the Indianapolis *Journal.*" Lincoln had long been in the habit of revising prepared speeches for later publication. This clipping shows how he followed this practice to revise his extemporaneous remarks for publication along the route from Springfield to Washington.[19]

LINCOLN'S SPEECH in Indianapolis was reported all across the country. "This little speech," declared the *Chicago Tribune,* "has electrified the true Republicans and has given the fishy ones 'fever and ague.'" The *New York Times* summarized Lincoln's prepared remarks, concluding that Lincoln had no sympathy with a viewpoint that believed the federal government was simply a "voluntary league of sovereign states" from which any state could secede.[20]

The *Cleveland Plain Dealer,* which had supported Douglas for president, saw Lincoln's performance at Indianapolis quite differently. "The President-elect has finally opened his mouth, and as Mrs. Partington would say, got his foot in it." Benjamin Penhallow Shillaber, in his *Life and Sayings of Mrs. Partington,* published in 1854, created the American Mrs. Malaprop, whose misapplication of words became a humorous part of popular conversation in these years. The *Plain Dealer* believed that the enthusiasm of the Hoosiers so affected Lincoln that it "carried away all his reserve, waked the 'old war horse' in him and he made a regular stump speech, instead of delivering a diplomatic Presidential address."[21]

THE TRAIN carrying Jefferson Davis reached Jackson, Mississippi, on the evening of February 11. Davis was surrounded by crowds of well-wishers upon his arrival at the train station. He spoke at the Capitol to an audience that "occupied every available inch of space." Davis said that he deplored war but would face it "with the stern serenity of one who knows his duty and intends to perform it." He asserted that England and France will "not allow our great staple to be dammed up within our limits." Finally, Davis promised—if war came—to "go forward . . . with a firm resolve to do his duty as God might grant him power."[22]

AT MIDMORNING the next day, February 12, Abraham Lincoln's presidential entourage made its way to Union Station in Indianapolis, where seven railroads converged. Lincoln was met at the train by Mary and the two younger boys. She had left Springfield on the evening of February 11 and had to travel all night to reach the Indiana capital just in time to meet the Presidential Special, which left on time at 11 A.M. on February 12. She greeted her husband on the morning of his fifty-second birthday. The Indianapolis and Cincinnati Railroad, supplying the locomotive and cars for the next portion of the journey, had provided a special apartment in an elegant car for the Lincoln family. Newspapermen reported that the president-elect, now reunited with his entire family, kept everyone laughing with his stories and humor.[23]

The new version of the Presidential Special was bedecked with American flags with thirty-four stars, as well as with red-white-and-blue bunting. As the train rolled through eastern Indiana, Lincoln was greeted at Greensburg by a brass band, a glee club, and a large crowd eager to sing patriotic songs. At Lawrenceburg, the Indianapolis and Cincinnati joined the Ohio and Mississippi Railroad for the ride into Cincinnati. The two railroads used different track gauges, but laying down a third rail solved the problem of transport into Cincinnati. As the train approached Cincinnati, the Lincolns could see private residences, workshops, and factories that were "elaborately decorated" for his arrival.[24]

LINCOLN'S TRAIN arrived somewhat after the appointed time of 3 P.M. in Cincinnati because the tracks coming into the city had to be cleared of enthusiastic citizens by the police and military. Cincinnati was the largest city in the West, proud that its population of more than 161,044 ranked it ahead of Chicago (112,112), Pittsburgh (49,217), and Cleveland (43,417). Poet Henry Wadsworth Longfellow had called Cincinnati the Queen City of the West.

Mayor Richard M. Bishop greeted Lincoln, who took his place in an open carriage. That the mayor was a Democrat afforded Lincoln the opportunity to respond that the reception offered him was not the result of party, but of the uniting of all peoples who enjoyed the benefits of free institutions. After initial speech making, Lincoln was greeted by "vociferous cheering" in a line of march that lasted one and a half hours through downtown Cincinnati. The correspondent for the *Chicago Tribune* celebrated the event in capital letters, declaring, "THE LIKE OF WHICH HAS NEVER BEEN SEEN IN THE NORTHWEST."[25]

Lincoln had spoken in Cincinnati once before, in September 1859, and he reminded his audience that in that earlier speech he had devoted many of his remarks to the citizens of Kentucky. At one point in the planning of this trip, Lincoln had hoped for a brief visit to his native state, just across the waters of the Ohio River from Cincinnati. The three pages of his remarks for Cincinnati and the five small pages of his speech intended for the Kentuckians were written on identical lined notepaper. On the back of the fifth page was attached a clipping from the first version of the First Inaugural Address.[26]

Lincoln quoted from his earlier speech. In 1859, before he was a candidate for president, Lincoln asked what would be the attitude of a new Republican administration toward Kentucky. He had answered:

> *We mean to treat you, as near as we possibly can, as Washington, Jefferson, and Madison treated you. We mean to leave you alone, and in no way to interfere with your institution; to abide by all and every compromise of the constitution. . . . We mean to recognize, and bear in mind always, that you have as good hearts in your bosoms as other people, or as we claim to have, and treat you accordingly.*[27]

Lincoln, the master of interaction with his audience, asked the crowd:

> *And now, fellow citizens of Ohio, have you, who agree with him who now addresses you, in political sentiment—have you ever entertained other sentiments towards our brethren of Kentucky than those I have expressed to you.*

He paused, dramatically, to hear their answer. The crowd responded with continuous cries of "No, no." Lincoln continued:

> *If not, then why shall we not, as heretofore, be recognized and acknowledged as brethren again, living in peace and harmony one with another?*

In response to Lincoln's question, the crowd thundered: "We will, we will."[28]

AT NINE the next morning, Lincoln and his party left Cincinnati on equipment provided by the Little Miami Railroad. From Cincinnati to Pittsburgh the Presidential Special would travel on six different railroads. It was February 13 and the weather was sunny and crisp. Stops were made in Milford, Loveland, Miamiville, Morrow, Corwin, Xenia, and London for brief speeches and to water the iron horse.

As the Presidential Special traveled through Ohio, Lincoln's thoughts surely were far away in Washington. This was the second Wednesday of February, the day the votes of the Electoral College would be counted. Lincoln had become concerned about this congressional confirmation of his election. Six weeks before, in answer to Seward's urgent appeal to postpone the trip and come to Washington earlier, he had replied, "It seems to me the inauguration is not the most dangerous point for us." Lincoln added, "Our adversaries have us more clearly at disadvantage, on the second Wednesday of February." Lincoln voiced his concern: "If the two Houses refuse to meet at all, or meet without a quorum of each, where shall we be?"[29]

The security in Washington had been entrusted to Gen. Winfield Scott. The general-in-chief of the army, now seventy-four, had fought in the War of 1812, the Blackhawk War, the Seminole Wars, and won lasting fame in the Mexican War. A huge man, six feet five inches tall, and now a rotund 350 pounds, he was known everywhere as Old Fuss and Feathers because of his penchant for colorful uniforms and his attention to detail. With secessionist tensions mounting, Scott moved his headquarters from New York to Washington.

As rumors grew in January of a plot to stop the vote confirming Lincoln's election, Lucius Eugene Chittenden, a Vermonter, expressed his alarm to Scott. The old general replied that if anyone attempted to obstruct the "lawful count of the electoral vote," that person "would be lashed to the muzzle of a twelve-pounder gun and fired out of a window of the Capitol." Asked what would happen if the villain were an elected representative, Scott replied, "I would manure the hills of Arlington with fragments of his body, were he a senator or chief magistrate of my native state!" Scott's native state was Virginia, and he was already under pressure to join the secessionists, but his response that day was, "It is my duty to suppress insurrection—*my duty!*"[30]

On February 13, Scott positioned military guards at all the entrances to the Capitol. Credentials were examined before one could enter. In the chair was Vice President John C. Breckenridge, a Kentuckian, who eventually became secretary of war in the Confederate States of America. On this day he presided over an orderly counting of the electoral votes. Vice President Breckenridge announced that Abraham Lincoln had been elected the sixteenth president of the United States.

THE SPECIAL arrived in Columbus punctually at 2 P.M. Lincoln went directly to the Capitol, where he was invited to address the Ohio legislature, the first of four legislatures he would address on his journey to Washington. In his prepared remarks he said:

> *I have not maintained silence from any want of real anxiety. It is a good thing that there is no more than anxiety, for there is nothing going wrong. It is a consoling circumstance that when we look out there is nothing that really hurts anybody. We entertain different views upon political questions, but nobody is suffering anything.*[31]

Lincoln's remark *there is nothing going wrong,* and again, *there is nothing that really hurts anybody,* started a controversy that would build toward his inauguration. Supporters contended that his remarks were part of a strategy of lessening public alarm. Critics countered that Lincoln's remarks at Columbus revealed a president-elect who was naive and out of touch with the forces gearing up for civil war.

AFTER ADDRESSING the Ohio legislature, Lincoln spoke to the crowd outside on the west steps of the Capitol. He told the audience that he recognized the *great difference of political sentiment* in the assembled crowd. He joked that *those agreeing with me* probably represented *the shortest row* of listeners. The crowd laughed. He then made his larger point:

> *I infer that you do me the honor to meet me here without distinction of party. I think this is as it should be. Many of you who were not favorable to the election of myself to the Presidency were favorable to the election of the distinguished Senator from the State in which I reside. If Senator Douglas had been elected to the Presidency in the late contest, I think my friends would have joined heartily in meeting and greeting him on his passage through your Capital, as you have me today. If any of the other candidates had been elected, I think it would have been altogether becoming and proper for all to have joined in showing honor, quite as well to the office, and the country, as to the man.*[32]

Lincoln had made this same point in Indianapolis and Cincinnati. In recognizing the diversity of political opinion and voting, in specifically mentioning other candidates in a positive way, Lincoln pointed beyond himself as he sought to foster loyalty to the Union.

When Lincoln finished his remarks, he was escorted inside the Capitol to the office of Gov. William Dennison, Jr. Here, Anson Stager, general superintendent of the Western Union office in Cleveland, who had been traveling on the Lincoln train, handed Lincoln a telegram reading: "The votes were counted peaceably. You are elected."[33]

THE PRESIDENTIAL SPECIAL chugged out of Columbus at 8 A.M. on Thursday, February 14. At the head of the train was a locomotive named Washington City. Stops were made at Newark, Frazeysburg, Dresden, Coshocton, Newcomerstown, Uhrichsville, and Cadiz Junction. At Steubenville, a port city on the Ohio River, some Virginians crossed the river to join the crowd.

The problem with speaking spontaneously was that Lincoln felt obliged to respond to the welcoming words of his host. These words sometimes led Lincoln down a track he did not want to travel. In such limited time, he sometimes arrived in the midst of an idea, and as the engine whistled, signaling it was time to leave, he did not know how to conclude.

At Steubenville he was welcomed by Judge W. R. Lloyd, whose remarks put Lincoln in an awkward place. Lloyd told Lincoln that Ohioans and Virginians were united in their attachment to the Constitution. Judge Lloyd went on to say that as Lincoln executed the laws in discharging his oath, he could expect the support of both sections.

At this point Lincoln's spontaneity got the best of him. Responding to Lloyd's welcome, Lincoln stated:

> *We everywhere express devotion to the Constitution. I believe there is no difference in this respect, whether on this or on the other side of this majestic stream.*

But Lincoln knew the issue was much more complicated, and he decided to step forward into that complexity by asking,

> *What are their rights under the Constitution?*

The issue became who would be the judge of those rights. Lincoln said that under the Constitution the majority rules. However,

> *By your Constitution you have another chance in four years. No great harm can be done by us in that time—in that time*

> *there can be nobody hurt. If anything goes wrong, however, and you find you have made a mistake, elect a better man next time. There are plenty of them.*[34]

When the engine whistled, Lincoln brought this speech to a swift end by concluding:

> *These points involve the discussion of many questions which I have not time to consider. I merely give them to you for your reflection.*

He then compounded the problems of his extemporaneous remarks by adding:

> *I almost regret that I alluded to it at all.*[35]

Lincoln was aware, again, of the problems that could develop when he allowed himself to speak spontaneously.

JEFFERSON DAVIS was in high spirits on February 14 as his train traveled through Mississippi and Alabama. Cannon and bonfires welcomed him at many stops. Veterans of his Mexican War regiment joined him all along the rail trip. Some of his former comrades held high their battle flags from Monterrey and Veracruz as they prepared for a new battle against old friends. Davis was so busy greeting people day and night that he slept in his clothes. In Stevenson, in northeastern Alabama, he predicted to the audience gathered at the one-story depot that the border states would join the Confederate States of America within sixty days. He also predicted that "England will recognize us, and . . . grass will grow in the northern cities where the pavements have been worn off by the tread of commerce." Davis told the enthusiastic crowd that he "hopes for peace but is prepared for war."[36]

ON THE MORNING OF Friday, February 15, Lincoln spoke from the balcony of the Monongahela House in Pittsburgh to a crowd of five thousand, standing under umbrellas. Sidestepping the crisis of an impending civil war, Lincoln spoke from a prepared text about the importance of the tariff. Lincoln brought out this central idea of Whig and now Republican economics. He declared that because there was no direct taxation, a tariff was necessary.

> *The tariff is to the government what a meal is to the family.*

Lincoln harked back to a plank in the Chicago platform of the Republican Party, which, he said,

> *should be regarded as law for the incoming administration*

He then made the unusual move of asking his private secretary, John Nicolay, to read the entire plank of the Republican Party platform.

At Pittsburgh the newspapers predisposed to support Lincoln were impressed. The *Pittsburgh Gazette* avowed that "the impression he made upon our citizens generally, by his personal bearing and public remarks, was highly favorable." The *Cincinnati Commercial* was of the same mind. Murat Halstead, their brilliant young news reporter, was a Republican liberal. The *Commercial* observed, "The temper of the remarks of Mr. Lincoln on the state of the country is that of a sincere, outspoken, honest man."[37]

Villard was not impressed. He characterized the Pittsburgh speech as "the least creditable performance" of the entire trip. "What he said was really nothing but crude, ignorant twaddle." He believed that this speech proved Lincoln to be "the veriest novice in economic matters."[38] The reporter for the *New York Herald* and the Associated Press was particularly critical of the several confessions Lincoln made in the speech. In speaking about protections for home industries, Lincoln stated:

> *I must confess that I do not understand this subject in all its multiform bearings . . .*

Regarding the Morrill tariff bill currently being debated in Congress, Lincoln admitted:

> *I confess I do not understand the precise provisions of this bill, and I do not know whether it can be passed by the present Congress or not . . .*[39]

For Villard, who had been reporting on Lincoln for three months, the Pittsburgh speech "strengthened my doubts as to the capacity for the high office he was to fill."[40]

IT WAS TIME to zag to Cleveland. Now Lincoln was entering greater New England, for the northern tier of Ohio was settled by westward-moving Yankees from the New England states. New England and, by extension, northern New York and northern Ohio were the regions most strongly antislavery.

The day dawned with rain and snow as the train retraced part of the previous day's journey. Lincoln was told that the elements might finally dampen the enthusiasm of the crowds and he could take a break from stopping and speaking. Not so. All along the route crowds assembled in the rain, snow, and mud. When the train slowed, but did not stop, Lincoln saluted with his stovepipe hat. At Hudson, he told the six thousand who had come out in the rain that he was quite hoarse and thus they would understand why he could not give a speech.

At 4:20 P.M. the train pulled into Cleveland. Cheering spectators lined Euclid Street despite standing in deep mud. Lincoln arrived at the Wedell House at five-thirty and stepped up to a platform adorned with colored lanterns to address the assembled crowd.

> *Frequent allusion is made to the excitement at present existing in our national politics, and it is as well that I should also allude to it here. I think that there is no occasion for any excitement. The crisis, as it is called, is altogether an artificial crisis.*[41]

These remarks at Cleveland added to the controversy started by Lincoln's remarks in Columbus. Did the president-elect not understand or did he underestimate the mounting crisis? Was this speech intended to calm the nerves of the North? Lincoln, in these remarks, was trying not to increase tensions, especially before he was in office in Washington, where he must be able to take action that would improve the situation.

LINCOLN LEFT CLEVELAND on the morning of February 16. The unpredictable Great Lakes winter had dawned with bright sunshine. The train traveled east again, through Ohio and across the northwest corner of Pennsylvania. Entering New York, the Presidential Special chugged along the shore of Lake Erie. A first stop was Westfield, where a banner was stretched across the tracks emblazoned, "Welcome Abraham Lincoln to the Empire State." Lincoln, by now bone-tired, appeared revived with the enthusiasm of the welcome.

Lincoln, who often began his remarks with self-deprecating humor, directed his words to the women in the crowd, telling them:

> *I am glad to see you; I suppose you are here to see me; but I certainly think I have the best of the bargain.*

He then told the crowd that three months earlier he had received a letter from a *young lady* from Westfield. His youthful correspondent advised him *to let my whiskers grow, as it would improve my personal appearance.* Lincoln had taken her advice, and now he wanted to know if she was present in the crowd. A small boy cried out, "There she is, Mr. Lincoln." Grace Bedell, a blushing eleven-year-old girl with black eyes, stepped from the crowd, and President-Elect Lincoln gave her several hearty kisses "amid the yells of delight from the excited crowd." Better than a speech on this memorable day in Westfield.[42]

An hour later, at Dunkirk, a crowd of twelve to fifteen thousand greeted Lincoln. As he stepped off the train on the station platform, he put his hand on a pole with the American flag blowing in the breeze coming in off Lake Erie. Lincoln exclaimed:

Standing as I do, with my hand upon this staff, and under the folds of the American flag, I ask you to stand by me so long as I stand by it.

The effect on the crowd was dynamic. They shouted, "We will, we will."[43]

THE PRESIDENTIAL SPECIAL arrived in Buffalo in the afternoon of Saturday, February 16. Lincoln was met at the Exchange Street depot by Millard Fillmore, the thirteenth president of the United States. As Lincoln and Fillmore walked toward the doors of the station, the crowd surged forward on both sides, eager to see this historic meeting of a former president and the president-elect. Numbers of people were hurt in the crush, including Maj. David Hunter, one of the officers accompanying Lincoln, who suffered a dislocated shoulder. Lincoln and Fillmore traveled through the streets of downtown Buffalo to the American House.

Lincoln's long train trip was at its halfway point, and he was exhausted. His throat was hoarse. The next day, February 17, was a Sunday, the Sabbath, and Lincoln would go to the Unitarian church with Fillmore, and then rest, not resuming his travels until Monday. Across the street from Lincoln's hotel was a banner on the Young Men's Christian Association building. The banner was inscribed with the words of the reply to Lincoln's farewell remarks at Springfield: "We Will Pray for You."[44]

FEBRUARY 16 would be Jefferson Davis's longest day of traveling and speaking. He arrived in Atlanta about four o'clock in the morning and at midmorning spoke at the Trout House for about thirty minutes. The *Atlanta Intelligencer* reported that Davis aimed some of his remarks at Northern abolitionism, especially "its systematic aggression upon the constitutional rights of the South for the last forty years."[45]

After the speech Davis boarded a special car on the Atlanta and West Point Railroad and headed west across Georgia. During the day he stopped to speak in Fairburn, Palmetto, Newnan, Grantville, La Grange, and West Point. At each stop he was greeted by cannon and by women waving their handkerchiefs. Entering Alabama, the Davis train stopped for speeches at Opelika and Auburn. By now Davis had worked out a basic speech. A correspondent for the *New York Tribune* reported that Davis would give elements of the same speech several times during the many stops of this day.[46]

On this same evening Davis completed his eight-hundred-mile train trip, arriving in Montgomery, Alabama, at 10 o'clock. He had spoken more than twenty times along the way. A dispatch from the *Charleston Mercury* described Davis's trip as "one continuous ovation." Now he traveled through the streets of Montgomery to his lodgings at the Exchange House, where eager crowds greeted him. After some brief remarks, Davis retired for the evening, anxious to spend more time preparing for his inaugural address, to be delivered on Monday, February 18.[47]

LINCOLN'S DEPARTURE from Buffalo, scheduled for Monday, February 18, at 6 A.M., was moved up to 5 A.M. to avoid the disorderly crowds of Saturday. On the train this morning was Horace Greeley, editor of the *New York Tribune.* Greeley had joined the train on Saturday briefly while on his way to deliver a lecture in Erie, Pennsylvania. Now he came aboard again for the ride to Albany.

Greeley was always determined to make his opinion count. He had visited with Lincoln most recently in Springfield. A man of complex motives, Greeley had formed a favorable impression of Lincoln, but he was eager to learn more.

The editor filed a story from Buffalo under the byline "From Our Special Correspondent." "The power of Mr. Lincoln," he wrote, "is not in his presence or in his speech, but in the honesty and gloriously refreshing sincerity of the MAN." Greeley offered his opinion about the success of Lincoln's train trip: "His passage through the country has been like the return of grateful sunshine after a stormy winter day. The people breathe more freely and hope revives in all hearts."[48] Greeley would rethink that opinion many times in the next four years.

WHILE LINCOLN'S TRAIN whistle-stopped through the Mohawk Valley toward Albany, he received news that Jefferson Davis had taken the oath of office as provisional president of the Confederate States of America. Lincoln's old friend from his single term in Congress, Alexander Stephens, took the oath of office as vice president.

Davis left the Exchange House at noon. Thousands of people gathered on Commerce Street, cheering and throwing flowers as Davis passed in an open carriage pulled by six iron gray horses. The destination was the Alabama Capitol Building, which had become the Capitol of the Confederacy. In the pomp and circumstance, without a national anthem, the band played the "Marseillaise."

Davis delivered his inaugural address at 1 P.M. on the portico of the Capitol Building. The speech was brief for one accustomed to long addresses. He had little time to prepare. The burden of his address was to justify the cause of the Confederacy. Davis spoke to his fellow Southerners, to the citizens of the United States—although he never mentioned Lincoln—and to foreign nations that had a vital interest in the availability of cotton. The speech was remarkably mild for some in the audience, who expected to hear a trumpet call to war.

As for rhetorical style, the second sentence of the address was typical.

> Looking forward to the speedy establishment of a permanent government to take the place of this, and which by its greater moral and physical power will be better able to combat with the many difficulties which arise from the conflicting interests of separate nations, I enter upon the duties of the office to which I have been chosen with the hope that the beginning of our career as a Confederacy may not be obstructed by hostile opposition to our enjoyment of the separate existence and independence which we have asserted, and, with the blessing of Providence, intend to maintain.[49]

This sentence of ninety-nine words reveals the limitations of this dimension of Davis's leadership. The sentences would only get longer as the speech unfolded. The contrast to Lincoln's economy of language and rhetorical artistry would become even more apparent in the next four years.

The inauguration of Davis was steeped in traditions refined over seventy-two years of the American republic. Religious symbolism was prominent from the opening invocation to Davis's swearing his oath of office on the Bible, which he kissed. After Davis's address an actress named Maggie Smith danced on the American flag.[50]

AS LINCOLN'S TRAIN approached the heights above Albany, the thunder of cannon announced his arrival in the capital city of New York. In his reply to the welcome by Gov. Edwin D. Morgan, Lincoln said, *I have neither the voice nor the strength to address you at greater length.*[51] He did give a prepared address to the New York legislature, meeting in joint session.

At 7:45 A.M. on Tuesday, February 19, the Lincoln party boarded the train for the trip south along the Hudson River to New York City. The train had to make a two-hour detour due to a midwinter thaw that freed masses of ice that roared down the Hudson River, demolishing several bridges in its path. Lincoln traveled on a fresh train with a new locomotive named Union.

LINCOLN ARRIVED in New York City at 3 P.M. with what surely were mixed emotions. He was returning to the scene of his triumph, where he had delivered his Cooper Union address of the previous winter, but he had received less than 35 percent of the vote in the city of New York, even though he carried the state.

New York was the largest city in the nation, with a population of 813,669 in 1860. Lincoln was greeted by a crowd estimated at more than two hundred thousand. Flags were everywhere, as were banners with special messages. Church bells greeted the procession. In the midst of the festivities, apprehension was also in the air.

The destination was the Astor House. An astute observer was Walt Whitman, who that afternoon found himself on the top of a

Broadway omnibus stalled in traffic. Whitman took the measure of Lincoln for the first time.

> I had, I say, a capital view of it all, and especially of Mr. Lincoln, his look and gait—his perfect composure and coolness—his unusual and uncouth height, his dress of complete black, stovepipe hat push'd back on the head, dark-brown complexion, seam'd and wrinkled yet canny-looking face, black, bushy head of hair, disproportionately long neck, and his hands held behind him as he stood observing the people. He look'd with curiosity upon that immense sea of faces, and the sea of faces return'd the look with similar curiosity.[52]

Whitman spied hostility as well as curiosity and admiration in the crowd. "Many an assassin's knife and pistol lurk'd in hip or breast-pocket there, ready, as soon as break and riot came."[53] Whitman, who would move to Washington early in the war, would observe Lincoln twenty to thirty times over the next four years.

At the Astor House Lincoln was ushered into the hotel's reception room. Told that this room was where Daniel Webster and Henry Clay had spoken in the past, Lincoln was invited to make a speech. Even in New York, to an eager audience, he replied:

> *I have been occupying a position, since the Presidential election, of silence, of avoiding public speaking, of avoiding public writing.*

He added:

> *I supposed it was peculiarly proper that I should do so until the time came when, according to the customs of the country, I should speak officially.*[54]

AN INTERESTED OBSERVER was George Templeton Strong. Strong, a lawyer, active Episcopal layman, and trustee of Columbia, was a careful observer of political events in New York City and the nation. Beginning in 1835, at age fifteen, he would write regularly in uniform blank books every evening before he went to bed. He wrote for the next forty years. The diary, ultimately comprising nearly four and a half million words, remained unknown to the public for more than fifty years after Strong's death, in 1875. Strong was a backer of Seward of New York for the Republican nomination. He was not quite sure what to make of "Honest Abe," his description of choice for Lincoln after the election in November 1860.

Strong had been following Lincoln's train tour as it wound its way toward New York. On Monday, February 18, he wrote an assessment of Lincoln. "Lincoln is making little speeches as he wends his way towards Washington, and has said some things that are sound and credible and raise him in my esteem." However, Strong also offered the opinion, "But I should have been better pleased with him had he held his tongue altogether."[55]

The New York lawyer walked uptown on Broadway at three-thirty the next afternoon to join the crowd welcoming Lincoln. At Saint Thomas's Church he met the Lincoln cortege as it moved slowly toward the Astor House. Strong recorded in his diary later that evening, "The great rail-splitter's face was visible to me for an instant, and seemed a keen, clear, honest face, not so ugly as his portraits."[56]

AS LINCOLN PREPARED to leave New York City, the *New York Herald* was not optimistic. James Gordon Bennett was the publisher of this Democratic newspaper not kindly disposed to Lincoln in February 1861. The paper had a wide influence because of its European circulation. Now the *Herald* editorialized, "The country balances upon the verge of chaos. Throughout the length and breadth of the land the throes of dissolution are being felt." The *Herald* believed the situation in New York was especially perilous. "Here in New York—from which, like the blood from the heart, throbs the life that sustains and quickens the whole commercial system—everything is stagnant; trade is paralyzed, merchants are breaking down and mechanics are unemployed."[57]

And what about Lincoln's ability to deal with a nation on the verge of chaos? Bennett and the *Herald* had not been impressed by Lincoln's visit to New York and his speeches. "Although we had a great many speeches, and a great deal of fuss and commotion during his visit to the commercial metropolis, yet from it all we cannot extract one ray of light thrown upon the disasters which are overshadowing the country like a pall."[58]

Henry Villard, whose stories were being printed both in the *New York Herald* and in many other newspapers through the Associated Press, left the trip upon the train's arrival in New York. He asked the *New York Herald* to be relieved of his duties. Villard said that "after ten days of the wearisome sameness of the 'performances'" he was "very sick of the 'traveling show.'"[59]

THE PRESIDENTIAL SPECIAL departed New York at 9:05 A.M. on Thursday, February 21. A program at Newark, New Jersey, was added at the last moment. The train slowed as it approached Princeton, and the students from the college greeted the president with thunderous cheers, what they called "skyrocket" yells, and college songs, which Lincoln acknowledged with bows and a tipping of his hat. The train reached Trenton, the state capital, at 11:50 A.M.

Lincoln was taken directly to the Senate chamber in the Capitol. He began his remarks by recounting how as a boy—in *the earliest days of my being able to read*—he obtained a copy of Parson Weems's *Life of Washington.* Lincoln told the New Jersey legislators that of all the accounts of the *struggles for liberties,* none remained so fixed in his mind as Washington crossing the Delaware and winning the battle at Trenton on December 26, 1776.[60]

For Lincoln, the past always became present. If Washington was the leader of that earlier American Revolution, in the present crisis Lincoln had his role.

> *I shall be most happy indeed if I shall be an humble instrument in the hands of the Almighty, and of this, his almost chosen people.*[61]

These words quickly became some of the most remembered of the twelve-day journey.

In his reply to Governor Morton at Indianapolis, Lincoln had spoken of himself as an *accidental instrument.* As Lincoln spoke in Trenton of his role as *an humble instrument,* he was suggesting something different. He believed that his role as a leader came not only from the people but from *the Almighty.* Lincoln contrasted *humble instrument,* as the portrayal of himself, with God, whom he described as *Almighty.*

Lincoln's depiction of the American people as an *almost chosen people* is one of his most enigmatic phrases. The notion that Americans were God's chosen people arrived with the Puritans. The first settlers had left Old England to establish a New England, which would be faithful to the word of God in the best tradition of the churches of the Reformation of the sixteenth century, now being advanced by the Puritans of the seventeenth century. This notion of God's chosen people flourished in the eighteenth century and, whether in secular or religious versions, undergirded the revolutionaries who founded a new nation in 1776. In the middle of the nineteenth century, Americans added the sense of "manifest destiny," the right and duty to inhabit and civilize the whole of the continent for the great experiment in democracy.

In the midst of all the certainties about God and nation, Lincoln's qualifying adjective, *almost,* is striking. In an era of absolutes, when Lincoln's various constituencies, from abolitionists to secessionists, were crying out for certainties, Lincoln could live comfortably with the uncertainties facing the nation.

LINCOLN REACHED Philadelphia at 4 P.M. on Thursday, February 21. Upwards of a hundred thousand people were in the streets to greet the president-elect as he traveled up Chestnut Street to the Continental Hotel. In response to greetings from Mayor Alexander Henry,

Lincoln declared his allegiance to the Declaration of Independence and the Constitution.

> *I have never asked anything that does not breathe from those walls. All my political warfare has been in favor of the teachings coming forth from that sacred hall.*

These sentiments were not new for Lincoln. Beginning in 1854, when he was aroused by the passage of the Kansas-Nebraska Act to reenter political life, Lincoln had repeatedly declared his fidelity to the principles of the Declaration of Independence and the Constitution.

> *May my right hand forget its cunning and my tongue cleave to the roof of my mouth, if ever I prove false to those teachings.*

Lincoln used biblical language and imagery (Psalm 137:5–6) to swear his allegiance. He placed the message above the messenger by invoking fervent language from the psalms.[62]

The next morning, February 22, the booming of cannon and the ringing of church bells announced the celebration of the birthday of George Washington. Early in the morning Lincoln traveled by carriage to Independence Hall. He was invited to raise the flag. In his remarks he confessed to the crowd:

> *I am filled with deep emotion at finding myself standing here in the place where were collected together the wisdom, the patriotism, the devotion to principle, from which sprang the institutions under which we live.*

He acknowledged:

> *I have never had a feeling politically that did not spring from the sentiments embodied in the Declaration of Independence.*

He had offered this sentiment a number of times since his reemergence into politics in 1854, but Lincoln must have taken special delight in affirming his loyalty to the Declaration of Independence at

Lincoln raised the flag at Independence Hall in Philadelphia. He is to be seen, bareheaded, standing close to the center of the flag. F. DeBourg Richards took this photograph shortly after sunrise on George Washington's birthday, February 22, 1861.

LIBRARY OF CONGRESS

the place where this sacred document was signed more than eighty-four years before.[63]

Inviting his audience to join him in this wonderful but frightening moment, Lincoln declared:

> *I have often inquired of myself, what great principle or idea it was that kept this Confederacy so long together.*

He answered that it was not the mere separation of the colonies from their motherland. Rather:

> *It was that which gave promise that in due time the weights should be lifted from the shoulders of all men, and that all should have an equal chance.*[64]

Having enunciated the basic promise of the Declaration of Independence, Lincoln asked:

> *Now, my friends, can this country be saved upon that basis?*

Lincoln pledged his life and work to this premise. To underline his commitment to this principle, he told the audience at Independence Hall:

> *I would rather be assassinated on this spot than to surrender it.*[65]

Lincoln concluded his remarks by telling the assembly:

> *My friends, this is a wholly unprepared speech. I did not expect to be called upon to say a word when I came here.*

He thought he was invited only to raise the flag. Lincoln, obviously concerned by his remarks, said further:

> *I may, therefore, have said something indiscreet.*

The crowd responded with cries of "No, no."[66]

ON THE PREVIOUS EVENING Lincoln had learned of a plan to kill him before he could reach Washington. At his lodgings at the Continental Hotel, Lincoln was introduced to Allan Pinkerton, a Chicago detective, whose company worked for the Philadelphia, Wilmington and Baltimore Railroad. Pinkerton informed Lincoln that his detectives had uncovered a plot to kill him as he changed trains in Baltimore. Lincoln's train car would be pulled by horse through the streets of Baltimore in the middle of the night, this slow transfer providing a perfect opportunity for mischief in a city swarming with pro-Confederate plug-uglies. Pinkerton and Norman Judd, an Illinois friend who had nominated Lincoln at the Republican convention at Chicago, insisted that he take a train for Washington that night. He refused. He was adamant that he would keep his date at Independence Hall. Lincoln would heed their warning and depart by night from Harrisburg. That same evening Frederick Seward, the son of William Seward, called on Lincoln to tell him that his father and General Scott had been informed by detectives in Baltimore of a plot to assassinate the president-elect. Seward's report was independent and confirmed the evidence of the plot.

The next morning Lincoln left Philadelphia at nine o'clock for the 106-mile trip to Harrisburg, the state capital of Pennsylvania. Stops and the slowing of the train at Haverford, Paoli, Downingtown, Coatesville, Leaman Place, Lancaster, Mount Joy, and Middleburg meant that the trip took four and a half hours. Gov. Andrew Curtin met Lincoln and took him to the state Capitol, where he addressed the legislature in joint session.

At dusk the plans for Lincoln's secret trip to Washington were put into action. Lincoln was spirited out of Harrisburg for the return trip to Philadelphia. Instead of traveling with his usual stovepipe hat, Lincoln wore a soft brown Kossuth hat given to him in New York. It was decided that only Ward Hill Lamon would accompany Lincoln and Pinkerton. At Philadelphia, Lincoln boarded a sleeping car, occupying a berth Pinkerton had reserved for an "invalid passenger." In Baltimore, Lincoln's car was transferred to the Camden Station, where he boarded a night train for Washington. He arrived at the B&O depot in the capital at 6:30 A.M., almost ten hours ahead of his scheduled late-afternoon arrival.[67]

The journey to Washington was completed. Lincoln had begun the journey with great expectations surrounded by a thousand of his friends and fellow townspeople. He ended his journey by arriving in Washington almost alone, unannounced and unrecognized.

NEWSPAPER PRESSES began to roll across the North and South, weighing in with their evaluations of Lincoln's preinaugural speeches. The *Baltimore Sun,* with strong Southern sympathies, reporting on "Lincoln and His Wayside Speeches," offered the opinion, "He approaches the capital of the country more in the character of a harlequin," or a character in a comedy. "There is that about his speechification which, if it were not for the gravity of the occasion, would be ludicrous."[68]

The pro-Lincoln papers were ready to respond to this kind of criticism. The *Chicago Tribune,* always a staunch friend of Lincoln, weighed in. "The wiseacres who indulge in criticism of the verbal structure of Mr. Lincoln's recent speeches" were off the mark. The *Tribune*'s defense, however, was mostly pointing out that Presidents Zachary Taylor, Andrew Jackson, and George Washington did not have the "gift of gab" when asked to speak extemporaneously.[69]

EVEN IF the criticism of Lincoln is marked off as the expected response of anti-Lincoln newspapers, some editors who were pro-Lincoln were also troubled. Samuel Bowles, publisher and editor of the *Springfield (Mass.) Republican,* had been impressed with Lincoln when he heard him speak in Boston in 1848. The *Springfield Republican,* an antislavery newspaper, supported Lincoln in the 1860 election. But Bowles was troubled as he read reports of Lincoln's speeches. On February 26, he wrote to Henry L. Dawes, a Republican member of Congress from Massachusetts, of his discouragement with Lincoln and the public disputes within the Republican Party. Bowles told Dawes, "Lincoln is a 'simple Susan.' "[70]

MORE SERIOUS YET was the confusion sown among Republicans in Congress by Lincoln's speeches. In some speeches, when Lincoln seemed to be advocating coercion of the South, his remarks were taken to be a repudiation of the labors at conciliation being led by Seward. In other speeches, Lincoln seemed to point toward a policy of moderation. Was Lincoln simply hesitating to state his position, or was he not certain of his own opinion?

Charles Francis Adams, whom Seward would soon recommend to Lincoln for the post of United States minister to England, was deeply concerned. Referring to Lincoln's speeches on the journey to Washington, Adams confided to his diary on February 20, "They betray a person unconscious of his position as well as the nature of the contest around him." Adams conceded that Lincoln was "good-natured, kindly," but he viewed the president-elect as also "frivolous and uncertain." All in all, in Adams's estimation, Lincoln's speeches "put to flight all notions of greatness."[71]

THE NATION'S greatest orator had also been reading Lincoln's speeches. Edward Everett, a native of Massachusetts, had served with distinction in a wide variety of offices for over four decades. He began as a young professor at Harvard in 1819 and returned a quarter century later as president of the nation's oldest college. Everett served Massachusetts as congressman, senator, and governor. He represented the United States as secretary of state and minister to England. Everett resigned from the Senate in 1854 at age sixty. He returned to Boston in poor health, but his health revived as he responded to speaking invitations from all across the country. He would give an address on George Washington hundreds of times.

Everett read with interest the first reports of Lincoln's speeches. He wrote in his diary for February 15, "These speeches thus far have been of the most ordinary kind, destitute of everything, not merely of felicity and grace, but of common pertinence." Everett, who believed that speeches were a mirror revealing the character and integrity of the person, had come to an opinion about Lincoln. "He is evidently a person of very inferior cast of character, wholly unequal to the crisis."[72]

LINCOLN'S SPEECHES and responses on the journey to Washington disclose the limitations as well as the potency of his still-developing speech making. Lincoln understood that the journey to Washington was his chance to campaign. He complimented the ladies, measured himself against tall men, and in brief speeches and remarks encouraged fidelity to the Union by cultivating trust in himself.

Certainly he spoke circumspectly about the issues of an impending war. He often contextualized his remarks to the city or crowd where he was speaking. Lincoln the politician knew how to work the audience. In his speeches he was continually asking questions or making statements that elicited enthusiastic vocal responses from the crowds. He understood that when he arrived in New York City he was not there this time to deliver a Cooper Union address to a select audience of political, business, and literary leaders, as he had one year before. Lincoln was often the down-home Lincoln, who was at home with crowds in Cadiz Junction, Ohio; Wellsville, New York; and Lancaster, Pennsylvania. These folk loved his self-deprecating humor and patriotic messages. He knew that he would have the opportunity to deliver a very different kind of speech on March 4, 1861.

The *Chicago Tribune* understood this difference also. "We attach little importance to the speeches which Mr. Lincoln has been compelled to make in response to complimentary receptions on the Presidential tour, because we know that the only complete and authoritative exposition of his policy will be found in his Inaugural."[73] But however the *Chicago Tribune* minimized the importance of the speeches on the way to Washington, it understood that the speeches of that cross-country trip only served to increase the stakes for what Lincoln would say in the most important speech of his life, coming quickly on March 4, 1861.

CHAPTER THREE

"THE MYSTIC CHORDS OF MEMORY"

FIRST INAUGURAL ADDRESS

MARCH 4, 1861

I hold, that in contemplation of universal law, and of the Constitution, the Union of these States is perpetual. Perpetuity is implied, if not expressed, in the fundamental law of all national governments. It is safe to assert that no government proper, ever had a provision in its organic law for its own termination. . . .

In your hands, my dissatisfied fellow countrymen, and not in mine, is the momentous issue of civil war. The government will not assail you. You can have no conflict, without being yourselves the aggressors. You have no oath registered in Heaven to destroy the government, while I shall have the most solemn one to "preserve, protect and defend" it.

I am loth to close. We are not enemies, but friends. We must not be enemies. Though passion may have strained, it must not break our bonds of affection. The mystic chords of memory, streching from every battlefield, and patriot grave, to every living heart and hearthstone, all over this broad land, will yet swell the chorus of the Union, when again touched, as surely they will be, by the better angels of our nature.

ABRAHAM LINCOLN ARRIVED in Washington incognito. But his unexpected early appearance quickly became the talk of the town. At daybreak on Saturday morning, February 23, Lincoln was taken by carriage to Willard's Hotel, at the corner of Pennsylvania Avenue and Fourteenth Street. The Willard was the grand hotel of the capital, boasting both water and gas in every room. Lincoln and his family were to be lodged in parlor number six, a suite of rooms on the corner of the second floor that overlooked the Executive Mansion.

Lincoln was met at the Willard by William H. Seward. Governor Seward, as he liked to be called, was a man of slight build, stooped, with graying hair and a pallid complexion. His dominant features were a beaklike nose and shaggy eyebrows. If Seward was not an imposing figure physically, he had become a leader of the Republican Party because of his impressive political abilities.

Why was Seward not at the train station to meet Lincoln? Seward, embarrassed, apologized to Lincoln. His explanation: he had overslept.[1]

SEWARD WOULD PLAY an intriguing role in the evolution of Lincoln's presidential rhetoric. Seward enjoyed a reputation as an excellent speaker, not because of his voice or gestures, but because of the political force of his words. On March 11, 1850, just months after assuming his seat in the United States Senate, he offered his first major speech in the midst of a debate that was riveting the nation. On January 29, 1850, as sectional bitterness in Congress was growing over attempts to strengthen the Fugitive Slave Law, Sen. Henry Clay of Kentucky had appealed for a compromise that would forbid the federal government from dealing with slavery. Seward, with his speech, assumed an immediate leadership position among those unwilling to compromise any longer over slavery. The speech became known as his "Higher Law" speech because he appealed to "a higher law than the Constitution." Seward did not mean to disparage the laws of the Constitution but rather to point beyond Caesar's law to God's law.[2]

On October 25, 1858, while campaigning for the Republican ticket in Rochester, New York, Seward drew national attention again with a speech about "an irrepressible conflict between opposing and enduring forces." Seward argued that "the United States must and will, sooner or later, become either entirely a slave-holding nation or entirely a free-labor nation."[3] Lincoln had spoken four months earlier in Springfield about "a house divided," but his speech did not draw the attention or the criticism of Seward's address.

LINCOLN AND SEWARD had been competitors for the Republican nomination in 1860. With a long career in New York and national politics, Seward led on the first two ballots at the Republican convention in Chicago. Seward's friends, anticipating victory, had moved a cannon near the Seward home in Auburn, New York. When the salutary news came from Chicago, the cannon would be fired in celebration of Seward's nomination. The good news came, not to Auburn, New York, but to Springfield, Illinois, and there was no cannon. After his election, President-Elect Lincoln reached out to his presidential rival and asked Seward to become secretary of state.

Seward and Lincoln had met once before. In September 1848, they both toured New England speaking on behalf of presidential candidate Zachary Taylor and the Whig ticket. Seward addressed a sizable audience at Tremont Temple. He was followed by Lincoln. Seward remembered that Lincoln gave "a rambling story-telling speech, putting the audience in good humor, but avoiding any extended discussion of the slavery question." The next evening Lincoln and Seward shared a room in Worcester, Massachusetts. Seward recalled, "We spent the greater part of the night talking about anti-slavery positions and principles."[4]

The New York politician passed through Springfield on October 1, 1860, in the midst of a campaign speaking tour in the West. Lincoln came on board the train and the two men conferred for twenty minutes. Charles Francis Adams, Jr., who was in Seward's traveling party, observed that Mr. Lincoln was good-natured but seemed shy in the presence of Seward in their new roles. It was as if Lincoln "had a realizing sense that properly the positions should be reversed."[5]

ON SATURDAY, February 23, Lincoln was briefed by Seward on the latest developments in the frenetic capital. Seward had tried to keep Lincoln abreast of events by writing frequent letters to the president-elect in Springfield. Because of the increasingly tense situation, Seward almost never signed his name, rather marking the letters "secret" or "confidential." Seward's handwriting was extremely difficult to decipher, but through these letters Lincoln started to get to know this man who would occupy an important place alongside the president. Now they were finally together in Washington.

They made their first order of business a call on President Buchanan and his cabinet at the Executive Mansion. Buchanan's manner suggested that he could not wait for the inauguration of the new president. In the afternoon Lincoln received visitors at the Willard, including Sen. Stephen A. Douglas and members of the Illinois delegation. Mary and the boys arrived in the late afternoon.

Lincoln dined that evening at six o'clock with Seward and Vice-President-Elect Hannibal Hamlin at the Seward residence. Governor Seward had enjoyed this first day with Lincoln and wrote that evening to his wife, Frances, of his initial impressions. "He is very cordial and kind toward me . . . simple, natural, and agreeable."[6]

At the end of the evening Lincoln made a request of Seward. Lincoln asked Seward if he would read his inaugural address and offer suggestions. Whether Lincoln had planned to ask Seward's help all along, or did so after they got on so well during their initial day together in Washington, is not known.

THE CITY THAT LINCOLN returned to was quite changed from the capital he had left as a congressman in March 1849. Lincoln would have seen immediately how much the city had grown. The census data give the raw figures of that increase.[7]

1840	23,364
1850	40,001
1860	61,122

Lincoln had arrived in Washington on December 2, 1847, and after spending a short time at Brown's Hotel, he took up lodging at the boardinghouse of Mrs. Ann Sprigg. Eight other Whig congressmen boarded with Mrs. Sprigg, in an area of the capital where the Library of Congress would later be built. Now Lincoln found himself in a city where many members of Congress who did not own or rent houses preferred to live in one of the many new hotels rising in the downtown area. In 1844 two four-story houses on the north side of Pennsylvania Avenue between Third Street and John Marshall Place were remodeled and became the United States Hotel. In the same year the older Gadsby's Hotel at Pennsylvania and Sixth Streets was extended and reopened by Samuel S. Coleman as the National Hotel. In 1847 the City Hotel at the northwest corner of Pennsylvania and Fourteenth Street was leased by Edwin D. and Henry A. Willard. The Willard brothers remodeled the City Hotel into the finest hotel in Washington and called it the Willard Hotel.[8]

THE TEN DAYS between Abraham Lincoln's private arrival in the capital and his public inauguration were wearying. Lincoln confronted a capital in turmoil. The city's inhabitants were divided in their loyalties. Southern sympathies spread through many of Washington's social and political circles. For the first seventy-two years of the federal government, Southern leaders had been dominant in Congress.

Washington was a slaveholding city. In 1860 there were 1,794 slaves and 9,209 free blacks in a total population of 61,122. Taken together, slaves and free blacks constituted 18 percent of the population. The capital was uncommon because it was one of only three cities where free blacks outnumbered slaves. The other two cities were Baltimore and St. Louis. Of cities with populations larger than 25,000 in 1860, only Charleston (42.3 percent), Richmond (37.7 percent), and Mobile (28.7 percent) had a greater percentage of blacks.[9]

Black codes continued to restrict the rights of blacks on the eve of the Civil War. In 1849, a little-known Congressman from Illinois, Abraham Lincoln, introduced a bill calling for a referendum on the abolition of slavery in the District of Columbia. The slave trade was outlawed in the District in 1850, but this step forward was balanced by a revision of the slave code in 1851 and compliance in the 1850s with the Fugitive Slave Law of 1850.[10]

NO INAUGURAL ADDRESS had ever been offered in such tumultuous and uncertain conditions. Wild rumors spread through hotels, bars, and on the streets about threats against Lincoln, attacks on Washington, and the prospects of more states joining the Confederacy. What to do about reinforcing Fort Sumter in Charleston harbor, South Carolina, was a continuing topic of debate. The rumors and gossip were fed by hundreds of discontented Southerners who were still in the capital with little means of returning home.

Lincoln found himself involved in one public reception, meeting, and event after another. Delegation after delegation called upon him at the Willard. Office seekers were not shy in pressing the president-elect for jobs. Henry Villard reported that Lincoln told him, "It was bad enough in Springfield, but it was child's play compared with the tussle here." Villard, after a brief respite from reporting on Lincoln in Springfield and on the train trip east, had been posted by the *New York Herald* to Washington. Lincoln complained, "I hardly have a chance to eat or sleep. I am fair game for everybody of that hungry lot."[11]

BEHIND THE PUBLIC president-elect, a private Lincoln struggled to find time to revise and edit his inaugural address. For this speech he departed from his usual pattern and decided to seek advice from friends and colleagues. He knew how much was riding on this address. He had raised the stakes himself by his silence before his inauguration. Lincoln wanted the counsel of those whose political instincts he trusted.

Before leaving Springfield, Lincoln asked Judge David Davis to read the draft of the entire speech. Davis, longtime friend, former legal associate, and Lincoln's campaign manager in 1860, appreciated the speech and made no suggestions.

He prevailed next upon Orville H. Browning, a friend and fellow lawyer who accompanied Lincoln on the train as far as Indianapolis. Lincoln gave Browning one of the copies of the address in the Indiana capital. He asked Browning to promise not to show the draft to anyone but his wife. Returning to Springfield, Browning reviewed the address and wrote in his diary on February 15, "I thought it well considered, and appropriate, and so informed him. It is, in my judgment, a very admirable document."[12]

On February 17, Browning wrote his response to Lincoln. He offered a single proposal, which he wrote at the bottom of the page of Lincoln's text. He suggested that Lincoln "modify" this passage:

> *All the power at my disposal will be used to reclaim the public property and places which have fallen; to hold, occupy and possess these, and all other property and places belonging to the government, and to collect the duties on imposts; but beyond what may be necessary for these, there will be no invasion of any State.*

Browning told Lincoln, "On principle the passage is right as it now stands. The fallen places ought to be reclaimed. But cannot that be accomplished as well, or even better without announcing the purpose in your inaugural?" Browning suggested revising the sentence to delete the clause

> *to reclaim the public property and places which have fallen*

Lincoln accepted Browning's deletion, thus removing a statement provocative to the South.[13]

Lincoln also turned to Francis P. Blair, Sr., an elder statesman nearly twenty years older than Lincoln. Blair had supported Edward Bates for the Republican nomination, but started offering advice to Lincoln immediately after the election. Blair read the speech and enthusiastically commended the whole address.[14]

DAVIS AND BROWNING were old friends. When Lincoln asked Seward to read his speech, he turned to a new colleague who had been his rival and was not yet his friend. He had relied upon Seward to manage things in Washington during the mounting secession crisis. Now he was not afraid to call upon Seward's abilities and experience at this critical moment.

On the next day, Sunday, Seward toiled over the speech as an editor. He numbered each line. On Sunday evening Seward sent Lincoln a six-page letter presenting him with no less than forty-nine suggestions.[15]

Seward began his letter with "General Remarks." He told Lincoln, "I have suggested many changes of little importance severally, but, in their general effect tending to soothe the public mind." Lincoln's future secretary of state told him, "Your case is quite like that of Jefferson." Thomas Jefferson won a contentious election that was not decided before thirty-six ballots were cast over five days in the House of Representatives, in February 1801. When Jefferson was inaugurated, on March 4, 1801, the anger of the defeated Federalists was almost visible in the air. Seward reminded Lincoln that Jefferson "sank the partisan in the patriot in his inaugural address, and propitiated his adversaries by declaring: 'We are all Federalists, all Republicans.' " Seward concluded with this counsel: "Be sure that while all your administrative conduct will be in harmony with Republican principles and policy, you cannot lose the Republican Party by practicing in your advent to office the magnanimity of a victor."[16]

In the days remaining until March 4, Lincoln worked with Seward's suggestions. Lincoln incorporated, even if sometimes recasting, twenty-seven of Seward's forty-nine suggestions into his rewriting.

LINCOLN WENT ABOUT the task of refining his address with great care. In Springfield, on the train, and now in Washington, Lincoln revised in several ways. In editing the "First Edition" he made a number of deletions, removing some whole paragraphs by crossing them out. Three of the paragraphs that he removed reappeared in the text of the speech he considered giving to the Kentuckians when he was in Cincinnati on February 12. He clipped other paragraphs and pasted them in a new arrangement. He also jotted ideas or words in the margins, to which he could return later.

In the second draft, now shortened from eight to seven pages, some of Seward's changes were added in red ink. Lincoln put in other changes on separate slips of paper. The revisions reveal him as a careful editor who thought about both the logic of his argument and the precision of individual words.

Thomas Nast, in his sketch The Inauguration Night in Washington, *which was published in the* New York Illustrated News *of March 9, 1861, captures the immense crowds who came for Lincoln's inauguration. In the background is the unfinished dome of the Capitol.*

COURTESY SPENCER RESEARCH LIBRARY, UNIVERSITY OF KANSAS LIBRARIES

In the case of his inaugural address, another factor was at work. He spoke about this consideration in a letter to an old friend. George D. Prentice was the editor of the *Louisville Journal.* It was founded as a Whig newspaper, but Prentice had nevertheless supported Douglas in the election of 1860. After Lincoln's election, however, Prentice began pestering Lincoln with questions and ideas. He wrote on January 31 requesting an advance copy of Lincoln's inaugural address. Lincoln's reply on February 2 offers yet another clue to his strategy of revising his address. "I have the document already blocked out; but in the now rapidly shifting scenes, I shall have to hold it subject to revision up to the time of delivery."[17] Lincoln determined to revise up to the last minute against the backdrop of the changing crosscurrents of the political scene swirling around him.

VISITORS BEGAN ARRIVING in the capital on Saturday and Sunday in preparation for the inauguration, on Monday, March 4. The hotels were overbooked. The Willard, all five stories, was crammed with visitors. Cots were placed in the hallways of the National and the Metropolitan. Those coming from outside the capital, whom the locals called "strangers," were mostly men.

Some visitors traveled long distances in difficult winter weather to attend Lincoln's inauguration. Charles Aldrich, a thirty-two-year-old Iowan, left an account of his trip. He lived in Webster City, which was located more than one hundred miles west of the terminus of the Dubuque and Sioux City Railroad. In the middle of February, Aldrich booked a seat with the Western Stage Company. In the summer the stage company ran a two-horse coach, but when the snows were deep they used a two-horse sleigh. Aldrich was picked up in front of the town hall in Webster City for the run to the first stage station, about twelve miles to the east. Staying overnight at a station twenty miles west of Cedar Falls, Aldrich and his fellow passengers awakened the next morning to a howling blizzard that delayed their trip east for two days. They amused themselves by playing euchre, parching corn by the open fireplace, and reading. On another occasion, the sleigh was upset and the passengers dumped into a snowdrift. Unhurt, they extracted themselves and continued on to Dubuque to begin the next phase of their journey, by railroad, to Washington City.[18]

Arriving in the capital some days before the inauguration, Aldrich recalled his "profound feeling of disgust" at "the great number of office seekers who had crowded into Washington." He heard rumors also that a gang of plug-uglies was coming from Baltimore. Whether the intent of these toughs was to harm Lincoln or simply to disrupt the celebrations by creating disturbances was unknown. Another story was circulating that Virginia horsemen would attempt to dash across the Long Bridge to abduct Lincoln on Inauguration Day.[19]

By Sunday evening thousands of people were walking the streets

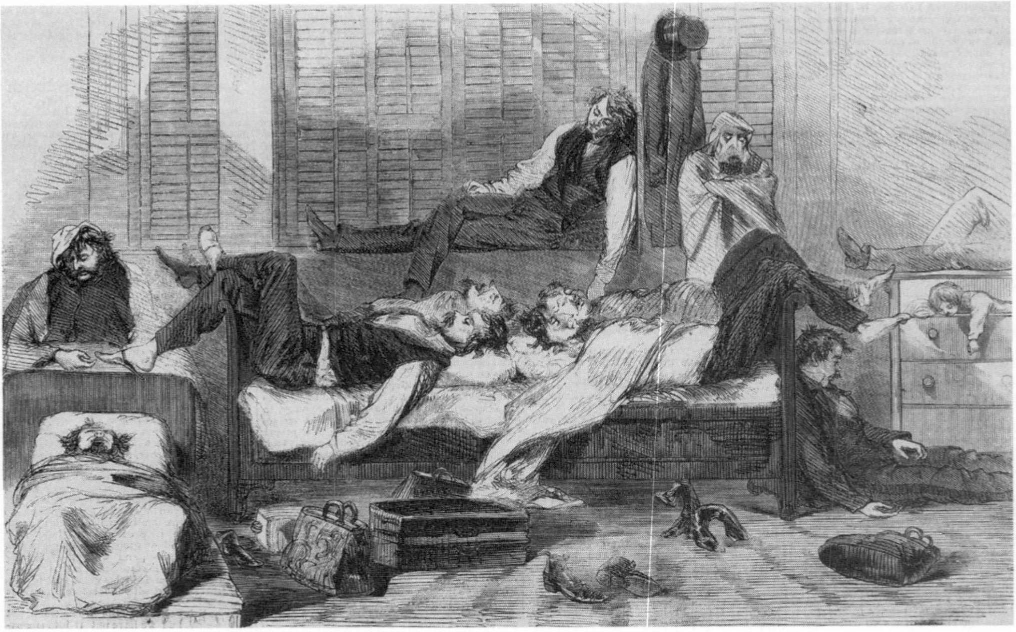

One Bedroom at Willard's Hotel, *a cartoon in the* New York Illustrated News *for March 9, 1861, depicts the cramming of visitors ino every available space even in the best hotels.*

COURTESY SPENCER RESEARCH LIBRARY, UNIVERSITY OF KANSAS LIBRARIES

of the capital. Many congregated around the lighted Capitol, where the Senate was meeting in an all-night session. Some visitors from the West, having found no accommodations, unrolled their carpetbags wherever they could find a place to sleep. This meant sleeping on piles of lumber or on market stalls. Others simply strolled on the streets all through the night.

MARCH 4 DAWNED blustery and cold. The *New York Times* captured the nation's expectations in its morning edition: "The great event to which so many have been looking forward with anxiety—which has excited the hopes and fears of the country to an extent unparalleled in its comparatively brief history—will take place today."[20]

The capital was alive early. Aldrich wrote, "Everyone was bestirring himself in preparation for the great event of the century."[21] The first editions of the Washington newspapers were being hawked by newsboys.

Early in the morning a few drops of rain fell on the first arrivals. A strong wind blew up the Washington dust, which made walking an arduous adventure in the days before streets were asphalted. The city had no system for dampening the streets.

Soldiers and district police were visible everywhere. General Scott had stationed riflemen atop the roofs on buildings along Pennsylvania Avenue. Cavalry patrolled all the major intersections. Expert riflemen watched the inaugural platform from windows in the Capitol. Plainclothes detectives were scattered throughout the arriving crowd. There were more volunteers present than either soldiers or police. The *New York World* reported, "The streets were thronged with volunteer soldiery hastening to their respective rendezvous."[22]

A few complained that Lincoln's inaugural was becoming a spectacle unlike any previous inauguration. Philadelphia's *Morning Pennsylvanian* worried in its March 4 edition that the day's events should "terrify the heart of every patriot." This would be the first time that a president would deliver his inaugural address "surrounded and guarded not by the honest hearts of the people, but safely esconced [*sic*] out of the people's reach, within a military cordon bristling with bayonets."[23]

A CROWD ESTIMATED at between twenty-five and thirty thousand swarmed the various approaches to the Capitol. The *Chicago Tribune* reported, "Every tree top bore its burden of eager eyes. Every fence and staging, and pile of building material, for the Capitol extension was made a 'coyn of vantage' for its full complement of spectators." It was reported that "scarce a Southern face is to be seen" in the crowd.[24]

Aldrich of Iowa, who had secured a guest ticket for the Senate chamber, decided to forgo that opportunity in order to get standing room for Lincoln's address. He wanted to arrive early enough to secure a place where he could hear Lincoln's words. Aldrich crossed the street from the northeast corner of the Capitol to be able to lean against an untidy fence "a distance of ten or twelve rods" from the platform extending to the east from the Senate wing.[25]

LINCOLN ROSE at 5 A.M. in suite six at the Willard Hotel. After an early breakfast, he "retired from his family circle to his closet, where he prepared himself for the solemn and weighty responsibilities which he was about to assume."[26]

At twelve noon, President Buchanan arrived at the Willard Hotel to escort Lincoln to the Capitol. The president-elect emerged from a side door and took his seat in an open barouche, a four-seated carriage with double seats facing each other. Lincoln was dressed in a new black suit, white shirt, and black boots. He wore a tall hat. He carried an ebony cane with a gold head.

In Lincoln's day the inaugural parade preceded rather than followed the inaugural address. One hundred marshals, dressed in blue, orange, and pink, guided their horses at the front of the parade. Nearly twenty different military groups marched in the parade. The local Republican association provided a float drawn by six white horses. The float was filled with little girls wearing laurel wreaths and representing the states of the Union.[27]

Flags were floating in the breeze along the line of march between the White House and the Capitol. Ranks of soldiers massed so densely about the carriage carrying Lincoln and Buchanan that it was not easy to get a look at the two leaders. Armed soldiers, positioned on the rooftops on each side of Pennsylvania Avenue, looked down on the thronged sidewalks and crowded windows. American flags were to be seen in many windows. As the procession passed the intersection of a street, a cavalry detachment stationed there fell into line.[28]

Ahead of Lincoln, towering above the Washington skyline, was the Capitol. The wooden dome, which Lincoln first saw in December 1847, when he arrived to begin his single term in Congress, had been pulled down. Congress made a commitment to build a new iron dome in 1855. Now, as Lincoln returned to Washington, this centerpiece of the inaugural ceremonies was uncompleted. The arm of a huge crane protruded from the unfinished dome.

THE PRESIDENTIAL PROCESSION ascended Capitol Hill as a detachment of United States cavalry and the president's mounted guard took

In Lincoln's day the inaugural parade preceded the inaugural speech. Mr. Lincoln on his way to the Capitol, to Be Inaugurated *appeared in* Frank Leslie's Illustrated Weekly *on March 16,1861.*

LIBRARY OF CONGRESS

up positions on each side of the carriageway. Lincoln and Buchanan entered the north wing of the Capitol arm in arm, and went to the Senate chamber. Buchanan appeared pale and cheerless. Lincoln's manner was grave, with his face somewhat flushed and his lips compressed.

Inaugural events were already under way inside the Senate chamber when the president and president-elect arrived. By midmorning a favored few political leaders and guests were allowed into the chamber. The men, dressed uniformly in black, pushed and struggled to get a better seat. A select number of ladies, dressed in colorful dresses, filled the ladies' gallery. The diplomatic corps, in full court dress, arrived early. Aged Chief Justice Roger Taney, born a year after the signing of the Declaration of Independence, and forever associated with the Dred Scott Decision of 1857, led a group of black-gowned justices into the chamber. John Breckenridge, the outgoing vice president, and Hannibal Hamlin, the incoming vice president, each gave short speeches. The oath of office was administered to Hamlin.

A crowd estimated at twenty-five thousand to thirty thousand was present on March 4, 1861, when Abraham Lincoln was inaugurated as the 16th president of the United States. The ceremonies were conducted at the east front of the Capitol so that the dome, uncompleted and with the arm of a huge crane protruding, formed the background.

LIBRARY OF CONGRESS

WHEN THE CEREMONIES were completed in the Senate chamber, the participants formed in line and walked through the rotunda out onto the special platform that had been erected on the east front of the Capitol. The platform was filled with frock-coated dignitaries. Many of the dignitaries were not aware that a company of soldiers was hunkered down in the space below the platform.

The appearance of the president-elect was greeted with immense cheering. Lincoln took his place in the front row. Sitting close to Lincoln was Stephen Douglas. A small wooden canopy covered the speakers' table.

Sen. Edward Dickinson Baker, from Oregon, Lincoln's longtime friend from their days together in Illinois, introduced the president-elect. As Lincoln rose, he seemed to realize that there was no place to put his cane and top hat. At that moment Douglas, his former rival, stepped forward and asked if he could hold them. Lincoln reached into his right pants pocket and took out a spectacle case. He opened it and drew out his steel-rimmed spectacles, adjusted them on his face, and stepped forward to the small table. He bent low to acknowledge the continuing applause and hurrahs of the crowd.

Abraham Lincoln prepared to speak.

> *Fellow citizens of the United States.*

Lincoln emphasized the word *United.* His voice was clear. His enunciation was distinct.

He continued:

> *In compliance with a custom as old as the government itself, I appear before you to address you briefly, and to take, in your presence, the oath prescribed by the Constitution of the United States, to be taken by the President "before he enters on the execution of his office."*[29]

This introduction seemed simple if not commonplace. At a second hearing or reading, however, Lincoln's simplicity often yields multiple levels of meaning. His opening words, without rhetorical flourish, recalled the history of the nation. *As old as the government itself* invoked the continuity of the Union. Lincoln, by calling attention to the oath to support the Constitution, which he would take at the conclusion of his address, set in place at the outset the permanence of the Constitution above any passing president.

After an initial self-reference—*I*—Lincoln began a pattern of directing attention away from himself. When he did refer to himself, he often did so in an almost tortured use of the third person. Thus, in the third paragraph he spoke of himself by saying:

nearly all the published speeches of him who now addresses you

Lincoln subsumed himself in the personae of larger political entities:

a Republican Administration
the Union
the American people
the national authority
the Constitution
the people

Lincoln worked hard to be nonpartisan in his language. His discussion of the prospective combatants seemed intended to lower emotions. We can hear his efforts to be evenhanded by charting a change from the first to the second draft. In the first draft he wrote:

on our side and yours

In the final draft he changed this sentence to say:

on your side of the North or yours of the South

thus balancing *your* and *yours* in a more inclusive spirit. In this same vein Lincoln adopted suggestions from Seward that changed key words from the second to the final text:

SECOND TEXT	*FINAL TEXT*
submit	*acquiesce*
treasonable	*revolutionary*

He evidently accepted these suggestions from Seward because they moderated his message further toward conciliation. At the time that the Northern press, as well as radicals within his own Republican Party, were using inflammatory language, Lincoln stayed away from volatile words such as "secessionists," "Confederacy," and "enemy."

MOST IN THE CROWD were observing and hearing Lincoln for the first time. Lincoln's lanky, and many would say homely, appearance was a surprise that could be an impediment to his initial connection with audiences who had never seen him before. The *New York Tribune*, which was used to reporting on Lincoln, observed that this day his bearing was "deliberate and impressive."[30]

William Herndon, from long observation, described Lincoln as a public speaker. "He always stood squarely on his feet, toe even with toe; that is, he never put one foot before the other." His portrayal of past speeches was also true of the inaugural address. "He neither touched nor leaned on anything for support. He made but few changes in his positions and attitudes."[31]

We have photographs but no audio recordings of Lincoln speaking. Reports about his speaking voice are remarkably rare, and normally just a sentence at the most. These usually brief comments often reflected the political biases or "journalistic excesses" of the day and were often reminiscences written years later. Nevertheless, a rendering of Lincoln's voice does emerge that is remarkably consistent.

Horace White, a reporter for the *Chicago Tribune*, began to write about Lincoln when he reemerged into the political limelight in 1854. White covered a speech that Lincoln gave in Springfield on October 4 of that year and wrote years later, "He had a thin, high-pitched falsetto voice of much carrying power, that could be heard a long distance in spite of the bustle and tumult of the crowd." White followed the Lincoln-Douglas debates throughout Illinois in 1858. Reporting on the debate in Ottawa, White wrote, "Lincoln began to speak in a slow and rather awkward way." He went on to describe the quality of Lincoln's voice: "He had a thin tenor, or rather falsetto voice, almost as high as a boatswain's whistle. It could be heard farther and it had better wearing qualities than Douglas' rich baritone."[32]

A correspondent for the *New York Herald,* in reporting on Lincoln's Cooper Union address in February 1860, described Lincoln's voice that evening as "sharp and powerful" with "a frequent tendency to dwindle into a shrill and unpleasant sound."[33]

How many could hear Lincoln in the open air? The reporter for Washington's *National Intelligencer* wrote that Lincoln spoke in such a "loud and distinct voice" that he was "quite intelligible by at least ten thousand persons below him." The reporter for the *Cincinnati Commercial* confirmed that Lincoln's "clear, ringing voice" was "easily heard by those on the outer limits of the crowd."[34] Lincoln enhanced the ability of his audience to hear him by his practice of speaking slowly.

IN THE SECOND printed draft, Lincoln had removed the original second, third, and fourth paragraphs by covering them with a pasted slip of paper. Seward had suggested that Lincoln's original second and third paragraphs, which included mention of the Chicago platform voted on at the Republican convention, sounded too Northern and sectional.[35]

On the pasted slip Lincoln wrote in a new second paragraph, in which he moved quickly to name the problem he, the audience, and the nation were facing. He told his audience first what the problem was not.

> *I do not consider it necessary at present for me to discuss those matters of administration about which there is no special anxiety or excitement.*

Lincoln knew that there was much conversation about his administration. He understood the anxiety around both his own leadership abilities and the makeup of his cabinet. He understated the level of concern, but he did so as a transition. Lincoln did not have time for a long introduction. His speaker's instinct told him to move directly to the real source of apprehension in his audience.

> *Apprehension seems to exist among the people of the Southern States, that by the accession of a Republican Administration,*

their property, and their peace, and personal security, are to be endangered. There has never been any reasonable cause for such apprehension. Indeed, the most ample evidence to the contrary has all the while existed, and been open to their inspection. It is found in nearly all the published speeches of him who now addresses you.

In identifying the apprehension, Lincoln also named a specific part of his audience. He deftly spoke of and to *the people of the Southern States.* By saying *Southern States,* he was affirming that they were still a part of the Union. He would not use the name Confederate States of America. He sought to allay their fears. Lincoln's initial rhetorical move was toward conciliation.

We can hear Lincoln's artistry in the structure and sound of this comprehensive sentence. *The people of the Southern States* felt that what was threatened was their

property
peace
personal security

Lincoln's use of alliteration—the repetition of initial consonant sounds in neighboring words—allowed his audience to hear and better understand the symmetry of his initial argument.

Lincoln's lawyerly tactic and tone dominated the structure and content of this crucial paragraph. Like a lawyer he argued, *There has never been any reasonable cause for such apprehension.* He introduced into his case *the most ample evidence* that this had not been so. What was the evidence? The evidence could be found in his previous speeches.

He even quoted himself. Lincoln did not identify the source, but his words came from a speech delivered at Columbus, Ohio, on September 16, 1859.

I have no purpose, directly or indirectly, to interfere with the institution of slavery in the States where it exists. I believe I have no lawful right to do so, and I have no inclination to do so.

Lincoln had offered almost identical words about his intentions not to interfere with slavery in his first debate with Douglas, at Ottawa, Illinois, on August 21, 1858, and in the sixth debate, at Quincy, on October 13, 1858. This *evidence,* he said, *has all the while . . . been open to their inspection.* Lincoln, the lawyer-politician, referred the jury-audience to the precedent of his own speeches. In the midst of the gathering storm he did not present himself as ready to do something new or innovative, but rather as following ideas and practices that he had advocated since the middle of the 1850s.[36]

> *There is much controversy about the delivering up of fugitives from service or labor.*

Lincoln bowed even further toward conciliation with the South when he said he would continue to support the Fugitive Slave Law. This law, revised as part of the Compromise of 1850, was enacted as an attempt to appease the South, but had helped increase the controversy growing in the past decade. Lincoln quoted from the Constitution.

> *"No person held to service or labor in one State, under the laws thereof, escaping into another, shall, in consequence of any law or regulation therein, be discharged from such service or labor, but shall be delivered up on claim of the party to whom such service or labor may be due."*[37]

Lincoln introduced a discussion of this controversial law because at this moment he must have believed there was more to gain from those who were in favor of the law than to lose from those in the North who opposed the law. He moved again to reach out to the South by using the Fugitive Slave Law as an example of his determination to abide by the Constitution.[38]

Lincoln's words on the Fugitive Slave Law did not elicit a great deal of comment in the newspapers in the North. Horace Greeley's *New York Tribune* was an exception, applauding Lincoln by saying his statement was "worthy the charge of a Chief Justice to a jury, and containing more sound law than is often found in charges twenty times its length."[39]

Introducing the Fugitive Slave Law so early in his address provided Lincoln the opportunity to announce his larger point. In taking the oath as president he intended to adhere to the Constitution in all matters.

> *I take the official oath to-day, with no mental reservations, and with no purpose to construe the Constitution or laws, by any hypercritical rules. And while I do not choose to specify particular acts of Congress as proper to be enforced, I do suggest that it will be much safer for all, both in official and private stations, to conform to, and abide by, all those acts which stand unrepealed, than to violate any of them, trusting to find impunity in having them held to be unconstitutional.*

Lincoln, as a lawyer, had always been wary of private opinions. The point of all of this constitutional language was to send a signal that the South had nothing to fear in this new president from Illinois.

> *I hold, that in contemplation of universal law, and of the Constitution, the Union of these States is perpetual. Perpetuity is implied, if not expressed, in the fundamental law of all national governments. It is safe to assert that no government proper, ever had a provision in its organic law for its own termination.*

Lincoln's words about the perpetuity of the Union were met with cheers. He had determined in Springfield that a central theme of his address would be the preservation of the indivisibility of the Union. Lincoln declared that states had the right to uphold their own domestic institutions, not on the basis of any state sovereignty, but rather because of their respective roles in the nation and national government.

At this point Lincoln offered a history lesson. He reminded his audience, *The Union is much older than the Constitution.* Now, almost as a teacher, Lincoln delighted in pointing out that the Union was

> *formed in fact, by the Articles of Association in 1774. It was matured and continued by the Declaration of Independence in 1776. It was further matured and the faith of all the then thirteen States expressly plighted and engaged that it should be perpetual, by the Articles of Confederation in 1778.*

Lincoln concluded his history lesson by returning again to the Constitution to assert that

> *one of the declared objects for ordaining and establishing the Constitution, was "to form a more perfect union."*

> *In doing this there needs to be no bloodshed or violence; and there shall be none, unless it be forced upon the national authority.*

Lincoln surely knew that he could not remain too long in the rarified air of constitutional argument. He must finally talk about the hard possibilities of *bloodshed* and *violence.* His larger purpose had been to establish a baseline: any violence will come from the other side. The initiative will not come from his administration. In another masterful choice of words, he now invented *national authority* to serve his purpose in a conflict with all lesser authorities.

He must have known that this passage on *national authority* would be a critical section of his address, for he made numerous revisions, accepting or refining Seward's suggestions. This was also the place where Lincoln accepted Browning's suggestion to eliminate his own more aggressive assertion that the government would act to "reclaim property."

LINCOLN NOW ADOPTED another of his favorite rhetorical strategies. He liked to ask questions, believing that listeners could often clarify their own thinking with their answers. Lincoln was convinced that there were many in the South who did not support secession but were being coerced by outspoken leaders. These leaders

seek to destroy the Union at all events, and are glad of any pretext to do it

Lincoln wanted to ask questions

to those, however, who really love the Union

His first question he revised considerably from his second edition to his speaking text. The original question was:

Before entering upon so grave a matter as the destruction of our national Union, would it not be wise to ascertain precisely why we do it?

As Lincoln moved to his speaking text, he struck the word *Union* and substituted

our national fabric, with all its benefits, it's memories, and it's hopes

—a phrase both more imaginative and evocative.

Plainly, the central idea of secession, is the essence of anarchy.

As Lincoln pivoted from conciliation to firmness, he began by characterizing the actions of those who were leading the secession movement. Its leaders had clothed themselves in a righteous second war of independence, trying to evoke memories of 1776, but Lincoln forcefully disrobed their actions by calling them *anarchy* and *despotism*. In a closely argued soliloquy on democracy, Lincoln, sounding like a constitutional law professor, made the case that

> *no State, upon its own mere motion, can lawfully get out of the Union,—that resolves and ordinances to that effect are legally void, and that acts of violence, within any State or States, against the authority of the United States, are insurrectionary or revolutionary, according to circumstances.*

Therefore, Lincoln declared that

> *in view of the Constitution and the laws, the Union is unbroken*

He understood it to be his duty as president to ensure

> *that the laws of the Union be faithfully executed in all the States*

Lincoln, as if remembering his conciliatory side, quickly added:

> *I trust this will not be regarded as a menace, but only as the declared purpose of the Union that it will constitutionally defend, and maintain itself.*

Lincoln put the focus, again, not on himself but on the Union and the Constitution.

> *Physically speaking, we cannot separate. We cannot remove our respective sections from each other, nor build an impassable wall between them. A husband and wife may be divorced, and go out of the presence, and beyond the reach of each other; but the different parts of our country cannot do this.*

Lincoln now employed figures from physical geography and marriage that would make this one of the memorable passages from his address.

The passage achieved its resonance from Lincoln's use of the relational imagery of the marriage and divorce of husband and wife. After using constitutional and legal arguments in most of the address to portray the binding notion of the Union, toward the end of his remarks Lincoln turned to a familial argument to make the conclusion of his case.

The *Boston Transcript* believed it was Lincoln's ability to speak the language of common people that was a key to his persuasiveness. "The language is level to the popular mind.—the plain homespun language of a man accustomed to talk with 'the folks' and 'the neighbors.' " The *Boston Transcript,* with a reputation as a cultured newspaper, appreciated in Lincoln the "language of a man of vital common sense, whose words exactly fit his facts and thoughts."[40]

> *In your hands, my dissatisfied fellow countrymen, and not in mine, is the momentous issue of civil war. The government will not assail you. You can have no conflict, without being yourselves the aggressors. You have no oath registered in Heaven to destroy the government, while I shall have the most solemn one to "preserve, protect and defend" it.*

Lincoln closed with two dramatic paragraphs, the next-to-last flung out as a challenge, and the last as a reaffirmation of faith in the Union. The first paragraph had been crafted in Springfield, and remained unchanged through three editions. The last was borrowed from Seward, but polished into prose akin to poetry by Lincoln. In these two paragraphs Lincoln evoked emotion and affection to balance his earlier dependence on law and reason.

When Lincoln spoke of *the momentous issue of civil war,* he moved from past to present. After downplaying the possibility of war, Lincoln had been widely criticized for failing to understand the gravity of the prospects of armed conflict. He named the crisis in this next-to-last paragraph. It was not so much that he had been denying the growing prospect of war. Lincoln was willing to speak about war only after he had the opportunity to place the coming storm in the larger context of the Constitution, his oath, and a shared history that he sought to evoke in his conclusion.

Lincoln broke dramatically with his own understated content and tone when he offered a challenge in his penultimate paragraph. Lincoln's fondness for parallel structures employed oppositions that he highlighted in his speaking text by underlining five key words. After first declaring that those whom he will now challenge are *fellow countrymen,* he introduced his first pair of images. Lincoln placed the responsibility for war, if it came,

1. *In <u>your</u> hands*	2. *not in <u>mine</u>*

He also wanted the record to be clear about who the aggressor would be. Thus he said in a forceful declarative sentence:

3. *The government will not assail <u>you</u>.*

Conciliation, the dominant motif for the bulk of the address, here gave way to firmness. Lincoln continued the opposition using the figure of oaths.

4. *<u>You</u> have no oath registered in Heaven to destroy the government*	5. *while <u>I</u> shall have the most solemn one to "preserve, protect and defend" it*

Lincoln had been employing the figure of the oath to abide by the Constitution since the beginning of his address. He raised the emotional level of his conciliatory feeling by declaring to those *dissatisfied* elements in the South that they could not appeal with integrity to *Heaven,* when their purpose was *to destroy* an authorized *government.* Lincoln, on the other hand, had a *solemn* oath *to preserve, protect and defend* the Constitution. Lincoln will take that oath momentarily. How we wish we could have heard the way Lincoln spoke this emotional paragraph.

I am loth to close. We are not enemies, but friends. We must not be enemies. Though passion may have strained, it must not break our bonds of affection. The mystic chords of memory,

William H. Seward, Lincoln's rival for the Republican nomination for president, served as secretary of state. Seward offered six pages and forty-nine suggestions for Lincoln's First Inaugural Address.

LIBRARY OF CONGRESS

> *streching from every battlefield, and patriot grave, to every living heart and hearthstone, all over this broad land, will yet swell the chorus of the Union, when again touched, as surely they will be, by the better angels of our nature.*

Lincoln concluded his address with an appeal to the South. The power of his plea built as he called to mind figures of common memory. Each of the figures he used evoked the enduring meaning of the Union.

In Lincoln's first and second drafts he had concluded with a question: "With you and not with me is the solemn question, 'Shall it be peace or a sword?' " Seward, after praising Lincoln's argument as "strong and conclusive," told him that something additional was needed "to meet and remove prejudice and passion in the South, and despondency and fear in the East." Seward urged Lincoln to conclude with "some words of affection—some of calm and cheerful confidence."[41]

Seward suggested an altogether different conclusion. He sent Lincoln two options for a new closing paragraph. The first paragraph, in Seward's handwriting, contained thirty-eight words. The second paragraph, in the handwriting of Seward's son Frederick, contained 139 words. Lincoln chose the first option. We are afforded a rare opportunity to look over Lincoln's shoulder as he took Seward's ideas and rewrote them to become his own memorable prose.

Lincoln's artistry with words can be seen by comparing the words in the sentences of the Seward and Lincoln conclusions.

	SEWARD	*LINCOLN*
1.	I close.	*I am loth to close.*
2.	We are not, we must not be, aliens or enemies, but fellow-countrymen and brethren.	*We are not enemies, but friends. We must not be enemies.*
3.	Although passion has strained our bonds of affection too hardly, they must not, I am sure they will not, be broken.	*Though passion may have strained, it must not break our bonds of affection.*
4.	The mystic chords which, proceeding from so many battlefields and so many patriot graves, pass through all the hearts and all the hearths in this broad continent of ours, will yet again harmonize in their ancient music when breathed upon by the guardian angel of the nation.	*The mystic chords of memory, streching from every battlefield, and patriot grave, to every living heart and hearthstone, all over this broad land, will yet swell the chorus of the Union, when again touched, as surely they will be, by the better angels of our nature.*

First, Lincoln condensed Seward's text in sentences two, three, and four. In sentence three he reduced Seward's twenty-one words to thirteen.

Second, Lincoln eliminated redundant words in Seward's paragraph. Thus, Seward's "aliens or enemies" became, in Lincoln, *enemies;* "fellow-countrymen and brethren" was changed to *friends.* Seward's "pass through all the hearts and all the hearths in this broad continent of ours" became *to every living heart and hearthstone, all over this broad land.*

Third, Lincoln employed assonance in his conclusion. Assonance brings close together words or syllables with similarity of sound. The result of expanding Seward's first sentence, "I close," to Lincoln's *I am loth to close* was to achieve a pleasing assonance in bringing together *loth* and *close.*

Fourth, alliteration was achieved by using the consonant *b* five times in the last two sentences of the address:

break
bonds
battlefield
broad
better

Lincoln, who had an auditory sense for words, was fond of alliteration, which promoted connection within the paragraph for the hearer.

Lincoln's tenor voice offered a peroration, or conclusion, of memorable words on the meaning of America that reach across time. He used symbolic images to forge a rhetoric of unity. Each element in his conclusion spoke across the growing divide to mutual feelings of union.

AFTER LINCOLN CONCLUDED, Chief Justice Taney stepped forward. Lincoln would be the ninth president sworn in by Taney. As Lincoln moved to one side of the table, Taney, standing on the other side, held out an open Bible. Lincoln placed his left hand on the Bible, raised his right hand, and repeated the oath of office.

> *I, Abraham Lincoln, do solemnly swear that I will faithfully execute the office of President of the United States, and will, to the best of my ability, preserve, protect, and defend the Constitution of the United States.*

Never, before or since, has there been such congruence between a speech addressing the meaning of the oath and the taking of the oath.

Almost before the oath was completed, the cheering began. Men waved their hats in the air. Artillery boomed salute after salute to the newly inaugurated sixteenth president.

THE WELL KNOWN and the unknown were in the crowd that day. Horatio Nelson Taft came to Washington to work as an examiner in the Patent Office in 1858. He was present to hear Lincoln's inaugural address. He wrote in his diary for March 4, "I stood near him and heard it distinctly." Taft's assessment was that Lincoln's "address seems to give general satisfaction." His daughter Julia celebrated her sixteenth birthday on March 4, 1861. That evening, at a reception at the White House, Horatio and his wife, Mary, and their children Bud and Holly, were introduced to Mary Lincoln. The Taft children were invited to become playmates of Willie and Tad Lincoln at the White House.[42]

GEORGE TEMPLETON STRONG was not present for the inaugural, but confided to his diary the sense of excitement the inaugural caused in New York City. He reported that there was "feverish anxiety in Wall Street" and that "news from Washington" was "awaited impatiently." Strong commented, "Everybody longing for the Inaugural." Newspapers were the chief source of information, and on this day different special editions were printed at noon and 1:30 P.M. A 2 P.M. extra reported on "Lincoln in triumphant procession along Pennsylvania Avenue." Strong read the first half of Lincoln's inaugural in the second edition of evening papers. He sent out for a later edition after dinner but was unable to procure one.[43]

The next day Strong had time to read the entire inaugural address. During the day he had talked with colleagues who liked its pacific and cautious approach. Strong, whose diary is fascinating because he brought in so many diverse opinions, offered his own. "I think there is a clank of metal in it." Strong believed that Lincoln's address "is unlike any message or state paper of any class that has appeared in my time." He appreciated its "absence of conventionalism of thought or diction." He thought it unlike typical public documents, "number one to number ten million and one." Rather, the inaugural "seems to introduce one to *a man* and to dispose one to like him."[44]

REACTIONS TO LINCOLN'S inaugural came quickly. Eager citizens gathered at newspaper offices waiting for telegraphic reports. Newspapers north and south weighed in with their editorial comments.

Newspapers ranged broadly in their responses. In a highly politicized press, critics read their partisan purposes into Lincoln's words. Many of the responses were expected, but not all were predictable.

Two newspapers in Illinois that had been longtime supporters of Lincoln applauded. The *Illinois State Journal* in Springfield proclaimed, "The Inaugural Address of our noble Chief Magistrate has electrified the whole country." The *Chicago Tribune* declared, "No document can be found among American state papers embodying sounder wisdom and higher patriotism."[45]

The *New York Times*, a conservative bellwether of opinion, editorialized that "conservative people are in raptures over the Inauguration." Horace Greeley's *New York Tribune* liked the firmness of Lincoln's remarks. "The avowal of purpose . . . is unequivocal, unhesitating, firm, and earnest." The *Indianapolis Daily Journal* praised Lincoln's ending. "The closing sentence, the only attempt at rhetorical display in the whole address, is singularly and almost poetically beautiful."[46]

The anti-Lincoln papers found nothing to praise and much to criticize. The *Chicago Times* deplored the address as "a loose, disjointed, rambling affair." The *New York Herald* criticized Lincoln's speech as "neither candid nor statesmanlike; nor does it possess any

This is the way the
North received it
This is the way the
South received it

This Thomas Nast cartoon in the New York Illustrated News *of March 23 portrays the different ways Lincoln's Inaugural Address was received in the North and the South.*

COURTESY SPENCER RESEARCH LIBRARY, UNIVERSITY OF KANSAS LIBRARIES

essential dignity or patriotism." Comparing Lincoln to his worthy predecessors, the *Herald* opined that the address "would have caused a Washington to mourn, and would have inspired a Jefferson, Madison, or Jackson with contempt." The *Philadelphia Evening Journal*, only five years old when Lincoln was inaugurated, declared it to be "one of the most awkwardly constructed official documents we have ever inspected."[47]

The citizens of California would not be able to read the speech in a newspaper until it was transported by telegraph and Pony Express and again by telegraph. The speech was first telegraphed from New York to Kearney, Nebraska. Lincoln's words were then placed in the saddlebags of Pony Express riders for their relay across plains and mountains to Folsom, California. The inaugural was then telegraphed to Sacramento and from there to other points in the far West.

THE REPORTER FOR the *New York Tribune* wrote that the inaugural address "was delivered in a clear and emphatic voice, which never faltered throughout, and reached nearly to the outskirts of the vast throng."[48]

A number of people offered comments on the quality of Lincoln's voice and the delivery of his inaugural address. His secretary, John G. Nicolay, recalled, "As Lincoln's voice, trained to open-air speaking, rang out, clear and resonant, above the vast throngs of people before him, the feelings of those who heard him were deeply stirred." Noah Brooks, correspondent for the *Sacramento Daily Union,* remembered that the inaugural address "was received with almost profound silence. Every word was clear and audible as the somewhat shrill and ringing tones of the Lincoln's voice sounded over the vast concourse."[49]

Southern newspapers did not hear any of the conciliation that Lincoln believed was one of the two pillars in the structure of his rhetoric. These newspapers attacked the content of Lincoln's policies and wasted little time analyzing the style of his address. In Charleston, the *Mercury* was an important voice whose editorials were often republished in Northern newspapers. The *Mercury* excoriated Lincoln's "lamentable display of feeble inability to grasp the circumstances of the momentous emergency." The *Richmond Enquirer* rejected the address as "the cool, unimpassioned, deliberate language of the fanatic." The *Enquirer* believed Lincoln's purpose as expressed in his address to be "the dismemberment of the Government with the horrors of civil war."[50]

The *New York Times* wondered aloud whether newspapers in the South had even taken time to read the address. "Before the Inaugural has been read in a single Southern State, it is denounced, through the telegraph, from every Southern point, as a declaration of war."[51]

EDWARD EVERETT, the nation's leading orator, followed closely the responses to Lincoln's oratory from his comfortable home on Summer Street in Boston. On March 4, after receiving the address in the evening by telegraph, he lauded Lincoln's "conciliatory" tone in his journal but expressed the opinion that Lincoln's firmness would "result in Civil War." On April 3, he noted that all of the opinions of the English press had arrived. "It is almost universally spoken of as feeble, equivocal, and temporizing. It has evidently disappointed public expectation."[52]

THE FIRST INAUGURAL is a signpost in the story of Lincoln's evolving eloquence over his next four years as president. Lincoln spent considerable time preparing this important speech. He sought the advice of former colleagues and a new friend. To appreciate the speech, we should view it not from hindsight, from the perspective of the end of the war or of our own day, but from Lincoln's viewpoint as he approached the darkening clouds of a great storm looming on the American horizon.

When Lincoln spoke on March 4, 1861, the situation in the nation was still ambiguous. Seven states had seceded. A new government had been formed in Montgomery, but Lincoln still hoped that war could be averted. Elected as a sectional candidate, he could have spoken forcefully as the champion of the North. Lincoln would have been applauded by many if he had demonized the South.

He determined to speak for the Union from the earliest beginnings of his work on the first draft in Springfield. The question facing Lincoln was how best to articulate that goal in the rhetoric of his inaugural address. Since this large speech and the series of small speeches were composed in the same space and time in Springfield, there is more overlap than has usually been noticed. To be sure, the inaugural address is a more formal, logical speech, but it elaborates ideas and themes already articulated by Lincoln on the journey to Washington.

The purpose of Lincoln's speech was political persuasion. The central components of his persuasion were conciliation and resolve. On his February journey from Springfield to Washington he had accented one or the other motif in various cities. Now, on March 4, he undertook a delicate balancing act so that within the same speech he sought both to assuage the South and to strengthen the resolve of the North.

IT IS LINCOLN the lawyer whom we hear first in this address. He carefully constructs a case to the jury, the people of the South and the North. In arguing his case Lincoln relies on precedent, referring the jury to his previous legal arguments—his political speeches—dating back into the late 1850s. Until his conclusion, Lincoln will use cogent argument and rational language more than imagination or emotion to plead the cause of union. Lincoln's confidence in reason as a moral force suffuses the entire address.

This speech at the beginning of Lincoln's presidency points as much to the past as it does to the future. We hear in it themes and even exact words from speeches that Lincoln delivered in the late 1850s. Although Lincoln deals briefly with the Fugitive Slave Law, he does not really discuss slavery, certainly not as a cause of war. The speech has little explicit reference to God, the Bible, or religion, themes that will become more prominent in the next years.

In appreciating Lincoln's inaugural we need to remember that the purpose of his speech in large measure controlled the rhetorical arsenal that he chose to use. Lincoln believed that in his first presidential speech, on the eve of a constitutional crisis, he needed to speak logically and rationally in support of the Constitution. It is a fair question whether Lincoln trusted too much in the power of rational argument. In this narrative of Lincoln's eloquence he will expand the range of his rhetoric even as he will be asked to speak in widely differing contexts in the next four years.

CHAPTER FOUR

"THIS IS . . . A PEOPLE'S CONTEST"

MESSAGE TO CONGRESS IN SPECIAL SESSION
JULY 4, 1861

. . . this issue embraces more than the fate of these United States. It presents to the whole family of man the question, whether a Constitutional republic, or a democracy—a government of the people, by the same people—can, or cannot, maintain its territorial integrity against its own domestic foes. . . .

This is essentially a People's contest. On the side of the Union, it is a struggle for maintaining in the world, that form and substance of government, whose leading object is, to elevate the condition of men—to lift artificial weights from all shoulders; to clear the paths of laudable pursuit for all; to afford all, an unfettered start, and a fair chance, in the race of life.

EARLY ON TUESDAY MORNING, March 5, Abraham Lincoln went to his new office on the second floor of the east wing of the White House and was handed a message needing urgent attention. A letter from Maj. Robert Anderson, commander of the Union garrison at Fort Sumter, in Charleston harbor, South Carolina, had arrived at the War Department on the day of Lincoln's inauguration. Major Anderson wrote that he had supplies to last only six weeks. Unless resupplied, he believed, he would be forced to surrender. The tension that Lincoln had attempted to straddle between conciliation and firmness in his inaugural address was about to be put to the test.[1]

IN LINCOLN'S FIRST DAYS in office everyone sought to take the measure of the new president. An experienced observer was William Howard Russell, special correspondent of the *Times* of London, who had seen a lot of fighting. He had earned an international reputation from twenty years of reporting on events in Ireland and India, and on the Crimean War. Russell arrived in New York in the middle of March. He hurried on to Washington as attention riveted on Lincoln and how he would respond to the growing crisis of Fort Sumter.

On March 27 the *Times* correspondent was taken to what he called "the moderate mansion, [the] White House." Russell recorded in his diary his first impressions of Lincoln in a word picture.

> Soon afterwards there entered, with a shambling, loose, irregular, almost unsteady gait, a tall, lank, lean man, considerably over six feet in height, with stooping shoulders, long pendulous arms, terminating in hands of extraordinary dimensions, which, however, were far exceeded in proportion by his feet. He was dressed in an ill-fitting, wrinkled suit of black, which put one in mind of an undertaker's uniform at a funeral; round his neck a rope of black silk was knotted in a large bulb, with flying ends projecting beyond the collar of his coat; his turned-down shirt-collar disclosed a sinewy, muscular yellow neck, and above that, nestling in a great black mass of hair, bristling and compact like a ruff of marching pins, rose the strange quaint face and head, covered with its thatch of wild republican hair, of President Lincoln.

Russell, known for his flair for descriptive prose, left his initial encounter with Lincoln "agreeably impressed with his shrewdness, humor, and natural sagacity."[2]

LINCOLN WAS NOT prepared administratively at the beginning of his presidency. He had been a legislator, but had never been in an executive position. He had served only one term in the House of Representatives and had been defeated in his aspiration to serve as a senator. He had not been a governor (as had Seward and Chase), a position in which he might have learned administrative abilities, as they did. He was not the leader of his own Republican Party. He came to the presidency with a lack of managerial experience, and his first days in office did not inspire confidence that he could take hold of running a new administration.

John Hay, who served with Nicolay as secretary to Lincoln, recalled, "There was little order or system about it." Hay reported, "Those around him strove from beginning to end to erect barriers to defend him against constant interruption, but the President himself was always the first to break them down." Sen. Henry Wilson of Massachusetts, who as chairman of the Military Affairs Committee would work closely with Lincoln, once remonstrated with him about his openness to people: "You will wear yourself out." Lincoln replied, "They don't want much; they get but little, and I must see them." Hay would conclude, "It would be hard to imagine a state of things less conducive to serious and effective work, yet in one way or another the work was done."[3]

Lincoln was well aware of his own inexperience in carrying out the duties of his new position. At first Lincoln attempted to do everything by himself. He admitted to Robert L. Wilson, a fellow member of the illustrious "Long Nine" of the Illinois House of Representatives in the 1830s, his struggles in administration. Lincoln told Wilson that "when he first commenced doing the duties, he was entirely ignorant not only of the duties, but of the manner of doing the business" of the presidency.[4]

IN ADDITION TO widespread criticism of Lincoln's administrative ability, there were some detractors who pointed to another concern. Behind the question of whether he was up to the job were qualms about his lack of education. Lincoln had attended schools for only brief periods in Kentucky and Indiana. Added together, Lincoln's periods of formal education amounted to less than one year in a schoolhouse.

Lincoln did not attempt to hide his lack of education. In 1858, Charles Lanman, preparing a *Dictionary of Congress,* sent to all members of Congress, past and present, a request for information about their lives. The first question asked was about education. Lincoln replied with a terse, one-word answer: "defective."[5]

In the fall of 1859, Jesse W. Fell, a fellow Illinois Republican, asked Lincoln for autobiographical information to be used with Eastern voters who knew little of Lincoln's life. In Lincoln's reply he spent considerable time talking about his education, mostly about its deficiencies. "There were schools, so called, but no qualification was ever required of a teacher, beyond '*readin, writin, and cipherin,* to the Rule of Three.'" The problem, as Lincoln looked back upon those years, was that "there was absolutely nothing to excite ambition for education." Lincoln averred of himself, "When I came of age I did not know much."[6]

In the summer of 1860 Lincoln supplied autobiographical materials to John L. Scripps of the *Chicago Tribune,* who was writing a campaign biography. In his twenty-five-hundred-word autobiography, whenever Lincoln spoke of himself, he did so in the third person. Lincoln continued to speak of his education with self-deprecation. "He was never in a college or Academy as a student." In the more extensive material he provided for Scripps, one senses his ambition for self-education. "He studied and nearly mastered the Six-books of Euclid, since he was a member of Congress."[7] Lincoln had studied Euclid, when he returned to the Eighth Circuit from his only term in Congress, as a means of strengthening his powers of reasoning.

IF LINCOLN LACKED formal education, and would struggle to learn the art of executive management, he brought with him one gift that he had worked hard to develop into an asset all his political life. Lincoln had become an artist with words. He had risen above political peers with more education and more political experience because he could articulate his political vision in spoken words that could both inform and inspire.

Stump speaking, so people said, was not the same thing as the kind of verbal communication Lincoln would be asked to do as president. Debates lasting more than three hours with Douglas, however popular they may have been in Illinois, did not prepare him for the kind of debates now taking place in Washington. His little speeches on the train trip from Springfield to Washington had not inspired but rather diminished confidence in Lincoln as a speaker. The jury that now counted—politicians and the public—was divided on the effectiveness of Lincoln's inaugural address.

AN EARLY FOUNDATION of Lincoln's ability to speak was laid in his reading of William Scott's *Lessons in Elocution.* His stepmother, Sarah Bush Lincoln, may have brought an 1806 edition with her from Kentucky. Scott's purpose was captured in the subtitle: . . . *for the Improvement of Youth in Reading and Speaking.* It was a large book, nearly four hundred pages, divided into two sections. Part I was entitled "Lessons in Reading," and Part II, "Lessons in Speaking." The second section included lessons with a compilation of soliloquies that the student was to practice. Lincoln acquired from Scott basic rules for public speaking. Among the eight rules were

1. Let your articulation be Distinct and Deliberate.
2. Let your pronunciation be Bold and Forcible.
6. In every sentence, distinguish the most significant words by a natural, forcible, and varied emphasis.
7. Acquire a just variety of Pause and Cadence.[8]

The book concluded with twenty-six speeches and soliloquies. These selections were in all probability the beginning of Lincoln's love affair with Shakespeare. From Scott's *Elocution* he memorized Falstaff's soliloquy on honor and King Claudius's soliloquy on his murder of Hamlet's father: "O, my offence is rank, it smells to heaven." The latter remained one of Lincoln's favorite passages.[9]

WHEN LINCOLN MOVED to New Salem he made the decision to master the English language by an intense study of grammar. While living in New Salem, Lincoln heard that a farmer, John Vance, owned a copy of Samuel Kirkham's *English Grammar.* Lincoln walked six miles to get it. He was twenty-three years old.

In William Herndon's biography of Lincoln, his law partner stated that Lincoln searched for a grammar because he "appreciated his inefficiency in a rhetorical sense, and therefore determined to overcome all these obstacles by mastering the intricacies of grammatical construction."[10] Lincoln's first motivation in studying grammar was to learn to speak well.

Kirkham's *English Grammar* was one of hundreds of grammars circulating in the first half of the nineteenth century. In his preface Kirkham stated that the grammar "professes not to instruct the literary connoisseur" but rather "attempts to accelerate the march of the juvenile mind."[11] Today's juveniles would surely find Kirkham's grammar book a tough assignment.

Kirkham divided his subject matter into four sections:

Orthography

Etymology

Syntax

Prosody

Lincoln devoured the Kirkham text. Sometimes he stretched out on the counter of Denton Offutt's store in New Salem as he committed whole sections of the book to memory. The student was asked to learn the lessons by rote. "Adverbs qualify verbs, adjectives, and other adverbs." The young Lincoln would wheedle his friends to help him practice the review tasks at the end of each chapter.[12]

To be able to master the text alone, however, was a daunting task, even for someone as motivated as Lincoln. Mentor Graham, a teacher in Kentucky and Illinois for nearly fifty years, told Herndon in a letter a few weeks after Lincoln's death that he had helped teach Lincoln grammar at New Salem. Graham reported that as soon as Lincoln had acquired the book, Lincoln had "turned his immediate & almost undivided attention to English grammar."[13]

The story of Lincoln studying grammar has been narrated in Lincoln biographies, but as a key to Lincoln's efforts to teach himself to write—whereas he said his first motivation was to teach himself to speak. Kirkham's final chapter, "Prosody," is the study of metrical verse. Lincoln, when supplying the autobiographical materials for Scripps in 1860, wrote, "He studied English grammar, imperfectly of course, but so as to speak and write as well as he now does."[14]

JUST AS LINCOLN was beginning his presidency, members of the House of Representatives were packing up to travel back to their home districts. The design for the ordering of Congress was imagined in the late eighteenth century. The original plans for annual sessions were calculated to coincide with the work patterns of citizen legislators, many of whom planned their lives according to the planting and harvesting seasons in an agricultural society. The nation's political business could be planted and harvested in Washington in the cold winter months of December, January, and February, when members could best be spared from their farms and plantations.

By the middle of the nineteenth century a plan had evolved whereby Congress, in its first so-called long term, met in a session that might go into the early summer. However, in the second, or last, year of a two-year term in the House of Representatives, they met in a short term, adjourning on March 4, thus being in session only three months.

ABRAHAM LINCOLN, given the biennial rhythm of Congress, found himself alone as the drama of Fort Sumter was being played out in early April. Everything changed when Confederate batteries, cloaked behind the small sandhills of Charleston harbor, fired on Fort Sumter on the morning of April 12, thirty-nine days after Lincoln's inaugural address.

As the war broke out, Lincoln had the freedom to act without the restraint of Congress. As commander-in-chief, under the war powers authorization of the Constitution, he issued an initial call for seventy-five thousand troops. But Lincoln knew he could not act alone. He needed the authorization of Congress in order to prosecute and to pay for the war. But the legislative branch of the government was not scheduled to convene—as the new Thirty-seventh Congress—until the first Monday in December.

On April 15, three days after the bombardment at Fort Sumter, Lincoln issued a proclamation calling for a special session of Congress to convene on July 4, 1861. The coming storm, of which Lincoln had spoken many times, had arrived in the waters off Charleston, South Carolina. Lincoln decided to offer an address to the special session. The preparation of that address would consume much of his imagination and time in the next two and a half months.

IN THE FOUR MONTHS between March 4 and July 4, Lincoln was confronted again and again by the same question: did he have a policy, either domestic or foreign?

He was asked that question by the person closest to him in his cabinet. William Seward, his secretary of state, had grown increasingly frustrated with Lincoln's leadership in this first month of the new administration. Finally, on Sunday afternoon, March 31, Seward drafted a letter, "Some thoughts for the President's consideration." The letter was dated April 1, copied by his son Frederick, and subsequently delivered to the president on Monday morning.

The first sentence surely received Lincoln's full attention. "We are at the end of a month's administration and yet without a policy either domestic or foreign." Seward cushioned his confrontation by admitting that the presence of the Senate, which continued in session until March 28, meant that much energy was taken up with appointments and patronage. Nevertheless, Seward's letter was no April Fool's joke. The secretary of state put the sword in deeper when he asserted, "But further delay to adopt and prosecute our policies for both domestic and foreign affairs would not only bring scandal on the Administration, but danger upon the country."[15]

What was the solution to this crisis of no policy? Seward suggested that "it must be somebody's business to pursue and direct it incessantly." And who should be the leader? "Either the President must do it himself, and be all the while active in it; or Devolve it on some member of his Cabinet." Guess who? Certainly Seward knew there was precedent in the first half of the nineteenth century for the secretary of state to assume a major share of leadership in the affairs of state.[16]

Lincoln wrote out a reply to Seward that very Monday. He responded point by point to Seward's letter. Lincoln acknowledged that they had disagreed over the question of resupplying Fort Sumter. The president stated that he did have a policy and reiterated the policy outlined in his inaugural address. He reminded Seward, who had been so helpful in reviewing the second draft of the address, "This had your distinct approval at the time." Finally, Lincoln said simply, "If this must be done, *I* must do it."[17]

We can only imagine Lincoln's feelings at receiving such a letter. What ultimately transpired between the two men is unknown to us. Lincoln's letter is in the Lincoln papers but there is doubt that it was ever sent. He may have delivered it personally, or he may have not given it to Seward, instead speaking to him that day. Remarkably, there was no knowledge of this exchange between the two leaders at the time. The letters came to light only three decades later, when Nicolay and Hay published their ten-volume biography in 1890. Future events, after April 1, 1861, would demonstrate that Seward's letter to Lincoln produced no lasting damage to their friendship.

BY THE END OF Lincoln's first month in office Seward was not alone in his concern about Lincoln's lack of a policy. Other leaders were distressed as well. Henry J. Raymond, founder of the *New York Times,* was a staunch Republican. Just two days after Seward's letter to Lincoln, however, Raymond printed an editorial: "Wanted—A Policy." He charged the new Republican administration with "a blindness and a stolidity without parallel in the history of intelligent statesmanship." Raymond focused his charge on Lincoln himself. "He must go up to a higher level than he has yet reached, before he can see and realize the high duties to which he has been called."[18]

LINCOLN'S SILENCE AFTER HIS inaugural address and his lack of public comment after the bombardment at Fort Sumter have raised questions, then and now. After we take into account a much different expectation of a presidential speech in the nineteenth century, the question persists.

But silence is speaking. In his silence he was offering resolve. He was silent before his inaugural address, and he struggled with what to say and not say on the train trip from Springfield to Washington, because he was preparing definitive remarks for March 4, 1861. He had now called for a special session of Congress to be convened and he was privately preparing for his definitive public message on July 4.

IN THE ANXIOUS DAYS in the spring of 1861, the city of Washington was running on two time schedules. The first schedule reflected the long-established time patterns of an unhurried Southern city. In Lincoln's first months in Washington, even with the preparations for a possible civil war, the ethos of official Washington lived on at a leisurely pace. In the early days of summer, people gathered under the shade of the alianthus trees on Pennsylvania Avenue to speculate about the latest news of impending war. Government offices closed at 3 P.M. and the dinner hour was set at 4 P.M. Those hours prevailed at the White House, too, although when there were special dinners, the hour was set at 5:30 P.M. It was the custom in the political season, after dinner, that citizens would join in a promenade on Pennsylvania Avenue, which concluded at the Capitol on Wednesdays and at the president's house on Saturdays, where the Marine Band would entertain.[19]

After the bombardment of Fort Sumter, and with the coming of military units from the North and West into the capital, a new pace emerged. Time speeded up. Soldiers from Maine, Massachusetts, Indiana, and Pennsylvania became a common sight, drilling all across the capital. A chain of forts grew up rapidly around the city. Tents could be seen dotting the hillsides. The Union flag was flying everywhere.

The leisurely ways of spring gave way to the up tempo of marching feet in a city preparing for war in the early summer of 1861.

After Lincoln's inaugural address in March, and again following the attack on Fort Sumter in April, Lincoln was largely silent in terms of public speeches and remarks. If his silence after his nomination and before his election can be explained by custom, and if his silence between his election and his inaugural address can be portrayed as his wariness not to misspeak before he was inaugurated in Washington, his long silences during his presidency are a lingering mystery.

In *The Collected Works of Abraham Lincoln,* editor Roy P. Basler classified Lincoln's speaking in five groups: addresses, speeches, remarks, replies, and responses. Most of these were not speeches, but were in the form of remarks, almost all in relation to his official duties as president. These do not include messages to Congress, which would be read by clerks in the House of Representatives and Senate. Taken together, Lincoln spoke fewer than one hundred times in a little more than four years in office. Most of his speaking was impromptu. Some remarks would have been at the suggestion of others, such as ceremonies presided over by Seward as secretary of state.[20]

Again and again, Lincoln rejected opportunities to give more formal speeches. He turned down a request to return to New York's Cooper Union to address a rally to enlist Northern recruits. He declined to speak at large events planned to honor the heroes Adm. David G. Farragut and Gen. Ulysses S. Grant.[21]

He almost never spoke away from Washington, and even then mostly at the White House. One can count Lincoln's major addresses on the fingers of one hand.

Why was Lincoln silent? If he rose to political prominence in Illinois in significant measure because of his remarkable stump speaking and debating abilities, why did he use this gift so seldom as president? We need to follow Lincoln into his first term as president before attempting to answer this question.

IN MAY, Lincoln began to compose his message to Congress. As president, Lincoln called a special session of Congress because, under the

Constitution, he had to secure congressional approval to pay for the war.

Lincoln had never written an executive report to a legislative body before. This would need to be a communication in a different form. He needed to explain his vision and actions after the outbreak of war. How could he bring his strengths as a speaker to a real audience in a report to be delivered by a clerk without Lincoln present?

By June reporters noted that President Lincoln was absenting himself from visitors to work on his address. As July 4 approached, his secretary John Nicolay reported that the president changed his open-door policy and now refused to see anyone, either for business or friendship, except for members of the cabinet or high officials. Just as before his inaugural address, a private Lincoln somehow found time and space away from the throngs who crowded the east wing of the White House each day, to work at writing and revising his message to Congress.[22]

Lincoln did have plenty of time for Seward. After their painful exchange of April 1, rather than separate, the two men came together. Lincoln, who did not hold grudges, valued Seward's intellect, abilities, and humor. Seward came to appreciate this gaunt Westerner, so unlike himself, who had deprived him of the highest prize of his life. Toward the end of June, in a letter to his wife, Frances, Seward wrote, "The President is the best of us."[23]

MANY OF LINCOLN'S writing habits had been developed working on cases in his career as a lawyer. Herndon reported that Lincoln preferred writing with his long legs at their full length and resting on a chair. He positioned any books he needed on a table nearby or in his lap.[24]

Lincoln was always writing notes to himself on odd scraps of paper, which he would then insert into the right place in his message. Herndon reported, for example, that Lincoln, in preparing his "House Divided" speech, delivered in Springfield in June 1858, wrote down ideas on scraps of paper and stray envelopes. Lincoln then put them into his circular file, "that miscellaneous and convenient receptacle, his hat."[25]

Noah Brooks, correspondent for the *Sacramento Daily Union,* confirmed a similar practice in the White House. He observed Lincoln writing in his armchair, his favorite position, sometimes with his legs crossed. Brooks reported that Lincoln wrote his speeches first with pencil on stiff sheets of white boxboard or pasteboard, which were five to six inches wide. He laid the sheets on his knee. Lincoln revised, crossing out words, until the text was ready to be copied as the final version of the address or speech to be delivered.[26]

CONGRESSMEN AND SENATORS began returning to Washington in the first days of July. There would be a presence of an absence for this special session. Stephen Douglas, "the Little Giant," Lincoln's longtime opponent, had died suddenly in early June. In recent months, Douglas, the 1860 northern Democratic candidate for president, had gone out of his way to signal his support for the man who was now president. Douglas's place in the Senate would be taken by Republican Orville H. Browning.

New York lawyer George Templeton Strong traveled from New York to Washington in this same time period. Strong recorded in his diary that Washington in early July was not for the fainthearted. "For all the detestable places, Washington is the first—in July, and with Congress sitting." He catalogued his experiences: "Crowd, heat, bad quarters, bad fare, bad smells, mosquitoes, and a plague of flies transcending everything within my experience." Strong, an active layman at the Trinity Episcopal Church in New York, resorted to Old Testament imagery to sum up his impressions of Washington and its best hotel. "Beelzebub surely reigns there, and Willard's Hotel is his temple."[27]

AS LINCOLN MOVED from the first to the second draft of his message to Congress, he invited his cabinet to look over the proof sheets. Seward reported that "various portions of the message had been the subject of several conferences" in the cabinet.[28]

Through the whole process Seward became the main contributor, as he had been with the inaugural address. The secretary of state made more than twenty suggestions, offered in the handwriting of his son and secretary, Frederick Seward. Lincoln accepted nearly all of Seward's suggestions. Lincoln made almost a hundred revisions of his own in the various versions of the text.[29]

On July 3, at noon, the message was reviewed a last time by the cabinet.

ON THE EVENING OF July 3, Browning called at the White House. Browning had arrived in the capital from Illinois the previous evening, and had checked into the National Hotel. At about 9 P.M. he came to pay his respects to the president. Nicolay told Browning that Lincoln was reviewing his message to Congress, but offered to send in Browning's card. Browning did not want to bother Lincoln and went to pay his respects to Mrs. Lincoln.

When Lincoln overheard Browning's voice, he sent for his old friend. He told Browning that "he had just finished his message." Browning reported in his diary that Lincoln "said he wished to read it to me."[30] Lincoln wanted to hear even this written message to Congress.

LINCOLN HAD SCHEDULED the special session of Congress to begin at noon on July 4. He does not say why he chose the Fourth of July. He may have wanted to take advantage of the anniversary of independence as he asked Congress to rededicate itself to this ultimate challenge to the independence of an undivided Union.

He may also have wanted the members of Congress to see and be seen on this particular Fourth of July. What a grand patriotic day in a still-young nation that felt very connected to beginnings stretching back only a little more than three quarters of a century! Citizens enjoying the holiday packed Lafayette Square. After months of worry about the defense of the capital, over twenty thousand troops marched along Pennsylvania Avenue, what locals simply called "the Avenue." Lincoln, with old Gen. Winfield Scott beside him, standing on a platform decorated with flags in front of the White House, received the salute of the largest display of military might ever seen in the capital.

One group stood out among the marchers. The Garibaldi Guards were made up entirely of foreign soldiers, many of whom had served in wars in Europe. The soldiers spoke six or eight languages. The colonel gave his commands in French. Each man wore a sprig of evergreen or a flower in his hat. As the Garibaldi Guards passed the reviewing stand where Lincoln stood with a number of Union officers, the soldiers took out their sprigs and flowers and tossed them toward the president in tribute. The whole dazzling parade increased the energy and the impatience of the lawmakers scheduled to assemble at noon.[31]

THE THIRTY-SEVENTH Congress assembled in marked contrast to its predecessor. This new Congress was loyal to the Union. The border states of Delaware, Maryland, Kentucky, and Missouri were represented. The Republicans had strong majorities in both houses. In the House of Representatives sat 105 Republicans and 43 Democrats. The Senate was composed of 31 Republicans and 10 Democrats. Secession cost the Democrats almost half of their representation in Congress. "War Democrats," those who supported Lincoln's war effort, such as Andrew Johnson from Tennessee and Reverdy Johnson of Maryland, were also prominent.

The first day's meeting was brief, devoted to organization.

THE PRESIDENT'S MESSAGE was actually sent up to Congress on July 5. Secretary Nicolay arrived at 2 P.M. with the message, which was to be read by a clerk in the recently completed impressive Senate chamber and the elaborate red-and-gold House of Representatives. In the middle of the nineteenth century the president was not expected to deliver his message in person.

George Washington and John Adams, the presidents in the first twelve years of the nation, had delivered their annual messages in person. Thomas Jefferson, the nation's third president, changed this tradition. Jefferson had a deep antipathy to the monarchical structures from which the colonies freed themselves. He believed that the symbol of the president speaking to Congress smacked of the old order in which the king or queen spoke from on high to Parliament. He declared a clean break from his two Federalist predecessors by saying he would not address Congress, but rather send up a written message.

Jefferson's practice lasted for more than one hundred years, all the way into the early twentieth century. Woodrow Wilson broke with this precedent in his first year as president when he decided to speak in person to Congress about the state of the union, in 1913. All presidents since Wilson have followed the practice of delivering their State of the Union address in person to both houses of Congress and invited guests.

The presidential message, delivered annually when Congress convened on the first Monday in December, had become by Lincoln's time a summation of the multiple actions and concerns of the president and his administration. The listeners did not expect, nor did they usually receive, any rhetorical dessert in the midst of the standard meat and potatoes of political fare.

Lincoln, starting with his message to the special session, did not abide by that tradition. When this message is placed within the whole range of his communications, it becomes clear that Lincoln crafted certain parts not as a report but as a speech. To be sure, his regular annual messages would contain a melting pot of political business. His message to the special session focused solely on the justification of the war. Even though his message would be read by a clerk, he infused it with artful language intended to inspire the imagination and passions of the nation.

> *Fellow-citizens of the Senate and House of Representatives:*
> *Having been convened on an extraordinary occasion, as authorized by the Constitution, your attention is not called to any ordinary subject of legislation.*

Lincoln began with one of his favorite rhetorical strategies, working with the juxtaposition of *extraordinary* and *ordinary.* Lincoln also placed the session under the Constitution, much in the spirit of his inaugural address.

The policy chosen looked to the exhaustion of all peaceful measures, before a resort to any stronger ones. It sought only to hold the public places and property not already wrested from the government, and to collect the revenue; relying for the rest, on time, discussion, and the ballot-box.

Lincoln, an experienced communicator even if not familiar with this form of communication, began by attempting to bring definition to an incredibly ambiguous situation. In the Congress and throughout the North he faced a muddle of frustrations and hopes. The nation had endured eighty days of almost bloodless war. Most on both sides expected a quick war. "Forward to Richmond" was the cry in the North. But Lincoln knew there were many problems.

At the outset Lincoln restated his policy, announced in his inaugural address, to pursue *all peaceful measures* to avoid war. Lincoln attempted to substantiate this policy by his use of the word *only* to underline the limited functions that the government attempted to exercise. He extended that spirit by reminding friend and foe that the strategy of his administration was to be content to rely on the peaceful measures of

time, discussion, and the ballot-box

And this issue embraces more than the fate of these United States. It presents to the whole family of man the question, whether a Constitutional republic, or a democracy—a government of the people, by the same people—can, or cannot, maintain its territorial integrity against its own domestic foes.

In these words we understand that his audience was more than Congress. He directed his remarks to the people of both the North and the South. He was even speaking to foreign governments that were deciding what their position should be toward the Union and the Confederacy. Lincoln, with these words, offered a new, expanded definition of the meaning of the American Civil War.

He employed an expansive figure—

the whole family of man

—to focus his remarks on what he believed was the real question of the war. That question was whether the American experiment, which Lincoln defined in three different ways, could maintain its territorial integrity against domestic foes. After starting with more formal definitions—*constitutional republic* and *democracy*—he turned to a populist definition:

a government of the people, by the same people

Lincoln enjoyed working with ideas, turning them over and over again in his mind as well as trying them out as parts of different speeches. He would keep working with this definition.

BY THE TIME CONGRESS assembled on July 4, Lincoln's suspension of the writ of habeas corpus was beginning to become a contentious issue. Soon after the surrender of Fort Sumter, Confederate supporters began burning bridges and cutting telegraph wires between Washington and Baltimore. On April 27, 1861, Lincoln ordered General Winfield Scott to arrest anyone between Washington and Baltimore believed to be involved in subversive speech or acts. The President told the commanding general of the army that if he were to "find resistance which renders it necessary to suspend the writ of Habeas Corpus for the public safety, you . . . are authorized to suspend that writ."[32]

Nearly one month later, on May 25, John Merryman, a Maryland state legislator who was drilling secessionist troops, was arrested and held at Fort McHenry. His attorney sought a writ of habeas corpus so that a federal court could look at the charges. Chief Justice Roger Taney, the author of the Dred Scott decision, interjected himself into the case as a federal district judge and heard the case. Merryman obtained a writ from Taney, who ordered that the Marylander be either tried before a regular court or released. Taney sent a copy to Lincoln.

Lincoln had been consulting with Attorney General Bates, but Lincoln did not respond, appeal, or order the release of Merryman. George Cadwalader, the commanding officer at Fort McHenry, also refused to comply, citing Lincoln's executive order.[33]

On July 2, two days before Congress was to meet in special session, Lincoln wrote again to Scott authorizing him to enlarge the scope of the suspension of habeas corpus to a line reaching from Washington to New York.[34] Lincoln would provide his answer to Taney and his critics in his Message to Congress in Special Session on July 4.

As Lincoln introduced the subject of the suspension of habeas corpus, his sometimes awkward prose spoke to his struggle over this divisive issue at the beginning of his presidency.

> *Soon after the first call for militia, it was considered a duty to authorize the commanding general, in proper cases, according to his discretion, to suspend the privilege of the writ of habeas corpus; or, in other words, to arrest and detain, without resort to the ordinary processes and forms of law, such individuals as he might deem dangerous to the public safety. This authority has purposely been exercised but very sparingly. Nevertheless, the legality and propriety of what has been done under it are questioned, and the attention of the country has been called to the proposition that one who is sworn to "take care that the laws be faithfully executed," should not himself violate them.*

Part of Lincoln's struggle, unknown to both his audience in Congess and the audience that would read his words in newspapers in the coming days, was with this new form of communication. Behind the scenes his secretaries, Nicolay and Hay, watched their boss write and rewrite. Years later, in their biography of Lincoln, which was published in 1890, they thought it worthwhile to include the first draft of the special message, believing that by reading the original autograph "we seem brought into direct contact with the living workings of Lincoln's mind." James G. Randall went a step further in 1926 and placed Lincoln's first draft and final version in two parallel columns.[35]

ORIGINAL AUTOGRAPH	*PUBLISHED MESSAGE*
Soon after the first call for militia *I felt it my duty* to authorize the commanding general, in proper cases . . . to suspend the privilege of the writ of habeas corpus . . .	*it was considered a duty*
At my verbal request, as well as by the general's own inclination, this authority has been exercised but very sparingly.	*This authority has purposely been excercised . . . sparingly.*
Nevertheless . . . *I have been reminded from a high quarter* that one who is Sworn to "take care that the laws should be faithfully executed" should not himself be one to violate them.	*the attention of the country has been called to the proposition*
Of course *I gave some consideration to the questions of power and propriety before I acted in this matter. The whole of the laws which I was sworn to [execute]* were being resisted . . . in nearly one-third of the States.	*. . . some consideration was given . . . before this matter was acted upon. The whole of the laws which were required to be faithfully executed,*
Must I have allowed them to finally fail of execution? . . . are all the laws but one to go unexecuted, and the government itself go to pieces, lest that one be violated? . . .	*Must they be allowed to finally fail*
But . . . I was not, in my own	*But it was not believed that*

judgment, driven to this ground. In my opinion, I violated no law. The provision of the Constitution . . . is equivalent to a provision . . . that [the] privilege may be suspended when, in cases of rebellion or invasion, the public safety *does* require	*this question was presented. It was not believed that any law was violated.*
it . . . *I decided* that we have a case of rebellion. . . .	*It was decided . . .*

The most striking alteration is Lincoln's editing from the active to the passive voice, from "I" to "it was." Did he do so to accommodate this new form of communication, a message read by a clerk rather than an address he would deliver? He disappears in his message, awkwardly, at the very moment where he surely knew that his own actions were being held up to review. I believe, at a deeper level, the change reflects Lincoln's concern regarding any appearance of military dictatorship on his part. He was unwavering in saying that his actions were determined both by circumstances and by his reading of the Constitution and not by any desire to overreach his authority.

Both suspension and arbitrary arrest confronted the powers of Congress and the Constitution. The terms in the Constitution read:

> *The privilege of the Writ of* Habeas Corpus *shall not be suspended, unless when in Cases of Rebellion or Invasion the public Safety may require it.*[36]

This section of Lincoln's message was rational and impersonal in tone. He did not mention the Merryman case. He seemed to admit that Congress was the appropriate place for such suspensions to take place. He went out of his way to assure those assembled that *Whether there shall be any legislation upon the subject,* he was content to rely on *the better judgment of Congress.*

The whole of the laws which were required to be faithfully executed, were being resisted, and failing of execution in nearly one-third of the States. Must they be allowed to finally fail of execution, even had it been perfectly clear, that by the use of the means necessary to their execution, some single law, made in such extreme tenderness of the citizen's liberty, that practically, it relieves more of the guilty, than of the innocent, should to a very limited extent, be violated? To state the question more directly , are all the laws <u>*but one*</u> *to go unexecuted, and the government itself go to pieces, lest that one be violated? Even in such a case, would not the official oath be broken, if the government should be overthrown, when it was believed that disregarding the single law, would tend to preserve it?*

Mark E. Neely, Jr., in *The Fate of Liberty: Abraham Lincoln and Civil Liberties,* asserts that "Lincoln stumbled" in speaking about habeas corpus in the special message: "The syntax of Lincoln's response was unusually labored." Neely states that this part of the message on July 4 revealed "the work of a fledgling president, uncertain of his legal ground and his audience."[37] Lincoln had much to learn.

Granting the validity of these observations of a Lincoln working in a new medium on a most difficult constitutional issue, at the end of this section he did recover his rhetorical balance when he asked:

To state the question more directly, are all the laws <u>*but one*</u> *to go unexecuted, and the government itself go to pieces, lest that one be violated?*

This is one sentence that remained unchanged from first to last draft. Seward had suggested replacing the last word in the sentence, *violated,* with *broken,* but Lincoln rejected the change. Lincoln underlined <u>*but one*</u> for stress, perhaps hoping that the clerks in the House and Senate would pick up his emphasis. His emphasis was to point beyond the immediate crisis to the ultimate preservation of the Union.

It might seem, at first thought, to be of little difference whether the present movement at the South be called "secession" or "rebellion." The movers, however, well understand the difference. At the beginning, they knew they could never raise their treason to any respectable magnitude by any name which implies <u>*violation*</u> *of law. They knew their people possessed as much of moral sense, as much of devotion to law and order, and as much pride in, and reverence for, the history and government of their common country, as any other civilized and patriotic people. They knew they could make no advancement directly in the teeth of these strong and noble sentiments. Accordingly they commenced by an insidious debauching of the public mind. They invented an ingenious sophism . . .*

Lincoln, at the center of the address, acted as a political guide eager to lead the way through a thicket of thorny definitions and recriminations. For Lincoln the lawyer-politician, definitions always mattered. It mattered most that this was not a war between the government of the United States and the government of the Confederate States of America. To use such terms would be to cede to the Southern states the constitutional prerogative of secession.

The conviction that animated Lincoln was that the Union was perpetual. Therefore, the Southern states, or rather individuals within those states, were acting in rebellion. Lincoln did call the conflict a civil war, but in the four years that lay ahead he much preferred the term *rebellion,* which he would use over four hundred times in speeches and letters.[38] States that were in rebellion could never be out of the Union.

In this section we hear a trait that marks the distinctiveness of Lincoln's rhetoric. Lincoln combined both homely with high language in a new kind of American communication. In his extended discussion of secession he referred initially to its proponents by saying:

they commenced by an insidious debauching of the public mind.

He continued his assault by arguing that

> *They invented an ingenious sophism*

—an argument ultimately invalid, even if correct in form. After speaking at this high level of oratory, Lincoln suddenly exclaimed:

> *With rebellion thus sugar-coated, they have been drugging the public mind of their section for more than thirty years . . .*

The government printer, John D. Defrees, objected to Lincoln's phrase *sugar-coated* when he received Lincoln's draft. Defrees had served as a member of the state legislature in Indiana, and was the head of the Indiana delegation at the Republican convention in Chicago. The politician and printer told Lincoln that *sugar-coated* "lacked the dignity proper to a state paper." Lincoln replied, "Well, Defrees, if you think the time will come when people will not understand what 'sugar-coated' means, I'll alter it; otherwise, I think I'll let it go."[39] In Lincoln's reply we hear his readiness to mesh homely and high language in his utilization of the full range of the American idiom.

> *This is essentially a People's contest. On the side of the Union, it is a struggle for maintaining in the world, that form and substance of government, whose leading object is, to elevate the condition of men—to lift artificial weights from all shoulders; to clear the paths of laudable pursuit for all; to afford all, an unfettered start, and a fair chance, in the race of life.*

The Civil War has been interpreted as a war to preserve the Union. Yet here at the beginning of the war, Lincoln declared that the Union was not an end, but a means to an end. The end was more than a particular system of political organization. It was rather an ecology of social and economic life that could nourish common persons' opportunity to pursue their dreams not limited by any artificial impediments.

Lincoln's words almost always had levels of intent and meaning. By an emphasis on *People* as opposed to states or nations, Lincoln was maintaining his position that the states of the Confederate States of America, an entity he would not dignify by naming it, were coercing millions of people who did not want this contest at all. Lincoln would insist on this point of view—be it fiction or nonfiction—for the next four years.

He combined a liberal end with a conservative means. He wanted to conserve a deep-rooted order and, after Fort Sumter, positioned the Union as the defender of the whole history of the nation. Lincoln's language is conservative when he speaks of defending an established system. Lincoln's language is liberal when he speaks of promoting and extending the rights of all people.

LINCOLN'S SPEECH TO Congress spoke to many of his critics.

Yes, Lincoln was in charge. As he had answered Seward's challenge directly in private, he now spoke in public. This speech was as much about establishing Lincoln's moral authority to lead as anything else.

Yes, Lincoln had a policy. In answer to the *New York Times* and other newspapers and politicians, Lincoln offered a policy that would then be acted upon in the more than seventy provisions Congress would pass in the remaining twenty-eight days of the special session.

GEORGE CURTIS READ Lincoln's message with keen interest. Curtis was an editorial writer for *Harper's Monthly* ("Easy Chair") and *Harper's Weekly* ("Lounger"), and he would be named the editor of *Harper's Weekly* in 1863. He was an independent-minded Republican who had been a delegate to the Republican national convention in Chicago. Living on Staten Island, Curtis went to Chicago to support his fellow New Yorker, Seward, for the Republican nomination for president. After Lincoln was elected, Curtis began to doubt that Lincoln had the abilities to carry the day.

The July 4 address became a turning point in Curtis's assessment of Lincoln. In a letter to a younger friend he offered his assessment of Lincoln's words. Curtis thought Lincoln's "message was the most truly American message ever delivered." As a literary critic he believed Lincoln's words were "wonderfully acute, simple, sagacious, and of antique honesty"! Curtis concluded, "I can forgive the jokes and the big hands, and the inability to make bows. Some of us who doubted were wrong."[40]

LINCOLN'S MESSAGE to the special session of Congress of July 4, 1861, is not as well known as it ought to be. It was a painstakingly prepared document. Read by a clerk, the message has received insufficient attention for both its political acumen and its rhetorical artistry. Lincoln presented an elucidation of the course of action he had taken in the Fort Sumter crisis as well as his plans to uphold the Union. Offered at the beginning of the war, in a time of ambiguity when everyone was seeking to define the meaning of the conflict, Lincoln's message is most prescient in already looking beyond the tempestuous present to articulate for the future a deeper meaning to the war.

This message is Lincoln's first of nearly one hundred speeches and communications authored while the nation was at war. Everything that went before, including the inaugural address, was written in the hope of avoiding war. In the first major message after the war had begun, Lincoln worked with ideas that he would develop in succeeding months and years. Lincoln's habit, as a person of ideas, was to launch a thought and then over time refine that thought in future speeches. In this message to Congress he worked with the idea of

a government of the people, by the same people

as a central definition of the meaning of the American experiment. He would make this definition more complete and symmetrical two and a half years later when he offered dedicatory remarks at a Pennsylvania battlefield.

A SPEAKER and a speech are significant for what they don't say as well as what they do say. Lincoln made no mention of slavery. In early July almost everyone in the North believed this would be a short war and a quick victory. Slavery was a reality, with a long history in the American story, that both North and South had dodged for 230 years. No one knew it on July 4, 1861, but before another year had come and gone, the dilemma of slavery would become central in Lincoln's thinking and speaking.

CHAPTER FIVE

"MY PARAMOUNT OBJECT IN THIS STRUGGLE"

REPLY TO HORACE GREELEY
AUGUST 22, 1862

I would save the Union. I would save it the shortest way under the Constitution. The sooner the national authority can be restored, the nearer the Union will be "the Union as it was." If there be those who would not save the Union, unless they could at the same time save slavery, I do not agree with them. If there be those who would not save the Union unless they could at the same time destroy slavery, I do not agree with them. My paramount object in this struggle is to save the Union, and is not either to save or to destroy slavery. If I could save the Union without freeing any slave I would do it, and if I could save it by freeing all the slaves I would do it; and if I could save it by freeing some and leaving others alone I would also do that.

ABRAHAM LINCOLN TO HORACE GREELEY, AUGUST 22, 1862

HORACE GREELEY, quixotic editor of the *New York Tribune,* penned a letter to Abraham Lincoln on August 19, 1862. The next day Greeley published the same composition as an open letter in the *Tribune* under the caption "The Prayer of Twenty Millions." Greeley protested that Lincoln was "strangely and disastrously remiss" in not proclaiming emancipation now.[1]

An impatient Greeley was calling out a patient Lincoln.

Greeley's letter created a firestorm. Coming toward the end of a long summer of Union discontent, Greeley's challenge to the president about the emancipation of slaves in Southern states was republished in newspapers across the North.

The editor of the *Tribune* was surprised when Lincoln did not blink, but raised the stakes with an immediate reply printed in Washington's *National Intelligencer.* The president's response was also republished in countless newspapers. The purpose and meaning of Lincoln's reply to Greeley has been discussed and debated ever since.

IMMEDIATELY AFTER Lincoln's message to the special session of Congress on July 4, 1861, the war intensified quickly. Bold talk about a short war was silenced by defeats at Bull Run on July 21 and at Ball's Bluff in October. At sea the Union naval blockade was far from successful in the first year of the war. Recognition of the Confederate States of America by Great Britain seemed a troublesome possibility. At the end of 1861 Southern spirits were soaring, with Confederate outposts located only a few miles from Washington, while the mood throughout the Union was sinking.

After the defeat at Bull Run, Lincoln appointed Gen. George McClellan commander of the Army of the Potomac, and with the retirement of Winfield Scott on November 1, he became general-in-chief as well. McClellan looked the part of a successful general as he organized, drilled, and prepared through late fall and early winter. In the opening months of 1862, Union spirits were lifted with the capture of Fort Henry and Fort Donelson, just below the Kentucky-Tennessee border, by an unknown brigadier general named Ulysses S. Grant. Nashville fell to Don Carlos Buell's Army of the Ohio on February 25, the first state capital in the Confederacy to be captured. In the same month, Gen. Ambrose E. Burnside won a series of battles in coastal North Carolina. Greeley's *New York Tribune* was enthusiastic over this string of successes. "Every blow tells fearfully against the rebellion. The rebels themselves are panic-stricken, or despondent. It requires no very far-seeing prophet to predict the end of the struggle."[2]

On April 6 and 7, in the Battle of Shiloh, in Tennessee, Grant secured victory from defeat in the largest and bloodiest battle of the war so far, but the cost of thirteen thousand federal casualties left many in the North stunned. Also on April 7, Union general John Pope, who had traveled with Lincoln on the train from Springfield, led twenty thousand troops in attacking and capturing Island No. 10 on the Mississippi River.

Union successes only heightened the pressure on McClellan to lead his large army into the field. He finally sailed his Army of the Potomac south to the peninsula between the James and the York Rivers in Virginia and on April 4 began the march up the peninsula toward Richmond. After a month of contradictory reports, Lincoln arrived on May 6 at Fortress Monroe to see for himself what General McClellan was or was not doing. By the end of May, the Union forces finally advanced to within six miles of Richmond.

In late May, Gen. Thomas J. ("Stonewall") Jackson, in part to relieve pressure on Richmond, began a dazzling campaign in the Shenandoah Valley of Virginia, where he outmaneuvered and outfought several Union armies. Jackson's mobility and quick successes even raised the prospect of a Confederate march on Washington. In June, Gen. Robert E. Lee assumed command of the Confederate forces defending Richmond, and at the end of the month he led a counteroffensive called the Seven Days' Battles that ended McClellan's Peninsular Campaign. By the Fourth of July 1862, one year after Lincoln's special message to Congress, it had become clear to the president and the North that McClellan's grand opportunity had been lost, Richmond had survived, and Lee and Jackson and their armies were on the rise.

In New York, lawyer George Templeton Strong took the measure of the Union state of mind in the summer of 1862. On July 11, he observed in a diary entry, "We have been and are in a depressed, dismal, aesthetic state of anxiety and irritability. The cause of the country does not happen to be thriving just now." Nearly a month later, on August 4, he wrote, "Prevailing color of people's talk is blue." Strong, who was growing in his admiration of Lincoln, understood that even with the fault of the generals, the criticism would ultimately be directed at the commander-in-chief. "What's very bad, we begin to lose faith in Uncle Abe."[3]

THE IMMEDIACY OF the Civil War was brought home in a new way to more people by newspapers, which were surging in growth in the middle of the nineteenth century. If in 1800 there were approximately 250 newspapers, by 1860 there were more than 2,500 newspapers, both weekly and daily. More newspapers were being published in the United States than in all of the rest of the world combined. Vicksburg, a little town in Mississippi with a population of forty-five hundred on the eve of the Civil War, could boast of six newspapers. In large cities newspapers often published multiple editions each day in order to keep up with the demand of a populace hungry for news of the war.

Horace Greeley had built the *New York Tribune* into a major newspaper in New York and the nation at the outbreak of the Civil War. It was one of the first penny newspapers. A weekly edition boasted a paid circulation of 214,000 by 1860. Even before the war broke out, however, many postmasters in the South refused to distribute "the black Republican" *Tribune.*

Many more people read newspapers than the paid subscribers. One copy was often read by several families. Numerous citizens heard editorials read aloud in an era that prized public reading. In countless general stores, neighbors gathered in the evening to listen to the reading of editorials from "Uncle Horace's Weekly Try-bune." As national issues heated up, people gathered by rural post offices to anticipate the stagecoach delivering their "newspaper Bible."

Ralph Waldo Emerson, writing to Thomas Carlyle, Scottish-born English historian and essayist, described traveling in the Midwest and discovering the power and reach of Greeley. He portrayed Greeley as "the right spiritual father of this region," who "prints and disperses 110 000 newspapers in one day." Greeley had preceded Emerson in Wisconsin and "people had flocked together, coming 30 & 40 miles to hear" the New York editor speak. Emerson told Carlyle that Greeley, through his weekly newspaper, "does all their thinking & theory for them, for two dollars a year."[4]

ON THE EVE OF the Civil War, the public mind identified the leading newspapers with larger-than-life personalities. Editors were not simply conduits of political news; they were often the news themselves. Editors were also politicians, or at the very least important political voices with far-reaching influence. Newspaper editors and correspondents clamored for political appointments, and they received scores of them in the first years of the Lincoln administration.

The Republicans could boast a phalanx of editors with national reputations. Henry J. Raymond had begun his career as an assistant to Greeley before founding the *New York Times* in 1851. He served as lieutenant governor of New York at the same time that he was editor of the *Times,* and would serve as chairman of the Republican National Committee during the Civil War. William Cullen Bryant, the gray-bearded poet and editor of the *New York Evening Post,* had introduced Lincoln at the Cooper Union. The following winter he pressured Lincoln about cabinet selections. Samuel Bowles of the *Springfield Republican,* after initial doubts, became one of Lincoln's strongest supporters, which helped transform his newspaper in a small city into a national voice. Joseph Medill, a founder of the Republican Party, moved from Ohio to Illinois in 1855, where he purchased the *Chicago Tribune.* He helped manage newspaper publicity for Lincoln in the 1860 election, and on the day before the convention opened, ran a three-foot-high editorial in the *Chicago Tribune* entitled "The Winning Man, Abraham Lincoln." After Lincoln was elected, these and other editors believed it was their duty to write Lincoln regularly, offering their advice and counsel on all manner of affairs of state.

All of these editors converged on the Wigwam in Chicago for the Republican convention in May 1860, where Lincoln would be nominated. The *New York Times,* an often bitter rival of the *New York Tribune,* nevertheless captured the importance of Greeley. "Mr. Greeley made a great sensation here. He is surrounded by a crowd wherever he goes, who besiege him for a speech, and failing in that seduce him into conversation, which inevitably becomes a speech ere he closes."[5]

HORACE GREELEY was born on a hardscrabble farm near Amherst, New Hampshire, in 1811. Departing from the farming ways of his ancestors, at age fifteen he apprenticed to an East Poultney, Vermont, printer. Seeking a larger world, he came to New York City in 1831 and found his first job with printer John T. West.

At age thirty, ten years later, he began the *New York Tribune,* on April 10, 1841. Greeley started the paper with one thousand borrowed dollars. He decided to name his new paper the *Tribune* because he wanted it to speak to and for the people. He was a reformer at heart and the *Tribune* would become his pulpit.

To appreciate the influence of the *Tribune* is to understand that it was far more than a New York newspaper. There were other newspapers that rivaled the *Tribune* within New York. James Gordon Bennett's *New York Herald,* an independent newspaper that would increasingly side with the Democrats after the beginning of the war, had the largest daily circulation in New York. Unrivaled was the *Tribune*'s influence as a national paper. A weekly edition was mailed to subscribers from Maine to California. Greeley's most concentrated audiences were in states that would become crucial to the Union cause. After New York, more people read Greeley's paper in Pennsylvania than in any other state in the Union. Next in order of subscribers were Ohio, Illinois, and Indiana.[6]

Greeley was a man with a large ego inside a slender body. Even his dress set him apart. He wore an old coat, a white duster that came just below his knees, baggy trousers, and a cravat always awry. Sometimes he was referred to as "the Man in the White Coat." His real trademark was an old Quaker hat, broad-brimmed and perched self-confidently on the back of his large head. When he came on board Lincoln's train from Springfield to Washington at Girard, Pennsylvania, on February 16, 1861, he conferred with Lincoln, and then was introduced to Mary Lincoln for the first time. He did not remove his hat.

The New York editor propagated his political views through his editorials, which he always signed "H.G." A curious mixture of conservative and liberal, he had been a vigorous opponent of slavery for years. In 1845, Greeley identified the reform trajectory of the

Horace Greeley's trademark was his old, broad-brimmed Quaker hat, perched self-confidently on the back of his large head.
LIBRARY OF CONGRESS

Tribune—"Anti-Slavery, Anti-War, Anti-Rum, Anti-Tobacco, Anti-Seduction, Anti–Grogshops, Brothels, Gambling Houses."[7]

Greeley fashioned his early antislavery position as much for economic as social reasons. He championed the rights of free labor in the East. In addition, he came to see the great potential of the West—"Go west, young man." Greeley believed that free labor, not slave labor, was the key to realizing the tremendous growth potential of a nation moving west.

He became a major proponent of the new Republican Party in the 1850s. He campaigned for politicians who received his imprimatur. Greeley sought to run for political office himself, but his ventures as a political candidate usually met with disappointment. Greeley's remarkable newspaper journey brought him to political power and influence just as the Republicans elected their first president, in November 1860. One cartoon in the winter of 1861 portrayed Greeley carrying the new president on his shoulders into the White House.[8]

WHEN HORACE GREELEY confronted Abraham Lincoln, he challenged a man who knew his way around newspapers. Lincoln had been captivated by newspapers his whole life. When he was appointed the United States postmaster in the village of New Salem in 1833, he particularly enjoyed perusing all the newspapers that passed through his hands. He announced his first candidacy for the Illinois House of Representatives in 1832 at age twenty-three in the pages of the *Sangamo Journal.* After entering politics, he reported on the Illinois legislature in the 1830s for the same newspaper. He enjoyed hanging out at the newspaper shop. He even enrolled subscribers. Lincoln occasionally wrote letters to the editor under assumed names. A favorite way to spend his evenings was to help a friend, editor Edward L. Baker, with editorials.

As Lincoln's political career began to rise in Illinois, "he made the newspaper his stump." He made friends with newspaper reporters and editors. Lincoln, who in his debates with Douglas spoke without the full text of a manuscript, was beholden to newspaper reporters, who acted as stenographers in recording his speeches. After an event he would often wander over to the newspaper office to check and revise the proofs before they were printed in the next edition. Lincoln delivered a lecture, "Discovery and Inventions," in several places in Illinois in the winter of 1859. In it he particularly praised printing, which "gave ten thousand copies of any written matter, quite as cheaply as ten were given before."[9]

Herndon recounted that Lincoln read mainly newspapers in their law offices in Springfield. Lincoln continued to read newspapers in the White House. On a small table in his office were usually found the Washington dailies—the *Daily Morning Chronicle*, *Washington Republican*, *National Intelligencer*, and *Star.* The war news reached him by telegraph before it could be printed in the newspapers, so he mostly glanced quickly at the local papers to check editorial comment.

A host of editors sent their newspapers to Lincoln hoping he would read their editorials. Francis B. Carpenter, an artist in residence in the White House from February through July 1864, reported that he observed in the secretary's quarters the *New York Tribune, Herald, Evening Post, World, Times,* and *Independent;* the *Chicago Tribune* and *Journal;* the *Philadelphia Press* and *North American;* the *Baltimore American* and *Sun;* the *Boston Advertiser, Journal,* and *Transcript;* the *Saint Louis Republican* and *Democrat;* the *Cincinnati Gazette* and *Commercial;* and the *Albany Evening Journal.*[10] Nicolay and Hay inspected these newspapers and reported important items to their boss. As president, Lincoln was even known to step outside the White House to ask a person walking by to send a corner newsboy to his front door with the latest newspaper.

Lincoln was both grateful for and on guard about newspapers. Newspaper editors were the butt of some of his biting humor. He enjoyed telling the story of being invited to inspect a newly invented repeating gun, the chief feature being a design to put a stop to the escape of gas. Lincoln commented, "Well, I do believe this really does what it is represented to do. Now have any of you heard of any machine, or invention, for preventing the escape of gas from newspaper offices?"[11]

HORACE GREELEY'S INITIAL impression of Abraham Lincoln was as a speaker. Greeley, already well known at age thirty-six, had traveled west in the summer of 1847 to attend a great-rivers-and-harbors convention in Chicago. Lincoln, a small-town lawyer who at thirty-eight had been elected to the Thirtieth Congress in 1846 but would not be seated until 1847, also made plans to attend. In July, Lincoln traveled by stagecoach for four days from Springfield to Chicago, a rising city of sixteen thousand residents. The purpose of the convention was to promote internal improvements, including protest of President James Polk's veto of an appropriation for river and harbor development. In the middle of the convention Lincoln rose to reply to a speech by David Dudley Field, a New York lawyer and law reformer. Greeley was one of the few who took much note of Lincoln that day. The new congressman's speaking made a favorable impression on Greeley, who wrote, "Hon. Abraham Lincoln, a tall specimen of an Illinoian, just elected to Congress from the only Whig District in the state, spoke briefly and happily in reply to Mr. Field."[12]

Twenty-three years later Greeley was sitting on the stage when Lincoln delivered his Cooper Union address in New York, on February 27, 1860. After the address Lincoln wandered over to the offices of the *Tribune* to correct the proofs of his address. The next morning, the *Tribune* published a story on the editorial page that glowed about Lincoln's speech. Greeley told his readers that "the speech of Abraham Lincoln at the Cooper Institute last evening was one of the happiest and most convincing political arguments ever made in this city to a crowded and appreciating audience." If Greeley liked the political content of the speech, he was even more taken by the oratorical gifts of the speaker. "Mr. Lincoln is one of nature's orators, using his rare powers solely and effectively to convince, though their inevitable effect is to delight and electrify as well." Greeley summed up Lincoln's performance at the Cooper Union by proclaiming, "No man ever before made such an impression in his first appeal to a New York audience."[13]

Greeley had been no enthusiast for Lincoln's candidacy. He had supported Judge Edward Bates of Missouri and was strongly against Seward at the Republican convention in Chicago. Nevertheless, once the campaign got under way, Greeley got behind "Honest Old Abe," as he liked to call him.

JOURNALISM AND POLITICS were closely intertwined during the Civil War. Editors from all parts of the North felt at liberty to dispatch personal letters to Lincoln offering their astute comments on all manner of subjects related to the war. Today we write letters *to* the editor. A phenomenon of Lincoln's day was letters *from* the editor. More than three hundred letters to the president from newspaper editors were received at the White House during Lincoln's presidency. The editors did not simply write Lincoln; they traveled to Washington to speak to him in person.

Joseph Medill, editor of the *Chicago Tribune*, seemed never to have a thought he did not want to share with Lincoln. In one of his

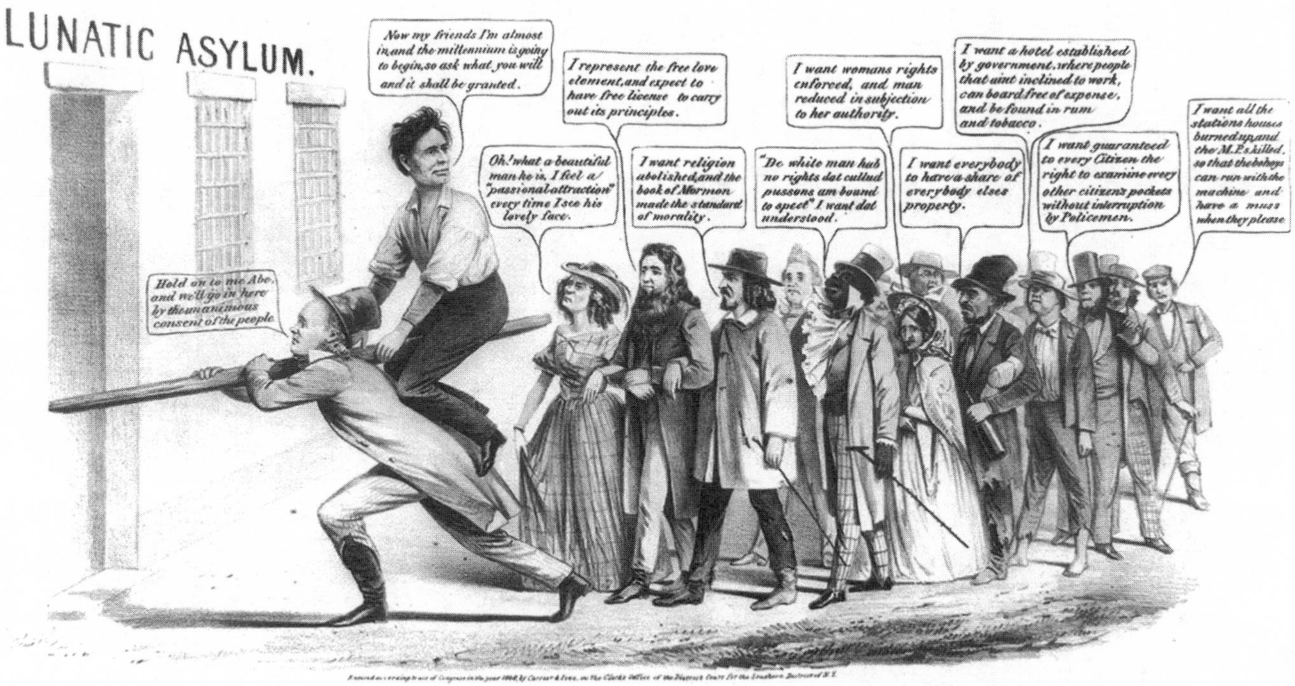

The Republican Party Going to the Right House.

The influence of Greeley ("Hold on to me Abe") is reflected in this Currier and Ives cartoon in the campaign of 1860.

LIBRARY OF CONGRESS

final letters, marked "private" and addressed to "Father Abraham," editor Medill wrote, "I am going home to Illinois in a few days and do not propose or desire to consume your time in personal interviews, but before leaving will jot down a few things, perhaps of no great account." Medill then gave Lincoln the benefit of his wisdom on cabinet appointments. "Could you do better on the whole than to make Gen Butler Sec of the Navy—in case its your intention to retain Stanton?" He also instructed Lincoln how to pursue war and peace. "Don't be in too much hurry for Peace. Don't coax the rebel chiefs but pound them a little more."[14] Lincoln was the beneficiary of numerous editors like Medill who offered him unsolicited advice on how he ought to conduct himself as president and commander-in-chief.

LONG BEFORE THE ERA of press conferences, Lincoln had learned how to communicate his ideas to the public through newspapers. He understood the partisan nature of newspapers. He figured out how to court editors. Part of Lincoln's political strategy was to correspond regularly with various editors.

After delivering a special message to Congress on March 6, 1862, in which he again recommended compensation to Southern states if they would end slavery, he wrote to Henry J. Raymond, editor of the *New York Times,* to complain gently that the *Times* got it wrong about how much such compensation would cost. He began, in typical Lincoln style, with an affirmation. He told Raymond that he was "grateful to the New-York Journals, and not less to the Times than to the others, for their kind notices of the late special Message to Congress." Lincoln was not just buttering up Raymond, for attached to Lincoln's letter in the Abraham Lincoln Papers at the Library of Congress are extracts Lincoln or his secretaries had cut from six New York newspapers—the *New York Times, Tribune, Evening Bulletin, Herald, World,* and *Evening Post*—all written on March 7, all supporting compensated emancipation.[15]

Even as Lincoln was struggling to find the right generals to lead the Union troops, he had to contend with the "newspaper generals" of New York. Greeley, Raymond, and Bryant saw their task as not

Horace Greeley was the self-appointed chief of staff of the New York newspaper generals. From his newspaper office he was one of the leading opinion-makers in the nation.

LIBRARY OF CONGRESS

simply informing people but shaping public opinion. Immediately after Fort Sumter, they began issuing calls for action from their offices on newspaper row near City Hall in New York. Throughout late April, May, and June, the newspaper generals counseled and cajoled the president. They advised that the war should be carried to Baltimore, Richmond, Charleston, Atlanta, and Montgomery. They argued that if the border states did not respond immediately to a call to arms, their populations should be treated as traitors.

Horace Greeley was the self-appointed chief of staff of the New York newspaper generals. Already by April 26, he had asked, "How much longer shall we wait?" "How much more disgrace shall we suffer?" In June, Fitz-Henry Warren, a *Tribune* correspondent in Washington who was in conversation with critics and radicals in the capital, sent to the *Tribune* the dictum "On to Richmond." Starting on June 26, managing editor Charles A. Dana placed a headline at the top of the editorial columns in bold italics:

Forward to Richmond! Forward to Richmond!
The Rebel Congress must not be allowed to meet there on the 20th of July.
By that date the place must be held by the National Army!

The Confederate capital was relocating from Montgomery to Richmond and was scheduled to convene for the first time on July 20. The same headline ran every day for eleven days until July 6.[16]

Greeley was traveling in the West while this whole episode and the subsequent headline developed. When he returned he was terribly upset and made it clear to both Warren and Dana that he did not approve of their daily iteration. The charge, after the disastrous Battle of Bull Run, in July 1861, was that Greeley and his newspaper had contributed to forcing this battle upon a yet unprepared Union Army. On July 25 Greeley published an apology for the masthead but also stated that the *Tribune* should not be held accountable for the "madness" of the Union strategy at Bull Run.[17]

IN THE FIRST MONTHS of the war in 1861, Lincoln appreciated the crucial role of the leading newspaper editors in molding public opinion. He understood Greeley's central role among the newspaper generals.

Greeley supported Lincoln in the opening months of the war. He was impatient with the hurry-up-and-win-the-war demands of many of his fellow Northern editors. By the end of 1861, with Northern armies not achieving battlefield successes, Greeley's support for Lincoln began to waver. His support became a four-days-a-week support. He would praise Lincoln on most days, but on other days he questioned the decisiveness of his leadership. After Bull Run, Greeley had called for the resignation of Lincoln's cabinet. He was coming to believe that Lincoln was temporizing in a crisis that called for bold action.

By early 1862, the New York editor assumed a more critical attitude. The president might be well-meaning, but by Greeley's estimation he was not up to the job. By the early summer of 1862, Greeley was discouraged by the silence coming from the White House.

In June, Greeley wrote Sen. Charles Sumner of Massachusetts and expressed his frustration with Lincoln. Sumner, elected to Congress in 1851, had become the Senate's leading opponent of slavery. During a speech on May 22, 1856, he was beaten unconscious on the floor of the Senate by Preston Brooks, a congressman from South Carolina. Greeley sprang to Sumner's defense and said that Brooks intended to kill the Massachusetts senator. Sumner's injuries prevented him from returning to the Senate floor for three years.

Now Greeley complained to Sumner that Lincoln seemed unwilling to act. He asked Sumner:

> Do you remember the old theological two-chapter book?
> *Chapter I—Hell.*
> *Chapter II—Hell, continued.*
> Well, that is the way "Old Abe" should be talked to.[18]

GREELEY DECIDED TO talk directly to the president through the most public medium he knew—his newspaper. His letter to President Lincoln appeared in the *Tribune* on August 20.

> On the face of this wide earth, Mr. President, there is not one disinterested, determined, intelligent champion of the Union cause who does not feel that all attempts to put down the Rebellion, and at the same time uphold its inciting cause, are preposterous and futile—that the Rebellion, if crushed out to-morrow, would be renewed within a year if slavery were left in full vigor. . . . I close as I began, with the statement that what an immense majority of the loyal millions of your countrymen require of you is a frank, declared, unqualified, ungrudging execution of the laws of the land, more especially of the Confiscation Act.[19]

The letter was Greeley all the way through. First, we hear the audacious supposition that he knew the minds and hearts of 20 million of his fellow Americans. Second, as a New York newspaper general, he knew better than the commander-in-chief both the substance and the timing of what needed to be done about emancipation.

Greeley's specific complaint was that Lincoln was not enforcing the Confiscation Act passed by Congress on July 17. This act, which was in part a response to a Confederate law that confiscated the property of Union supporters in the South, authorized seizing the property of disloyal citizens engaged in "armed rebellion against the United States"; among such property were slaves, who "shall be deemed captives of war and shall be forever free."[20]

Lincoln initially objected to some of the language of the Confiscation Act, and believed the law was badly written in parts. He was especially concerned about the act's dispossession of property without a criminal hearing or conviction. Lincoln expressed his objections to Congress, but ultimately signed the bill.

THE RESPONSE TO Greeley's letter was immediate from other armchair generals. The *New York Times* indicted Greeley for his presumption, saying it was "a bold assumption to claim to represent the view of so vast a constituency." The *Times* chided Greeley's self-importance, such that "the President," not having yet seen "the propriety of abdicating in behalf of our neighbor [Greeley], consoles him with a letter that assures the country of abundant sanity in the White House."[21]

THAT LINCOLN WOULD respond to his letter publicly was surely not expected by Greeley. After the publication of the letter in the *Tribune*, the president drafted an immediate reply. Lincoln's letter appeared in Washington's *National Intelligencer* on Saturday, August 23, at the head of the editorial column, as "A Letter from the President." The tightly written letter contained four paragraphs and 396 words. Lincoln, with his careful concern for words, specified that eleven words be printed in italics.

Lincoln began:

> *I have just read yours of the 19th addressed to myself through the New-York Tribune. If there be in it any statements, or as-*

sumptions of fact, which I may know to be erroneous, I do not, now and here, controvert them. If there be in it any inferences which I may believe to be falsely drawn, I do not now and here, argue against them. If there be perceptable in it an impatient and dictatorial tone, I waive it in deference to an old friend, whose heart I have always supposed to be right.

This portion of the letter, often omitted in biographies and studies of Lincoln, sets the tone for all that follows. Lincoln, who must have been stung by Greeley's high-handedness, began his response in a spirit of magnanimity.

In this opening paragraph Lincoln started the second, third, and fourth sentences with *if*. The word *if* introduces a clause of condition or supposition. In all three sentences, Lincoln employs *if* to extend the benefit of the doubt to the New York editor. Lincoln already knew that Greeley was being criticized for the letter in other newspapers. In this political exchange, Lincoln, who had received a contentious thrust from Greeley, parries with a generosity of spirit.

As to the policy I "seem to be pursuing" as you say, I have not meant to leave any one in doubt.

A brief second paragraph is the transition to the main body of the letter. Instead of a forceful declaration, such as "I did not leave any one in doubt," Lincoln adopts a gentler *I have not meant to* as the introduction to clarifying his ideas and policy.

I would save the Union. I would save it the shortest way under the Constitution. The sooner the national authority can be restored, the nearer the Union will be "the Union as it was." If there be those who would not save the Union, unless they could at the same time <u>save</u> slavery, I do not agree with them. If there be those who would not save the Union unless they could at the same time <u>destroy</u> slavery, I do not agree with them. My paramount object in this struggle <u>is</u> to save the Union, and is <u>not</u> either to save or to destroy slavery. If I could

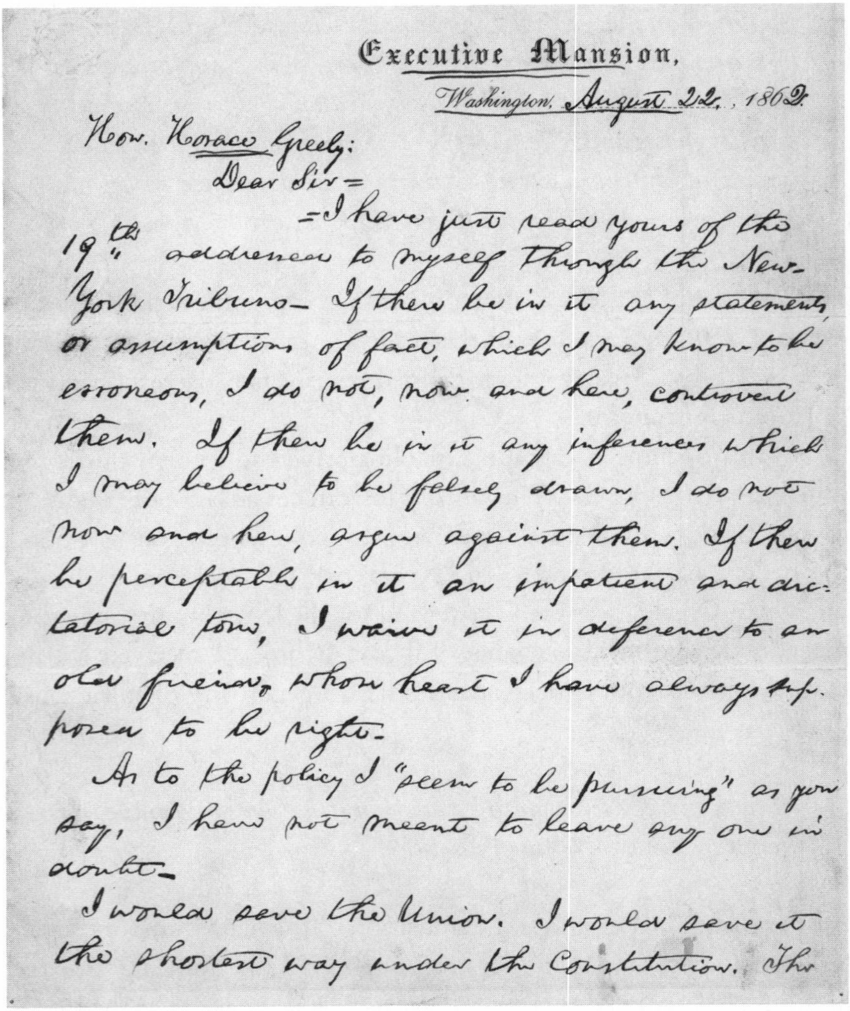
Executive Mansion,
Washington, August 22, 1862.

Hon. Horace Greely:
Dear Sir=
=I have just read yours of the 19th. addressed to myself through the New-York Tribune— If there be in it any statements, or assumptions of fact, which I may know to be erroneous, I do not, now and here, controvert them. If there be in it any inferences which I may believe to be falsely drawn, I do not now and here, argue against them. If there be perceptable in it an impatient and dictatorial tone, I waive it in deference to an old friend, whose heart I have always supposed to be right—

As to the policy I "seem to be pursuing" as you say, I have not meant to leave any one in doubt—

I would save the Union. I would save it the shortest way under the Constitution. The

Lincoln's letter to Greeley.

WADSWORTH ATHENEUM MUSEUM OF ART, HARTFORD. GIFT OF MISS ELIZABETH L. DIXON

save the Union without freeing any slave I would do it, and if I could save it by freeing all the slaves I would do it; and if I could save it by freeing some and leaving others alone I would also do that. What I do about slavery, and the colored race, I do because I believe it helps to save the Union; and what I forbear, I forbear because I do not believe it would help to save the Union. I shall do less whenever I shall believe what I am doing hurts the cause, and I shall do more whenever I shall be-

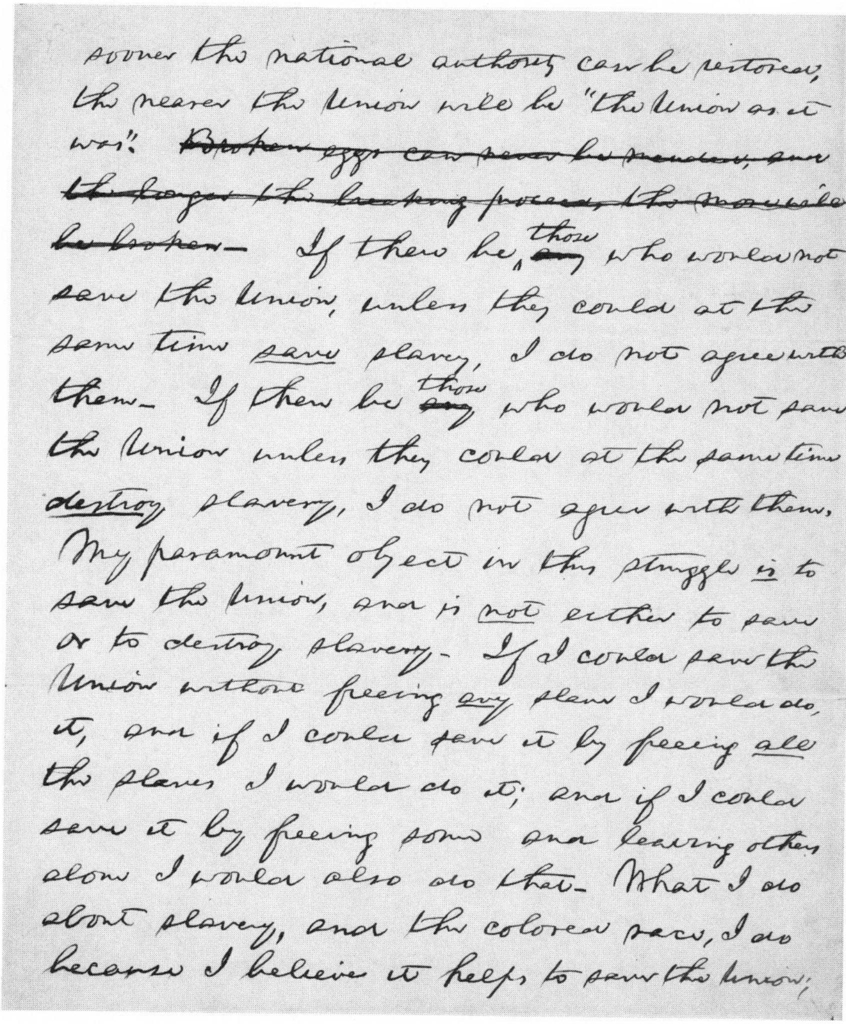
sooner the national authority can be restored; the nearer the Union will be "the Union as it was". ~~Broken eggs can never be mended, and the longer the breaking proceeds, the more will be broken~~— If there be ~~any~~ those who would not save the Union, unless they could at the same time save slavery, I do not agree with them— If there be ~~any~~ those who would not save the Union unless they could at the same time destroy slavery, I do not agree with them. My paramount object in this struggle is to save the Union, and is not either to save or to destroy slavery— If I could save the Union without freeing any slave I would do it, and if I could save it by freeing all the slaves I would do it; and if I could save it by freeing some and leaving others alone I would also do that— What I do about slavery, and the colored race, I do because I believe it helps to save the Union;

lieve doing more will help the cause. I shall try to correct errors when shown to be errors; and I shall adopt new views so fast as they shall appear to be true views.

When Lincoln informed Washington's *National Intelligencer* that he was writing a response, he invited an editor to come to the White House. If you were a person of culture in Washington, you wanted it known that you read the *Intelligencer.* James C. Welling was dispatched. When Welling has been remembered it has been as the political editor of the *Intelligencer,* but he described himself as the literary

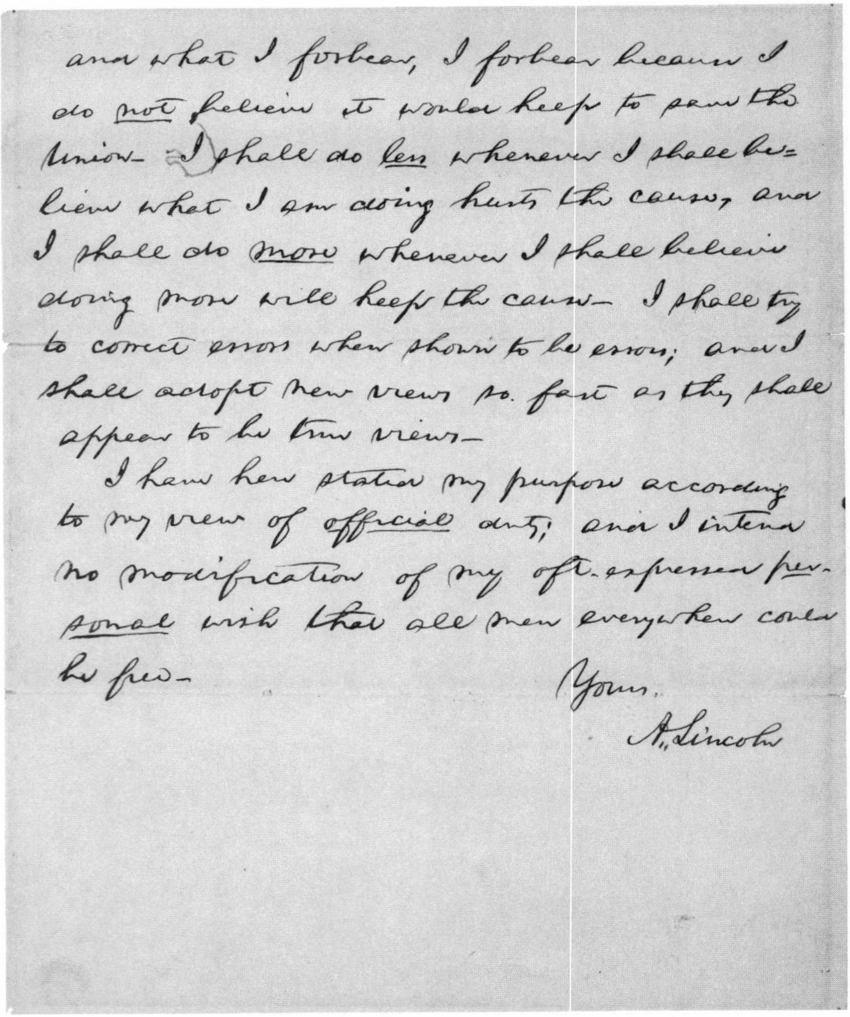

and what I forbear, I forbear because I do *not* believe it would help to save the Union— I shall do *less* whenever I shall believe what I am doing hurts the cause, and I shall do *more* whenever I shall believe doing more will help the cause— I shall try to correct errors when shown to be errors; and I shall adopt new views so. fast as they shall appear to be true views—

I have here stated my purpose according to my view of *official* duty; and I intend no modification of my oft-expressed *personal* wish that all men everywhere could be free—

Yours.

A. Lincoln

editor, qualified by education to work with Lincoln on revising his letter. He was a bright young man who had graduated first in his class at Princeton at age nineteen in 1844. At the White House he went over the letter with Lincoln word by word.[22]

Welling suggested that one sentence be "erased." This sentence would have been the fourth sentence in the third paragraph, coming right after "*the Union as it was.*" The sentence that read, "Broken eggs can never be mended, and the longer the breaking proceeds the more will be broken," did not make it into the final version of the reply.[23]

The young literary editor recalled that Lincoln acceded "with some reluctance." Why did he resist? Welling doesn't tell us Lincoln's reason, but he offered his own. This sentence "seemed somewhat exceptional, on rhetorical grounds, in a paper of such dignity."[24]

Welling took a position exactly like printer John D. Defrees's response to *sugar-coated* in the message to Congress of the previous year. Each wished to correct Lincoln about what was and was not dignified speech. Printers and editors had the temerity to suggest that Lincoln's homely American figures did not fit the decorum of the occasion.

ACTUALLY, LINCOLN did not give up on this metaphor. Four and a half months later, in a letter to John A. McClernand, a former Democratic congressman from Illinois and now a Union general, Lincoln defended the Emancipation Proclamation, issued one week earlier. In the first paragraph of his letter, Lincoln turned again to broken eggs.

> *Still, to use a coarse, but an expressive figure, broken eggs can not be mended. I have issued the emancipation proclamation, and I cannot retract it.*

It surely was Welling, the literary editor of the *Intelligencer,* who informed Lincoln the previous August that this figure was *coarse.* But Lincoln, who probably had worked with this figure long before Welling told him it was uncouth, continued to work with it, only now he felt the need to defend the figure in his letter to McClernand because he believed it was *an expressive figure.*[25]

THE AUTHORITY OF Lincoln's reply to Greeley is grounded in the majesty of the architecture of his composition. Lincoln composed his letter with a structural design that began with a simple foundation:

> *I would save the Union.*

He started with this foundation of but five words, after which he would clarify and expand his initial premise. When we read these words in linear sentences compacted into a paragraph, however, we may not grasp the architecture of Lincoln's design. Thus, in Lincoln's structure, the second sentence, exactly double the number of words of the first sentence, built upon Lincoln's intention.

> *I would save the Union.*
> *I would save it the shortest way under the Constitution.*

In the middle of the paragraph he would expand yet a third time, clarifying the scope to now include a discussion of slavery. At the center of the letter, Lincoln offered a thesis sentence that spells out further the meanings of the first and second sentences.

> *My paramount object in this struggle <u>is</u> to save the Union,*
> *and is <u>not</u> either to save or to destroy slavery.*

In this central thesis sentence Lincoln declared both what he would save and what he would not save.

Lincoln also understood what we have forgotten. He knew that his letter, printed in newspapers, would be read aloud in the family parlor by the father or mother, or among neighbors at the general store. Reading out loud was the pattern of teaching and learning in American schools until early into the twentieth century, when teachers, for the first time, began asking children to read silently to themselves. Lincoln, in his customary style of writing, would have spoken the word *save* aloud, surely emphasizing it over and over again. When heard aloud, *to save the Union* becomes the leitmotif, or recurring theme, of Lincoln's reply to Greeley, sounding again and again on the ear.

THE VERB *save* pulsates twelve times through the ten sentences of Lincoln's structure in this central third paragraph of his letter. We may better sense the use of *save* by portraying Lincoln's structure:

If there be those who would not save
the Union, unless they could at the same
time save slavery,
I do not agree with them.
If there be those who would not save
the Union unless they could at the same
time destroy slavery,
I do not agree with them.
My paramount object in this struggle is to save the Union, and
is not
either to save or to destroy slavery.
If I could save the Union without freeing
any slave I would do it,
and
if I could save it by freeing all the
slaves I would do it;
and
if I could save it by freeing some and
leaving others alone I would also do that.

When Lincoln's ideas are laid out in this format, we can grasp better the structure of his thinking.

WELLING CALLED LINCOLN's letter "syllogistic." The young *Intelligencer* literary editor was insightful. Aristotle argued that a syllogism is the truest form of knowledge. A classical syllogism is a deductive form of argument:

A. All men are mortal.

B. Socrates is a man.

C. Socrates is mortal.

In rhetoric, after a universal premise is made, other premises follow in deductive order. Greeley argued in his letter to Lincoln:

A. Slavery is the cause of the rebellion.

B. Abraham Lincoln wants to put down the rebellion.

C. Abraham Lincoln must eliminate slavery.

Welling, with his background in both philosophy and literature, saw Lincoln's reply as a syllogism. Thus:

A. The Union must be saved, with or without slavery.

B. Abraham Lincoln intends to save the Union.

C. Abraham Lincoln will do so with or without eliminating slavery.[26]

Welling's perception about the syllogism at the heart of the reply to Greeley was confirmed independently by Lincoln's friend James C. Conkling. A fellow Springfield lawyer, Conkling, from long observation, noted that "every proposition submitted to his mind was subjected to the regular process of a syllogism, with its major proposition and its minor proposition and conclusion."[27] Lincoln used this process of thinking, and sometimes of writing, as a test of the reasonableness of his arguments. Lincoln's penchant for syllogism did not come from a college class in philosophy but from a lawyer's practice in the courtroom. In the letter to Greeley he was now appealing to the court of public opinion.

AS A LAWYER or debater, Lincoln used the conditional *if* five times. He posited different broad points of view. Standing behind each of these positions were millions of people. Lincoln assumed that most, but not all, in the South wanted to save slavery. In addition, when he referred to

"the Union as it was"

in the third sentence, he was referring to the growing opposition among Democrats and some Republicans to any move to free the slaves. "The Union as it was," then, was the watchword for the first point of view, which favored returning the Union to the time of Lincoln's election before there was any secession. The argument being advanced in the North, after more than one year of war, was that the abolition of slavery and the mounting casualties were too high a price to pay. In response to this position Lincoln offered a resounding

I do not agree with them.

The second point of view, very vocal and articulate, was represented by the abolitionists, who included many Republicans in Lincoln's own party. Republican Charles Sumner of Massachusetts was the most vocal spokesman in the Senate. Horace Greeley had become a leading spokesman in the press. Now Greeley presented himself as representing 20 million.

A third group, to whom Lincoln was especially sensitive, even if they go unnamed in his letter, was the common soldiers. He knew that many of them were saying they signed up to save the Union, and not to free the slaves. Many soldiers believed that African-Americans would be all right to help the war effort behind the lines, but not fight the war on the front lines.

A shrewd Lincoln, given an unexpected opportunity by Greeley's letter, used this public forum to speak to all these groups at once.

WILLIAM W. SEATON, editor of the *National Intelligencer,* added his comments to Lincoln's letter. "We supposed he [Greeley] had little idea that his communication, if ever reaching the eye of his distinguished correspondent, would receive from that correspondent the honor of a response." Seaton continued, "We hope, however, that when Mr. Greeley has duly pondered the pithy sentences of the President's letter, he will be able to rejoin, if he proposes to continue the 'correspondence' in a spirit which shall be slightly less arrogant, dictatorial, and acrimonious."[28]

Yet another irony in this exchange was Lincoln's choice of the *National Intelligencer* to publish his reply to Greeley. Lincoln had admired Seaton and the *Intelligencer,* in part for its literary qualities, long before he came to Washington as president. But the paper had not always been a strong supporter of the president and had not hidden its empathy with slavery. Did Lincoln choose the *Intelligencer* as yet another way to tweak Greeley?

LINCOLN'S ANSWER has sometimes been printed without Greeley's complaint. Throughout 1862 "General" Greeley, along with other newspaper editors, had driven the debate about emancipation as much as politicians in Washington. Now Greeley argued in his letter that the only way to "put down the Rebellion" was to emancipate the slaves.

Many readers, then and now, have read Lincoln's reply to Greeley as indicating a lack of interest in emancipating the slaves. Lincoln concluded his reply to Greeley with a poignant if brief final paragraph.

> *I have here stated my purpose according to my view of official duty; and I intend no modification of my oft-expressed personal wish that all men everywhere could be free.*

This final paragraph needs to be heard for any full appreciation of Lincoln's reply to Greeley. Often forgotten, this final sentiment was consistent with the creative tension in Lincoln between duty—under the constraints of his office and the Constitution, which he took an oath to uphold—and his personal wishes. The letter to Greeley was not about his personal ethics or sentiments. Lincoln's reply, crafted by a shrewd politician, was about his official duty, through which he hoped to pull as many people as possible into the largest tent possible: the Union.

ABRAHAM LINCOLN was on a long road to emancipation. At first, emancipation was hardly included in his public remarks. Thus, in his inaugural address and in his message to the special session of Congress, slavery was almost invisible. At this early point in the war, Lincoln had a pressing concern to keep the border states of Kentucky, Maryland, Missouri, and Delaware in the Union.

By the middle of 1862, union and emancipation were coming together for Lincoln as the inseparable goals in a rebirth of the nation. The framers of the Constitution, needing to keep all the colonies on board a fragile ship of liberty sailing in rough waters, purposely decided to sidestep the issue of slavery at the birth of the nation. Lincoln was convinced the Founders believed that slavery would die out in time, succumbing to death by natural causes. But it did not.

Lincoln, sometimes pictured as most interested in preserving the values of the past, was also quite capable of changing his mind. As he told Greeley,

> *I shall try to correct errors when shown to be errors; and I shall adopt new views so fast as they shall appear to be true views.*

In these months, Lincoln would surprise his cabinet, his party, and much of the nation with his ability to *adopt new views.*

LINCOLN'S REPLY to Greeley did not really answer Greeley's appeal. But that was not Lincoln's purpose. Instead the president made his own appeal—to save the Union. He had shrewdly outflanked the leading New York general, and on his own territory, the newspaper.

And Greeley knew it. The best commentary on the purpose and effectiveness of Lincoln's letter comes from Horace Greeley himself. Lincoln "added insult to injury by answering my 'Prayer of Twenty Millions,' which asked only for the honest enforcement of an existing law, as if it had been a demand for the abolition of slavery." Greeley, who took pride in his ability to discern the attitudes of the public, grasped that he had been outmaneuvered. Lincoln "adroitly" used Greeley "to feel the public pulse, and making me appear as an officious meddler in affairs that properly belong to the government."[29] Greeley understood the brilliance of Lincoln's political eloquence.

THE PRESIDENT HAD a high postmaster's bureau with wooden doors in his office, against the south wall and between the windows. He used the cabinet as a file into which he crammed letters and notes. The cabinet was divided into pigeonholes, each of which was lettered alphabetically in his own hand. A few were marked for one individual, mostly reserved for generals—McClellan, Grant, and Halleck. Lincoln had reserved a separate pigeonhole for Horace Greeley, the self-appointed chief of staff of the New York newspaper generals.[30]

In the evolution of Lincoln's rhetoric, his reply to Greeley is a signpost that points to his grasp of the politics of persuasion. The letter, written quickly, nevertheless attained a splendid structure, even if written for a newspaper, which deprived him of the immediate interaction of speaker and audience. The letter is unusual in its absence of metaphors or figures, once literary editor Welling persuaded a reluctant Lincoln to throw out the eggs. But the letter achieved immediate as well as lasting prominence because of the poetry, which gave voice and symmetry to his politics.

The reply to Greeley will be misconstrued if it is interpreted as a simple and uncomplicated declaration. This letter was crafted at the very moment Lincoln was preparing his Emancipation Proclamation. Lincoln had become adroit at keeping his own counsel and moving forward on his own timing. Greeley, unwittingly, gave Lincoln the opportunity to take the North into his confidence and at the same time explain his policies to the South, just as he would shortly announce his plans for emancipation.

CHAPTER SIX

"GOD WILLS THIS CONTEST"

MEDITATION ON THE DIVINE WILL
SEPTEMBER 2(?), 1862

The will of God prevails. In great contests each party claims to act in accordance with the will of God. Both may be, and one must be wrong. God can not be for, and against the same thing at the same time. In the present civil war it is quite possible that God's purpose is something different from the purpose of either party—and yet the human instrumentalities, working just as they do, are of the best adaptation to effect His purpose. I am almost ready to say this is probably true—that God wills this contest, and wills that it shall not end yet. By His mere quiet power, on the minds of the now contestants, He could have either saved or destroyed the Union without a human contest. Yet the contest began. And having begun He could give the final victory to either side any day. Yet the contest proceeds.

ABRAHAM LINCOLN CONVENED an emergency meeting of his cabinet on Tuesday, September 2, 1862. The public outcry was growing. After predictions of a Union victory at Manassas Junction, in northern Virginia, Northern troops were soundly defeated at what the North called the Second Battle of Bull Run, named for a meandering river several miles north of the junction. Gen. John Pope, who had predicted victory but whose men called him "Boastful" Pope behind his back, had been overwhelmed by troops led by Stonewall Jackson and Robert E. Lee. The Union troops retreated in disarray all the way back to the outskirts of Washington. The Northern press criticized the president, the generals, and the Army of the Potomac. The Southern press and people were euphoric.

In this bitter moment Lincoln summoned his cabinet to the Executive Mansion. Attorney General Edward Bates recorded Lincoln's somber mood at the beginning of the cabinet meeting. Bates, a small, compact man from Missouri with black, piercing eyes, who had been one of Lincoln's rivals for the Republican nomination in 1860, wrote in his diary that the president was disheartened after early predictions of victory had turned into reports of a devastating defeat. Bates reported that Lincoln "seemed wrung by the bitterest anguish—said he felt almost ready to hang himself."[1]

LATER THAT SAME DAY, Lincoln sat at his desk and wrote out a private musing. He wrote on a small piece of lined paper. He did not date his reflection. As he pondered and wrote, Lincoln sought to discern the will of God among the cacophony of voices all around him after news of one of the most discouraging defeats of the war.[2]

Lincoln's reflection was framed in theological language. We are able to listen in on a dialogue Lincoln is having with himself. He regularly went through exercises of differentiating choices. In this rumination the language is not yet the finely crafted rhetorical language of an address.

Lincoln's brief contemplation would remain unknown during his lifetime. John Hay, the president's young secretary, found it after his death. The private musing was one of the few Lincoln papers Hay kept for himself. In 1872 Hay gave it the title "Meditation on the Divine Will."[3]

We have no witnesses to the writing of this reflection. Hay and Nicolay, in their biography of Lincoln published in 1890, remarked simply, "This meditation was not meant to be seen by men."[4]

THE PRIVATE Meditation on the Divine Will is significant in the story of the evolution of Lincoln's rhetoric even though he never offered it as a public speech. It needs to be taken account of for two reasons. First, behind Lincoln's finished public addresses were many bits and pieces of notes to himself. These fragments are the largely unknown building blocks of important Lincoln speeches. Lincoln's habit was to write ideas on odd strips of paper and backs of envelopes. He deposited these notes in his tall hat or in a desk drawer for future retrieval. He usually left these fragments untitled. These notes were given the name "fragments" by Roy Basler and the editors of the Abraham Lincoln Papers. Some of these fragments can be traced forward to a future speech or address.

The presence of these fragments points to the process of Lincoln's thinking, writing, and speaking. He took pleasure in working with an idea over time. He would turn ideas over and over in his mind in the course of months and even years. Only after he was satisfied that he had thought through his idea, chosen just the right words to express its many dimensions, and polished the grammar of its expression was he ready to share it with the public. This small Meditation points to Lincoln's private process of planting and watering that bore such rich fruit in his public speaking. The reflection of September 2, 1862, is a remarkable example of a private musing that would become grist for an important future speech, his Second Inaugural Address, to be delivered two and a half years later.

Second, this rumination, unknown during Lincoln's life, is a chief signpost that points to the growth and intensity in Lincoln's religious thinking under the pressures of the Civil War. A question has been asked of Lincoln, as must be asked of all political leaders: did Lincoln, as a shrewd politician, use religion in his political speeches because he knew that religious language would play well with his churchgoing audience? This document is critical in answering that question. The profound theological thinking and ideas in the Meditation on the Divine Will were written not for public consumption, but for Lincoln's eyes only.

LINCOLN BEGAN his reflection:

> *The will of God prevails. In great contests each party claims to act in accordance with the will of God. Both may be, and one must be wrong. God can not be for, and against the same thing at the same time.*

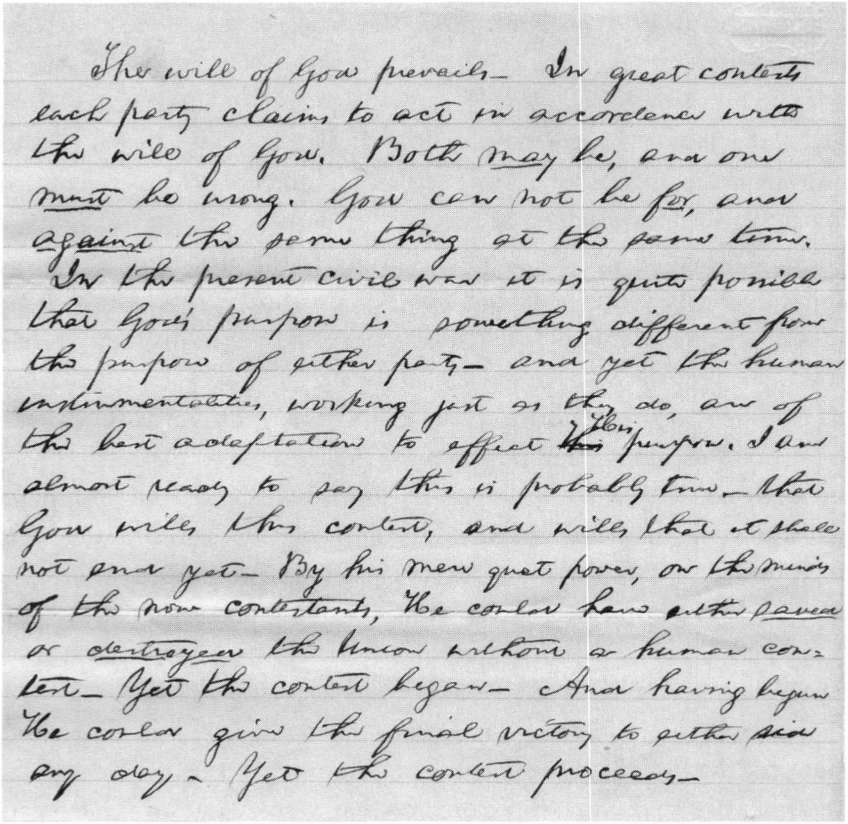

The will of God prevails— In great contests
each party claims to act in accordance with
the will of God. Both *may* be, and one
must be wrong. God can not be *for*, and
against the same thing at the same time.
In the present civil war it is quite possible
that God's purpose is something different from
the purpose of either party— and yet the human
instrumentalities, working just as they do, are of
the best adaptation to effect His purpose. I am
almost ready to say this is probably true— that
God wills this contest, and wills that it shall
not end yet— By his mere quiet power, on the minds
of the now contestants, He could have either *saved*
or *destroyed* the Union without a human contest— Yet the contest began— And having begun
He could give the final victory to either side
any day— Yet the contest proceeds—

This private reflection is undated, but Lincoln may have written it shortly after learning of the disastrous results of the Second Battle of Bull Run in September 1862. It was discovered after Lincoln's death by his young secretary, John Hay, who gave it the title "Meditation on the Divine Will."

LINCOLN COLLECTION, JOHN HAY LIBRARY, BROWN UNIVERSITY

He started with an affirmation:

The will of God prevails.

We wish we could enter into the mood with which Lincoln commenced his musing. Did he write these words in a feeling of grateful acceptance? Or was his sense more of passive resignation? Or both?

Lincoln's deliberations were written in the form of a theological reflection. In his logical mind he was attempting to work out the dilemma of the presence of God in the war. He employed the same kind of logic that he had used only days before in his public reply to Horace Greeley.

But what he was dealing with was not an abstract problem in philosophy or theology. The impetus for his musing grew out of the very real forces pressing in upon him as president. He was the recipient of *claims* presented to him on a regular basis from delegations and groups saying, in effect, that "God is on our side."

Lincoln was weighing the validity of those claims. He was well aware that the very same claims were being made by politicians and preachers in the South. How to reconcile such divergent claims? His first response:

> *Both may be, and one must be wrong.*

His language, *may be,* is typical of Lincoln as he thinks his way into a problem. He was at first often tentative in his judgments. His penchant was to look at all sides of a problem.

Our tendency is to read his reflection in a linear fashion, with no pauses between the sentences. I believe that Lincoln may have paused for a long time after *Both may be, and one must be wrong.* He might have pondered this conclusion that had been coming to him after more than a year of hearing claims and counterclaims from delegations of politicians and church leaders.

Then, perhaps after some time, Lincoln was ready to write a preliminary conclusion to his query. The rational Lincoln, as if working through the logic of a syllogism, came to the conclusion that both of the claimants may be wrong and one must be wrong. Why?

> *God can not be for, and against the same thing at the same time.*

Lincoln frequently underlined words of contrast.

His answer presumed something about the nature and purposes of God. This God was not simply an original first cause. Lincoln's meditation is about a God who acts in history.

> *In the present civil war it is quite possible that God's purpose is something different from the purpose of either party—and yet the human instrumentalities, working just as they do, are of the best adaptation to effect His purpose.*

This poignant sentence may be the best clue to Lincoln's ultimate understanding of *God's purpose* in the war. Lincoln appears to be seeking to maintain an equilibrium between God's action and human actions. In his profound balancing act is a line running from the apostle Paul through Augustine in North Africa to John Calvin in Geneva to the Puritans in Old and New England to Lincoln in Washington. Forced by the war to go deeper into the Bible and into theological reflection, he emerged broader than his contemporaries in discerning the ways of God. Instead of coming down where everyone else did, North and South, with God being on one side or the other, Lincoln mused that

> *God's purpose is something different from the purpose of either party*

even though he qualified this observation with

> *it is quite possible.*

By September 1862, despite the political and religious chauvinism all around him, Lincoln had arrived at a remarkable declaration about *God's purpose* in the war.

Lincoln's affirmation achieved its power when juxtaposed to the external pressures that he faced almost every day. His point of view was not the assertion of a host of political and religious partisans seeking to cajole him with a steady litany of "God is on our side."

Lincoln was equally confident about the other side of the equation. He became convinced that those who wanted to act within God's will did so by carrying out their ordinary activities. The action of God never meant the inactivity or passivity of human beings. Rather, God's action was through the activity of *human instrumentalities.*

On the trip from Springfield to Washington, Lincoln had called himself one of those *human instrumentalities* on several occasions. In his address to the New Jersey Senate on February 21, 1861, he had said:

> *I shall be most happy indeed if I shall be an humble instrument in the hands of the Almighty.*[5]

In making this point he employed the word *adaptation.* Lincoln wrote slowly, allowing himself to deliberate over the use of words. He was his own thesaurus, whispering or speaking words out loud until he came up with just the right word that he needed for his purposes. The noun *adaptation* suggests the act or process of adjustment to external conditions. In qualifying *adaptation* with the word *best,* Lincoln was again affirming that God had chosen to work through the human side of the historical equilibrium.

What was the purpose of the human beings in history, *working just as they do*? It was ultimately *to effect His purpose.* Lincoln keeps his balance by affirming free will or human action even as this central section of his reflection begins with *God's purpose* and concludes with *His purpose.*

> *I am almost ready to say this is probably true—that God wills this contest, and wills that it shall not end yet. By His mere quiet power, on the minds of the now contestants, He could have either saved or destroyed the Union without a human contest. Yet the contest began. And having begun He could give the final victory to either side any day. Yet the contest proceeds.*

Lincoln offered here an astonishing assertion:

> *God wills this contest*

With the word *almost,* he suggested a point of view to which he was only now arriving. He qualified this affirmation further by the use of a second adverb, *probably,* which means "without much doubt." Lincoln's statement combined both doubt and faith.

Even more surprising was his judgment that God

wills that it shall not end yet

At the moment when Lincoln, as commander-in-chief, was working night and day in mobilizing every resource at his disposal to bring the war to an end, in private he was writing that God seemed to be deciding that the war would continue.

Lincoln described a God who acted in *quiet power.* At first glance this was a curious way to portray a deity whom Lincoln usually referred to as the *Almighty.* The God whom Lincoln had encountered in the revivalism of his youth was a noisy God. The God of Civil War jingoism, the God who was on our side, was a strident God. In the midst of the noise and stridency of the Civil War, Lincoln pointed to a God whose *quiet* purposes were at work in the world.

This *power* of God, however *quiet,* was so commanding that

He could have either <u>saved</u> or <u>destroyed</u> the Union without a human contest.

Lincoln, whose solitary purpose at the outset of the hostilities was to save the Union, now ascribed to God the singular might to save or obliterate his beloved Union.

At this point in his very logical dialogue with himself Lincoln used the word *yet* twice:

Yet the contest began.
Yet the contest proceeds.

The use of the terse conjunction *yet* helped Lincoln maintain the creative tension between divine action and human action. His forceful prose, even if for his eyes only, accented the drama of the divine-human interaction in the progress of the war.

THE CONTENT OF the Meditation on the Divine Will illuminates how far Lincoln had moved in his journey from fatalism to providence. Early in his life, Lincoln encountered a form of fatalism called the doctrine of necessity. He spoke of this doctrine in a handbill published in the heat of his campaign for Congress in 1846 against Methodist minister Peter Cartwright. "It is true that in early life I was inclined to believe in what I understand is called the 'Doctrine of Necessity'—that is, that the human mind is impelled to action, or held in rest by some power, over which the mind itself has no control." Lincoln hastened to add, "The habit of arguing thus however, I have entirely left off for more than five years."[6]

Historians and biographers have continued to use Lincoln's engagement with fatalism as a young man as the main rubric to understand his religious thought as president.[7] This approach, static in its engagement with a changing Lincoln, fails to do justice to the growth and change in Lincoln's thinking, especially during the Civil War. If Lincoln was drawn to a doctrine of necessity in the 1840s, the ideas and words in the Meditation on the Divine Will give evidence of a quite different perspective on the nature of God's involvement in history. Instead of the appeal to *some power* as in the handbill of 1846, Lincoln writes in the Meditation on the Divine Will of *God's purpose* and that *God wills,* language growing from an understanding of a purposeful God who acts in history.

The suggestion of biographers that fatalism and providence are part of a continuum would have surprised Protestant theologians and ministers in the middle of the nineteenth century. In 1859, a year before Lincoln was elected president, Francis Wharton described fatalism as "a distinct scheme of unbelief." Wharton, the author of *A Treatise on Theism, and on the Modern Skeptical Theories,* singled out fatalism as a heresy or an opponent of Christianity because it did not acknowledge a God who acted in history. Wharton, an evangelical or low church Episcopalian, who would later become a professor at the Episcopal Theological School in Cambridge, Massachusetts, contrasted fatalism with the God of Christianity known by "his watchful care and love."[8]

A BELIEF IN FATALISM was also far different from the preaching of providence Lincoln was hearing at the New York Avenue Presbyterian Church in the month leading up to his reflection on the divine will.

When the Lincolns arrived in Washington, they were wooed by many church suitors who would have been honored to have the new president and his family worship in their congregation. On the first Sunday after his inauguration, March 10, the Lincolns attended the New York Avenue Presbyterian Church. The church was located on New York Avenue at the intersection of Thirteenth and H Streets, only three blocks from the White House. Lincoln was present again on April 14, the Sunday after the attack on Fort Sumter.

When the church was informed of their decision to become regular attenders, a deacon came to the White House so that the Lincolns could choose a pew. They selected pew B-14, which was located in the seventh row from the front on the right side of the center aisle. The vacant pew had formerly been occupied by President James Buchanan. On June 30, Lincoln sent a first payment on an annual pew rental of $50.[9]

Lincoln began attending New York Avenue on a more regular basis than he had First Presbyterian Church in Springfield. But he never joined the church. A persistent story has circulated down through the years that Abraham Lincoln did decide that he would join the church on April 16, 1865, which was Easter Sunday, but this story cannot be confirmed.

At the center of Presbyterian worship in the nineteenth century was preaching. The Reverend Phineas Densmore Gurley, minister at New York Avenue, was a preacher whose reputation reached beyond Washington. Gurley had studied at Princeton Theological Seminary, the leading seminary in the Presbyterian Church. Gurley graduated first in his class in 1840. In the words of a fellow student, Gurley "was regarded as our foremost man."[10]

At Princeton, Gurley sat in the classes of Professor Charles Hodge, one of the foremost theologians of the nineteenth century, who was near the beginning of a teaching career that would span more than fifty years at the seminary. Hodge was an expositor of a Calvinism that stressed the government and sovereignty of God. He said of providence, "An infinitely wise, good, and powerful God is everywhere present, controlling all events great and small, necessary, and free, in a way perfectly consistent with the nature of his creatures and with his own infinite excellence."[11] Gurley would preach these same themes in his ministry at Dayton, Indianapolis, and Washington.[12]

Why was Lincoln attracted to New York Avenue and Gurley? The Presbyterian denomination had divided in 1837 between Old and New School traditions. Lincoln, although he never became a member of any church, made the decision to attend not simply Presbyterian churches but Old School Presbyterian churches in both Springfield and Washington. The break between the Old School and the New School encompassed many issues. The New School, centered in New York, was more open to revivalism and experiential faith and also more willing for the church to speak out on social issues, with many of its ministers advocating an antislavery position. The Old School, centered in Pennsylvania, was suspicious of the emotionalism sometimes associated with revivalism and placed its faith in a rational religion articulated in the Westminster Confession of Faith. The Old School believed the church was a "spiritual" institution that should not speak out on social issues, including slavery.

Gurley embodied the characteristics of Old School Presbyterianism. His preaching was learned and thoughtful. The Calvinism he preached presented a high view of God and providence. By the middle of the nineteenth century Calvinism was under attack by both secular and religious critics for its supposedly stark theology, especially its emphasis on human depravity. An admirer described Gurley as the best representative of Calvinism, commending that his preaching was "Calvinism presented in his beautiful example and spirit" and was a "practical and irresistible refutation of the calumnies so often heaped upon it by those who know little of it."[13]

Chicago sculptor Leonard Volk, remembered for his life mask of Lincoln, claimed that Lincoln told him that when it came to preaching, "I don't like to hear cut and dried sermons. No—when I hear a man preach, I like to see him act as if he were fighting bees!" Lincoln, in Volk's studio, extended his long arms to demonstrate what he meant. Gurley, from the reports of contemporaries, was far from fighting bees in his sermons. One friend described Gurley's preaching as "slow and stately solemnity." Lincoln was drawn to Gurley's preaching probably more for the thoughtful content of the sermons than for the style. Lincoln said of his paster, "I like Gurley. He don't preach politics. I get enough of that through the week, and when I go to church, I like to hear the Gospel."[14]

GURLEY, IF HE did not preach politics, did preach providence. Less than seven months before Lincoln would write out his private musing on the divine will, he invited Gurley to preach the funeral sermon for Willie Lincoln on February 24, 1862, at the White House. Willie, of the four Lincoln boys, was most like his father in looks and character. His death on February 20 cast a dark cloud over the White House that never really lifted for Mary Lincoln.

The relationship between Gurley and Lincoln deepened in these difficult days. We will never know what words were exchanged between pastor and president, but Gurley was a frequent visitor at the White House. The death of Willie, a personal tragedy, and the deaths of so many young soldiers, a public tragedy, prompted questions in Lincoln about the meaning of life and death.

Into this scene of mourning Gurley attempted to bring a message of consolation and hope in his funeral sermon. After Gurley began by identifying with the grief of the parents over the death of a young child, he made a transition to words of comfort. "It is well for us, and very comforting on such an occasion as this, to get a clear and scriptural view of the providence of God." He went on to affirm, "His kingdom ruleth over all."[15]

Gurley, steeped in the Calvinism he had learned from Hodge, was a thoughtful preacher who seemed to anticipate questions as well as proclaim answers. He told the grieving parents that sometimes providence appears as "a mysterious dealing." His final counsel was to "acknowledge His hand, and hear His voice, and inquire after His will."[16]

Not many months later Lincoln would write out of his brooding about his own understanding of a "mysterious dealing."

IT IS IMPORTANT to notice not simply what is present in the Meditation but what is absent. Lincoln offered no indication that God was on the side of the Union. Not even a hint. Religion has become captive again and again to patriotism in times of war. Lincoln met religious patriots, both clergy and laity, regularly in his office at the Executive Mansion. Even as he pondered the ultimate questions of the nature and activity of God in this Meditation, he did so by suggesting alternate possibilities. He was *almost* convinced that above and beyond the human actors—the president, the generals, the soldiers—

> *God wills this contest*

And yet the certainty of this religious conviction was balanced by his reluctance to equate God's will with the actions of either side.

> *In the present civil war it is quite possible that God's purpose is something different from the purpose of either party . . .*

War, in any era, calls forth proponents on both sides who espouse the rightness of their cause with absolute certainty. This has been true in all the wars in which the United States has been involved since the Civil War. The greatest demagoguery churned out by politicians has usually occurred in the midst of war. All of this makes Lincoln's honest wrestling with God's purposes in the Meditation the more remarkable.

REINHOLD NIEBUHR, a leading twentieth-century American theologian and social ethicist, wrote an article for the *Christian Century* in 1965 asserting that "Lincoln's religious convictions were superior in depth and purity to those held by the religious as well as by the political leaders of his day." Niebuhr believed that Lincoln's faith "was informed primarily by a sense of providence." What struck Niebuhr as the "purity and profundity of Lincoln's sense of providence" was his ability to resist "the natural temptation" to do what nearly every political leader has done throughout history: "identify providence with the cause to which he was committed."[17]

Niebuhr appreciated Lincoln's attainment precisely because the sixteenth president was comfortable with ambiguity. Niebuhr's early work *Moral Man and Immoral Society* had challenged the liberal idealism of educational and religious leaders because both sets of leaders, buoyed by an optimistic belief in progress, were unable to admit the limitations and ambiguities of human achievement. In looking through the lens of his own realistic social ethic, Niebuhr believed that "Lincoln had a sense of historical meaning so high as to cast doubt on the intentions of both sides."[18]

Niebuhr believed this "human achievement" of Lincoln was unique among statesmen. Niebuhr, whose counsel was listened to by leaders of the Franklin D. Roosevelt administrations in the 1930s and 1940s, and who ran for political office in New York State, had come to believe that "it is the very nature of political commitments that those who make them claim more ultimate virtues for their cause than either a transcendent providence or a neutral posterity will validate." He believed that Lincoln's gift was his ability "to put the enemy into the same category of ambiguity as the nation to which his life was committed."[19]

Niebuhr offered his assessment of Lincoln as part of his wide-ranging critique of Western culture. Niebuhr believed an "evil by-product" of the dynamism of Western culture "was a fanaticism which confused partial meanings and contingent purposes with the ultimate meaning of life itself." Niebuhr admired Lincoln's "lack of fanaticism" and "his spirit of magnanimity." Lincoln embodied decisive political and religious commitments and at the same time, as in the Meditation, was able to recognize the "partiality of all historic commitments."[20]

WHO, THEN, is this God of whom Lincoln speaks?

He was a God who *wills.* Four times, in the 151 words of the Meditation, Lincoln described God as a God who *wills.*

The will of God prevails.

In great contests each party claims to act in accordance with the will of God.

. . . God wills this contest,
and wills that it shall not end yet.

Lincoln's repetitive use of the noun *will* and the active verb *wills* underscored the main point of his meditation, that God was the primary if *quiet* actor in the war.

ALTHOUGH LINCOLN'S MEMO of September 2, 1862, was for his eyes only, two of his conversations within the next twenty days would reflect some of the same ideas and spirit.

On September 13, Lincoln welcomed two Chicago ministers to the Executive Mansion. Earlier in the month, "Christians of all denominations" had gathered in a large public meeting that was "filled to overflowing" in Bryan Hall in Chicago to express their support for emancipation. William W. Patton and John Dempster, representing that assembly, presented Lincoln with memorials in English and German.[21]

In his reply Lincoln offered words that picked up the tenor of the dilemma he had written about in his private reflection eleven days earlier. Speaking of the advice he was receiving about emancipation, Lincoln said:

> *I am approached with the most opposite opinions and advice, and that by religious men, who are equally certain that they represent the Divine will. I am sure that either the one or the other class is mistaken in that belief, and perhaps in some respects both.*[22]

The syntax and words of his private memo and public remarks are remarkably similar.

MEDITATION	*MEMORIAL*
In great contests each party claims to act in accordance with the will of God.	*I am approached with the most opposite opinions and advice, and that by religious men, who are equally certain that they represent the Divine will.*

Both may be, and one must be wrong. God can not be for, and against the same thing at the same time.

I am sure that either the one or the other class is mistaken in that belief, and perhaps in some respects both.

Lincoln spoke to the delegates from Chicago of his own desire.

I hope it will not be irreverent for me to say that if it is probable that God would reveal his will to others, on a point so connected with my duty, it might be supposed he would reveal it directly to me; for, unless I am more deceived in myself than I often am, it is my earnest desire to know the will of Providence in this matter.

He concluded:

And if I can learn what it is I will do it!

Lincoln underlined this affirmation and put an exclamation point to underscore his conviction!

FOUR DAYS LATER, on September 17, Gen. Robert E. Lee's first invasion of the North was turned back at the Maryland village of Sharpsburg, in what the North called the Battle of Antietam. Lincoln convened a special cabinet meeting on Monday, September 22. Two members of Lincoln's cabinet confided to their diaries some of Lincoln's words of explanation behind his historic decision to issue an Emancipation Proclamation. Salmon P. Chase, secretary of the Treasury, recorded that Lincoln told them that "when the rebel army was at Frederick," he had "determined" that if they be "driven out of Maryland," he would issue a "Proclamation of Emancipation." Lincoln continued, "I said nothing to any one; but I made the promise to myself, and"—here Chase indicated that Lincoln found himself hesitating a little—"to my Maker. The rebel army is now driven out, and I am going to fulfill that promise."[23]

Gideon Welles, secretary of the Navy, had been writing detailed entries in his diary for almost every day since January 1862. His diary entry confirmed independently the account by Chase. Welles recorded that the president began by informing the cabinet that regarding emancipation, "the question was finally decided, the act and the consequences were his," but he wanted to invite the cabinet's "criticism" of the paper he had prepared. In the course of the discussion, Welles recorded that Lincoln "remarked that he had made a vow, a covenant, that if God gave us the victory in the approaching battle, he would consider it an indication of Divine will, and that it was his duty to move forward in the cause of emancipation." He continued: "It might be thought strange, [Lincoln] said, that he had in this way submitted the disposal of matters when the way was not clear to his mind what he should do." Welles reported that Lincoln summed up his remarkable discourse by telling them, "God had decided this question in favor of the slaves."[24]

FINALLY, THE Meditation on the Divine Will is an intriguing example of Lincoln's humility. The reflection is suffused with his growing conviction that God was the primary actor in this war. What was most remarkable, in an atmosphere charged with religious fervor and hyperpatriotism, was Lincoln's new belief that God's purposes may not be able to be identified with either side. What sets him apart, in this musing, from his contemporaries in both North and South was his absence of pretension. He neither touted his own sagacity nor claimed that God was on his or the Union's side. Lincoln, who never wore his religious beliefs or feelings on his sleeve, here pondered just how it was that God, as the unseen, *quiet* actor in the war, was working out his will through human instruments.

The public and politicians knew nothing about Lincoln's Meditation. He continued to work out his own understanding of the trajectory of God's *will* in the privacy of his own thoughts. When he was ready, this private musing would form the core of what he would come to believe was his finest address, offered at the beginning of his second term as president.

CHAPTER SEVEN

"WE CANNOT ESCAPE HISTORY"

ANNUAL MESSAGE TO CONGRESS
DECEMBER 1, 1862

The dogmas of the quiet past, are inadequate to the stormy present. The occasion is piled high with difficulty, and we must rise with the occasion. As our case is new, so we must think anew, and act anew. . . .

Fellow-citizens, we cannot escape history. We of this Congress and this administration, will be remembered in spite of ourselves. No personal significance, or insignificance, can spare one or another of us. The fiery trial through which we pass, will light us down, in honor or dishonor, to the latest generation. We say we are for the Union. The world will not forget that we say this. We know how to save the Union. The world knows we do know how to save it. We—even we here—hold the power, and bear the responsibility. In giving freedom to the slave, we assure freedom to the free—honorable alike in what we give, and what we preserve. We shall nobly save, or meanly lose, the last best, hope of earth.

"NEVER HAS SUCH a paper been delivered to the National Legislature under auspices so grave, and rarely, if ever, has one been awaited with equal solicitude by the people of the country." Washington's *National Intelligencer* understood immediately the import of Abraham Lincoln's annual message to Congress on December 1, 1862.[1] Coming at the end of a difficult summer and fall of military setbacks, and after September's significant but controversial victory at Antietam, Lincoln's annual message was also delivered after fall elections that were disastrous for Republicans in both state and national voting. Lincoln sent up his second message on the opening day of the final, rump session of the Thirty-seventh Congress, which had been elected in 1860.

Annual presidential messages to Congress before Lincoln had not been known for their literary or rhetorical style. What we call today the State of the Union address had consisted typically of reports, usually written by heads of departments, and of a president's proposals for future congressional action.

Lincoln's annual messages rose above the limits of the event. Before the press conferences of the next century, he used his annual messages as an opportunity to speak through Congress to the American people. In the body of this message he addressed the timely questions converging at the end of 1862, while in its conclusion Lincoln spoke words of timeless expression. Of all his regular and special messages to Congress during his four-plus years as president, the annual message of 1862 rose to the zenith of his presidential eloquence.

LINCOLN COMPOSED his second annual message to Congress exactly one month before he was scheduled to sign the controversial Emancipation Proclamation, on January 1, 1863. Lincoln's decision, in the summer of 1862, to offer such a proclamation took both his friends and his foes by surprise. When Lincoln assembled his cabinet on July 22 and began to read a preliminary draft of a proclamation promising emancipation, none were prepared for its conclusion. Lincoln's purpose was not to ask their assent, but to inform them of his plan of action. The last sentence contained the heart of his intention. Lincoln, as commander-in-chief, authorized *as a fit and necessary military measure* that on January 1, 1863, *all persons held as slaves within any state or states, wherein the constitutional authority of the United States shall not then be practically recognized . . . shall then, thenceforward, and forever, be free.* Lincoln had come to the determination that the preservation of the Union and the liberation of the slaves were inseparable.[2]

Secretary of State Seward and Secretary of the Navy Gideon

Welles were the only members of the cabinet who knew of Lincoln's plans in advance. Seward suggested that to issue the proclamation at a time of continuing defeats by Union armies might appear to be an act of desperation. Why not wait until a significant military victory would place the proclamation in a more positive light? Lincoln took Seward's remarks to heart.

LINCOLN'S PLAN TO issue an Emancipation Proclamation cost him the backing of many moderates within his own party, but did not bring him the full support of radical Republicans. Throughout the war, but especially in 1862, he suffered merciless scolding from conservatives and radicals within his own party. Conservative Republicans believed Lincoln was being bullied by and had finally capitulated to the radicals and their abolitionist allies. Radical Republicans welcomed Lincoln's new proposal, but after initial elation cast a critical eye on what it did not do. The proclamation was only a wartime measure and limited to the rebel territory. The ultimate goal of the radical Republicans and their abolitionist allies was an amendment that would abolish slavery forever. Moderate Republicans and border-state unionists were worried about the implications for the border states of Kentucky, Maryland, and Missouri. Democrats, who had opposed Lincoln from the start, exploded with anger at this presidential authoritarianism, but after a while some of them believed they now had the issue by which they could appeal to a nation tiring of war and death.

The political landscape changed with the disastrous biennial elections. The elections of 1862 offered a crazy-quilt schedule that incited interest from spring to late fall. Twenty-three states voted, in elections held in April, June, August, September, October, and November. No national body supervised the elections as voters went to the polls in the spring in New England and in late summer and fall in the West. The course of the war, the preliminary emancipation proclamation (on September 22), and the suspension of the writ of habeas corpus (on September 24) all became factors in the elections. Lincoln was concerned and realistic, remembering that he and his fellow Republicans had won as a minority party in 1860, contending with opponents who were divided.[3]

The Democrats garnered a net increase of thirty-four seats in the House. Five key states in which Lincoln had won every electoral vote in 1860 now elected Democratic majorities in Congress: New York, Pennsylvania, Ohio, Indiana, and Illinois. Republicans did pick up five seats in the Senate. In state contests the results were dismal. New York and New Jersey elected a Democrat as governor. Criticizing Lincoln as an abolitionist dictator, Democrats gained control of the state legislatures in Illinois and Indiana. Illinois elected nine Democrats and only five Republicans to the House of Representatives. In Lincoln's home district, John Todd Stuart, Lincoln's first law partner and political guide, defeated the Republican candidate, Leonard Swett, a leader in the campaign to secure the Republican nomination for Lincoln in 1860. The *New York Times,* surveying the results, opined that the elections could be summed up as a "vote of want of confidence" in the president.[4]

BY EARLY NOVEMBER, Lincoln was hard at work preparing his annual message. In order to make time to write, he reversed his open-door policy and instructed his secretaries to limit his times for public receptions to two hours daily.

Right at this time Albert Chandler was a frequent observer of Lincoln's method of writing. Chandler was one of the three cipher operators in the Military Telegraph Service in the War Department building. Albert E. H. Johnson, custodian of military telegrams, enjoyed referring to Chandler and his fellow operators, Charles Tinker and David Homer Bates, as the "Sacred Three."[5]

Once the war began, Lincoln developed the habit of visiting the War Department several times a day. The War Department, located on the southeast corner of Pennsylvania Avenue and Seventeenth Street, was the nerve center of the Union war effort. Edwin M. Stanton, eccentric but hardworking secretary of war, from his office overlooking the White House, and with a huge map placed near his desk, used his considerable energy to support the far-flung efforts of the Union armies. The telegraph office was housed in several locations in the War Department in the first two years of the war. In the spring of 1862, it was moved to a permanent location in the old library room on the second floor, adjoining the quarters of Secretary Stanton.[6]

Lincoln came to the telegraph office as early as 6 A.M. In the evening he would sometimes walk through the tree-lined grounds between the Executive Mansion and the War Department as late as 11 P.M. in order to read firsthand the latest news from the battlefronts. A deep box was made for Lincoln where all messages for him, or messages he ought to see, were placed. All of the operators remembered that when the president finally got to the bottom of the box and had read the last report, he often made some remark that caused laughter in the office. The telegraph office in the War Department became Lincoln's ear to hear of the fast-moving events of the war. He also found that the telegraph office provided him a quiet retreat away from the always busy Executive Mansion where he could read, think, and write.

Chandler described Lincoln's habits of writing. Lincoln, often wrapped in a gray plaid shawl, after reading the various messages, would sit down at the table opposite Chandler to write. "His composition, in writing, was slow and apparently somewhat labored." While Lincoln was writing, Chandler said, he often saw the president move his lips. The cipher operator was observing a pattern that Lincoln had developed over the years. Lincoln would whisper or speak out loud words or phrases before writing them down. Chandler also noted Lincoln talking to himself, observing this behavior both inside the telegraph office and several times when he saw Lincoln walking between the White House and the War Department.[7]

Chandler supported the reports of other witnesses when he said that Lincoln usually read his words aloud. The telegrapher reported that alliteration and peculiar names seemed to hold "a charm for him." He would repeat these particular words over and over. The telegrapher offered another observation when he reported that Lincoln "would occasionally purposely mispronounce words and misplace inflection and accent, as if musing as he read." Chandler believed that a major reason Lincoln wrote so slowly was that he was deliberating as he wrote, as if carrying on a conversation with himself about the meaning and direction of his thinking.[8]

SEN. ORVILLE H. BROWNING, returning from Illinois for the convening of Congress, called on the president on November 29 at the White House. Browning and Lincoln had been friends in Illinois. Their friendship had warmed since Browning came to Washington. As Browning's initial votes in the Senate stamped him as a conservative, many Republicans in Illinois, including the *Chicago Tribune,* were turning against him.

Browning feared that Lincoln was being unduly influenced by the radical leaders in the Republican Party. As close as he was to the president, Browning did not know of Lincoln's intentions about the freedom of the slaves until the preliminary emancipation proclamation was announced on September 22. Browning confided to his diary on October 14 that he had met that day with Judge Thomas Drummond, United States district judge in Illinois, and they spoke about Lincoln and the emancipation proclamation. Browning and Drummond agreed: "The President's proclamation unfortunate—He was not satisfied of its constitutionality but to say nothing of that, it was ill advised as it could do no possible good, and certainly would do harm in uniting the rebels more firmly than ever."[9]

Browning believed he could speak frankly with Lincoln. He wrote in his diary on the evening of November 29, "I told him that his proclamation had been disastrous to us."[10]

ON THE SAME DAY that Browning visited Lincoln, a story about the president ran in the *Springfield (Mass.) Republican,* a strong supporter of Lincoln. Beneath the heading "The President and His Critics," the *Springfield Republican* published a story from its correspondent in Washington. The reporter told how Mr. Lincoln had been sent a batch of "newspaper criticisms upon him and his conduct of the war." Lincoln told a friend that, having an hour to spare on a Sunday, he had read the editorials. Lincoln said that when he was finished reading, "I asked myself, 'Abraham Lincoln, are you a man *or* a dog?' "[11]

LINCOLN'S ANNUAL MESSAGE was taken by Lincoln's secretary John G. Nicolay to Congress on the morning of December 1. Lawrence A. Gobright, Washington bureau chief for the Associated Press, wrote a hurried note to Nicolay with an enclosed envelope. "I will be on the lookout for you at the door of the Senate, after you shall have delivered the Message to that body. Please have two copies for me in the envelope, for the better convenience of transmission." The Associated Press was prepared to dispatch the message immediately to its member papers.[12]

John W. Forney, secretary of the Senate, also wrote a note to Nicolay on that same morning. Forney, editor of the *Washington Chronicle,* was yet another newspaper editor who doubled in politics. Though Forney was a lifelong Democrat, Lincoln had helped him secure his position in the Senate, and he in turn became an ardent champion of the president and his policies.

Forney wrote to Nicolay from the Senate, "The Senate is filling with Senators." He promised the president's secretary, "I will do justice to the message in reading." At the same time, as editor of the *Chronicle,* he wanted to position his paper to publish the annual message first, before other Washington papers or the Associated Press. He began the *Chronicle* as a weekly in 1861, but had expanded it to a daily in 1862, partly on the urging of Lincoln. The *Chronicle* also was becoming the unofficial organ of the Republican Party in the capital. "I hear that the Star is resolved to beat the Chronicle in getting it out. We'll see."[13]

LINCOLN BEGAN his annual message:

> *Since your last annual assembling another year of health and bountiful harvests has passed. And while it has not pleased the Almighty to bless us with a return of peace, we can but press*

> *on, guided by the best light He gives us, trusting that in His own good time, and wise way, all will yet be well.*

Tucked in introductory words that might sound formulaic were some of Lincoln's basic beliefs. He began with gratitude, spoken in alliteration, for

> *health and . . . harvests*

These words were from a man from the prairies who had not forgotten his roots in the land. His reference to God, in his favorite ascription, *the Almighty,* was not gratuitous. For Lincoln, God was the author of peace; on earth our task is to *press on,* yet we do so *by the best light He gives us.*

Lincoln began on the upbeat even as he understood that many in Congress who came to hear his message read were down and discouraged. Republicans were agitated for different reasons. Lame ducks, mostly conservatives who had lost their seats to Democrats, were downcast. Radical Republicans were concerned that Lincoln, reading the results of the election, might step back from the promise of the proclamation and adopt a more conservative posture. Democrats, buoyed by the election results, could be counted upon to be more aggressive in this session.

Lincoln's annual message for 1862 would encompass a broad range of topics, including a long section on foreign relations, with most of the language coming from Seward, as well as reports on other government departments, using words supplied by department members. A large amount of the message followed custom. But Lincoln was not going to let custom take up the entirety of this opportunity, not only to speak to Congress but to mobilize public opinion in towns and cities where his message would be read and spoken aloud from countless newspapers.

EARLY ON, Lincoln spoke of the prospects for colonization, a topic he had been discussing with Congress since the beginning of the war. One last time in this annual message he would speak of its benefits.

Later in his message, after reminding the Congress of his preliminary emancipation proclamation of September 22, he called their attention to *compensated emancipation.* What was surprising was the rhetoric he chose to frame the discussion. Instead of legal arguments he offered a mini lecture in geography, with a political conclusion. In this message he began by defining a nation as consisting of

> *its territory,*
> *its people,*
> *and its laws*

But he observed:

> *The territory is the only part which is of certain durability.*

Lincoln underscored his observation by a quotation from Ecclesiastes 1:4:

> *"One generation passeth away, and another generation cometh, but the earth abideth forever."*

Lincoln moved from this biblical remark to the particular territory of the United States, declaring that the land itself helped define one nation. It

> *is well adapted to be the home of one national family; and it is not well adapted for two, or more.*

What was more:

> *Steam, telegraphs, and intelligence, have brought these, to be an advantageous combination, for one united people.*

In Lincoln's rhetorical architecture, he often looked at an idea from both the negative and the positive points of view. He now turned to the negative, what he called

> *the total inadequacy of disunion, as a remedy for the differences between the people of the two sections*

In this discussion Lincoln stated that he could not improve upon the discussion in his inaugural address, so he took the unusual step of repeating two paragraphs from an address he had given twenty-one months before.

In descriptive prose he spoke about possible boundaries if there were to be two nations. He began with a topic sentence:

> *There is no line, straight or crooked, suitable for a national boundary, upon which to divide.*

He tried out possible dividing lines:

> *a little more than one-third of its length are rivers*

and

> *nearly all its remaining length, are merely surveyor's lines . . .*

But rivers are easy to cross and people walk back and forth over surveyors' lines without any consciousness of their presence.

Lincoln, still working with the hypothesis of a divided nation, forecast a future with greater difficulties. He launched into a picturesque description of

> *the great interior region, bounded east by the Alleghanies, north by the British dominions, west by the Rocky mountains, and south by the line along which the culture of corn and cotton meets*

He named the twelve states and three territories that made up this region.

> *A glance at the map shows that, territorially speaking, it is the great body of the republic.*

Lincoln argued that the other parts of the nation were *but marginal borders* to this heartland. He did pay tribute to

> *the magnificent region sloping west from the Rocky Mountains to the Pacific, being the deepest, and also the richest, in undeveloped resources*

Despite the incredible promise of the interior region, there was a major problem:

> *. . . this region has no sea-coast, touches no ocean anywhere.*

As part of one nation, the *people* of the region will *forever find*

> *their way to Europe by New York,*
> *to South America and Africa by New Orleans,*
> *and to Asia by San Francisco*

But if the nation was to be divided, the people of each nation would be cut off from one or more of these ocean outlets. Lincoln was arguing from physical geography—the land—against the madness of disunion.

If the land was permanent, human beings were impermanent. The land would go on and on, but people can change their destiny within a generation.

> *Our strife pertains to ourselves—to the passing generations of men; and it can, without convulsion, be hushed forever with the passing of one generation.*

He concluded this pictorial discussion by declaring that the problems building through many generations could be solved by the present generation.

HAVING SKETCHED in a broad picture of the problem of disunion, Lincoln turned to specific resolutions by proposing three constitutional amendments that might yet provide unity. Lincoln's goal was to provide an end of slavery by peaceful means even while still in the midst of war.

1. The first amendment called for each state where slavery existed to abolish slavery by January 1, 1900. In return that state would receive interest-bearing bonds conditioned on their abolition of slavery. If slavery continued to be tolerated or was reintroduced, the state would refund the proceeds to the United States.
2. All slaves who had been freed during the war should remain free. Their owners, if they had not been disloyal to the Union, would be compensated at the same rates as the states.
3. Congress could appropriate money to provide for the colonization of African-Americans outside the United States.

Lincoln summarized the meaning of these amendments by stating:

> *Without slavery the rebellion could never have existed; without slavery it could not continue.*

Lincoln, by the end of 1862, was willing to speak directly of slavery as the cause of the war. Without mentioning here the Emancipation Proclamation by name, he was defending emancipation as the answer to this cause of the rebellion.

Lincoln recognized, however, that *among the friends of the Union*, there was a *diversity* of opinion about slavery. He named those opinions:

> *Some would perpetuate slavery;*
> *some would abolish it suddenly, and without compensation;*
> *some would abolish it gradually, and with compensation;*
> *some would remove the freed people from us,*
> *and some would retain them with us . . .*

In Lincoln's habit of validating all voices, he listed five options. He did so in the best words their proponents would use. However, Lincoln averred:

> *Because of these diversities, we waste much strength in struggles among ourselves.*

Compromise was the only solution. Lincoln put forward his three amendments as a plan for mutual concessions. He then discussed how persons advocating each of the five positions could see strengths and weaknesses in the amendments.

LINCOLN TOOK TIME toward the end of this second annual message to pay tribute to his senior colleagues even as he asked them to understand the passion of his leadership. In a gracious but astute political gesture he told them:

> *Nor do I forget that some of you are my seniors, nor that many of you have more experience than I, in the conduct of public affairs.*

Yet, Lincoln said, he hoped that

> *in view of the great responsibility resting upon me, you will perceive no want of respect to yourselves, in any undue earnestness I may seem to display.*

LINCOLN TURNED QUICKLY to his conclusion.

> *The dogmas of the quiet past, are inadequate to the stormy present. The occasion is piled high with difficulty, and we must rise with the occasion. As our case is new, so we must think anew, and act anew.*

Although Lincoln appealed explicitly for support of his proposals, and implicitly for the Emancipation Proclamation, his rhetoric expanded his appeal beyond any particular agenda to a willingness to embrace a new and different future.

Lincoln did not say what he meant by

the dogmas of the quiet past

Did he mean the dogma of the Constitution on slavery that was fashioned in the revolutionary era to ensure that Southern states would sign on to the Constitution of the new republic? Was he suggesting the dogmas of the proslavery position? Was he referring to his earlier belief, stated in his inaugural address, that the Constitution forbade him from attacking slavery where it already existed? Perhaps he was referring to all of the options within the North that he had summarized earlier in his message.

When he located these *dogmas* in the *quiet past,* he was suggesting a more peaceful, prewar past. It was one thing to debate the merits of slavery and colonization and abolitionism and compensated emancipation in relative peace. This sentence can be read so that Lincoln included himself as one who debated these dogmas, as in those nights long ago in Boston and Worcester, or in debates in Illinois with Stephen Douglas.

Lincoln contrasted the *quiet past* with the *stormy present.* A favorite image of the developing war was to compare it to an emerging storm. In this storm Lincoln was subjected to noisy voices that were constantly telling him what he should do about the raging storm.

Piled high suggests that Lincoln had learned on the job that even if the goal of the war was the preservation of the Union, and now the complementary goal of liberty, as president he had to deal with all kinds of nettlesome *difficulty.* When Lincoln called for three hundred thousand volunteers on July 1, 1862, he was met with a disappointing and sometimes acrimonious response. On September 24, 1862, when Lincoln extended his suspension of the privilege of the writ of habeas corpus "throughout the United States," he was criticized for stifling the words of those who opposed his war aims. These and other contentious issues spoke to the growing *difficulty* with which Lincoln had to contend. The home front often seemed to present as many difficulties to Lincoln as the war front.

. . . we must rise with the occasion.

The full sentence can best be understood if we add an unvoiced "because" at the beginning of the sentence:

[Because] the occasion is piled high with difficulty . . .

this is why we must *rise* and change. Lincoln was including himself. He *must rise with the occasion.* Stung by criticism in 1860 and early 1861 that he had underestimated the determination of the South to go its own way, he made no such misjudgments now about what was at stake or how long the war might go on. He said to his fellow countrymen, Northerners and Southerners, Republicans and Democrats, that we could not continue to live in the past.

Lincoln had come to embrace the phrase "the right to rise" in articulating his economic philosophy. Beginning as a Whig, and continuing as a Republican, Lincoln championed the equality of all individuals to rise just as far as their abilities might carry them. We dare not miss this economic component in his hatred of slavery, for this system of subjugation denied blacks the right to rise.[14]

Lincoln embodied his own principle as president. In terms of policy, he was rising in relation to slavery and emancipation. In terms of rhetoric, the studied, rational argument of his inaugural address was being replaced or enhanced by rising to a more evocative rhetoric better able to resonate with both the emotional fears and the longings of his audience.

As our case is new, so we must think anew, and act anew.

These words, and the trajectory to which they point, have often been mislaid or forgotten because of the dramatic final words of the address that followed.

Presidential politics is the ability to articulate a compelling vision. Those to whom we have accorded the mantle of our greatest presidents have exercised their leadership by articulating the ideals of America for their time, and in a few cases for all time.

For the first year and a half of the war, the burden of Lincoln's rhetoric had been to show that he was acting with fidelity to the great ideals of the past, especially as they were enshrined in the Declaration of Independence and the Constitution. Lincoln, with his finely honed sense of history, appealed to the nation's founding documents to argue for the perpetuity of the Union. At the same time he argued that it was the Confederate States of America that was presenting a novel and illegitimate understanding of the ideals and sacred texts of the nation's past.

By the summer and fall of 1862, Lincoln became willing to change the definition of the war. In his Meditation on the Divine Will, written three months earlier on September 2, 1862, Lincoln indicated a willingness to *think anew* by rejecting the reigning religious and political orthodoxies of his day—"God is on our side"—espoused by Union and Confederate politicians and preachers, and to consider that

> *in the present civil war it is quite possible that God's purpose is something different from the purpose of either party . . .*

Lincoln, after the Second Battle of Bull Run, voiced not fatalism or resignation but a desire to discern the often inscrutable will of God in human affairs.

Lincoln's decision on emancipation, which he had mulled over by himself for months, and which he presented to his cabinet on July 22 and on September 22, was a primary example of his willingness to

> *think anew, and act anew*

> *Fellow-citizens, <u>we</u> cannot escape history. We of this Congress and this administration, will be remembered in spite of ourselves. No personal significance, or insignificance, can spare one or another of us.*

Lincoln joined history and memory in the appeal that marks his conclusion. From his first reading of Parson Mason Weems's biography of George Washington as a boy to the delivery of his first major speech, the address to the Young Men's Lyceum in Springfield in 1838, as a young man, Lincoln could not escape the allure of history. He held himself accountable to the great ideals both of the Founding Fathers and of the primary documents of the nation. Now he desired that Congress join him in a new accountability.

If Lincoln had evoked symbols of the past in his inaugural address in making his appeal for the Union, in his 1862 annual message to Congress he appealed to the future. It will be *the latest generation,* the distant future, that will judge the actions of Lincoln and his contemporaries.

Lincoln asked the Congress to unite behind him. He was aware of all the political divisions represented in the representatives who would assemble to hear his message. He must have wished he could have addressed Congress in person. The closest he could get was to guide editor Forney in the Senate and the clerk in the House by his use of italics, which he designated for emphasis.

In addition, in his conclusion he used inclusive plural pronouns—*we, ourselves, us*—to underscore the personal responsibility he wanted each member of Congress to feel.

> . . . *we cannot escape history*
> *We . . . will be remembered*

There is no "I" but rather a *we* that energizes this peroration. Lincoln is the president, but he is calling on the Congress, as the people's representatives, to join him.

He links *Congress* and *administration* to suggest that the divisions that do exist must now be put aside because of the urgency of the task before us. *Personal significance* or *insignificance* must disappear in face of the tasks that confront each person who hears his words.

> *The fiery trial through which we pass, will light us down, in honor or dishonor, to the latest generation.*

On September 26, 1862, Lincoln received a visit from Eliza P. Gurney, a Quaker minister from Philadelphia. She and three friends had sought an interview with the president for the purposes of comforting and exhorting him. They ended up organizing a prayer meeting in the president's office.

Lincoln was sympathetic to the particular dilemma of the Quakers. As pacifists they abhorred war. He appreciated that they had been among the first antislavery activists in America. Mrs. Gurney, following her sermon about the necessity to seek divine guidance, knelt and offered a prayer "that light and wisdom might be shed down from on high, to guide our President."[15]

Lincoln, who was more often than not reticent to speak about his deepest feelings, especially his religious feelings, became surprisingly candid in a correspondence he began with Mrs. Gurney. In his first letter, on October 26, he thanked her for "your sympathy and prayers." He then remarked, "We are indeed going through a great trial—a fiery trial."[16] The "indeed" in his comment may indicate that he was responding to her sermon, in which she had commended Lincoln for the steadfastness of his leadership in such a difficult time. Lincoln's image of "a fiery trial" surely comes directly from 1 Peter 4:12; the letter was written to people undergoing persecution and hard times: "Beloved, think it not strange concerning the fiery trial which is to try you, as though some strange thing happened unto you." On December 1, Lincoln would invoke this same biblical image, used just five weeks earlier, at the time he was beginning to compose his annual message.

> *In <u>giving</u> freedom to the <u>slave</u>, we <u>assure</u> freedom to the <u>free</u>—honorable alike in what we give, and what we preserve. We shall nobly save, or meanly lose, the last best, hope of earth.*

As an audience, then and now, we respond to the expressiveness of Lincoln's words, but we may not be aware of what it is in his artistry with words that produced such eloquence. In Lincoln's final two sentences he offered a complex rhythmic balance of ideas that was completed by a decisive final sentence expressed in simple but powerful monosyllables.

The pattern of rhythmic balancing was a hallmark of Lincoln's rhetoric. He had offered it in his Farewell Address at Springfield, on February 11, 1861. In that brief address Lincoln elegantly balanced three expressions of the ubiquity of God—

Trusting in Him,
who can go with me,
and remain with you
and be every where for good

—with a simpler, decisive conclusion, a crescendo of six monosyllables expressing hope for the future:

. . . let us confidently hope
that all will yet be well.

Nearly three years later, in the second annual message, he offered an almost musical balancing:

In giving freedom to the slave,
we assure freedom to the free—
honorable alike in what we give,
and what we preserve.

Lincoln moved from this nicely balanced pair of ideas—

We shall nobly save,
or meanly lose,

—to his decisive conclusion, spoken in six final monosyllabic words:

the last best, hope of earth

DAVID ZAREFSKY, a dean of teachers of rhetoric and speech communications, when asked to choose from the entire Lincoln canon the text that most embodied Lincoln's "rhetorical leadership," selected the 1862 annual message. He said that he made his choice over the more obvious choices of the First and Second Inaugural Addresses, the Gettysburg Address, and the Emancipation Proclamation.[17]

Zarefsky makes the case for "rhetorical leadership": the power of the president does not stem simply from official duties granted by the Constitution, but grows from his personal powers of persuasion. Certainly presidents are not free to construct their vision of reality without taking into account the political restraints of their times. After almost two years in office, Lincoln had learned much about both the restraints and the possibilities of presidential power.

Zarefsky argues that the 1862 annual message reveals at least two dimensions of Lincoln's rhetorical leadership. First, he is responsive to the pressing rhetorical and political situation. Lincoln is working within the constraints of the practical politics of the moment. He is conscious of the anxieties and hopes of his audience.

Second, Zarefsky contends, Lincoln crafts an alternative vision of reality. Although Lincoln presents specific arguments for compensated emancipation, Zarefsky argues that the message "subtly subverts" Lincoln's own immediate political proposal for emancipated compensation, "implicitly conceding the impracticality of what it explicitly proposes." This move creates rhetorical space for Lincoln to offer a "more radical alternative." In the end Lincoln is asking his listeners to move beyond their limited worldviews and embrace a future that cannot yet be known.[18]

THE ANNUAL MESSAGE of December 1, 1862, was Lincoln's finest message to Congress. His words transcended the limitations of the event. He used this occasion not simply to report to Congress but to mobilize public opinion. He offered a powerful appeal to history, but also invited Americans to think in the future tense. Lincoln's message represented a breadth of conception and height of imagination in his expanding rhetorical arsenal. He expressed the prospect for democracy in words that deserve to be known alongside the Gettysburg Address and the Second Inaugural Address.

CHAPTER EIGHT

"YOU SAY YOU WILL NOT FIGHT TO FREE NEGROES"

LETTER TO THE RALLY AT SPRINGFIELD
AUGUST 26, 1863

*You say you will not fight to free negroes. Some of them seem willing to fight for you; but, no matter. Fight you, then, exclusively to save the Union. I issued the [*emancipation*] proclamation on purpose to aid you in saving the Union. Whenever you shall have conquered all resistance to the Union, if I shall urge you to continue fighting, it will be an apt time, then, for you to declare you will not fight to free negroes. . . .*

The signs look better. The Father of Waters again goes unvexed to the sea. Thanks to the great North-West for it. Nor yet wholly to them. Three hundred miles up, they met New England, Empire, Key-Stone, and Jersey, hewing their way right and left. The Suny South too, in more colors than one, also lent a hand. On the spot, their part of the history was jotted down in black and white. . . . Nor must Uncle Sam's web-feet be forgotten. At all the watery margins they have been present. Not only on the deep sea, the broad bay, and the rapid river, but also up the narrow muddy bayou, and wherever the ground was a little damp, they have been, and made their tracks. Thanks to all. For the great republic—for the principle it lives by, and keeps alive—for man's vast future,—thanks to all.

Peace does not appear so distant as it did. I hope it will come soon, and come to stay; and so come as to be worth the keeping in all future time. It will then have been proved that, among free men, there can be no successful appeal from the ballot to the bullet; and that they who take such appeal are sure to lose their case, and pay the cost. And then, there will be some black men who can remember that, with silent tongue, and clenched teeth, and steady eye, and well-poised bayonet, they have helped mankind on to this great consummation; while, I fear, there will be some white ones, unable to forget that, with malignant hearts, and deceitful speech, they have strove to hinder it.

ABRAHAM LINCOLN RECEIVED a request on August 14, 1863, that surely caused his heart to jump. He was invited to speak at what organizers were calling the largest popular meeting of the war in support of the Union. The location of the gathering immediately arrested Lincoln's attention. A "Grand Mass Meeting" would be held in Springfield, Illinois, on September 3.

James C. Conkling, chairman of the Committee on Arrangements, tendered the invitation. Conkling was Lincoln's longtime friend in Springfield. Born in New York in 1816, educated at Princeton, he had moved to Springfield in 1838, one year after Lincoln had arrived. Mercy Levering Conkling became a close friend of Mary Todd Lincoln. A fervent Whig, James C. Conkling was a central figure in a small group of influential Springfield leaders with antislavery commitments. When the Republican electors gathered in Springfield to cast their ballots for Lincoln on December 5, 1860, they were entertained at dinner at the Conkling home, at the northeast corner of Fourth and Monroe Streets. Now Conkling told the president, "Not only would thousands who will be here be prepared to receive you with the warmest enthusiasm but the whole country would be eager to extend to you its congratulations on the way." He concluded his letter with a plea: "Can you not give us a favorable reply?"[1]

Conkling made Lincoln a tempting offer. After successes at Gettysburg and Vicksburg six weeks earlier, in July 1863, supporters of the Union believed prospects for victory were on the rise again. Conkling was convinced the Springfield meeting offered Lincoln the opportunity to speak about his policies at a critical moment in the

James C. Conkling, Springfield lawyer, invited Lincoln to return to speak at a large rally in Springfield on September 3, 1863.

ABRAHAM LINCOLN PRESIDENTIAL LIBRARY

war. Lincoln could expect that appreciation and vindication would be his traveling companions on the train trip home to Springfield. Would he accept the invitation?

LINCOLN REPLIED TO Conkling six days later by telegraph. He wrote on August 20, "Your letter of the 14th is received. I think I will go, or send a letter—probably the latter."[2]

Lincoln's secretaries, John G. Nicolay and John Hay, both from Illinois, appreciated the emotional tug-of-war they observed in their boss. "For a moment the President cherished the hope of going to

Springfield, and once more in his life renewing the sensation, so dear to politicians, of personal contact with great and enthusiastic masses, and of making one more speech to shouting thousands of his fellow-citizens."[3]

Conkling wrote once more on August 21. He stepped up his persuasion. "While it would afford the many thousands of loyal men assembled together on that occasion, great pleasure to hear from you, by Letter . . . they would infinitely prefer to see you in person." Conkling concluded by telling Lincoln that "the importance of our meeting . . . at the capital of a State, which has sent so many soldiers into the army, and which exercises such a controlling power in the West, cannot be overestimated."[4] Conkling was speaking for ardent Republicans from Illinois and across the Midwest who were planning to travel to Springfield to hear the president.

THERE WAS LITTLE TIME now before the event. Lincoln had to make his decision. Finally, on August 26, after thanking Conkling for the invitation, Lincoln gave his answer: *It would be very agreeable to me, to thus meet my old friends, at my own home; but I can not, just now, be absent from here, so long as a visit there, would require.*[5] The remainder of the letter to Conkling contained the speech Lincoln wanted his friend to read on his behalf on September 3. A clerk copied Lincoln's final draft, at which point Lincoln made some corrections and signed the letter.

The next day, August 27, Lincoln wrote to Conkling again, this time on stationery with a War Department letterhead.

My dear Conkling:

I can not leave here now. Herewith is a letter instead. You are one of the best public readers. I have but one suggestion—Read it very slowly.

And now God bless you, and all good Union-men.

Yours as ever

A. LINCOLN

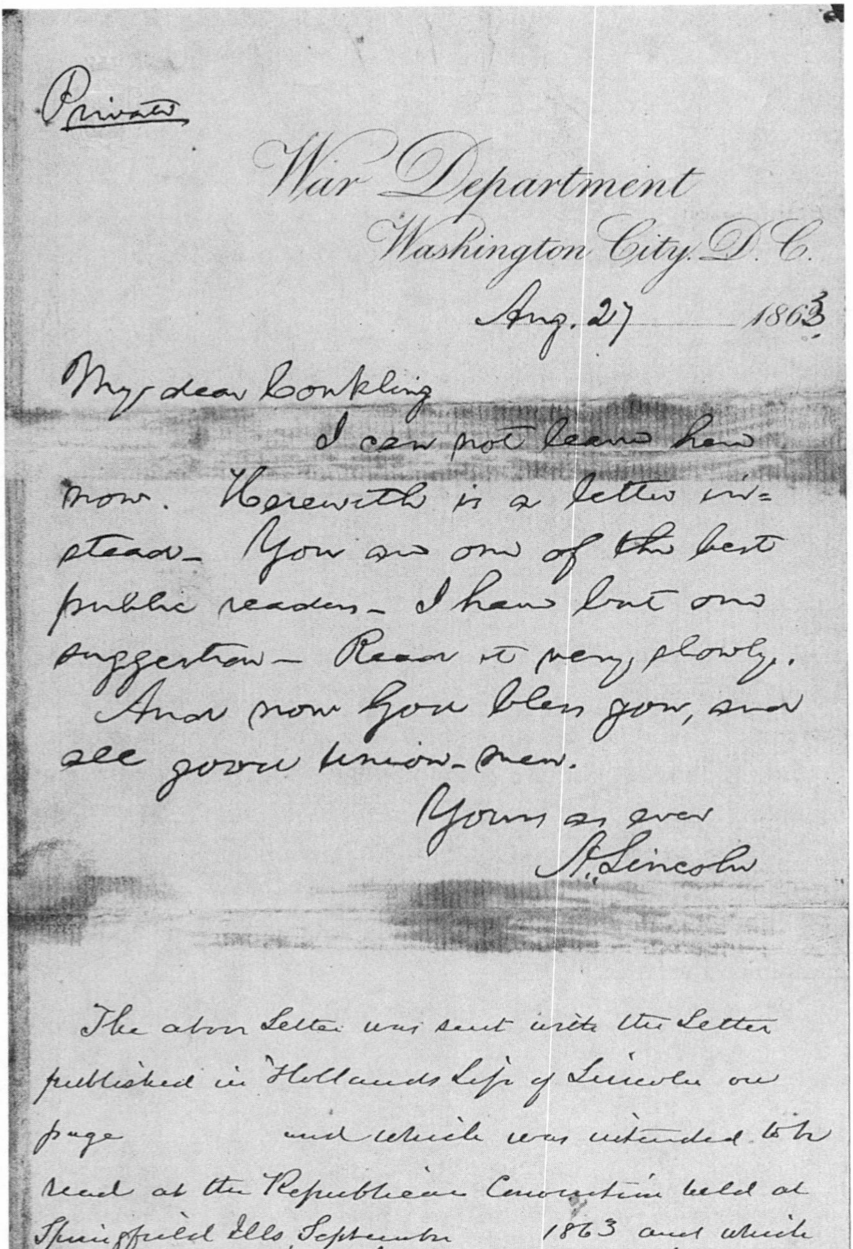

Private

War Department
Washington City. D.C.
Aug. 27 1863.

My dear Conkling

I can not leave here now. Herewith is a letter instead— You are one of the best public readers— I have but one suggestion— Read it very slowly. And now God bless you, and all good Union-men.

Yours as ever
A. Lincoln

The above Letter was sent with the Letter published in Hollands Life of Lincoln on page and which was intended to be read at the Republican Convention held at Springfield Ills September 1863 and which was read at that time James C Conkling

Lincoln's telegram to James C. Conkling including a single instruction for his letter to the Springfield rally: "Read it very slowly." This is one more indication of the way Lincoln intended to deliver his speeches.

ABRAHAM LINCOLN PRESIDENTIAL LIBRARY

Lincoln, who knew Conkling was a fine speaker and public reader, bundled the letters from August 26 and 27 together and sent them off to Conkling.[6]

ON AUGUST 29 William Herndon wrote to Lincoln about some legal business but he added his endorsement of the upcoming mass meeting. "We will have a great time here on the 3d Septr and it is thought it will be the largest crowd ever Convened here." Herndon had his own expectations for what the meeting could accomplish. "I hope it will—hope it will give us confidence, back-bone vigor & energy." He did not yet know whether Lincoln was coming or not, but he wanted to add his enthusiasm.[7]

TWO WITNESSES GIVE information about the composition of the letter to Conkling. Lincoln evidently made up his mind by August 23 to send a letter, for on that day Hay, the first witness, wrote in his diary that in the afternoon Lincoln "went to the library to write a letter to Conkling."[8]

William O. Stoddard, the second witness, served as an additional secretary, assisting Nicolay and Hay from 1861 to 1864. In his diary Stoddard recounted a scene when Lincoln invited him into his office. He did not give a date, but this was probably the same incident that Hay had described on Sunday, August 23. Stoddard, who later achieved fame as the author of more than seventy books for boys, sometimes exaggerated the closeness of his relationship with Lincoln, but he was at his best in describing the atmosphere of the working Lincoln White House.

Upon entering the office Stoddard observed that the president was sitting at the end of the long oak cabinet table in the center of the room. The table was draped with a cloth covering. Cluttered about the table were a variety of newspapers, rolled-up maps, and assorted odds and ends of letters and orders. Lincoln was writing slowly on sheets of foolscap paper. The president asked if he could read aloud what he was writing. Lincoln said, "I can always tell more about a thing after I've heard it read aloud, and know how it sounds." He continued, "Just the reading of it to myself doesn't answer as well, either."

Stoddard asked Lincoln if he could read the letter aloud.

"No, no; I'll read it myself. What I want is an audience. Nothing sounds the same when there isn't anybody to hear it and find fault with it."[9]

Stoddard portrayed a remarkable scene. He captured the way Lincoln wrote, and his need to hear his writing read aloud.

NEITHER OF THE WITNESSES, Hay or Stoddard, speaks to the question of which version of the letter to Conkling their boss was writing. It was written in pencil. The numbered pages, seven to eleven, suggest an eleven-page document, but the first six pages are missing. Two options exist. First, the fragment may simply be an early version, prepared toward the end of August. Such versions are in keeping with what we have learned of Lincoln's habits of writing and rewriting. Second, it may be that the fragment was part of his general writing in defense of emancipation and the arming of black troops. In the months after the Emancipation Proclamation of January 1, 1863, Lincoln knew that opportunities would present themselves when he could articulate his policies. As we have observed, he was always writing notes about important and timely topics. By the reasoning of this second option, he used this fragment in writing and revising the letter to Conkling.[10]

THE MEETING ON September 3 was planned in part as a response to a large Midwest "peace meeting" held three months earlier, also in Springfield. Throughout 1863, desperate attempts were made by peace Democrats, or Copperheads as their Republican opponents called them, to gain control of states in the Northwest.

Lincoln's preliminary announcement of the Emancipation Proclamation on September 22, 1862, had cost Republicans at the polls in the fall of the year, both in Illinois and in other states in the

Midwest. Soldiers in Illinois regiments were deeply divided about emancipation, their point of view often depending upon where they were from in the state. Most soldiers had signed up to save the Union. For soldiers from southern and western Illinois—areas settled by immigrants from Kentucky, Tennessee, and the Carolinas—the issue of emancipation was sometimes explosive. A citizen of McDonough County wrote to his nephew in the Sixteenth Illinois in the spring of 1863, "Richard take a fool's advice and come home if you have to desert." He added, "You will be protected—the people are so enraged that you need not be alarmed if you hear of the whole of the Northwest killing off abolitionists." Yes, there was plenty of Copperhead action in McDonough County, but the sentiment against Lincoln's Emancipation Proclamation spread like a contagion even in Republican areas.[11]

One rallying point of efforts to oppose emancipation and the continuing of the war was mass meetings held in the spring and summer of 1863. The largest of these meetings was held in Springfield on June 17. On a warm summer's day a large crowd listened to furious oratory critical of Lincoln, the Emancipation Proclamation, and the arming of black troops. The culmination of the day's events was the adoption of twenty-four resolutions calling for peace now. The general sense of the resolutions was "that a further offensive prosecution of this war tends to subvert the Constitution and the Government, and entails upon this nation all the disastrous consequences of misrule and anarchy." The meeting asked for "peace upon a basis of restoration of the Union." It called for a national convention that would set the terms of peace. In the hometown of Lincoln, the boisterous assemblage churned out anti-Lincoln sentiment as it called for peace.[12]

ON AUGUST 14, the day that Conkling wrote to Lincoln, a call went out to "Unconditional Union men of the State of Illinois, without regard to former party associations," to meet in Springfield on September 3. The call was signed by several hundred men from more than two-thirds of the counties in the state. The invitation went to people of all walks of life. "Come from the remotest extremities of the State. Come from the farm and the workshop. Come from the office and the counting-room." Let "the farmer leave his plow, the mechanic his tools, the merchant his store, the professional man his business."[13]

Come they did. People started arriving on September 1 and 2. Men, women, and children came from farms and small towns all over Illinois—walking, on horseback, or in wagons. The men were nearly all older men. The young men of Illinois were off fighting for the Union. A good number of people, individuals and groups, also came from other states. The arriving throng was far too large to be accommodated in Springfield hotels, so people slept in their wagons or on the streets.

As September 3 dawned, the *Illinois State Journal* underscored the meaning of the day's events in its morning editorial, "The Duty of the Hour." The *State Journal,* long a friend of Lincoln, believed the purpose of the events was "to sustain the Government in the hour of its trial."[14]

Anna Ridgely, now twenty-one years old, observed the arriving crowds from her vantage point of a carriage ride. She noted later in her diary, "The town was full of country people." A reporter for the *Chicago Tribune* wrote, "The state capital looks like a bee hive in swarming time."[15]

Early in the morning, delegations converged from every direction on the town square. Marshals struggled to disentangle the more than three hundred "vehicles of all descriptions" and form a parade line. At around 9 A.M., the parade began moving from the city square to the fairgrounds in the western part of Springfield. People walked, rode horses, and were transported, packed into wagons, to the accompaniment of "the braying of music" and "the roll of drums." Battle-torn flags flapped in the breeze. As the marchers wound their way through residential sections they were greeted by cheering spectators who waved miniature flags. Reaching the fairgrounds, the marchers were welcomed by the booming sounds of a cannon salute.[16]

The meeting began at 11 A.M. With such a huge crowd, the organizers had arranged for the speaking and the reading of letters to take place into the twilight at a half dozen stands. The first order of business was to read the letters of distinguished persons who could not be present. Letters were read from Edward Everett, Congressman Daniel S. Dickinson of New York, Congressman Schuyler Colfax of Indiana, and Maj. Gen. Benjamin F. Butler. Finally, Conkling drew out his letter from Lincoln. He started to read—slowly.

LINCOLN BEGAN HIS LETTER with a thank-you that acknowledged the pull of Springfield.

> *It would be very agreeable to me, to thus meet my old friends, at my own home . . .*

And he offered a tribute to

> *all those who maintain unconditional devotion to the Union*

After this brief thanks, Lincoln set the tenor for a speech that must have taken aback many in his audience.

> *There are those who are dissatisfied with me. To such I would say: You desire peace; and you blame me that we do not have it. But how can we attain it? There are but three conceivable ways. First, to suppress the rebellion by force of arms. This, I am trying to do. Are you for it? If you are, so far we are agreed. If you are not for it, a second way is, to give up the Union. I am against this. Are you for it? If you are, you should say so plainly. If you are not for force, nor yet for dissolution, there only remains some imaginable compromise. I do not believe any compromise, Embracing the maintenance of the Union, is now possible.*

One of the primary challenges of any speaker, as Aristotle had stated centuries before, was to assess the mind of the audience. Lincoln's practice of listening is at much variance with modern practice. We have become accustomed, in nearly fifty years of televised news conferences, to watching a pattern. A question is asked of a president, almost any president, and too often instead of hearing him answer the question, we hear a statement we suspect was rehearsed in advance with aides, that sidesteps the question.

Lincoln's practice validated both the question and the questioner. He developed a practice of continuing to revise his speeches up to the last moment because he wanted to listen carefully to what people were asking and saying on the eve of an address. For this address, Lincoln's practice was complicated by the fact that he would not be present at Springfield to listen and then revise.

Yet Lincoln had been listening for years to the people to whom he would be speaking. He had lived with them, represented them in the state legislature, in court, and in Congress. In the last two and a half years he had been corresponding with many friends and critics in Illinois and the Midwest. From the perspective of modern politics we would expect Lincoln to "rally his base." If a crowd came to hear a candidate or elected official, that official would spend plenty of time saying what he knew they wanted to hear. Lincoln, from a distance of nearly eight hundred miles, had pondered what he would say to loyal supporters gathering in Springfield.

Lincoln began by saying what many in the crowd did not want to hear. He acknowledged the dissatisfaction of some within this largely Republican audience. He could have taken an easy way and simply called for support for his policies. Why did he, rather, pursue the approach of question and confrontation?

BECAUSE LINCOLN LISTENED. Today we evaluate politicians primarily by the quality of their speaking. Lincoln believed that an initial way to appraise a speaker was by the quality of his listening. He traveled around Illinois listening to Stephen Douglas before he responded with his own speeches. The debates themselves were punctuated by questions and comments from the audiences that forced the debater to be an active listener.

When, in the early months of his presidency, Lincoln was criticized for his open-door policy at the White House, he replied that he could not be president without his "public opinion baths," because they kept him in touch with the "plain people" who had elected him. Hay wrote later that Lincoln "continued to the end receiving these swarms of visitors." Hay observed that Lincoln "disliked anything that kept people from him who wanted to see him." Lincoln "gained much information" from these visits. He especially liked speaking with soldiers and sailors and learning about the war through their eyes. Long before polls, Lincoln, in his conversations with all manner of people who came to see him, was conducting his own regular survey of public opinion.[17]

At the outset of his letter, Lincoln decided to speak to his critics as much as to his supporters. Lincoln went against what the public has come to expect of politicians by demonstrating that he had heard and understood the criticism of himself and his conduct of the war.

The plea of the critics was peace. In the summer of 1863, the victories at Gettysburg and Vicksburg, hailed by the Union, were understood quite differently by peace Democrats. Many Democrats, and some Republicans, greeted these victories as an opportunity to bargain for peace and end this cruel war.

Lincoln, sounding as if he had returned to the Eighth Circuit, argued that there were three ways to pursue peace—force of arms, ending hostilities, or compromise. After he stated briefly the first two possibilities, he asked a question of the audience:

> *Are you for it?*

He then went on to explain why compromise was not a real possibility.

In this introduction Lincoln was fostering a conversation. He was the master of a dialogical address. His listening and speaking were always an exchange with his audience—even from a distance.

> *But, to be plain, you are dissatisfied with me about the negro. Quite likely there is a difference of opinion between you and*

> *myself upon that subject. I certainly wish that all men could be free, while I suppose you do not. . . .*
>
> *You dislike the emancipation proclamation; and, perhaps, would have it retracted. You say it is unconstitutional—I think differently. I think the constitution invests its Commander-in-Chief, with the law of war, in time of war.*

When Lincoln wrote *to be plain,* he was speaking in vernacular American English. His plain talk was part of his departure from the high-toned oratory that dominated much political speech in the first half of the nineteenth century. To those assembled in Springfield he was saying: Let's get to the real point of your disagreement with me.

He recognized that their conflict with him was over the Negro. He understood that many in Illinois disliked the Emancipation Proclamation. Lincoln believed it was better to be up-front about differences of opinion.

Lincoln knew the kinds of people who lived in Illinois and the Midwest. Illinois became a territory in 1809, the year of Lincoln's birth. Illinois became a state within nine years, in 1818, one of six new Western states established within a span of just five years.

Settlers pushed west into Illinois in streams of migration from five areas to the east and south. The major groups of settlers of Springfield came from Tennessee, the Carolinas, Kentucky, Ohio, and Pennsylvania. The largest group came from Kentucky, Lincoln's native state.[18]

The Ordinance of 1787 had prohibited slavery in the Northwest Territory. The Illinois Constitution of 1818 had stated that slavery could not be introduced into the state. However, black codes were introduced in 1819 that stripped blacks of their civil rights. In 1848 a new constitution was ratified that included a provision banning free blacks from entering Illinois. Whatever the actions of the state legislature, Lincoln knew that Illinois, from north to central to south, had responded to slavery in quite different ways in the half century before the Civil War. Slavery became the central topic in the debates between Lincoln and Stephen A. Douglas in 1858.

Lincoln was clear about his own opinion. He used here almost the same words with which he ended his reply to Horace Greeley:

> *I certainly wish that all men could be free . . .*

However, in his Greeley letter, written almost exactly one year before, he differentiated between his personal wish and his duty under the Constitution. A year later, this division between personal and public views was not present in the letter to Conkling.

> *You say you will not fight to free negroes. Some of them seem willing to fight for you; but, no matter. Fight you, then, exclusively to save the Union. I issued the [*emancipation*] proclamation on purpose to aid you in saving the Union. Whenever you shall have conquered all resistance to the Union, if I shall urge you to continue fighting, it will be an apt time, then, for you to declare you will not fight to free negroes.*

These fiery words quickly gave the Springfield letter its identity. With Lincoln's outspoken affirmation of the willingness of black soldiers to fight for whites, we hear how far Lincoln had traveled on the road to emancipation. In tracing the evolution of Lincoln's political rhetoric, this letter stands in stark contrast to the loud silences about the aspirations of black Americans in his inaugural address and the message to the special session of Congress on July 4, 1861.

Even while he was preparing the ground for the Emancipation Proclamation in the summer of 1862, Lincoln had been reticent about the arming of black soldiers. The Confiscation Act of July 1862 had allowed for black enlistments, but Lincoln believed that the prospect of blacks fighting alongside whites in the Union Army would dismay many Northerners. Lincoln thought that blacks could definitely help behind the lines, but he was not at all certain how blacks would do as soldiers at the front. He also believed there would be dissatisfaction, if not dissension, among white troops in the Union armies.

BLACK LEADERS HAD been encouraging the arming of black troops since the start of the war. Frederick Douglass, black abolitionist editor and reformer, had been dismayed at the conciliatory approach to the South in Lincoln's inaugural address, as well as his intention to continue to abide by the Fugitive Slave Law. As blacks were officially barred from the Union military in the first year and a half of the war, Douglass, from his editor's writing desk in Rochester, and on platforms throughout the North, criticized the president for fighting a war with his white hand while his black hand was tied behind his back.

Douglass was overjoyed with the signing of the Emancipation Proclamation on January 1, 1863, and immediately began to act upon its promise. In February 1863, Douglass traveled two thousand miles to speak at jubilee meetings and encourage black enlistment. Douglass, in his tour, encountered the colliding of twin emotions—white Northern discouragement with the war effort, and eagerness on the part of blacks to enlist and serve.[19]

By the early summer of 1863, after his initial enthusiasm over the Emancipation Proclamation and his extensive recruiting trips in the North, Douglass had become discouraged. Draft riots erupted in New York City in mid-July, with many blacks beaten to death, while their homes and churches were burned. Lincoln had to deploy federal troops to restore order. Douglass found that the Union Army was too often treating black soldiers poorly and not offering equal pay. Maj. George Luther Stearns, wealthy Boston abolitionist, who had appointed Douglass and other black leaders as agents for recruitment across the North, encouraged Douglass to lay his concerns before Lincoln.

LINCOLN HAD CONCLUDED his letter to Greeley by stating:

> *I shall adopt new views so fast as they shall appear to be true views.*

In the spring of 1863, Lincoln adopted a new view of the role of the black soldier. As the Union armies suffered severe losses, with thousands of soldiers absent without leave and thousands of others about to complete their enlistments, with too few volunteers enlisting and the results of the latest conscription act not yielding results quickly enough, Lincoln supported the use of black troops.

Events were moving quickly in the three weeks in August before Lincoln drafted his letter to Conkling. On August 9, in a letter to Gen. Ulysses S. Grant, Lincoln brought up the issue of the arming of black troops. He commented that Gen. Lorenzo Thomas was attempting to raise black troops, and now conveyed this possibility to Grant. He offered his opinion: "I believe it is a resource which if vigourously applied now, will soon close the contest."[20]

The next day, August 10, a card was passed into Lincoln's office in the White House from an unexpected visitor. Within minutes after presenting his card, Frederick Douglass was invited in to meet President Lincoln for the first time. Lincoln stood up to welcome Douglass. In their meeting Douglass pressed upon Lincoln the need for more official recognition of black troops. They spoke together about the troublesome issue of unequal pay for blacks.

Douglass was pleasantly surprised by the tone and substance of their conversation. Several months later, in Philadelphia, Douglass spoke of his sense of his first meeting with Lincoln. "I never met with a man, who, on the first blush, impressed me more entirely with his sincerity, with his devotion to his country, and with his determination to save it at all hazards."[21] Although Douglass was not in agreement with all of Lincoln's views, after meeting the president he decided he could work with him in promoting the role of black soldiers in the Union effort.

ON AUGUST 23, Grant replied to Lincoln, "I have given the subject of arming the negro my hearty support. This, with the emancipation of the negro, is the heaviest blow yet given the Confederacy." The exchange with Grant and the meeting with Douglass took place just at the moment Lincoln was pondering the request from Conkling and writing initial drafts of a message to the Springfield convention.[22] Lincoln was looking for an opportunity to defend both emancipation and the valor of black soldiers.

Grant's reply probably did not reach Lincoln before he had sent off his letters to Conkling on August 27. Lincoln's habit was to continue to revise a speech right up to the last moment as he listened to the audience and received new information. He now determined to add the insights from Grant to the reply he had already sent to Conkling. Thus, on August 31, Lincoln wrote to Conkling yet again, asking that he insert the following paragraph after the sentence ending *since the issue of the proclamation as before* and before *You say you will not fight.* The new paragraph read:

> *I know, as fully as one can know the opinions of others, that some of the commanders of our armies in the field, who have given us our most important successes, believe the emancipation policy, and the use of colored troops constitute the heaviest blow yet dealt to the rebellion; and that at least one of those important successes could not have been achieved when it was, but for the aid of black soldiers. Among the commanders holding these views are some who have never had any affinity with what is called abolitionism, or with Republican party politics, but who hold them as purely military opinions.*
>
> *I submit these opinions as being entitled to some weight against the objections, often urged, that emancipation, and arming the blacks, are unwise as military measures, and were not adopted, as such, in good faith.*

Lincoln, now that he had a reply from the hero of Vicksburg, wished to strengthen his speech to the Springfield convention by arguing that the arming of black troops was useful from a military standpoint, and that these opinions came from military leaders who were neither abolitionists nor supporters of the Republican Party. This addition was copied by a secretary, but the signature was in Lincoln's hand.[23]

LINCOLN SELECTED CONKLING to read the letter not simply because he was a friend. Lincoln asked Conkling because, as he said in his telegram on August 27, "You are one of the best public readers."[24]

Public reading was an art form in the nineteenth century. A public reader acquired recognition through practice and performance in civic and religious events. Washington's Farewell Address was read in Congress every year on February 22. The Declaration of Independence was read on July 4 on the village green or town square in small towns and large cities. John Bunyan's *Pilgrim's Progress* and, lately, Harriet Beecher Stowe's *Uncle Tom's Cabin* were favorite texts to be read aloud in churches. Lincoln was not saying Conkling was an orator, but that he was an excellent public reader.

Even so, Lincoln added, "I have but one suggestion—read it very slowly."[25] Absent any audio of Lincoln speaking, we have a definitive word from Lincoln. He had always read slowly, much more slowly than the average person. Lincoln now wrote to Conkling and his only instruction was to read his words slowly.

> *The signs look better. The Father of Waters again goes unvexed to the sea. Thanks to the great North-West for it. Nor yet wholly to them. Three hundred miles up, they met New England, Empire, Key-Stone, and Jersey, hewing their way right and left. The Suny South too, in more colors than one, also lent a hand. On the spot, their part of the history was jotted down in black and white.*

Lincoln's rhetoric soared when he allowed his imagination free rein as he did in this letter. A sign signifies something beyond itself. What did these signs point toward? The preservation of the Union.

If Lincoln told Greeley he would save the Union, he told Conkling what kind of Union is worth saving. In this letter, speaking to the people of his home state, Lincoln argued poetically for the interdependence of all the parts of the Union. He was a son of the South and had married a woman of the South. As a young man he descended *the*

Father of Waters on a flatboat on a three-month trip all the way to the lower Mississippi. On the wharves of New Orleans a young Lincoln saw firsthand the inhumanity of slavery, with husbands separated from wives and children as all stood waiting to be sold at auction as property. His greatest triumph before his presidency may have been his Cooper Union address in New York.[26] After that address he undertook an often forgotten speaking tour of New England. He did not heed Seward's instructions to cancel his long train trip to Washington, because he wanted to meet the citizens of eight states who embodied the rich diversity of the Union.

As much as Lincoln is remembered as a child of the South, he was even more a child and then an adult of what his contemporaries called the Great Valley. Lincoln understood, even if many in the East refused to admit, that it was in the Mississippi Valley that the future of the nation was being worked out. Americans of Lincoln's generation believed there was the promise of a bright future for the Rocky Mountains and the far West, especially California, but for Lincoln's day the nearer promise was the lands in the great interior section of the nation watered by the Mississippi and its tributaries.

Lincoln, the man from the West, understood early on the significance of the Western theaters of the Civil War. Even as Lincoln prepared his letter, the attention of the press and politicians was focused on the victory at Gettysburg much more than Vicksburg in the summer of 1863. Lincoln drew his best generals, Ulysses S. Grant (Illinois) and William Tecumseh Sherman (Ohio), as well as his successful admiral, David Glasgow Farragut (Tennessee), from the Great Valley. Lincoln inherited the title commander-in-chief, but he taught himself to be general-in-chief. Central to his strategy was his early realization that control of the Mississippi was critical.[27]

NOWHERE IS LINCOLN'S political and military strategy expressed in more picturesque rhetoric than in this letter written not long after the fall of Vicksburg. Instead of detailing a long list of military battles and victories, Lincoln invited his audience to stand with him on the mighty Mississippi. For people whose lives radiated around rivers, Lincoln could not have chosen a more open metaphor.

It is difficult for most people in the twenty-first century to grasp the importance of rivers for people of the nineteenth century. Before railroads and highways, rivers were the thoroughfares of transportation. Whether it was up the Hudson River in New York, down the Mississippi in the Great Valley, or Lewis and Clark exploring the West up the Missouri, explorers, pioneers, and huge numbers of settlers traveled waterways to their destinations. New Englanders moved west using the Erie Canal, which was finished in 1825. Early settlers came to Illinois on the Ohio, Cumberland, and Tennessee Rivers. Starting in the 1830s, steamboats brought people to northern Illinois on the Great Lakes. Once in Illinois, settlers homesteaded along the Mississippi and Illinois Rivers.

THE FATHER OF WATERS was the name the first explorers and missionaries heard from the Indians as their name for the magnificent Mississippi. The Mississippi, fed by its arteries, could once again go *unvexed,* unharassed, to the sea. Why? Lincoln offered his

> *thanks to the great North-West for it*

—the people who were hearing his letter—but

> *Nor yet wholly to them.*

Lincoln wanted this Western audience to appreciate, as he had over the last two and a half years, all the partners in making the Mississippi free again. How to offer those thanks? He could have extended his appreciation by listing the partners, but he preferred to picture them because he was writing for the ear.

> *Three hundred miles up, they met New England, Empire, Key-Stone, and Jersey . . .*

At the heart of writing for the ear is to show your audience and not tell your audience. He could have said New England, New York,

Pennsylvania, and New Jersey, but these would have been static, one-dimensional images. He used rather the familiar names—

Empire, Key-Stone, and Jersey

—that he had come to know firsthand in his traveling from Springfield to Washington on the way to his inauguration.

His images were active as Lincoln described these allies working together to free the mighty Mississippi,

hewing their way right and left

Hew is a vigorous verb that was familiar to most in the audience, who had to hew their lands and farms from the wilderness. Farmers also hewed with an axe, a much-loved tool of Lincoln even as he now used a favorite word from his past in Illinois.

Lincoln's images were not finished. He wanted to thank every region for its part, so he even doffed his hat to the South:

The Suny South too, in more colors than one, also lent a hand. On the spot, their part of the history was jotted down in black and white.

He applauded the region in vivid language by his upbeat use of *Sunny* as the modifier of *South.*

Up until now the images had all been geographical, which is one kind of diversity in an interdependent Union. At this point Lincoln changed the metaphors of diversity when he painted a word picture:

in more colors than one

He said to the naysayers and doubters in the audience that even the South had

lent a hand

and that this part was acted out by both

black and white

Douglass had accused Lincoln of fighting with his white hand while his black hand was tied behind his back. Lincoln now used the same metaphor of the hand to affirm the black hand, which was a sign pointing beyond itself to the courageous actions of black soldiers. The great majority of black soldiers who would fight for the Union were from the South. One more time, in a different kind of language, Lincoln took the opportunity to commend their contributions.

Finally, he combined all of these rich pictorial images of the contributions to be

their part of the history

Sooner or later, in every one of Lincoln's significant speeches—"House Divided," Cooper Union, First Inaugural, Gettysburg, Second Inaugural, and now in the letter to Conkling—he placed immediate ideas or actions in the framework of the longer vision of history.

> *Nor must Uncle Sam's web-feet be forgotten. At all the watery margins they have been present. Not only on the deep sea, the broad bay, and the rapid river, but also up the narrow muddy bayou, and wherever the ground was a little damp, they have been, and made their tracks.*

Lincoln relied on illustrative imagery in buttressing his special thanks for *Uncle Sam's Web-feet.* If the Eastern theater received publicity over the Western theater, the army received attention over the navy. Lincoln now set out to redress that imbalance. He did so by continuing to speak in sensory images. Water was the central image, but Lincoln also chose to work with the borders or boundaries, *watery margins,* suggesting that the activities of the navy were not as noticeable but nevertheless vital. The power of Lincoln's watery images was in its cumulative effect:

the deep sea,
the broad bay,
and the rapid river

But Lincoln was not finished. To these images, with such upbeat modifiers, he added:

but also up the narrow muddy bayou,
and wherever the ground was a little damp

In the letter to the Springfield convention Lincoln worked again and again with contrasts. Thus *deep* and *broad* was contrasted with *narrow.* The final two images are quite removed in grandeur from *sea, bay,* and *river.* Finally, the *tracks* of *Uncle Sam*^{s} *web-feet* are visible to anyone who has spent time in nature and by rivers. Lincoln, with these natural images, was hoping that his audience would see and be grateful for the now quite visible *tracks* that were leading the Union forces to victory.

Thanks to all. For the great republic—for the principle it lives by, and keeps alive—for man's vast future,—thanks to all.

Lincoln offered thanks again, but in a different trajectory and spirit. At the beginning of the letter he offered thanks for

all those who maintain unconditional devotion to the Union

The symmetry of this passage exhibited the way Lincoln thought and spoke. It can better be appreciated if it is placed in a symmetrical way on the page:

Thanks to all.
For the great republic—
for the principle it lives by, and keeps alive—
for man's vast future,—
thanks to all.

Lincoln has often been depicted as a fatalist, one who was resigned, passively, to a relentless march of events over which humans had little control. Lincoln struggled every day in the White House with turmoil, both inner and outer. In this letter he stepped beyond that tumult to offer a vision, actively, for the future of America.

Peace does not appear so distant as it did. I hope it will come soon, and come to stay; and so come as to be worth the keeping in all future time. It will then have been proved that, among free men, there can be no successful appeal from the ballot to the bullet; and that they who take such appeal are sure to lose their case, and pay the cost.

In a grand transitional sentence Lincoln moved from images of space to images of time. He allowed himself to think in the future tense about the shape of peace. It was as if he were standing on the Illinois prairie and looking west toward the horizon. If in 1861 most believed the war would be short, by early 1863 many wondered how long the war might be. The length of the war, with its mounting casualties, was central to the speeches of that other Springfield mass meeting, the previous June.

He expressed his sense of hope by repeating the image of *come* three times:

come soon
come to stay
so come as to be worth the keeping in all future time

This balanced sentence creates in the listener a crescendo of expectation toward the future.

If and when peace comes, a great truth shall *have been proved.* Lincoln, sometimes the lawyer, at other times the teacher, now taught a history lesson. Although he was speaking to Illinois citizens, he was also speaking to the citizens of the world. He grew up in a generation that still spoke of the American republic as an experiment. In the greatest test to the survival of that experiment, Lincoln declared that

> *among free men*

this awful war had a large purpose, which should demonstrate for all time that a minority cannot get by war what they could not win by free elections. That truth had been uttered a thousand times by hundreds of politicians. Lincoln offered this truth economically and with one of his favorite rhetorical devices, alliteration:

> *. . . there can be no successful appeal from the ballot to the bullet.*

Lincoln made yet another shift of metaphor when he spoke of

> *no successful appeal*

and asserted:

> *. . . they who take such appeal are sure to lose their case, and pay the cost.*

Now Lincoln sounded like an old country lawyer utilizing the language and imagery learned from his many years in court. For those who would be in the audience who knew Lincoln from his days of the Eighth Circuit, this was yet another way to connect. The favorite indoor sport in Illinois in Lincoln's day was litigation. But Lincoln knew he was writing to more than Illinois and the Midwest. His appeal was to the court of history, with the whole wide world as spectators.

And then, there will be some black men who can remember that, with silent tongue, and clenched teeth, and steady eye, and well-poised bayonet, they have helped mankind on to this great consummation; while, I fear, there will be some white ones, unable to forget that, with malignant hearts, and deceitful speech, they have strove to hinder it.

Lincoln's next-to-last paragraph is one of the most compelling in the whole vast array of Lincoln speeches. Lincoln offered a contrast between the courage of black soldiers and the malevolence of some whites. His words connected with the audience, then and now, because he did not rely on words of analysis but rather words of vital description. The *black men* that Lincoln extols are portrayed

with silent tongue,
and clenched teeth,
and steady eye,
and well-poised bayonet

—whereas the white men are portrayed

with malignant hearts,
and deceitful speech

Again Lincoln worked with contrasts to heighten his message. The *black men* are *silent* whereas the *white ones* are noisy with *deceitful speech.* The final, telling contrast was of two quite different results. The black soldiers, who had won Lincoln's admiration, he praised because

they have helped mankind on to this great consummation

whereas some white men

have strove to hinder it

The passion in these words is remarkable for so many reasons. First, Lincoln's colleagues from his Illinois days reported that Lincoln, often nervous and almost passive at the beginning of a speech, was roused to fervor by interaction with the audience, but now the real audience was far removed. Second, Lincoln's appeal to reason, which so dominated the First Inaugural and the July 4 special message to Congress, had been replaced by a conclusion brimming over with passion. And there is no evidence that Seward or anyone else had a hand in the composition of the letter to Conkling. This is Lincoln's emotion alone. Third, Lincoln, who not long before had been reticent about the fighting possibilities of black soldiers, now extolled their valor with unlimited praise. Finally, Lincoln did not just praise the courage of blacks; he did so in contrast to the deceitfulness of whites.

Because we have no audio of Lincoln, and it was Conkling who read Lincoln's words, it would appear we cannot know how he would have said these words to an audience. How we would like to know Lincoln's tone and emphasis as he spoke.

It turns out that Lincoln had spoken these same words aloud ten days earlier. Secretary William O. Stoddard, in his remembrance of his conversation with Lincoln, took particular note of one sentence in the letter to Conkling. Stoddard recalled, "I noted the singular emphasis which he put upon the words: 'And there will be some black men who can remember with silent tongue, and clenched teeth, and steady eye, and well poised bayonet, they have helped mankind on to this great consummation.' "[28]

Stoddard is a witness to the weight Lincoln gave to these words of affirmation about black soldiers, even if Lincoln was speaking to an audience of one.

CONKLING WROTE TO Lincoln on September 4 to report on the meeting and the reception of Lincoln's letter. The mass meeting was a huge success. Estimates of attendance ran from forty thousand to seventy thousand. Conkling wanted the president to know that "the Letter was received by the Convention with the greatest enthusiasm." Conkling, no neophyte at political thinking, offered the president his own commentary on the importance of the letter. "It indicates another step in the onward progress of our government towards its only true position, and that which it ought always to have occupied viz the establishment and protection of universal Liberty."[29]

GEORGE TEMPLETON STRONG read Lincoln's letter to Conkling in the morning paper in New York on September 3. That same evening he recorded his response in his diary. "Lincoln's little letter defending his war policy is very good; a straightforward, simple, honest, forcible exposition of his views." The New York lawyer was aware how this letter from Lincoln might be criticized by some of his class—"There are sentences that a critic would like to eliminate"—but Strong believed "they are delightfully characteristic of the 'plain man' who wrote it." The New Yorker understood how Lincoln's language appealed "directly to the great mass of 'plain men' from Maine to Minnesota."[30]

LINCOLN WAS FURIOUS when he discovered that many newspapers printed the letter on the same date it was read in Springfield. On the same day, September 3, he wrote to Conkling, "I am mortified this morning to find the letter to you, botched up, in the Eastern papers, telegraphed from Chicago. How did this happen?"[31]

Conkling replied on September 4. He explained that in order for the Saint Louis, Chicago, and Springfield papers to publish the letter as soon as possible, and therefore publicize the meeting and Lincoln's words, "copies were sent to the two former places with strict injunctions not to permit it to be published before the meeting or make any improper use of it." Someone, Conkling did not know who, perhaps connected with the *Chicago Tribune*, "is chargeable with this breach of faith."[32]

Lincoln may have been "mortified," but his good friend John W. Forney, editor of the *Daily Morning Chronicle*, wrote him immediately on September 3 to place his interpretation on an admittedly surprising development. "The appearance of your letter in the Chronicle of this morning may surprise, but cannot, I hope, offend you." Forney told Lincoln that the *Chronicle* received the letter from Lawrence A. Gobright of the Associated Press. Forney understood better than Lincoln the boon this immediate publication could be. "To-morrow we will republish it, accompanied by a strong editorial endorsement." Despite Lincoln's ire, the fact that the letter was printed immediately and widely contributed to its success.[33]

IN THE DAYS FOLLOWING, a wide circle of people commended the letter. Horace Greeley, one year after his public exchange with Lincoln, praised the letter to the Springfield convention the very day it was published in Eastern newspapers: "The most direct honesty of purpose and the most vigorous common sense mark the letter." Greeley appreciated that Lincoln used a Republican rally to defend the Emancipation Proclamation. "'God Bless Abraham Lincoln!' The Promise must be kept!"[34]

John Z. Goodrich wrote from the Collector's Office of the Custom House in Boston: "I cannot permit the day to pass without thanking you for your letter, published in the Boston papers this morning." He mentioned that he had already been in conversation with many prominent citizens, and he cited three by name. Goodrich applauded "the logic" that he believed was "characteristic" of Lincoln. He concluded by quoting back to Lincoln the passage that had particularly arrested his attention:

> *But Negroes, like other people, act upon Motives. Why should they do anything for us if we do nothing for them? If they stake their lives for us, they must be prompted by the strongest motives, even the promise of freedom; and the promise being made must be kept.*[35]

ABOLITIONISTS RESPONDED to this letter with an enthusiasm they had not accorded earlier Lincoln speeches. Lincoln had been held in suspicion by many abolitionists early in this war for his tardiness in supporting emancipation. Charles Sumner wrote from Boston on September 7. Sumner and Lincoln were opposites in many ways. Sumner, handsome, Harvard-educated, well traveled, was one of those who wondered in 1861 if Lincoln was up to the job. Sumner, as a fine speaker, had cringed when Lincoln called the rebellion *sugar-coated* in his message to Congress on July 4, 1861. Over the next two years, however, Sumner and Lincoln formed a relationship based on genuine respect for each other that grew into a friendship. Now Sumner wrote, "Thanks for your true and noble letter. It is an historical document. The case is admirably stated, so that all but the wicked must confess its force. It cannot be answered."[36]

Sumner's Senate colleague from Massachusetts, Henry Wilson, who headed the important Senate Committee on Military Affairs, also wrote Lincoln: "God Almighty bless you for your noble, patriotic, and Christian letter." Wilson understood the importance of the letter in the crosscurrents of conversation of the day. "It will be on the lips, and in the hearts of hundreds of thousands this day."[37]

John Murray Forbes, a leader in the railroad industry who had helped to organize African-American troops in Massachusetts, wrote to Lincoln on September 8: "Your letter to the Springfield Convention . . . will live in history side by side with your [emancipation] proclamation." Forbes believed Lincoln's letter to Conkling spoke to a wide audience on the vexing question of emancipation and the role of black soldiers. "It meets the fears of the timid and the doubts of the reformer." Forbes had copies printed to distribute to blacks fleeing to Union lines.[38]

Lincoln especially appreciated a letter from Josiah Quincy, whose lengthy career included service as a congressman, judge of the Boston Municipal Court, state representative, mayor of Boston, and president of Harvard College. Now ninety-one, Quincy wrote to Lincoln expressing "my gratitude for your letter to the Illinois Convention, happy, timely, conclusive & effective." Quincy, reviewing Lincoln's course of action that culminated in the Emancipation Proclamation, believed these actions were "due to truth, and to your own character, shamefully assailed as it has been."[39]

On September 10, George Opdyke, the mayor of New York, stopped in at the White House. Opdyke was a wealthy merchant who joined the Republican Party in part because of its antislavery posture. Hay noted in his diary that when Opdyke arrived at the White House he told Lincoln's young secretary that he felt he had been treated "cavalierly" by Lincoln on a previous visit, but today he wanted to thank the president "for his recent admirable letter to the Springfield Convention."[40]

HAY, A WITNESS TO the writing of the letter, now understood its import. Writing to Nicolay on September 11—"His last letter is a great thing"—Hay acknowledged that the hastily written letter included "some indecorums," but his overall assessment was that "the whole letter takes its solid place in history as a great utterance of a great man." Hay, who always defended Lincoln's oratorical artistry, could not resist a jibe at those who thought they might do better. "The whole Cabinet could not have tinkered up a letter which could have been compared with it."[41]

EDITORS OF OPPOSITION newspapers were always keen to reprint any article that disparaged Lincoln. In this pursuit they found the London press a boundless resource. On September 17, the *Times* of London printed a long editorial on Lincoln that especially took Lincoln's letter to Conkling to task. The editorial began:

> Among the marvels and paradoxes of the American Revolution there is none greater than the part played by President Lincoln himself. That such a man should have been called upon to guide the destinies of a mighty nation during a grand historical crisis is surely strange enough, but that he should have blundered and vacillated as he has, without for a mo-

ment losing confidence in himself, or altogether forfeiting that of his countrymen, is stranger still.

This fierce criticism of Lincoln could be attributed solely to political motives by a newspaper that was supportive of the Confederacy. At the heart of the editorial, however, was an indictment of Lincoln the orator. Even as the letter was being praised in many circles in the United States, it was trashed by the *Times* of London. "How any man in his sober senses could have sat down to compose such a rhapsody as this, or having composed it could have read it over with gravity and ordered it printed, passes our comprehension." The *Times* could not mask its contempt as it piled on a mixture of literary epithets. "It is something between a prophecy and an oracular expression, with a dash of Yankee slang and terms of expression which remind us alternately of Ossian, of the incoherent utterances of the Maori Chiefs, and of schoolboy translations of corrupt choruses in Greek tragedy." In condescension the English newspaper concluded, "One is really tempted to think Mr. Lincoln cannot have been himself when he penned so grotesque a production."[42]

The *Times* editorial would be read by thousands of Americans in succeeding months in newspapers that were hostile to Lincoln.

LINCOLN'S LETTER TO the Springfield rally, not well known today beyond Lincoln circles, was heralded in Lincoln's time. George Templeton Strong believed Lincoln's letter was "likely to be a conspicuous document in the history of our times."[43] Nicolay and Hay, writing from the hindsight of nearly a quarter century, said, "It may be called his last stump-speech, the only one made during his Presidency."[44]

Stoddard, reflecting on Lincoln speaking the words of the letter, described the metamorphosis in Lincoln as he was roused from writer to speaker. "He is more an orator than a writer, and he is quickly warmed up to the place where his voice rises and his long right arm goes out, and he speaks to you somewhat as if you were a hundred thousand people of an audience, and as if he believes that fifty thousand of you do not at all agree with him. He will convince the half of you, if he can, before he has done with it."[45]

Surprising in content and tone, this speech to the Springfield convention is far removed from the Lincoln of the First Inaugural. The letter points to the growth of Lincoln in both his political vision and his more forceful rhetoric in support, first of emancipation, and then of the arming and the courage of black troops. This public letter demonstrated in vivid rhetoric, aimed at both friend and foe, that Lincoln intended not only to fulfill the promise of the spirit and letter of the Emancipation Proclamation, but to support and applaud the valor of the newly armed black troops.

CHAPTER NINE

"THIS NATION, UNDER GOD, SHALL HAVE A NEW BIRTH OF FREEDOM"

GETTYSBURG ADDRESS

NOVEMBER 19, 1863

Four score and seven years ago our fathers brought forth on this continent, a new nation, conceived in Liberty, and dedicated to the proposition that all men are created equal.

Now we are engaged in a great civil war, testing whether that nation, or any nation so conceived and so dedicated, can long endure. We are met on a great battle-field of that war. We have come to dedicate a portion of that field, as a final resting place for those who here gave their lives that that nation might live. It is altogether fitting and proper that we should do this.

But, in a larger sense, we can not dedicate—we can not consecrate—we can not hallow—this ground. The brave men, living and dead, who struggled here, have consecrated it, far above our poor power to add or detract. The world will little note, nor long remember what we say here, but it can never forget what they did here. It is for us the living, rather, to be dedicated here to the unfinished work which they who fought here have thus far so nobly advanced. It is rather for us to be here dedicated to the great task remaining before us—that from these honored dead we take increased devotion to that cause for which they gave the last full measure of devotion—that we here highly resolve that these dead shall not have died in vain—that this nation, under God, shall have a new birth of freedom—and that government of the people, by the people, for the people, shall not perish from the earth.

THE VILLAGE OF GETTYSBURG was less than a hundred years old in 1863, having been settled by James Getty in 1780. By the early 1860s the town's population had grown to around twenty-five hundred. The small town was proud of its two institutions of higher education, the Pennsylvania College of Gettysburg (now known as Gettysburg College) and the Lutheran Theological Seminary. Carriage making had become a major industry, with Gettysburg being home to ten carriage plants. Like carriage spokes, eleven roads radiated out from Gettysburg to surrounding cities, towns, and hamlets.

At the end of June 1863, two huge armies converged up the spokes of the wheel toward the hub. On July 1, 2, and 3, warm summer days, 170,000 Union and Confederate soldiers fought in the orchards and on the hillsides, on Seminary Ridge and Cemetery Hill, and across the fields with their symmetrical white fences and running stone walls. When the battle was over, more than fifty thousand dead, wounded, and missing lay on the battlefields or in hospitals or were carried painfully with the retreating Confederate Army. The meaning of the courage and the carnage of those three days of fighting and dying at Gettysburg would quickly acquire a central place in American memory.

THE GETTYSBURG ADDRESS has usually been treated in splendid isolation from the rest of Lincoln's speeches. Whole generations of Americans steadfastly used to memorize the Gettysburg Address in school. Even if memorization has fallen into disuse, if one mentions "Lincoln's speeches," an overwhelming majority would respond: "Gettysburg Address." It takes nothing away from an appreciation of the Gettysburg Address to examine its significance within the full range of Lincoln's developing eloquence.

A purpose of this book is to see Lincoln's speeches as a string of pearls. Each pearl, although of different color and size, possesses its own beauty. Even if one comes to the conclusion that the Gettysburg Address is the most beautiful pearl of all, it can be best understood, not when it stands starkly alone, but rather when it is compared and contrasted to Lincoln's other pearls.

Battlefield at Gettysburg.

LIBRARY OF CONGRESS

IN THE LONG HISTORICAL AFTERGLOW of the Gettysburg Address it has been forgotten that it was not certain whether Lincoln would accept the invitation to speak at the dedication ceremonies for the new national cemetery on November 19, 1863. As a politician on the rise in Illinois, Lincoln accepted any and all requests to speak. In the last months of 1859, when Lincoln understood for the first time that he might be a candidate for the Republican nomination for president, he took on invitations that entailed traveling more than four thousand miles, to speak in Iowa, Indiana, Ohio, and Wisconsin, concluding with an eight-day speaking tour of frontier Kansas in early December. But after his inauguration in March 1861, Lincoln turned down nearly all requests to speak.

As president, Lincoln spoke outside Washington only twice before November 19, 1863. In late June 1862, he made an unannounced trip to West Point for a consultation with Gen. Winfield Scott. Upon his return he was greeted by a small crowd at the train station at Jersey City, New Jersey. He spoke only four sentences, telling the crowd, *The Secretary of War, you know, holds a pretty tight rein on the Press, so that they shall not tell more than they ought to, and I'm afraid that if I blab too much he might draw a tight rein on me.*[1] In early October 1862, while visiting the battlefields in the vicinity of Sharpsburg, Maryland, the scene of the Battle of Antietam two weeks earlier, Lincoln offered two brief spontaneous speeches in Frederick, Maryland, site of the headquarters of the Army of the Potomac. He began his first brief speech with what was by now a standard apology: *In my present position it is hardly proper for me to make speeches.*[2]

Two months before Gettysburg, Lincoln had wrestled with the invitation to speak in Springfield, Illinois, but ended up sending a letter to James C. Conkling to be read at the Springfield convention. As commander-in-chief he preferred to stay close to the War Department and its telegram office, where he could closely monitor the fast-moving events of the conflict. The trip from Washington to Gettysburg involved traveling on three separate trains. Some of the dignitaries as well as reporters did not make it to Gettysburg in time for the dedication because of breakdowns with trains. What prompted Lincoln to say yes?

IN LATE SEPTEMBER, Massachusetts senator Charles Sumner brought to Lincoln's attention a letter from John Murray Forbes, the Boston industrialist who had written to the president on September 8. Forbes wrote to commend Lincoln's letter to the Springfield convention and to tell the president he was impressed with the wholehearted response to the letter throughout the North. Sumner came to the Executive Mansion to underscore a suggestion at the end of the letter. Forbes had written, "My suggestion then is that you should seize an early opportunity and any subsequent chance to teach your great audience of <u>plain people</u> that the war is not North against South but <u>the People against the Aristocrats</u>." Forbes continued, "If you can place this in the same strong light that you have the Negro question you will settle it in men's minds as you have that."[3] Sumner wanted to encourage the president to be open to "any subsequent chance" to speak.

Benjamin P. Thomas, whose 1952 biography of Lincoln remains a master narrative after more than half a century, suggested that Forbes's letter "may have induced him to accept the invitation to Gettysburg."[4] Thomas pointed out that the members of Lincoln's cabinet were surprised when the president accepted the invitation to Gettysburg. Thomas, in an unpublished autobiographical sketch completed after his biography of Lincoln, had become even more convinced of the role of Forbes's suggestion. "I do believe it was his letter that induced him to accept the invitation to speak at Gettysburg."[5]

WITHIN DAYS AFTER the Battle of Gettysburg, plans were set in motion that would lead to a national soldiers' cemetery. American soldiers in all previous wars were buried where they fell in battle. This remained the pattern into the first two years of the Civil War as well. Graves were marked in makeshift ways that too often were not permanent. All this began to change on the battlefields in 1862 and reached a new dimension at Gettysburg in 1863.

Andrew G. Curtin, the Republican governor of Pennsylvania who had introduced Lincoln in his speech to the joint legislature at the state Capitol in Harrisburg in February 1861, toured portions of the battlefield on July 10. Curtin was accompanied by thirty-two-year-old David Wills, a successful Gettysburg attorney. They observed that graves were crudely marked, here by a piece of fencing, there by boards from ammunition or cracker boxes. Before returning to Harrisburg, Curtin asked Wills to be his agent, taking charge of plans to properly bury the dead even as farmers sought to resume their farming in these same fields.[6]

The diligent Wills became a prime mover in formulating plans for a national cemetery for a national army. He accumulated possession of seventeen acres for the new cemetery. The governors of all eighteen states in the Union were contacted. An interstate commission was formed. William Saunders, an architect in the employ of the Depart-

This photograph by Alexander Gardner was taken in Washington on November 8, 1863, ten days before Lincoln would travel to Gettysburg to deliver his address.

LIBRARY OF CONGRESS

ment of Agriculture, was invited in August to come to Gettysburg to plan and execute the layout of the new cemetery. Representatives of states, and some family members, were making plans to return the bodies of their husbands, fathers, sons, and brothers to native soil, but Saunders's symmetrical plan would provide burial places for soldiers of each state at Gettysburg. The hope was that this new kind of cemetery would be a place that family members of those who fought and died would be able to visit in future years.

THE DECISION WAS MADE early on that such a national cemetery required a national dedication. The planners set October 23 for the dedication, a fall day that would still ensure good weather that would bring citizens from across the North and West to the small Pennsylvania town just eight miles north of the border with Maryland.

Exactly one month before, on September 23, Edward Everett was invited to offer the central address. Everett had become the most celebrated speaker in the United States. After his resignation as United States senator from Massachusetts in 1854, Everett had raised his voice over the next six years on behalf of national concord and peace. Everett's delivery was in the grand manner, committed to an ornate style of rhetoric.[7]

Everett replied immediately that a month would not be sufficient time for the research and preparation of a totally new address. He responded that he would not be ready to deliver such an important address until November 19. Thus it was that Everett set the date for the dedication ceremonies.

Wills also invited some of the leading literary artists of the day to participate. Henry Wadsworth Longfellow, John Greenleaf Whittier, and William Cullen Bryant were requested to prepare a poem or ode for the occasion. Each declined.

ABRAHAM LINCOLN was the last speaker invited. Wills wrote to the president on November 2, just seventeen days before the event: "I am authorized by the Governors of the different states to invite you to be present, and participate in these ceremonies, which will doubtless be very imposing and solemnly impressive." Wills's invitation included a brief word about the nature of the remarks the president was being asked to give:

> It is the desire that, after the Oration, You as Chief Executive of the Nation formally set apart these grounds to their Sacred use by a few appropriate remarks.[8]

Lincoln was not being invited to give an "Oration."

It is probable that Lincoln received a spoken invitation before receiving a written invitation. No reply from Lincoln has been discovered.

On the same day, the Gettysburg lawyer sent a second letter inviting Lincoln to spend the night at his large three-story home on the town square.

A MAJOR PROBLEM confronting the planners was the reburial of thousands of bodies. The change of dates from October 23 to November 19 precipitated an alteration in plans. Wills did not put out bids to rebury the bodies until October 22, planning to bury the bodies in November before the dedication ceremonies. Thirty-four bids were received. The lowest bidder, F. W. Biesecker, was awarded the contract at $1.59 per body. The contract called for work to begin between October 26 and November 1. A haunting description of the battlefield on October 23, the original date set for the dedication, described the disarray. "The battlefield had been over run by thousands of sorrowing friends in search of lost ones, and many of the graves opened and but partially or carelessly closed." The undertakers "performed their work in the most careless manner, invariably leaving the graves open, and often leaving particles of bone and hairs laying around. These things were frequently to be seen in every part of the battlefield."[9]

LINCOLN'S SPECIAL four-car presidential train arrived at the little depot on Carlisle Street at sundown on Wednesday, November 18. As he stepped from the train, Lincoln could see hundreds of coffins on the station platform. He was met by Wills, Everett, and Ward Hill Lamon, who had been appointed marshal-in-chief for the dedication.

Lincoln was driven to the Wills residence, the largest home on the town square, or "the Diamond," as the locals called it. Lincoln was shown up the steep front stairs to his bedroom on the second floor, immediately over Wills's law office. Seward stayed next door at the home of Robert G. Harper, editor of the *Adams County Sentinel.*

PEOPLE HAD BEEN arriving in Gettysburg for days before the dedication. The eleven roads leading into Gettysburg were packed with people in Conestoga wagons, spring wagons, carriages, and buggies. Old-fashioned wagons drawn by four or six horses, usually used for conveying cargo, now were overloaded with people. Many citizens came by train. A good number of visitors walked.

A reporter for the *Indianapolis Daily Journal* described the hazards of getting to Gettysburg by train in time for the ceremonies. "Our excursion from Harrisburg was certainly the worst conceived, arranged and executed expedition of the war, not excepting the Peninsula campaign." Everything that could go wrong did go wrong. "We ran fifteen miles, and the engine, which seems to have been 'copper' fastened (which politically is disunion) broke away from the tender and tore the water-pipes of the tank in two." How to spend the time waiting? "The interval was pleasantly divided between sitting on the logs of Goldsboro, and hunting permissions."[10]

There were far too many people for beds, even with the accepted custom of two and three in a bed. The American House, Eagle, and McClellan hotels, as well as all the boardinghouses, were full. Where there were no beds, people slept in hotel lobbies and boardinghouse parlors. Churches opened their doors so that people could sleep on pews.

AFTER DINNER on November 18, a crowd gathered outside the Wills home. The president was serenaded by the band of the Fifth New York Artillery. A group of young women sang, "We are coming, Father Abraham, three hundred thousand strong." After frequent requests, Lincoln consented to offer some words.

> *I appear before you, fellow-citizens, merely to thank you for this compliment. The inference is a very fair one that you would hear me for a little while at least, were I to commence to make a speech. I do not appear before you for the purpose of doing so, and for several substantial reasons. The most substantial of these is that I have no speech to make.* [Laughter.] *In my position it is somewhat important that I should not say any foolish things.*

A person in the crowd called out, "If you can help it." Lincoln, who again evidenced discomfort speaking extemporaneously, was nevertheless comfortable in dealing with interruptions from an audience. Without missing a beat, Lincoln picked up the respondent's word "help" and continued:

> *It very often happens that the only way to help it is to say nothing at all. [Laughter.] Believing that is my present condition this evening, I must beg you to excuse me from addressing you further.*[11]

John Hay, who had listened to the president's words, recorded in his diary, "The President appeared at the door said half a dozen words meaning nothing & went in."[12] Everyone agreed that these were not among Lincoln's finest words. Not a good omen for a president charged with speaking on the morrow.

THE STORY of the composition of Lincoln's address has threatened to overshadow the content of the address itself. Down through the years the persistent story has developed of a Lincoln who hastily composed his dedicatory remarks on a discarded piece of paper on the train to Gettysburg. Although the story is filled with conflicting accounts, much of it reminiscence dating from long after the events themselves, this tangled tale has had remarkable staying power.

If we treat Gettysburg not alone, however, but within a string of rhetorical pearls, it will help to place the composition of the Gettysburg Address within the larger story of the habits Lincoln had developed in preparing his presidential addresses and messages for nearly three years now. It is then possible to posit a number of assumptions and follow up with some questions.

First, Lincoln's pattern was to begin his preparation for speeches not hastily, shortly before an event, but unhurriedly, long before he was to speak. He began work on his First Inaugural Address and his 1861 Message to Congress in Special Session months in advance of the date of delivery.

Question: when did he begin his preparation for Gettysburg?

Lincoln did not have a long lead time for the Gettysburg Address, unlike his inaugural address or his annual messages to Congress, which were fixed by the calendar. He received a formal invitation only seventeen days in advance of the ceremonies. If we grant that he received an oral invitation before November 2, this probably added a week or two to his notice of the event. Based on his pattern of preparation, it is safe to assume he started to mull over ideas for the address close to the moment he accepted the invitation.

The notion that Lincoln wrote out his remarks on the train to Gettysburg was present almost from the beginning. Isaac N. Arnold, a scholarly Chicago lawyer who had been a friend of Lincoln for twenty years, was the first to suggest in print that Lincoln wrote the address on the train. In *The History of Abraham Lincoln and the Overthrow of Slavery,* published in 1866, Arnold wrote that Lincoln was not informed that he was to speak until on his way from Washington to Gettysburg. Arnold then narrated, "Retiring a short time, he prepared the following address."[13]

From Arnold's brief observation would grow larger and more fanciful tales through the years. Many people got into the act. The story was passed on and embroidered by everyone from Harriet Beecher Stowe to Andrew Carnegie.[14]

The story of Lincoln writing the address on the train refused to die and took on new life with an even wider audience in the early twentieth century. Mary Raymond Shipman Andrews published *The Perfect Tribute* as a short story in *Scribner's Magazine* in July 1906. A month later the story became a forty-seven-page book published by Charles Scribner's Sons. A school edition was published in 1910.

The Perfect Tribute was based on the remembrance of her fourteen-year-old son, Paul, who heard a story about the composition of the address from his history teacher, Walter Burlingame. Mr. Burlingame's story in turn went back to a boyhood memory of a conversation with his father, Anson Burlingame. The elder Burlingame remembered Edward Everett telling him that Lincoln wrote his address on a scrap of brown paper on the train to Gettysburg.

Andrews was a successful writer of sentimental novels. She had a deep veneration for Lincoln. She combined her admiration with her literary skills to produce a book that in the next thirty years sold more than five hundred thousand copies. *The Perfect Tribute* was placed on required reading lists for high school courses in English, which helped to swell the number of readers.

Most readers were evidently not overly concerned with the veracity of the tale. Everett could hardly have given such an account to Anson Burlingame because the New England orator was not on the train with Lincoln. The purpose behind Andrews's elaboration of this myth may have been to suggest that Lincoln's creative genius was largely spontaneous. The truth was that Lincoln's genius grew not from spontaneity but from hard, painstaking work with words.

Shortly after the book was published and was enjoying enormous success, Judd Stewart, a prominent Lincoln collector, invited Andrews to join his Lincoln Club. She replied, "I am flattered to be thought eligible, but my little book on Lincoln is all I know."[15]

WARD HILL LAMON stirred the pot when he wrote an open letter to the *Chicago Tribune* in 1886 purporting to tell the real story of that fateful day. Remembrance is so often characterized by the intent to place the rememberer close to Lincoln, usually closer than other mortals. Lamon offered from memory whole conversations with Lincoln, Seward, and Everett on that celebrated day at Gettysburg. Lamon expanded on this account in his reminiscences, edited by his daughter and published in 1895. In chapter 11, "The Gettysburg Speech," he added to the myth that Lincoln had gone to Gettysburg unprepared. Lamon asked his audience to believe that a day or two before the dedication ceremonies, Lincoln produced from his hat a memorandum for the intended address and read it to Lamon. After its delivery at Gettysburg, Lamon said, Lincoln expressed regret that the speech was not more carefully prepared, and offered his own judgment of his remarks. "Lamon, that speech won't *scour*! It is a flat failure, and the people are disappointed." Lamon also asserted that Seward and Everett believed the president's address a failure.[16]

TWO PERSONS close to Lincoln have left more reliable accounts. Noah Brooks, Lincoln's newspaper friend from Sacramento, reported that shortly before November 19 he accompanied the president to a long-standing appointment to Alexander Gardner's photography studio on Seventh Street. As they came down the stairs of the Executive Mansion, the president recalled that he had forgotten a paper and returned to his office, presently reappearing with a long envelope in his hand. When Brooks asked the president about his forthcoming remarks at Gettysburg, he replied the speech was "written but not finished." Lincoln brought the speech along in hopes of continuing to work on it while waiting for the photographer's preparations. As it turned out there was no time for Lincoln to edit his speech at the studio.

Brooks's account has been faulted because he said he saw Lincoln also take out of the envelope at the studio printed proof sheets of Everett's address. The difficulty with this part of the recollection was that the New England orator's speech was not printed in Boston until November 14. The comment about Everett does not in itself invalidate his report about Lincoln's work on the Gettysburg Address.[17]

As the debate swirled about the composition of the address, John G. Nicolay attempted to set the record straight. Writing in the *Century Magazine* in 1894, Nicolay declared, "There is neither record, evidence, nor well-founded tradition that Mr. Lincoln did any writing, or made any notes, on the journey between Washington and Gettysburg." His former secretary quickly added that the "rockings and joltings" of the train would have made such writing "virtually impossible."[18] It is worth recalling that Lincoln had tried writing down his Farewell Address after departing Springfield on February 11, 1861, but gave up the effort and dictated his words to Nicolay. His secretary was clear that there had been no writing and no dictation on this train.

SECOND, LINCOLN'S SPEECHES usually drew upon previous speeches, notes, or earlier spontaneous remarks. His use of such sources was evident in the preparation of his inaugural address. Lincoln never started out to write a speech from scratch.

Question: what previous think pieces or speeches did he draw upon?

Lincoln's opening words—

Four score and seven years ago

—achieve even greater poignancy when contrasted with an awkward antecedent. On July 7, when news of the victory at Vicksburg was finally confirmed in Washington, crowds erupted in cheers and celebrations. At 8 P.M., a huge throng assembled at the National Hotel and marched up Pennsylvania Avenue to the Executive Mansion. Reaching the White House, the crowd serenaded the president until Lincoln appeared at a window and offered an impromptu response. After thanking both the assemblage and "Almighty God," Lincoln asked a question: *How long ago is it?—eighty odd years—since on the Fourth of July for the first time in the history of the world a nation by its representatives, assembled and declared as a self-evident truth that "all men are created equal"?*[19]

In four and a half months the words "eighty odd years" would become *four score and seven years ago.* Lincoln was adept at reusing and then rewriting earlier ideas.

THIRD, LINCOLN WAS his own editor, revising and editing all his speeches. He had spent considerable time editing and revising his inaugural address and his message to Congress of July 4, 1861. Sometimes he did rely upon others, chiefly Seward, to look over a speech or state paper and offer suggestions.

Question: did Seward or anyone else assist Lincoln at Gettysburg?

Secretary of State William H. Seward was a conspicuous presence at Gettysburg. He accompanied Lincoln on the four-car train. He would sit next to Lincoln during the ceremonies the next day. In between he conferred with Lincoln on at least two occasions. What was his role in assisting Lincoln with the Gettysburg Address?

There is no indication of Seward's involvement with the address before Lincoln left Washington. Once they were in Gettysburg, however, the story is not so clear.

After dinner at the Wills home, and the serenade that followed, Lincoln spent some time in his room, where he may have continued to revise his address. Wills recalled later that Lincoln asked him to bring him some writing materials. Later in the evening Lincoln came downstairs and told Wills he wanted to see Seward. Together they walked next door to the Harper home, where Seward was staying. What was the purpose of Lincoln's visit? By now Seward had become Lincoln's closest confidant in the cabinet. Based on his past consultations with Seward, on both his inaugural address and the message to the special session of Congress on July 4, 1861, it is safe to presume he read the address to Seward. Did Seward make any suggestions? Whereas Seward gave Lincoln six pages of suggestions aimed at improving the inaugural address, no notes from Seward remain with suggestions for revising the Gettysburg Address.

The next morning, after an early breakfast, Lincoln and Seward took a bumpy buckboard ride to inspect the battlefield. They rode up to the grounds of the Lutheran seminary where the fighting had churned during the first day of the battle. Did Lincoln and Seward talk about the address?

FOURTH, LINCOLN'S PRACTICE was to continue revising right up to the moment of his delivery. This pattern has already been observed in the editing of his inaugural address, the Message to Congress in Special Session, and the annual message to Congress on December 1, 1862.

Question: did Lincoln continue to revise his remarks after his arrival in Gettysburg?

The answer is yes. In contrast to Everett, Lincoln did not send a copy of his address to the press in advance. Why? Because Lincoln intended to continue writing his few remarks.

It was after his morning conversation with Seward that Lincoln returned to his room to complete the final writing and revising of his first draft. At 9 A.M. secretary Nicolay reported to his boss in the

Wills home. When he arrived, Nicolay said, he found Lincoln writing and revising his speech. The first page of the address, nineteen lines, was written in ink in Lincoln's firm hand on official white letter paper with the heading

EXECUTIVE MANSION

Washington, , 186

There was no blot or erasure. The last line on the first page read:

> *It is for us, the living, to stand here . . .*

Nicolay observed Lincoln writing with a lead pencil on a second page, on bluish gray foolscap supplied by his host, Wills. Lincoln had crossed out the last three words of the first page—

> *to stand here*

—and substituted in their place:

> *to here be dedicated*

Nicolay estimated that Lincoln worked for not much more than an hour as he completed the last nine and a half lines of the address.[20]

Lincoln then prepared, as Nicolay reported, a second text, which would serve as his speaking text. He did make a few changes for this delivery text as he continued to search for the most appropriate words for his purposes.

None of the recollections speak to the question, when did Lincoln begin to draft the address? Nicolay argued persuasively that Lincoln "probably followed his usual habit in such matters, using great deliberation in arranging his thoughts, and molding his phrases mentally, waiting to reduce them to writing until they had taken satisfactory shape."

When Lincoln finally finished writing and revising, he folded up this speaking text and tucked it in the left breast pocket of his coat.

Lincoln rode in this parade along Baltimore Street in Gettysburg on the morning of November 19, 1863. Large crowds thronged the parade route.

NATIONAL ARCHIVES

CHIEF MARSHAL LAMON struggled to assemble the dignitaries in the Diamond outside the Wills home at 10 A.M. Lincoln came outside at the appointed hour dressed in a black suit with a frock coat. He was wearing his usual tall silk hat, to which he had added a wide mourning band in memory of his son Willie, who had died at the White House in February 1862. Lamon had decided to transport the dignitaries with horses rather than carriages. Lincoln, with white riding gloves, was assigned a bay horse so small that the president's long legs nearly touched the ground. It was almost an hour later before Lamon could get the procession moving toward the battlefield.

All along the route up Baltimore Street, homes were draped with American flags. Evidences of the fierce battle fought less than five months before were to be seen in buildings pockmarked with bullet

Edward Everett, New England politician and former president of Harvard, was invited to be the featured speaker at Gettysburg.

LIBRARY OF CONGRESS

holes. The most incongruous scene was children at little stands selling cookies and lemonade and also bullets and buttons—even cannonballs.

THE PROCESSION REACHED the site of the dedication.[21] Many in a large crowd, estimated at fifteen or twenty thousand, had been waiting for hours for Lincoln, Everett, and the other dignitaries to arrive. Lamon escorted Lincoln up the steps of the twelve-by-twenty-foot wooden platform to a chair in the first row. The ceremonies were finally ready to begin.

The invocation was offered by the Reverend Thomas H. Stockton, chaplain of the House of Representatives. Although many commended the prayer, which was longer than Lincoln's address, the

In this enlarged photograph taken before his address, Lincoln is in the center, hatless, with part of his face covered by the hat of a soldier.

NATIONAL ARCHIVES

young Hay wrote in his diary that it was "a prayer which thought it was an oration."[22]

After a hymn by Benjamin B. French, hastily composed after the poets had declined to participate, Edward Everett stepped forward to deliver his oration. As expectations grew in the days leading up to the dedication of the national cemetery, Everett had become a center of attention. He was the logical person to offer the main address. Everett was the protégé and successor to the great New England orator

Daniel Webster. Lincoln respected Everett because the New England orator had delivered a lecture on George Washington across the nation. He donated nearly $100,000 of the proceeds from his addresses to the restoration of George Washington's home at Mount Vernon.

In 1860 Everett had been opposed to what he believed was the too aggressive stance of the Republican Party. Once the war came, however, he quickly supported Lincoln and the war effort.

Everett placed his manuscript on a table in the center of the platform. He always delivered his speeches from memory. The New England orator's voice had enormous carrying power.

Lincoln followed Everett's address attentively. Seward sat with his hat drawn over his eyes because of the day's low, bright sun. The president stirred when Everett, in a slip of the tongue, spoke of "General Lee." Lincoln, turning to Seward, provided the correction, "General Meade."

Everett, after speaking for two hours and eight minutes, finally concluded. He bowed to the audience in response to polite applause.

CHIEF MARSHAL LAMON introduced President Lincoln. The crowd was restless after such a long oration. A photographer who had pitched his equipment directly in front of the platform was busy adjusting his camera as he prepared to get a photograph of the president speaking. The president rose, adjusted his spectacles, and took out of the left breast pocket of his frock coat his dedicatory remarks. Beyond the sprawling crowd Lincoln could see row upon row of soldiers' graves. He shifted his speaking text to his left hand.

Lincoln began:

> *Four score and seven years ago our fathers brought forth on this continent, a new nation, conceived in Liberty, and dedicated to the proposition that all men are created equal.*

Lincoln spoke in a high tenor voice well practiced in the art of speaking to large crowds in outdoor settings. He spoke from memory, glancing occasionally at the text in his left hand.

Four score and seven was not a simple way to say eighty-seven. Lincoln was asking his audience to calculate backward quickly to discover that the nation's starting point was not the Constitution, nor the election of George Washington as the first president, but 1776 and the signing of the Declaration of Independence.

The opening words that resonated to the ear were about cadence as well as content. He began with two rhyming words—

four score

—that set in motion a symphony of melodious sounds. The Hebrew cadence, rendered in Elizabethan English, would have been stated slowly by Lincoln.

THE BIBLICAL RING of his opening words was rooted in lines from Psalm 90:

> The days of our years are threescore years and ten;
> And if by reason of strength they be fourscore years . . .[23]

The psalms were a favorite portion of the Bible for Lincoln. At noontime in the Executive Mansion, or early in the morning at the Soldiers Home—multiple observers have left independent reports of Lincoln's love of reading the Bible, especially the psalms. At Gettysburg he was not only retrieving biblical words, but employing a biblical cadence expressed in the rhythms of the King James Version that he thought appropriate for the solemnity of the day.[24]

Lincoln never named the Bible, or quoted directly from the Bible in his remarks, as he would do so prominently in less than sixteen months in his Second Inaugural Address, but the whole of his speech was suffused with both biblical content and cadence.

LINCOLN BUILT the Gettysburg Address upon a structure of past, present, and future time. Following the opening sentence, the address is erected with three sets of three sentences, dedicated to past, present, and future. Lincoln had used this same temporal arrangement in his other celebrated short speech, the farewell at Springfield in February 1861.[25]

PRESIDENT LINCOLN STARTED in the past by placing the dedication of the battlefield at Gettysburg in the larger context of American history. His opening words highlighted historical continuity. Lincoln's beginning encouraged the listener to enter into the intellectual and spiritual content and tone Lincoln was setting up at the outset of his dedicatory remarks. He began with a biblical allusion that accented permanence and at the same time noted that the nation's continuity had already surpassed the biblical time frame for life and death. In speaking of

our fathers

Lincoln both invoked a common heritage of the Founding Fathers and, at the same time, identified himself with his audience.

THE TRAJECTORY OF Lincoln's crucial first sentence was to underscore the timeless American truth that

. . . all men are created equal.

Lincoln had sounded this note in his recent letter to the Springfield convention. The Boston industrialist John Murray Forbes had urged Lincoln to look for an opportunity to enunciate this truth, and Forbes's friend Sen. Charles Sumner had seconded the motion. When Lincoln reaffirmed this truth at the beginning of the dedicatory remarks at Gettysburg, he was asserting that the war was about both liberty and union.

A word in this first sentence that protruded for some was

proposition

Sumner did not like the word. English poet Matthew Arnold was supposed to have objected to this long Latinate word interrupting Lincoln's Saxon prose poem.[26]

Lincoln's employment of *proposition* was not new, however; it was a favorite word, which he had used nearly three hundred times in previous addresses and letters. To be sure, it was a term more at home with Euclid's theorems than Shakespeare's poetry. It is also untrue—though it has been suggested—that Lincoln used Saxon words almost exclusively, for Lincoln knew that a dash of Latinate words flavored the best of Shakespeare's Elizabethan poetry.

Even as Lincoln began his address by invoking the Declaration of Independence, his use of the word *proposition* spoke to a different certainty than did Jefferson's "truths" that were "self-evident." It was not that Lincoln did not accept Jefferson's understanding of truth as a moral and political principle. Lincoln had appealed to Jefferson in numerous speeches after 1854.

Lincoln chose to emphasize at Gettysburg that the United States was an experiment still in process. On July 4, 1861, in his message to Congress, Lincoln said:

> *Our popular government has often been called an experiment. Two points in it, our people have already settled—the successful establishing, and the successful administering of it. One still remains—its successful maintenance against a formidable internal attempt to overthrow it.*[27]

Lincoln, in using the word *proposition,* was appealing to reasoned argument as he had in his inaugural address. But this was a different Lincoln from the new president who had spoken and written in March and July 1861. He had come to understand the fragility of the Union. In the architecture of his speech the word *proposition* functioned as a turning point wherein Lincoln shifted his trajectory from past ideas to present realities.

> *Now we are engaged in a great civil war, testing whether that nation, or any nation so conceived and so dedicated, can long*

endure. We are met on a great battle-field of that war. We have come to dedicate a portion of that field, as a final resting place for those who here gave their lives that that nation might live.

After his long introductory sentence, Lincoln traveled rapidly forward from the Revolution to the Civil War. With quick brush strokes he recapitulated the meaning of the war. As a speaker he was sparing with his adjectives, but on this occasion he modified both *civil war* and *battle-field* with *great.* Unlike Everett, he spent none of his words on the details of the battle. His purpose was to transfigure the dedication with a larger meaning of the purpose of the *nation*—a word he would use five times in his address. The Civil War was a *testing* of the founding ideals of the nation to see whether they *can long endure.*

Lincoln employed many rhetorical devices in his artistry, but his mature speeches are especially characterized by grammatical parallelism, antithesis, alliteration, and repetition. He would use all four strategies in his brief address at Gettysburg.

At the beginning of the body of his address he used two perfect parallels:

that nation	*any nation*
so conceived	*so dedicated*

He resolved this beautifully balanced sentence with a strong conclusion:

can long endure[28]

As Lincoln spoke about different dimensions of the past, he constructed the content of his political purposes by the repetition of key words.

great civil war	*great battle-field*
so dedicated	*come to dedicate*

Lincoln's use of repetition allowed him to underscore his rhetorical purpose even though he had been limited by Wills to offer only "a few appropriate remarks."

It is altogether fitting and proper that we should do this.

But, in a larger sense, we can not dedicate—we can not consecrate—we can not hallow—this ground. The brave men, living and dead, who struggled here, have consecrated it, far above our poor power to add or detract.

Lincoln's intonation of *fitting* and *proper,* parallel adjectives, befitted the solemn occasion. But he was not about to use up his brief time in only dedicating a battlefield.

His words *But, in a larger sense* were his clue to the audience that he was about to expand the parameters of his intentions for this day. He was announcing his purpose to speak to a *larger* subject. With this transition he began his appeal from the past battle to the present dedication.

But before he lifted their eyes beyond the battlefield, Lincoln started by telling the audience what they could not do:

we can not dedicate
we can not consecrate
we can not hallow

Lincoln, the logical thinker, started with the negative side of the argument. Lincoln sounded like the lawyer in the courtroom speaking to a jury. Stating the negative first served to prepare the audience to agree with his evocation of what each person in the audience could do. These three parallel clauses focused on the present space: *this ground.*

At this point Lincoln employed a dramatic antithesis. He contrasted

the brave men

with

our poor power

At the same time he framed his words

living and dead

at the beginning of the sentence, and

add or detract

at the end of the sentence, in another striking parallelism.

> *The world will little note, nor long remember what we say here, but it can never forget what they did here. It is for us the living, rather, to be dedicated here to the unfinished work which they who fought here have thus far so nobly advanced. It is rather for us to be here dedicated to the great task remaining before us—that from these honored dead we take increased devotion to that cause for which they gave the last full measure of devotion—that we here highly resolve that these dead shall not have died in vain—that this nation, under God, shall have a new birth of freedom—and that government of the people, by the people, for the people, shall not perish from the earth.*

In the last three sentences of the address, Lincoln shifted the focus a final time. In the architecture of his address Lincoln had recalled the past and what the nation did at its beginning, then recited what the soldiers did in the near present. He now prepared to open out the future and speak to the responsibility of the hearers.

In the first sentence he pointed away from words—there had been more than two hours of words already—to deeds. In yet another grammatical antithesis he contrasted *what we say here*

with

what they did here

Although Lincoln spoke in the plural *we,* his tone continued the personal self-effacement that had characterized his whole address.

THE WORDS OF LINCOLN'S next-to-last sentence achieved their energy from his use of contrasts. First,

us the living

is contrasted with

they who fought here

In addition,

the unfinished work

was an invitation to finish the work. Although Lincoln extolled the

work which they who fought here have thus far so nobly advanced

the emphasis had clearly shifted from what they did to what he would ask the audience to do.

LINCOLN'S CLOSING SENTENCE, in a speech known for its brevity, was a surprising, long, complex sentence of eighty-two words. The simplicity of Lincoln's speeches has often been oversold.

In his closing sentence Lincoln continued his use of repetition.

to be dedicated here	*to be here dedicated*
we take increased devotion	*the last full measure of devotion*

His use of repetition had the rhetorical effect of reiterating the accountability of the audience.

Lincoln, who always took much time in choosing his words, used here the words *dedicate* and *devotion.* They were both religious words, which conjured up the call to commitment present in the revival services of the Second Great Awakening and in the Presbyterian and other Protestant churches Lincoln was attending in Washington during the war.

AT THIS POINT Lincoln made his only extemporaneous addition to his speaking text. He added the words

under God

Did he add these two words on the spot? If he did, this addition was uncharacteristic for a speaker who did not trust extemporaneous speech.

His speaking text read:

that this nation shall have a new birth of freedom

He inserted *under God* after the word *nation* and before the phrase *shall have a new birth of freedom.* We do not know what prompted Lincoln to add these two words. Unlike extemporaneous words in some earlier speeches, after the Gettysburg Address there was no apology for the interjection of *under God.* Lincoln decided to include these words in all three subsequent copies he prepared at later dates.

The interjection of *under God* pointed backward and forward. The words pointed backward to *this nation.* Lincoln, the Whig and the Republican, had always insisted that the American nation drew its breath from both political and religious sources. His words were consistent with invocations of God in almost all of his major presidential speeches. Lincoln, as president, walked back and forth across the line between religion and politics.

The words *under God* pointed forward to *shall have a new birth of freedom.* In the first years of the Civil War, Lincoln found himself wrestling in new ways with the purposes of God in history. The death of so many soldiers brought him face-to-face with the meaning of life. With the death of his son Willie, in February 1862, he was confronted with the meaning of eternal life. His evocation of *a new birth* had deep meaning for the evangelical Protestantism that intersected his life with increasing frequency and intensity in his presidential years.

The phrase *a new birth of freedom* was layered with both political and religious meanings. In each case the metaphor starts with a contrast with the old. As Lincoln looked into the faces of a mournful audience, many of whom had lost a son, husband, father, or brother, he sought to find words of comfort and assurance. The *new birth* that slowly emerged in Lincoln's politics meant that on November 19 at Gettysburg he was no longer, as in his inaugural address, defending an old Union but proclaiming a new Union. The old Union contained and attempted to restrain slavery. The new Union would fulfill the promise of liberty, the crucial step into the future that the Founders had failed to take.

The *new birth* in Christian preaching and theology contrasted the old physical birth by which men and women came into the world with a new spiritual birth that often came suddenly by means of conversion. This spiritual *new birth* offered both abundant life now but also eternal life.

The *new birth* was a paradox in both politics and religion. Lincoln had come to see the Civil War as a ritual of purification. The old Union had to die. The old man had to die. In death there was a preparation for a new Union and a new humanity. As Lincoln had said in his annual message to Congress the previous December,

> *As our case is new, so we must think anew, and act anew.*

Almost one year later, at Gettysburg, Lincoln was more ready to speak of *a new birth of freedom.*

AS LINCOLN APPROACHED the unexpected climax of his address, he uttered the words that would be most remembered from the address:

> *. . . and that government*
> *of the people,*
> *by the people,*
> *for the people,*
> *shall not perish from the earth.*

Much of the scholarly detective work on the sources of the Gettysburg Address has centered on earlier words by New England politician and orator Daniel Webster and New England Unitarian minister Theodore Parker.

Lincoln considered Webster's "Reply to Robert Hayne" of January 27, 1830, to be one of America's greatest speeches. Speaking before a crowded gallery, Webster asked Senator Hayne of South Carolina, "Is it [the government] the creature of the State legislature, or the creature of the people?" Webster continued, "It is . . . the people's Constitution, the people's government, made for the people, made by the people, and answerable to the people."[29] Lincoln consulted these stirring words in his preparation for his inaugural address. A full-length portrait of Webster hung in the White House during Lincoln's residency. While appreciative of Webster, Lincoln, in his mature speeches, moved away from Webster's florid rhetoric to a tauter eloquence, exemplified in his conclusion to the Gettysburg Address.

Lincoln's law partner William Herndon was enamored with Parker and called Lincoln's attention to the writings of the Boston Unitarian minister. Parker, in a speech in 1850 to an antislavery convention in Boston, defined democracy as "a government of all the people, by all the people, for all the people." This triple axiom appears in a number of places in Parker's speeches and writings.[30]

Lincoln was surely conscious of Webster's and Parker's words. But this historical detective work has tended to overshadow the fact that he was more apt at Gettysburg to be building on his own words.

The primary sources of Lincoln's words may be found closer to home, in two of Lincoln's previous presidential speeches.

In his First Inaugural, Lincoln had declared:

> *The chief Magistrate derives all his authority from the people.*

In his Message to Congress in Special Session on July 4, 1861, he wrote that *the affair at Fort Sumter* had provoked the question

> *whether a Constitutional republic, or a democracy—a government of the people, by the same people—can, or cannot, maintain its territorial integrity against its own domestic foes.*[31]

Lincoln was working with a definition of democracy that he expanded and refined from the First Inaugural to the special message of July 4, 1861, to the Gettysburg Address.

LINCOLN WAS FINISHED. The audience was expecting a longer speech. They were surprised when Lincoln stopped after speaking for less than three minutes. He concluded before the photographer could begin. A hymn was sung and the Reverend Dr. Henry L. Baugher, president of Gettysburg College, pronounced the benediction.

Although we have no photograph of Lincoln speaking at Gettysburg, we would do well to see his speech through multiple lenses.

First, this was a profoundly political speech, in which Lincoln was defending his administration and its record. Lincoln came to speak at Gettysburg in November, just as he wrote to the Springfield convention in late August, well aware of the power of the conservative argument for a return to "the Union as it was." Lincoln may have been concerned that Everett, given the New England orator's past speeches, might add his voice to this movement. In his recent letter to the Springfield convention, Lincoln had spoken against any option of a negotiated settlement with the Confederacy. At Gettysburg he built on the Springfield letter by emphasizing his belief that the United States was a nation whose origins in 1776 preceded the Constitution in 1789. Lincoln, although admiring the Constitution, had labored under its constraints for the first years of the war. At Gettysburg he chose to emphasize the liberties emblazoned in the Declaration of Independence.[32]

LINCOLN WELL UNDERSTOOD the power of rhetoric to delineate the aims of politics and war. Against those who wanted to return to "the Union as it was" and end the carnage, so evident at Gettysburg, Lincoln argued forcefully why the war, with all of its revulsions, must be continued through to a just and peaceful conclusion.

Second, the sentences of the Gettysburg Address exhibit Lincoln's preference for the cadences of what people of his day called "Saxon" words. The King James Bible was called the Saxon Bible in Lincoln's time. Saxon words were down-to-earth words derived from Old English as opposed to elevated words derived from Latin or Greek.

SAXON	*LATINATE*
herds of cows	cohorts of bovines
lie	prevaricate
stop	desist
end	terminate

Saxon words are briefer. They bring more clout.

The King James Bible was often called the Saxon Bible in the nineteenth century. The Bible's popularity was rooted in its ability to speak to both low and high culture. The English in the Saxon Bible is at times coarse, but the opening of Genesis, the psalms, and the gospel of John can also be sublime.

Kenneth Cmiel, in *Democratic Eloquence: The Fight over Popular Speech in Nineteenth-Century America,* asserts that Lincoln's speeches are "saturated in Saxon eloquence." He knew the Bible well and could quote from the psalms and the gospels. In the progression of his speeches as president one senses Lincoln attempting to ennoble his writing and speaking. Cmiel observes that in Lincoln "the sublime appears in the simplest dress."[33]

Lincoln achieves his eloquence by a remarkable combination of the humble and the lofty. We see his mediating style at work in the Gettysburg Address. The formal language, *four score,* with which Lincoln begins the Gettysburg Address is balanced by the familiar language, *that government of the people, by the people, for the people, shall not perish from the earth,* with which he closes. Poet James Russell Lowell, in early 1864, praised Lincoln's style as "familiar dignity."[34]

Lincoln's Springfield friend James C. Conkling paid close attention to the sources of Lincoln's gift of oratory. "He used plain Saxon words, which imparted strength to his style, at the expense, it may be of elegance, but which were understood and appreciated by the masses of people."[35] At Gettysburg his use of Saxon words was a foundation of his elegance.

Third, the voice that we hear in the Gettysburg Address is not an individual voice. The address is full of first-person references, but every one is plural. Ten times Lincoln uses the plural *we* and three times *us.*[36]

Edwin Black, a professor of communication arts, asks the question "What was the single most important instance of rhetorical leadership by Lincoln during his presidency?" Black's answer is not to choose a speech from a list of Lincoln speeches. He answers rather that the most significant occasion of rhetorical leadership "was his disappearance." Lincoln's disappearance became more and more evident in his speeches and public letters in the latter part of his presidency. This trait is evident in the Gettysburg Address, as it will be in the Second Inaugural. Black observes, "In place of his vanished ego, he proposed a set of principles of which he became the personification."[37]

In the Gettysburg Address, Lincoln says nothing of himself. At a first hearing or reading, we are aware of what is being said and not of who is saying it. Yet at a second or third hearing or reading, Lincoln's character, the *ethos* or credibility, which is the first principle of Aristotle's rhetoric, is everywhere present. His very reticence to speak about himself—how different from modern politicians—is what makes his voice by the end of the address so decisive. "Lincoln was to be believed because he did not ask to be believed."[38]

NEWSPAPERS RAN THE WHOLE range in their responses. Most of the larger newspapers in the major cities had set up their page forms with type set in advance with Everett's text, which they had had for days. Most newspapers decided to shirttail Lincoln's words below Everett's without comment. The newspapers that were traditionally supportive of Lincoln found much to praise in his remarks at Gettysburg. The *Chicago Tribune,* always in Lincoln's corner, editorialized, "The dedicatory remarks of President Lincoln will live among the annals of the war."[39]

Josiah Holland, associate editor to Samuel Bowles of the *Springfield (Mass.) Republican,* was one of the first editors to grasp the importance of Lincoln's succinct address. Writing on November 20, he penned, "Surprisingly fine as Mr. Everett's oration was in the Gettysburg consecration, the rhetorical honors of the occasion were won by President Lincoln." Holland continued, "His little speech is a perfect gem, deep in feeling, compact in thought and expression, and tasteful and elegant in every word and comma."[40]

James Burrill Angell had become the editor of the *Providence Daily Journal* in 1860. A graduate of Brown University, in 1866 he would become president of the University of Vermont, and in 1871 of the University of Michigan. Only one day after Lincoln's speech, Angell editorialized, "We know not where to look for a more admirable speech than the brief one which the President made at the close of Mr. Everett's oration." Angell asked, "could the most elaborate and splendid oration be more beautiful, more touching, more inspiring than those few words of the President?" Two New England editors instantly understood the import of the Gettysburg Address. Angell concluded, "It had the charm and power of the very highest eloquence."[41]

Despite much praise, the myth of the address as a failure has continued on doggedly. Criticism from Lincoln's political opponents in the press was instant. The *Chicago Times* responded, "The cheek of every American must tingle with shame as he reads the silly, flat, and dishwatery utterances of a man who has to be pointed out to intelligent foreigners as the President of the United States."[42] Thirty-six miles from Gettysburg, the *Harrisburg Patriot and Union* spoke acrimoniously: "We pass over the silly remarks of the President; for the credit of the nation, we are willing that the veil of oblivion shall be dropped over them and that they shall no more be repeated or thought of."[43]

Far away, the *Times* of London continued to criticize Lincoln's American eloquence. Reporting on Gettysburg, the *Times* editorialized, "The ceremony was rendered ludicrous by some of the sallies of that poor President Lincoln."[44]

If the speech was not fully noticed and appreciated immediately, praise grew in the days and weeks that followed. On December 5, *Harper's Weekly* commented, "The few words of the President were from the heart to the heart. They cannot be read, even, without kindling emotion. . . . It was as simple and felicitous and earnest a word as was ever spoken."[45]

EVERETT, IN HIS QUITE FULL account of the day in his diary, did not mention the president's dedicatory remarks. The following day, however, he wrote to Lincoln, "Permit me . . . to express my great admiration of the thoughts expressed by you, with such eloquent simplicity & appropriateness, at the consecration of the cemetery." Everett, who had almost three years earlier confided to his diary his criticisms of Lincoln's speaking abilities when Lincoln traveled from Springfield to Washington, now offered his opinion that "I should be glad, if I could flatter myself, that I came as near to the central idea of the occasion, in two hours, as you did in two minutes."[46]

That same day Lincoln replied magnanimously, "In our respective parts yesterday, you could not have been excused to make a short address, nor I a long one."[47]

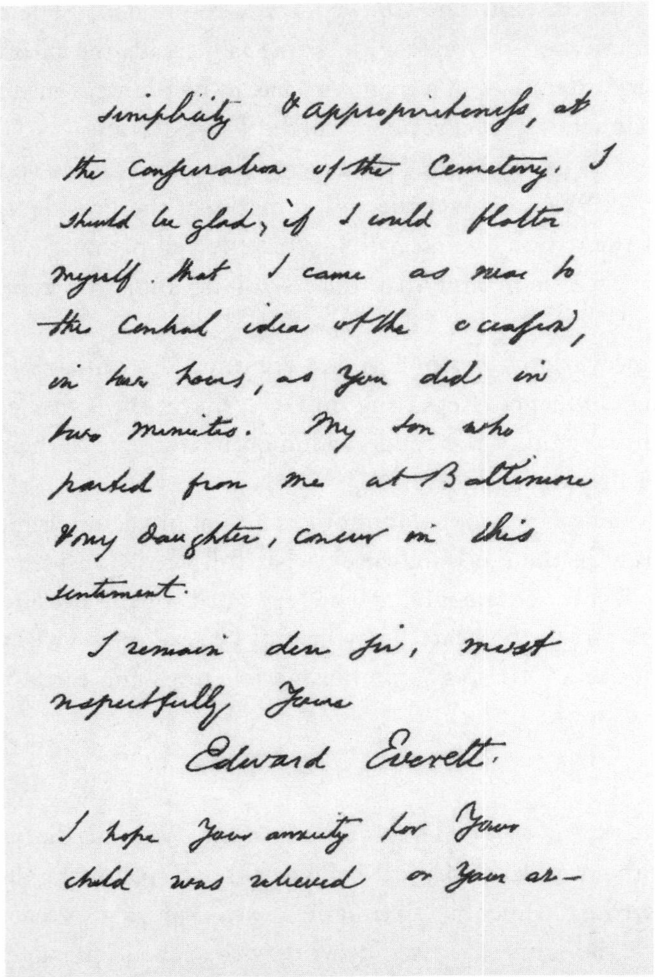

simplicity & appropriateness, at
the Consecration of the Cemetery. I
should be glad, if I could flatter
myself that I came as near to
the central idea of the occasion,
in two hours, as you did in
two minutes. My son who
parted from me at Baltimore
& my daughter, concur in this
sentiment.

I remain dear Sir, most
respectfully Yours
Edward Everett.

I hope your anxiety for your
child was relieved on your ar—

A portion of the generous letter of commendation Edward Everett wrote to Lincoln on the day after he and Lincoln spoke at Gettysburg.

LIBRARY OF CONGRESS

THE GETTYSBURG ADDRESS was a distinctive pearl in Lincoln's expanding American eloquence. Small in size, if not fully appreciated at the time, it has grown in splendor in the American memory of Lincoln and the Civil War. Often examined alone, it can best be appreciated when it is compared and contrasted with all of Lincoln's speeches.

There was one visitor in Gettysburg who knew these truths well.

When Lincoln's dedicatory remarks were completed, one of those present, surely remembering the public knowledge of Seward's role in Lincoln's inaugural address, asked Secretary of State Seward if he had helped Lincoln with that address also.

Seward replied, "No one but Abraham Lincoln could have made that address."[48]

CHAPTER TEN

"I CLAIM NOT TO HAVE CONTROLLED EVENTS"

"LITTLE SPEECH" TO ALBERT G. HODGES
APRIL 4, 1864

"I am naturally anti-slavery. If slavery is not wrong, nothing is wrong. I can not remember when I did not so think, and feel. And yet I have never understood that the Presidency conferred upon me an unrestricted right to act officially upon this judgment and feeling. It was in the oath I took that I would, to the best of my ability, preserve, protect, and defend the constitution of the United States. I could not take the office without taking the oath. Nor was it my view that I might take an oath to get power, and break the oath in using the power. I understood, too, that in ordinary civil administration this oath even forbade me to practically indulge my primary abstract judgment on the moral question of slavery." . . .

I add a word which was not in the verbal conversation. In telling this tale I attempt no compliment to my own sagacity. I claim not to have controlled events, but confess plainly that events have controlled me. Now, at the end of three years struggle the nation's condition is not what either party, or any man devised, or expected. God alone can claim it. Whither it is tending seems plain. If God now wills the removal of a great wrong, and wills also that we of the North as well as you of the South, shall pay fairly for our complicity in that wrong, impartial history will find therein new cause to attest and revere the justice and goodness of God.

ABRAHAM LINCOLN WELCOMED his three visitors to the Executive Mansion with apprehension. It was Saturday morning, March 26,

1864, and these leaders had traveled all the way from Kentucky, a key border state, to talk bluntly with Lincoln about the consternation growing in Kentucky from the recent recruiting by the Union Army of black troops in the state.

The leader of the delegation was Thomas E. Bramlette, the governor of Kentucky. Bramlette had raised and commanded the Third Kentucky Infantry Regiment in the Union Army before being nominated for governor as a Union Democrat in 1863. Archibald Dixon, the second member of the delegation, had served both as a lieutenant governor of Kentucky and as a United States senator, completing the unexpired term of Henry Clay from 1852 to 1855. Albert G. Hodges, the third visitor, had founded the *Frankfort Commonwealth* in 1833 and built it into a preeminent newspaper in the state. A former Whig, Hodges became a unionist during the war.

Lincoln granted a long interview. At the end of the meeting, he asked if he could make "a little speech." He talked with them about why he felt compelled to change course, from the assurances offered in his inaugural address that he would not interfere with slavery to his actions resulting in the Emancipation Proclamation and the arming of black troops.

Editor Hodges was so impressed with Lincoln's "little speech" that he returned in the afternoon to ask if he could take a copy of the president's remarks back to Kentucky. Lincoln responded that what he had spoken was extemporaneous and not written. Lincoln advised him to return home. He would write a letter to him with the words of his speech.

On April 4, 1864, Lincoln wrote his promised letter to Hodges. At the end of the letter Lincoln told him that he had decided to

add a word which was not in the verbal conversation

This meeting with the Kentucky visitors, one of hundreds convened with political leaders in the Executive Mansion during the Civil War, generated one of Lincoln's most compelling declarations about his views on slavery and his understanding of his role in the war.

Lincoln's letter to Hodges was both personal and public. He wrote in response to his conversation with his three visitors. He also understood that the letter might be published. In the tradition of his earlier reply to Horace Greeley, his letter to Hodges offered Lincoln the opportunity to present his views and respond to criticism, both elements present in this public letter. In the days before press conferences, and when there were long periods in his presidency during which he did not offer formal speeches, Lincoln became adroit at crafting public letters.

Always identified by editors and compilers of Lincoln's writings as the "Letter to Hodges," Lincoln thought of it as his "little speech." And in writing to Hodges he appended a second speech. The content and the form of these speeches point to Lincoln's mature articulation both of his views on slavery and of his thinking about the tension between the actions of man and the actions of God in the Civil War. A major reason why these speeches resonate long after the particular details that occasioned them have been forgotten or grown dim is that Lincoln offered his insights with such remarkable eloquence.

LINCOLN HAD ALWAYS felt a special affection for Kentucky. The state was his birthplace. He had lived there as a child and had returned several times as an adult. Mary Todd Lincoln was from Lexington. Joshua Speed, his best friend, moved from Illinois back to Louisville, where Lincoln had visited him.

Once the war began, Kentucky became the foundation of Lincoln's strategy for keeping the border states in the Union. He knew that his Emancipation Proclamation, followed by the arming of black troops, threatened to produce cracks in this foundation. By March 1864, the disagreements arising from the need for black troops prompted this trip to Washington by Kentucky leaders eager to speak with Lincoln in person.

THE VISITORS STOPPED first at the office of Edward Bates. The attorney general was also from a border state, Missouri. Later that day Bates wrote in his diary that "the Governor's mission is to have a better understanding with the Genl. Govt., about negro enlistments in Ky." Bates added that Bramlette told him, "The draft will not be opposed, if conducted in a simple and honest way—i.e. enlist the men and march them off, without making it a pretence to insult, and rob, and dominate every neighborhood—as in Maryland!"[1] They had traveled all this way to present this message to Lincoln.

THE PROBLEMS THAT BRAMLETTE, Dixon, and Hodges spoke about to Lincoln had been festering for more than a year. After Lincoln issued the Emancipation Proclamation, on January 1, 1863, the enrollment of blacks stirred up resistance in the commonwealth of Kentucky. Early on, a number of slaves joined the Union Army, but they enlisted outside the state borders. The General Assembly of the commonwealth insisted that no encampments be established within the state that might tempt slaves to leave their masters.

When Bramlette was elected governor in 1863 he grudgingly accepted the recruitment of blacks, but only if this was to make up the quota of troops from Kentucky not filled by whites. The War Department responded by promising to enroll only free blacks, or slaves who sought out military service. Loyal owners were to receive $300 for each slave.[2]

Despite what Bramlette believed to be assurances from the War Department about policies for recruiting blacks, problems continued to develop. Throughout 1863, masters complained that their agricultural production was falling dramatically because of a scarcity of labor. At the beginning of 1864, Bramlette decided to write directly to Lincoln.

Bramlette telegraphed the president on January 5, 1864, to protest that Maj. Gen. John G. Foster had announced his intention to move troops raised in Kentucky for the commonwealth's defense to the state of Tennessee. The governor told Lincoln that this action will "expose us to ruin." He reminded Lincoln that only the president had "the power to remove these troops." He asked that "this order as to these troops be countermanded."[3]

Lincoln replied on January 6 that he knew nothing about the order but that it must have been authorized by General Grant. Lincoln told Governor Bramlette that he did not "understand how doing so is bad faith or dishonor; nor yet how it exposes Kentucky to ruin."[4]

Thomas E. Bramlette, governor of Kentucky, led a delegation to meet with Lincoln in the White House on March 26, 1864, to discuss the growing consternation over the recruitment of black troops in his state.

KENTUCKY HISTORICAL SOCIETY

Bramlette telegraphed Lincoln again on January 8. He wrote that he appreciated Grant, "the first Gen'l of the age," but he believed Grant might not know of this order, which strained the emotions of the people of Kentucky.

Lincoln replied on January 17, now admitting that he did know that Grant was with General Foster in Nashville and thus Grant must have known of the order. Lincoln informed Bramlette that Grant would be passing through Kentucky and encouraged the governor to have a conference with him.[5]

The conflict between the federal and state governments continued to escalate. On March 12, Bramlette wrote to the provost marshal in Boyle County, "If the president does not, upon my demand, stop the negro enrollment, I will. I am awaiting his answer."[6]

Just three days later, however, Governor Bramlette softened his stand in a proclamation that asked Kentuckians to accept the enrollment plan. He understood their feelings, but "your indignation should not move you to commit crimes of violence, nor to unlawful resistance."[7] The proclamation of March 15, 1864, may have been the prudent measure, but it did not end Bramlette's distress. He now decided to take his concerns to Washington and requested a meeting with Lincoln.

BRAMLETTE, DIXON, AND HODGES left the Executive Mansion after their interview with Lincoln convinced that they had been heard. Governor Bramlette led the delegation, but it was editor Hodges whose name would be remembered for words that Lincoln would speak and write.

Two days later, on Monday, March 28, Lincoln spoke to Attorney General Bates, conveying his sense of the conversation with the visitors from Kentucky. That day Bates added a marginal note to his diary: "The President tells me that he made an arrangement with Gov. Bramlette that seemed to be satisfactory, all around."[8]

Orville H. Browning, no longer a senator from Illinois but now practicing law before the Supreme Court, called on the president on the evening of April 3. Lincoln told Browning of the visit of Bramlette, Dixon, and Hodges. Browning recorded in his diary that Lincoln told him that in the midst of his discussion with his visitors from Kentucky "he asked them to let him make a little speech to them." He recalled how Mr. Hodges came back later and requested a copy of his remarks. Lincoln told Browning that he had finally "written the letter today, Sunday, and wished to show it to me, as he felt the need of sympathy & advice. He then read it to me." Lincoln wanted to hear the letter before he sent it.[9]

LINCOLN BEGAN his letter of April 4:

> *I am naturally anti-slavery. If slavery is not wrong, nothing is wrong. I can not remember when I did not so think, and feel.*

Lincoln's beginning minced no words. He started his speech with a fervent affirmation of his antislavery beliefs. None of the participants left a record of the conversation that preceded Lincoln's words. If we know anything about Lincoln, it can be surmised that he spent some time listening to the concerns of his visitors, who had traveled the long distance from Kentucky to Washington to speak with him.

The first words of his speech were unequivocal. He offered them in the first person singular. He began with the bedrock of his own beliefs. Lincoln, who acted often as a moderator between the extremes, on this occasion owned his personal position as *anti-slavery.*

The words achieve even more power when we remember to whom he was speaking. Lincoln was not talking with Senators Charles Sumner and Henry Wilson of Massachusetts, strong abolitionists, but with leaders of Kentucky, all unionists, but men who brought with them deep concerns about the effects of Lincoln's Emancipation Proclamation.

We long to know what were the experiences—*I can not remember when*—behind Lincoln's words. Was he recalling his own boyhood in Kentucky and Indiana? The Lincoln family lived in Hardin County, Kentucky, where there were not many slaves. Their cabin was located along the Cumberland, or National, Road and Lincoln would have been a spectator to the regular sight of slaves being driven like cattle to market. Lincoln would surely have been told that his parents' opposition to slavery was one of their motives for moving from Kentucky to Indiana when he was seven.[10]

Lincoln's speaking strategy was often to affirm an idea not once but twice. This repetition is so reminiscent of the psalms, one of Lincoln's favorite books in the Bible. Thus Lincoln says:

> *I am naturally anti-slavery.*

He then emphasizes this truth by repeating it in a slightly different form:

> *If slavery is not wrong, nothing is wrong.*

Lincoln chose to describe his attitudes as *think* and *feel.* As he became a young adult, the rational Lincoln wished to ground all of his beliefs and actions in his thinking. And yet, in his early encounter with slavery, it was no doubt feeling that triggered his thinking. As a young man, at the end of a journey by boat down the Mississippi, Lincoln had experienced deep feelings of outrage at the sight of slaves being held against their will on the wharves in New Orleans. If this was a *natural* outgrowth of his childhood, his opening statement can allow for a commitment that grew even as the young Lincoln developed in ideas and experience.

> *And yet I have never understood that the Presidency conferred upon me an unrestricted right to act officially upon this judgment and feeling. It was in the oath I took that I would, to the best of my ability, preserve, protect, and defend the constitution of the United States. I could not take the office without taking the oath. Nor was it my view that I might take an oath to get power, and break the oath in using the power. I understood, too, that in ordinary civil administration this oath even forbade me to practically indulge my primary abstract judgment on the moral question of slavery.*

The opening words of the letter to Hodges can be understood only within the meaning of the entire first paragraph. Lincoln's words need to be seen and understood as part of a larger argument about the tension he felt between slavery and the Constitution.

Lincoln, as president, was not a private citizen but a public official. And not just any public official, but one who as the chief executive of the government of the United States took an oath to

> *defend the constitution of the United States*

One of Lincoln's political purposes in this letter was to underscore the tension between private opinion and public duty. He had spoken of this same tension in his reply to Horace Greeley:

> *I have here stated my purpose according to my view of official duty; and I intend no modification of my oft-expressed personal wish that all men everywhere could be free.*

In the letter to Hodges he set up the political tension with rhetorical artistry:

> *I could not take the office without taking the oath.*

In this one sentence Lincoln employed at once parallel structure, opposition, and assonance. First, he used the verb *take* twice in his parallel structure. Second, he opposed *office* with *oath.* Finally, he conveyed his idea in a sound pleasing to the ear by choosing two words, *office* and *oath,* that were assonant.

If, as seems likely, Lincoln had in the intervening days edited his extemporaneous words in preparation for sending them in a letter, the finished product was a model of balanced structure and rhythm. Thus his contrast between *oath* and *office* was emphasized in an opposition:

take an oath to get power	*break the oath in using the power*

The rhyming of *take* and *break* and the opposition of *get* and *using* made a pleasing sentence for the ear. Lincoln, whose penchant was to say the same thing two or three times in different ways, concluded this thought by saying once again that it was his *oath* that *forbade* him from indulging his personal judgment on slavery.

> *When, in March, and May, and July 1862 I made earnest, and successive appeals to the border states to favor compensated emancipation, I believed the indispensable necessity for military emancipation, and arming the blacks would come, unless averted by that measure, They declined the proposition; and I was, in my best judgment, driven to the alternative of either surrendering the Union, and with it, the Constitution, or of*

> *laying strong hand upon the colored element. I chose the latter. In choosing it, I hoped for greater gain than loss; but of this, I was not entirely confident.*

Lincoln recalled his struggles over the issue of emancipation with the border states. First, he reminded his listeners that he had overruled attempts at emancipation by Gen. John C. Frémont in the border state of Missouri; an initiative to arm black troops by Simon Cameron, at the time secretary of war; and another effort, by Gen. David Hunter, to effect what Lincoln called *military emancipation* in South Carolina.[11]

Second, as stated in the above text, he recalled his own three appeals for *compensated emancipation* in 1862. He made the last appeal in his annual message to Congress on December 1, 1862. He reminded his listeners that all of those appeals were rebuffed.

Lincoln rehearsed this narrative in some detail in order that the Kentuckians might appreciate that in the latter part of 1862, he was *driven to the alternative of either surrendering the Union, and with it, the Constitution* or of arming Southern slaves. If, at the beginning of his letter, Lincoln spoke of his antislavery beliefs in moral terms, by the middle of the letter he spoke about the arming of black slaves in strategic terms.

The undergirding principle throughout was Lincoln's intention and duty to preserve the Union. As he told it, at the beginning of the war he believed he could preserve the Union without freeing and arming the slaves. By the middle of the war he had changed his mind. His conclusion, not reached hastily, was that the only way to preserve the Union was by freeing and arming the slaves. Although he did not say so here, the freeing and arming of the slaves did not occur at once, but were themselves two acts in response to the changing events of the war.

Lincoln was remarkably candid in admitting the ambivalence in his decisions:

> *I hoped for greater gain than loss; but of this, I was not entirely confident.*

That Lincoln was willing to discuss his ambivalence is a distinguishing characteristic of his rhetorical leadership. What Lincoln didn't say, but what his listeners certainly knew, was how much Lincoln was criticized in the North for the slowness of that decision. In the midst of his present resolve, Lincoln was willing to admit his earlier lack of confidence in the path he was choosing.

> *And now let any Union man who complains of the measure, test himself by writing down in one line that he is for subduing the rebellion by force of arms; and in the next, that he is for taking these hundred and thirty thousand men from the Union side, and placing them where they would be but for the measure he condemns. If he can not face his case so stated, it is only because he can not face the truth.*

Lincoln was fully aware that his letter would be read by more than the three leaders. They were representatives from Kentucky. It is not known for sure why the letter was addressed to Hodges. He was the one who went back in the afternoon to ask for a copy of Lincoln's words. Bramlette had been a Democrat, whereas Hodges was formerly a Whig and had become a dedicated Union man.

As a speaker, Lincoln was always asking himself how his audience would respond to this argument or that point. Lincoln anticipated questions before they were asked. In this instance he anticipated the *Union man who complains of the measure.* His response was to pose a *test.* He suggested that Union men write down that they are *for* not only

> *subduing the rebellion by force of arms*

but also, at the same time,

> *taking these hundred and thirty thousand men from the Union side*

In arguing the *case* of arming black soldiers from Kentucky, we hear the lawyer employing logic showing that the end or goal cannot be achieved if the means to the end are removed. In words betraying uncharacteristic impatience, Lincoln concluded by issuing a challenge:

> *If he can not face his case so stated, it is only because he can not face the truth.*

As Hodges came to the end of the "little speech" he had heard the president speak in the Executive Mansion, he must have been surprised to see that the letter continued:

> *I add a word which was not in the verbal conversation.*

Lincoln added not a word but six sentences, 111 words. Why he decided to add this new material is a fascinating question. He must have believed he had something of great importance to say that would put his previous remarks in perspective.

He began:

> *In telling this tale I attempt no compliment to my own sagacity. I claim not to have controlled events, but confess plainly that events have controlled me.*

Lincoln started with words of self-deprecation. He had just recounted a long, twisting journey leading to emancipation. At the end of the journey he had surprised everyone. He had stunned the Republican radicals, trumped Horace Greeley in his clever reply to the New York editor's "Prayer of Twenty Millions," and frustrated conservative Democrats who wanted to return the nation to "the Union as it was."

But Lincoln told Hodges he would take no credit. What was Lincoln doing, rhetorically, by starting his final words with this negation? What was he saying when he told Bramlette, Dixon, and Hodges that he had not *controlled events,* and declared that *events have controlled me*? Was this modesty? Was it self-deprecation? Hodges was surely eager to read on.

AT FIRST GLANCE, the ideas in the final paragraph of the letter may seem quite unlike the content of Lincoln's "little speech" of March 26. But with a second reading, it is possible to see the connection. The first four-fifths of the letter, the "little speech," was a detailed defense of Lincoln's actions. Perhaps Lincoln reread it and thought to himself that it came across as magnifying his wisdom if not his shrewdness in all that had transpired. Did he feel the need, given the passing of nine days, to reframe the emphasis of his extemporaneous remarks?

> *Now, at the end of three years struggle the nation's condition is not what either party, or any man devised, or expected. God alone can claim it. Whither it is tending seems plain. If God now wills the removal of a great wrong, and wills also that we of the North as well as you of the South, shall pay fairly for our complicity in that wrong, impartial history will find therein new cause to attest and revere the justice and goodness of God.*

The weight of the paragraph is not about Lincoln's passivity. As if a circuit-riding lawyer in a courtroom, Lincoln began his case with three negative statements:

1. *I attempt no compliment to my own sagacity*
2. *I claim not to have controlled events*
3. *The nation's condition is not what either party, or any man devised, or expected*

These three negative assertions—building in crescendo from the negation of Lincoln to the wider negation of *either party* to a universal negation of *any man*—were meant to prompt a question from the jury, now become the three leaders: What, then, was the source of *the nation's condition*?

At this point the jury would know that something was coming.

Lincoln answered in four positive suggestions that balanced the previous three negative assertions:

1. *God alone can claim it*
2. *If God now wills the removal of a great wrong*
3. *and wills also that we of the North as well as you of the South, shall pay fairly for our complicity in that wrong*
4. *to attest and revere the justice and goodness of God*

The central meaning of the paragraph becomes clear. By employing the verb *devised—*

> *Now, at the end of three years struggle the nation's condition is not what either party, or any man devised, or expected.*

—Lincoln was speaking about agency, the politicians and generals responsible for carrying out the war. He did not exempt himself.

The trajectory of the paragraph was to point rather to the action of God. Crafting it with a lawyer's logic, Lincoln pointed beyond himself as president or commander-in-chief to God as the primary actor. Lincoln was quite willing at the outset to acknowledge his passivity as his way of pointing to the larger truth of the activity of God.

THIS LAST PARAGRAPH has been interpreted in quite different ways. David H. Donald, in his biography *Lincoln,* chose one line from this final paragraph as the epigraph:

> *I claim not to have controlled events, but confess plainly that events have controlled me.*

Donald says in his preface, "This biography highlights a basic trait of character evident throughout Lincoln's life: the essential passivity of his nature."[12]

Albert G. Hodges, editor of the Frankfort Commonwealth, *received Lincoln's letter on April 4, 1864. Lincoln transformed his "little speech" of March 26 into a public letter that would be republished broadly and used as a campaign document in 1864.*

KENTUCKY HISTORICAL SOCIETY

Throughout this examination of Lincoln's eloquence, a continuing emphasis has been put on reading and hearing Lincoln's individual sentences in the larger architecture of Lincoln's political rhetoric. Many of the recent debates about Lincoln's attitudes toward slavery have forgotten this counsel. Interpreters have fastened upon a particularly quotable sentence, but torn it from the intent of the speech as a whole, to say nothing of its date and place. Such practice invariably distorts Lincoln's overall argument and meaning.

The trouble with choosing this sentence from the letter to Hodges to highlight Lincoln's passivity is that it neglects the overall meaning of the paragraph. Certainly Donald constructs his interpretation of Lincoln from many sources and not just this one sentence. Yet this highly quotable sentence, used by other interpreters as well, does not adequately reflect Lincoln's meaning. Rather, examined closely in the full meaning of the paragraph, Lincoln's willingness to admit his passivity is a rhetorical move. A close reading of the paragraph reveals that Lincoln is intent on pointing beyond himself and his activity to God's activity in history.

ALBERT G. HODGES received Lincoln's letter with delight. Hodges published it in the *Frankfort Commonwealth* on April 25. He wrote to Lincoln on April 22 thanking him for the letter "received by due course of mail." He went on to tell Lincoln, "I have shown it to some of the prominent Union men here and from other parts of the State . . ." Lincoln, in person, and now by letter, made such a strong impression on Hodges that he began corresponding regularly with the president, supplying all kinds of information and opinions about affairs in Kentucky. Starting on April 22, he would write twelve letters to Lincoln in 1864, and two more in 1865.[13]

The language of the first and last paragraphs of the letter to Hodges did not stay put. The meaning of Lincoln's language about slavery—

> *I am naturally anti-slavery. If slavery is not wrong, nothing is wrong. I can not remember when I did not so think, and feel.*

—has been debated ever since. Beginning in the 1960s, these words became one of the key passages in a reexamination of Lincoln's attitudes toward slavery.

Eleven months later, the ideas and language of the final paragraph would become the basis of the opening sentences of the third paragraph of Lincoln's finest speech. In a story repeated over and over again in Lincoln's presidency, the ideas and rhetoric of one speech become the building blocks of a future speech. What Lincoln said briefly to Hodges on April 4, 1864, would be amplified in his Second Inaugural Address, eleven months to the day in the future.

This photograph of Lincoln was taken on February 5, 1865, one month before his Second Inaugural Address. For many years this Alexander Gardner photograph was incorrectly dated as having been taken five days before Lincoln's death, and was thus believed to be the last photograph of him. Compare this photograph with the one taken just before his departure from Springfield in 1861 and a remarkable aging is revealed through the four tumultuous years of the Civil War.

LIBRARY OF CONGRESS

CHAPTER ELEVEN

"WITH MALICE TOWARD NONE; WITH CHARITY FOR ALL"

SECOND INAUGURAL ADDRESS

MARCH 4, 1865

The Almighty has His own purposes. "Woe unto the world because of offences! for it must needs be that offences come; but woe to that man by whom the offence cometh!" If we shall suppose that American Slavery is one of those offences which, in the providence of God, must needs come, but which, having continued through His appointed time, He now wills to remove, and that He gives to both North and South, this terrible war, as the woe due to those by whom the offence came, shall we discern therein any departure from those divine attributes which the believers in a Living God always ascribe to Him? . . .

With malice toward none; with charity for all; with firmness in the right, as God gives us to see the right, let us strive on to finish the work we are in; to bind up the nation's wounds; to care for him who shall have borne the battle, and for his widow, and his orphan—to do all which may achieve and cherish a just, and a lasting peace, among ourselves, and with all nations.

ABRAHAM LINCOLN WAS LOOKING forward to the beginning of a second term as Inauguration Day, March 4, drew near in the early months of 1865. Although he would not make any predictions, the Civil War appeared to be finally drawing to a close. Coming to the end of four years as a war president, Lincoln relished the opportunity to be a peace president for the next four years. Gamblers were even wagering that Lincoln would be inaugurated to a third term in March 1869.

In the days leading up to the inauguration, smoking steam engines led jammed trains into the gleaming Baltimore and Ohio depot. The hotels spilled over with guests. The Willard, the National, and the Metropolitan were crammed, with people sleeping on cots in parlors and hallways. Churches, firehouses, and homes offered places to sleep.

Soldiers were everywhere. Many came for this special day from the more than forty hospitals scattered throughout the city. The sprawling Mount Pleasant Hospital was placed in service in March 1862 and just kept expanding. The hospital was a rebuilt army barracks surrounded by more than fifty large tents to accommodate the overflow of wounded men. Churches, schools, and fraternal lodges as well as hotels were transformed into quarters for the wounded and sick. Soldiers on cots were to be found all through the Capitol Building itself.

Many of the soldiers were marked by their wounds. Amputation became a sign of Civil War medicine: 75 percent of Civil War surgeries were amputations. Weapons were far ahead of tactics. Once wounded, the wait for treatment could be a day or two. Many doctors were introduced to surgery on the battlefield. Many visitors to the inaugural ceremonies were stunned at the sight of so many soldiers with amputated legs and arms.

FOUR MONTHS AFTER Lincoln's election to a second term, hope and despair were mingled in the thirty-five to forty thousand people who made their way to the capital on March 4, 1865. Hope was in the air as Lincoln was beginning to receive credit for his leadership in a Civil War that seemed to be in its last gasps.

Lathrop C. Keith, a thirty-eight-year-old soldier from Braintree, Massachusetts, was in the crowd that day. Keith, a carpenter by trade, had been mustered into "C" Company of the Massachusetts 4th Heavy Artillery on August 9, 1864. Seven months later, he found himself in Washington eager to attend Lincoln's second inaugural.

At ten o'clock the next morning, Keith wrote to his wife, Fannie, about some of his impressions of the previous day's events. He wrote that "the morning was dull and rainy & showery and the ground exceedingly muddy but I was too much in earnest about going to the Inauguration to be hindered by small obstacles."[1]

Despair, even anger, was also present because nearly every person in attendance at the inaugural would have lost someone to death or horrible disability during the war. Anger was in John Wilkes Booth, who was making his way to a place where he would stand about thirty-five feet above and behind Lincoln.

At the end of the conflict the final figures would reveal that 623,000 died in the Civil War—as many as in all of the other American wars put together. We are now celebrating the generation passing from us who fought in World War II. Approximately 407,000 Americans died in that war. If one compares the United States in 1860, a small nation with just over 30 million inhabitants, to the United States in 1940, with over 130 million citizens, the comparable losses in World War II would have been more than 2.6 million dead.

Residents and visitors walking toward the Capitol encountered armed patrols on horseback at every major intersection. Rumors swirled about that Confederates, knowing that defeat was looming, would attempt to abduct or even assassinate the president. Sharpshooters were placed on top of and in the windows of the buildings near the Capitol, where the inaugural ceremonies would take place.

Relentless rains and gale winds flogged the parade that preceded the inauguration. At his first inauguration Lincoln saw a half-finished dome on the Capitol. On this day the new iron dome shone above the president, the dignitaries, and the crowds. The presence of many blacks, both soldiers and spectators, changed the scene dramatically from that of Lincoln's first inauguration.

THE CROWD BURST into sustained applause when Lincoln was introduced. The president stood up, put on his steel-rimmed eyeglasses, and stepped forward to a white iron table constructed by Maj. Benjamin Brown French. Lincoln held in his left hand his Second Inau-

This Alexander Gardner photograph of Lincoln delivering the Second Inaugural Address is the only photograph we have of Lincoln speaking. Lincoln is seen holding his speaking text. John Wilkes Booth can be seen, hatless, above and to the right of center.

LIBRARY OF CONGRESS

gural Address. Exactly at the moment he started to speak, the sun broke through the clouds.

Soldier Keith of Massachusetts, even though he was far out in the crowd, captured that moment in his letter to his wife, Fannie: "At about one, the Sun in the heavens and the Son of the Backwoodsman came in sight almost at the same moment, the one to cheer the natural world, and the other to take upon himself, God sparing him, four more years of labor, care and responsibility such as never rested upon mortal before." Keith quickly added, "May the time of his office be like the days of his inauguration."[2]

Lincoln began:

> *At this second appearing, to take the oath of the presidential office, there is less occasion for an extended address than there was at the first. Then a statement, somewhat in detail, of a course to be pursued, seemed fitting and proper. Now, at the expiration of four years, during which public declarations have been constantly called forth on every point and phase of the great contest which still absorbs the attention, and engrosses the enerergies of the nation, little that is new could be presented. The progress of our arms, upon which all else chiefly depends, is as well known to the public as to myself; and it is, I trust, reasonably satisfactory and encouraging to all. With high hope for the future, no prediction in regard to it is ventured.*

Almost nothing is known about the composition of the Second Inaugural. A lone voice has left a spare account. On the Sunday evening preceding the inauguration, February 26, Francis B. Carpenter, an artist who had earlier lived for six months at the White House, was in Lincoln's office. Carpenter was speaking with two men from Ohio and New York who were there for a scheduled meeting with Lincoln. Carpenter reported that when Lincoln arrived, he was "holding in his hand a roll of manuscripts." Upon seeing Carpenter, Lincoln offered, "Lots of wisdom in that document, I suspect. It is what will be called my second inaugural, containing about six hundred words. I will put it in my drawer until I want it."[3]

From this brief account it is possible to make some observations based on what we have learned of Lincoln's habits of composition. First, the Second Inaugural was written out in advance; it was not written hurriedly, not on an envelope or scraps of paper, at the last moment. Second, because Lincoln mentioned an address of six hundred words, he may have continued to edit and expand his remarks in the week leading up to the inauguration on Saturday, March 4. We have observed his practice of continuing to rewrite up to the last moment. Third, there is no evidence of any other hand at work as an editor. Seward, who had offered editorial comment on the First Inaugural and the Message to Congress in Special Session of July 4, 1861, does not mention any role in the editing of the Second Inaugural. By now, at the end of four years as president, Lincoln worked alone.

LINCOLN'S SECOND INAUGURAL ADDRESS is 701 words (703 words if the later addition of *Fellow Countrymen* is counted). It is the second shortest Second Inaugural. George Washington offered the shortest, 135 words, speaking at an occasion with no tradition yet in place.

The address is arranged in four paragraphs, with twenty-six sentences. Five hundred and five words are of one syllable.

Lincoln wrote the address on foolscap, a kind of paper approximately thirteen and a half by seventeen inches in size. He wrote in two columns. A careful writer, he wrote for the ear and thus his pattern was often to speak the words aloud before writing them. His handwritten address was then set in type and pasted on white boards.

A feature that sets the address apart is its biblical and theological language. Within 701 words Lincoln mentions God fourteen times, quotes the Bible four times, and invokes prayer three times.

LINCOLN'S OPENING WORDS, *at this second appearing*, were not lost on his audience. Newspapers had been underlining the fact that Lincoln would be the first president to be elected to a second term in thirty-two years in a nation that was only seventy-six years old. Andrew Jackson had been the last president inaugurated for a second term, way back in 1833. A whole generation of Americans had lived through the intervening decades of undistinguished single-term presidents.

As recently as the previous summer, many of Lincoln's supporters were apprehensive that he would become another of those one-term presidents. In the early summer of 1864, with Grant's troops fighting a determined enemy in the Battle of the Wilderness in Virginia, and Sherman's progress uncertain as he led his army through

Georgia toward Atlanta, the Northern populace was growing anxious. Casualty counts from Grant's forces that sometimes reached two thousand a day were weakening the resolve of many in the North to fight on.

On August 22, Henry J. Raymond, chairman of the Republican National Committee, wrote a bleak letter to Lincoln. "I feel compelled to drop you a line concerning the political condition of the country as it strikes me. I am in active correspondence with your staunchest friends in every state and from them all I hear but one report. The tide is setting strongly against us."[4]

The next day, August 23, Lincoln brought a private memorandum to the afternoon cabinet meeting. He showed it to the members of his cabinet, but folded it so that the text was not able to be seen. He requested that each of the cabinet members sign the back of the memorandum. Lincoln had written: "This morning, as for some days past, it seems exceedingly probable that this administration will not be reelected. Then it will be my duty to so cooperate with the President-elect as to save the Union between the election and the inauguration; as he will have secured his election on such ground that he cannot possibly save it afterwards."[5]

Everything changed nine days later, when Atlanta was abandoned by Confederate forces on September 1. Sherman led his victorious troops into the city on September 2.

A renewal of support for the Union changed the whole tenor of the election. Lincoln won a second term in November with a decisive victory over his Democratic opponent, Gen. George McClellan. Lincoln received 2,203,831 votes to McClellan's 1,797,019. Lincoln won a tremendous victory in electoral votes, 221 to 21.

LINCOLN'S OPENING LINE, if noteworthy for the surprise of Lincoln *appearing*, does not stand out for its elegance. Compare it to the opening sentence of the "House Divided" speech of 1858:

> *If we could first know <u>where</u> we are, and <u>whither</u> we are tending, we could then better judge <u>what</u> to do, and <u>how</u> to do it.*

Or contrast it to the American ideals announced in the first sentence of the Gettysburg Address:

> *Four score and seven years ago our fathers brought forth on this continent, a new nation, conceived in Liberty, and dedicated to the proposition that all men are created equal.*

The opening sentence was part of a first paragraph in which Lincoln spoke as if he wanted to lower expectations. He achieved this with a steady litany of negatives, present in three of the five sentences in the paragraph.

> Sentence one: *less occasion for an extended address*
>
> Sentence three: *little that is new*
>
> Sentence five: *no prediction in regard to it is ventured*

There is nothing in the first paragraph that suggests the meaning that is to follow.

THE TONE OF Lincoln's opening words is completely different from that of previous second inaugural addresses. George Washington, who did not want to serve a second term, offered the first and the shortest second inaugural. He began:

> I am again called upon by the voice of my country to execute the functions of its Chief Magistrate. When the occasion proper for it shall arrive, I shall endeavor to express the high sense I entertain of this distinguished honor, and of the confidence which has been reposed in me by the people of united America.

The remainder of his brief 135 words was about the meaning and obligations of the oath he was about to take.[6]

Starting with Thomas Jefferson, the rhetoric of second inaugural addresses changed. Jefferson, in 1805, began his second inaugural address:

> Proceeding, fellow citizens, to that qualification which the constitution requires before my entrance on the charge again conferred upon me, it is my duty to express the deep sense I entertain of this new proof of confidence from my fellow citizens at large, and the zeal with which it inspires me, so to conduct myself as may best satisfy their just expectations. On taking this station on a former occasion, I declared the principles on which I believed it my duty to administer the affairs of our commonwealth. My conscience tells me that I have, on every occasion, acted up to that declaration, according to its obvious import, and to the understanding of every candid mind.[7]

Jefferson began a tradition of second inaugural addresses in which the president offered thanks for the confidence of the citizens in electing him to a second term.

James Madison, in 1813, began:

> About to add the solemnity of an oath to the obligations imposed by a second call to the station in which my country heretofore placed me, I find in the presence of this respectable assembly an opportunity of publicly repeating my profound sense of so distinguished a confidence and of the responsibility united with it. The impressions on me are strengthened by such an evidence that my faithful endeavors to discharge my arduous duties have been favorably estimated, and by a consideration of the momentous period at which the trust has been renewed.[8]

Madison, who ran unopposed, combined thanks to the people with speaking of his sense of responsibility to them.

James Monroe, in 1821, offered:

> I shall not attempt to describe the grateful emotions which the new and very distinguished proof of the confidence of my fel-

> low-citizens, evinced by my reelection to this high trust, has excited in my bosom. The approbation which it announces of my conduct in the preceding term affords me a consolation which I shall profoundly feel through life. The general accord with which it has been expressed adds to the great and never-ceasing obligations which it imposes.[9]

In 1832, for the first time, candidates were selected in national nominating conventions. Andrew Jackson ran for a second term against Lincoln's favorite politician, Henry Clay of Kentucky. After a rancorous campaign, Jackson began his second inaugural address:

> The will of the American people, expressed through their unsolicited suffrages, calls me before you to pass through the solemnities preparatory to taking upon myself the duties of President of the United States for another term. For their approbation of my public conduct through a period which has not been without its difficulties, and for this renewed expression of their confidence in my good intentions, I am at a loss for terms adequate to the expression of my gratitude.[10]

Each of these five presidents began his inaugural address with a reference to the "confidence" of their fellow citizens. One cannot miss, however, the self-referential quality that was advanced by many different personal pronouns in each of their opening words. There was a steady staccato of "I" in all of these inaugural addresses.

Except for Lincoln's. The opening words in his Second Inaugural are all the more remarkable when heard against the backdrop of the five previous second inaugural addresses. He nowhere speaks of the "confidence" or "approbation" of the electorate. He uses personal pronouns only twice, *I* and *myself,* in the first paragraph, and never again. Because we approach the Second Inaugural through the larger lens of his previous speeches, we should not be so surprised. He never spoke of himself, did not use one personal pronoun, in the Gettysburg Address.

All of his rhetoric, from the outset of the address, is directed away from himself.

> *On the occasion corresponding to this four years ago, all thoughts were anxiously directed to an impending civil war. All dreaded it—all sought to avert it. While the inaugeral address was being delivered from this place, devoted altogether to saving the Union without war, insurgent agents were in the city seeking to destroy it without war—seeking to dissole the Union, and divide effects, by negotiation. Both parties deprecated war; but one of them would make war rather than let the nation survive; and the other would accept war rather than let it perish. And the war came.*

If Lincoln does not speak of "I," he does speak of *all* and *both.* His second paragraph is marked by his use of inclusive language. This is the first clue to the larger purpose of his address.

War always elicits calls for exclusive language. Parties in any war have a very difficult time understanding the aspirations or point of view of the other side. Lincoln knew the audience would have cheered him if he chose to demonize the South.

But he chose a different path. The signs along this path were spelled *all* and *both.* These inclusive pronouns signal that Lincoln was about to portray a path that North and South could now travel together.

The objection can be raised that Lincoln does say of the South,

> *but one of them would make war rather than let the nation survive*

It is what Lincoln doesn't say that is important. Rather than *one of them,* he might have characterized those who would make war as "Confederates" or "the enemy" or "rebels." He didn't use those words, which would have raised the emotional tone of his address by many more decibels than *one of them.*

ONE IMAGE DOMINATES the second paragraph. Nine times in ninety-nine words Lincoln refers to war, seven times as a noun (*war*) and twice as a pronoun (*it*). The image of *war* builds and expands in the hearer's consciousness.

Lincoln was not trying to solve some abstract philosophical problem about war. He rather entered the dilemma of the meaning of the war standing close to the soldiers who had asked about the war's meaning while they prepared to enter into the agony of battle. After the battles were over, Lincoln had visited them, both Union and Confederate soldiers, in the many hospitals in Washington. He had seen firsthand what some in the crowd that day saw for the first time, that many of the soldiers left these same hospitals with legs and arms amputated.

When the war began, nearly four years earlier at Fort Sumter, everyone in the North expected a war of short duration. People in the North were surprised at both the length and the cost of four years of war. To cite the statistic of 623,000 dead can never capture the real cost. One out of nine soldiers in the Union Army died in the war.

The deaths in the whole Revolutionary War were estimated at 4,000, whereas the deaths at Antietam alone in September 1863 were approximately 4,800. The death of young men whose whole lives were out in front of them was felt in each community. Worcester, Massachusetts, sent 4,277 young men off to battle; 398 did not return.[11]

Lincoln's surprise is his conclusion to the paragraph:

And the war came.

He had spent almost the entire paragraph describing the various parties to the war, and their intentions about war. The people who begin a war almost always do so with the sense that they are in charge. Lincoln, looking back with the hindsight of four years, is suggesting that the generals, the soldiers, and the commander-in-chief were not completely in control of the war. This final sentence is not only a conclusion but also a transition to Lincoln's discussion of yet other dimensions of the meaning of the war.

Up until now *war* has been the direct object, both historically and grammatically, of actions and inactions of both the North and the South. In the last sentence Lincoln reversed the drama by making *war* the subject. *And the war came.*

> *One eighth of the whole population were colored slaves, not distributed generally over the Union, but localized in the Southern part of it. These slaves constituted a peculiar and powerful interest. All knew that this interest was, somehow, the cause of the war. To strengthen, perpetuate, and extend this interest was the object for which the insurgents would rend the Union, even by war; while the government claimed no right to do more than to restrict the territorial enlargement of it. Neither party expected for the war, the magnitude, or the duration, which it has already attained. Neither anticipated that the cause of the conflict might cease with, or even before, the conflict itself should cease. Each looked for an easier triumph, and a result less fundamental and astounding.*

Lincoln's meaning flows out in several trajectories in this largest paragraph of the Second Inaugural. First, Lincoln intimates that the North, even when it spoke of defending the Union, knew—*somehow*—that slavery was the key moral issue underneath its political rhetoric. Second, he suggests that the South, even when it spoke of the right to be independent, knew—*somehow*—that slavery was foundational to its way of life. In an address filled with inclusive language, Lincoln intends to situate slavery as an inclusive problem that was the responsibility of the whole nation.

Lincoln had come a long way since his first major address of 1861 (what was now being called his First Inaugural), in which he said he would leave slavery alone, and his long Message to Congress in Special Session on July 4, in which he did not speak about slavery at all.

Lincoln is at his most argumentative when repeating his contention that, regarding slavery, *the government claimed no right to do more than to restrict the territorial enlargement of it*

Actually, his language is quite mild in tone. However, four years later he no longer restricts his rhetoric to what he as president cannot do. He goes far beyond this starting point in his discussion of slavery.

No one knew it yet, but Lincoln was preparing his audience to hear about God's purposes by rehearsing the finitude of human purposes. In a masterful rhetorical passage Lincoln points up the irony that both sides failed to understand adequately both the cause and the result of the civil strife. He made this point about the limitations of human judgment from three different vantage points:

1. *Neither party expected for the war, the magnitude, or the duration, which it has already attained.*
2. *Neither anticipated that the cause of the conflict might cease with, or even before, the conflict itself should cease.*
3. *Each looked for an easier triumph, and a result less fundamental and astounding.*

Neither . . . neither . . . each is Lincoln's way of emphasizing a truth about the limitations of human judgment.

The victors usually write the story of war. Many in the audience expected Lincoln to offer assurances that God was on the side of the Union. Instead, Lincoln asks rather than answers. No sentence in this section is framed grammatically as a question, but it is clear that Lincoln, as president, is asking a question, four years later, about human wisdom in both North and South.

Both read the same Bible, and pray to the same God; and each invokes His aid against the other. It may seem strange that any men should dare to ask a just God's assistance in wringing their bread from the sweat of other men's faces; but

> *let us judge not that we be not judged. The prayers of both could not be answered; that of neither has been answered fully.*

When Lincoln introduced the Bible and prayer, he was adding one more emphasis of inclusive language. *Both* functions the same as *all. Both* Confederate and Union soldiers read the *same Bible.* By extension, Lincoln was saying, Union people and Confederate people *read the same Bible, and pray to the same God.*

Lincoln was reading the Bible. As the war heated up, Lincoln spent increasing time living in the cooler climate at the Soldiers' Home, located a few miles from the White House in the northwest quadrant of the District along the road to Silver Spring, Maryland. In 1864 the Lincoln family began its third season at the Soldiers' Home on July 4 and would not return until mid-October. The usual pattern was for Lincoln to work at the White House by day and be at his cottage at the Soldiers' Home in the evening.

David V. Derickson, a forty-four-year-old businessman from Meadville, Pennsylvania, was a captain in Company K of the Pennsylvania Volunteers. Derickson was the officer in charge of the detail guarding Lincoln as the president traveled back and forth between the White House and the Soldiers' Home each day. Derickson recounted that he would enter the Lincoln cottage at the Soldiers' Home each morning about six-thirty, often observing the president "reading the Bible or some work on the art of war."[12]

The Bible was also at the center of the intermittent revivals taking place among both Northern and Southern soldiers. When we ask the question why soldiers on both sides fought, we find faith as a central ingredient in any answer. James M. McPherson, in *For Cause and Comrade: Why Men Fought in the Civil War,* states that "Civil War armies were, arguably, the most religious in American history." We know why these soldiers fought because never have two armies conveyed their aspirations and anxieties, including their religious beliefs, so fully in diaries and letters.[13]

Lincoln, who never joined a church, began at this point in his address to use the church's book, the Bible, with telling insight.

LINCOLN ALSO INVOKED prayer four times in this address. In his first layer of meaning Lincoln was inclusive. His observation

Both . . . pray to the same God

was a wholly positive affirmation of the practice of prayer. The Union soldiers and the Confederate soldiers *pray to the same God.*

Immediately, however, Lincoln offered reservations about the way prayer was practiced:

and each invokes His aid against the other.

Lincoln understood from his own experience how both the Bible and prayer could be both used and misused. He had met many delegations of politicians and ministers who told him that God was on the side of the Union. The Bible was becoming a weapon in the religious patriotism that grew with the war. He was well aware of similar practices in the South.

This indictment sounds similar to ideas he had been wrestling with in his private writing two and a half years earlier. In his Meditation on the Divine Will, written when political jingoism and religious chauvinism were heating up on both sides, Lincoln had observed,

Both may be, and one must be wrong. God can not be for, and against the same thing at the same time.[14]

LINCOLN NOW ELABORATED on what he deemed a misuse of prayer by referring to a first passage from the Bible. Quoting Genesis 3:19, where God orders Adam and Eve out of the garden because of their disobedience, Lincoln observed:

It may seem strange that any men should dare to ask a just God's assistance in wringing their bread from the sweat of other men's faces

For a moment it may have appeared that Lincoln was breaking his inclusive rhetorical strategy. Lincoln employed this verse from Genesis in order to speak about whites in the South who appealed that God was on their side even as they ate what was produced and harvested by the work of their black slaves.

But ever so quickly Lincoln balances judgment with mercy by quoting directly from Jesus' Sermon on the Mount (Matthew 7:1):

> *but let us judge not that we be not judged*

Speaking to an audience so ready to judge, Lincoln invoked the authority of Jesus in the New Testament to restrain an all too human impulse.

The audience does not know it yet, but in this transitional section Lincoln is about to connect human purposes, with their tendency toward pretentiousness, to what will emerge as the central theme in this address, the purposes of God.

> *The Almighty has His own purposes. "Woe unto the world because of offences! for it must needs be that offences come; but woe to that man by whom the offence cometh!" If we shall suppose that American Slavery is one of those offences which, in the providence of God, must needs come, but which, having continued through His appointed time, He now wills to remove, and that He gives to both North and South, this terrible war, as the woe due to those by whom the offence came, shall we discern therein any departure from those divine attributes which the believers in a Living God always ascribe to Him?*

With the affirmation

> *The Almighty has His own purposes*

Lincoln had arrived at the architectural center of his address. After chronicling a variety of purposes and intentions, Lincoln presented his own meaning of the war, to be found in the purposes of God.

Lincoln is not speaking here of a private God whom men and women know in solitude, but rather of a public God who is involved in the tumult of war and slavery. When he uses the language *the providence of God,* he is not offering a closed theoretical construct but rather an open window through which he will invite his audience to see the relationship of God's *providence* to the American *offence* of *Slavery.*

In affirming God as subject, Lincoln chooses the description *Living God.* All of his ideas in this address finally come back to the touchstone of the *Living God.* If the Declaration of Independence was the sheet anchor of his belief that all men are created equal, faith in a *Living God* will allow him to go forward in the remainder of his address to speak both of judgment and of reconciliation.

The Second Inaugural is the last pearl in a string of pearls. However, it is deeply connected in content with at least two earlier gems of Lincoln's rhetoric, one private and one public.

In the fall of 1862 Lincoln wrote for his own eyes the Meditation on the Divine Will. The Meditation was unknown during Lincoln's life. Let us observe the connections between the Meditation on the Divine Will and the Second Inaugural Address.

MEDITATION ON THE DIVINE WILL	*SECOND INAUGURAL ADDRESS*
The will of God prevails.	*The Almighty has His own purposes.*
Both may be, and one must be wrong. God can not be for, and against the same thing at the same time.	*The prayers of both could not be answered; that of neither has been answered fully.*
I am almost ready to say this is probably true—that God wills this contest, and wills that it shall not end yet.	*He now wills to remove. . . . Yet, if God wills that it continue . . .*

The connections are more in beliefs than in precise language. The Meditation is more speculative, whereas Lincoln will become more specific and tangible in the Second Inaugural.[15]

Lincoln's public letter to Albert G. Hodges on April 4, 1864, is a second antecedent. We need to recall that Lincoln added a concluding paragraph that was not in his original conversation with Bramlette, Dixon, and Hodges. The first continuity related to the expectations of the various parties:

LETTER TO ALBERT G. HODGES	*SECOND INAUGURAL ADDRESS*
Now, at the end of three years struggle the nation's condition is not what either party, or any man devised, or expected.	*Neither party expected for the war, the magnitude, or the duration, which it has already attained.*

Lincoln's point in both the letter and the address was the limitation of human opinions about the war.

If the first continuity is about human judgments, the second is about the purposes of God. Again, note the comparisons with the letter to Hodges:

If God now wills the removal of a great wrong, and wills also that we of the North as well as you of the South, shall pay fairly for our complicity in that wrong, impartial history will find therein new cause to attest and revere the justice and goodness of God.	*. . . He now wills to remove, and that He gives to both North and South, this terrible war, as the woe due to those by whom the offence came, shall we discern therein any departure from those divine attributes which the believers in a Living God always ascribe to Him?*

The ideas in the public letter and public address, written exactly eleven months apart, are remarkably similar. If Lincoln spoke in the

Second Inaugural about the *attributes* of a *Living God,* in the letter to Hodges he was more specific in attesting the *justice and goodness of God.*[16]

LINCOLN CHANGED THE TONE of his address again when he recited a third biblical verse (Matthew 18:7):

> *"Woe unto the world because of offences! for it must needs be that offences come; but woe to that man by whom the offence cometh!"*

This withering indictment by Jesus is the beginning of Lincoln's attack on slavery.

The issue of slavery dominates the central paragraph of his address. All of the critics of Lincoln's views and policies on slavery must account for the reality that Lincoln decided to spend a full one-third of this second-shortest presidential inaugural address speaking about slavery.[17]

Lincoln connected the there and then of the biblical world with the here and now of the United States in the 1860s when he said,

> *If we shall suppose that American Slavery is one of those offences . . .*

Once again he begins a discussion of a central idea with inclusive language. He could have said "slavery" or "Southern slavery," or simply located slaves as residing in the South. Instead he uses the inclusive *American Slavery.*

HOW ARE WE TO understand Lincoln's readiness in the Second Inaugural to shine so much light on the darkness of slavery? I believe that standing behind the composition of Lincoln's muscular words about the evils of slavery was his immediate memory of the recent wrestling in the halls of Congress over a constitutional amendment that would abolish slavery forever. If the Emancipation Proclamation had been intended as a body blow to slavery, right away questions were raised about its scope and permanence. Some argued that it was only a wartime measure by a commander-in-chief. Might it be outlawed by a future Congress? Would it be declared unconstitutional by the courts?[18]

Into this vortex of questions came a surge of proposals for a constitutional amendment outlawing slavery. A central problem for any amendment was the increasing reverence for the Constitution that had grown up by the 1860s. The Constitution had been amended only twice since the ratification of the Bill of Rights in 1791. There had been no amendments for sixty years.

Lincoln was silent as debates over various proposed amendments went forward in the winter and spring of 1864. He did work behind the scenes to encourage the drafting of antislavery constitutions in Louisiana and other Southern states. On June 15, 1864, a proposed Thirteenth Amendment failed to receive the necessary two-thirds majority, falling short by thirteen votes in the House of Representatives.

Lincoln had decided that he desired such an amendment to be part of the platform of the Republican convention that would meet in Baltimore on June 7 and 8. He proposed to Edwin D. Morgan, senator from New York, that the amendment be the "key note" of the opening address.[19]

After his reelection in November, Lincoln made it known that he wanted an antislavery amendment passed before his second inauguration. The election had produced a strong Republican majority in Congress, but that new body would not be convened until December 1865. Some Republican leaders advised Lincoln to wait for positive action by the new Congress. Another option was for Lincoln to call a special session of the new Congress, as he had in July 1861. He decided he would not wait.

Lincoln went into action. Lincoln and Seward lobbied various Democratic congressmen to encourage them to change their votes. Formal debate in Congress began in January 1865, less than two months before the Second Inaugural. As Michael Vorenberg tells the story, "no piece of legislation received more of his [Lincoln's] attention than the Thirteenth Amendment."[20]

On January 31, 1865, a final vote was scheduled in the House of

Representatives. The galleries were packed, including women who had been pressing for universal emancipation. The new chief justice, Salmon P. Chase, arrived on the floor of the House. In the gallery was Charles Douglass, eldest son of Frederick Douglass. Rumors flew that Confederate peace envoys were on their way to Washington. Now was not the time, so opponents of the amendment argued, to upset the prospects for peace.

The clerk called the roll. The final tally was 119 to 56, with eight members absent. The House erupted in shouts and cheers. In the galleries people embraced. Both blacks and whites wept for joy. Blacks were jubilant. Charles Douglass wrote to his father, "I wish that you could have been here, such rejoicing I have never before witnessed . . . (white people I mean)."[21]

LINCOLN JOINED THE CELEBRATION the next day. He was so pleased by the measure that he signed the Thirteenth Amendment in a ceremony, even though the Constitution did not require a president to sign an amendment. Lincoln was immediately criticized by detractors who spoke about growing presidential power.

That evening, February 1, in response to a serenade at the White House, Lincoln spoke with overflowing emotion. Unfortunately his remarks at the signing ceremony were preserved only in a summary fashion from a reporter's hand. Nevertheless, one phrase does leap from Lincoln's remarks. Lincoln declared,

This amendment is a King's cure for all the evils.[22]

Fondly do we hope—fervently do we pray—that this mighty scourge of war may speedily pass away. Yet, if God wills that it continue, until all the wealth piled by the bond-man's two hundred and fifty years of unrequited toil shall be sunk, and until every drop of blood drawn with the lash, shall be paid by another drawn with the sword, as was said three thousand

> *years ago, so still it must be said "the judgments of the Lord, are true and righteous altogether."*

Lincoln believed that the Thirteenth Amendment codified in law for all time what the Emancipation Proclamation had begun as a timely order by the commander-in-chief. The threads of the Emancipation Proclamation, woven into the taut rhetoric of his public letter to Conkling, had become an unbreakable cord in the Thirteenth Amendment. Now in the Second Inaugural he decided to speak about slavery once again, but this time depicting it in the larger frames of American and biblical history:

> *the bond-man's two hundred and fifty years of unrequited toil*

> *as was said three thousand years ago, so still it must be said*

In his First Inaugural Address Lincoln oriented his remarks around political and legal texts. Lincoln buttressed his words by quoting from the Constitution and citing words from the Republican platform. His address was a careful, legal definition of what he and the federal government were prepared not to do about slavery.

Lincoln's discussion of slavery in the Second Inaugural was on an entirely different plane. What we hear is not the legal Lincoln of the First Inaugural but a theological Lincoln. His meaning is buttressed by quotations from the Bible. In his debates with Stephen Douglas in 1858, he referred to the Founders' ideas codified in the Constitution. In March 1865, he appealed to the ideas of the prophets, the poetry of the psalmist, and the searching words of Jesus. If Lincoln had become known previously for his entreaty to get behind the Constitution to the Declaration of Independence, he now appealed behind both the Constitution and the Declaration of Independence to a God who had been at work in history for at least three millennia.

FONDLY AND *FERVENTLY* are affecting words that reveal the deep feeling of one who had not revealed much of his sentiments in earlier speeches. They reach out to the emotions of the listener. Lincoln utilized two of his favorite rhetorical devices, parallel structure and alliteration, as he lingered between hope and judgment. Lincoln had moved a long way from the *less, little,* and *no* of the opening paragraph.

As much as these words sounded a kind of Victorian sentimentality, Lincoln did not linger there for long. His use of *yet* stopped *hope* in its tracks. This truculent conjunction was Lincoln's signal that he was returning to a discussion of the incredible costs of slavery in a moral universe. There is a price to be paid. The religious dimension of Lincoln's argument would be clearly understood by the audience. The abolition of slavery was the only way to purge the nation of its sins.

LINCOLN SUMMARIZED HIS depiction of slavery and its consequences for the nation by making use of a fourth biblical verse (Psalm 19:9):

> *"the judgments of the Lord, are true and righteous altogether"*

Lincoln had told numerous friends of his fondness for the psalms. Whether in the morning in his cottage at the Soldiers' Home or after the midday meal at the White House, sprawled in his comfortable chair in his large stocking feet, Lincoln enjoyed reading the psalms. He had told Rebecca R. Pomeroy, a nurse who had resided at the White House after Willie's death in 1862, of his love of the psalms. "They are the best, for I find in them something for every day of the week."[23]

Now Lincoln found just the right words from the psalms to summarize his argument. This final quotation from the Bible brought the weight of accepted authority and history to bear upon this contemporary if ancient issue.

Lincoln accepted, along with almost all of his fellow citizens in the middle of the nineteenth century, a belief in the special destiny of America. Lincoln's courage at the moment of his highest triumph—

his second inauguration, at the conclusion of the Civil War—was his courage to say that judgment is the other side of justice.

NEWSPAPERS NOTED that throughout the address the audience produced only sporadic applause. The reporter for the *New York Herald* noted one remarkable exception. About halfway through the address the large number of African-Americans in the audience began a sturdy "Bress de Lord" at the conclusion of more or less every sentence.[24]

Frederick Douglass, who had been indignantly disappointed in Lincoln's First Inaugural, was in the crowd to hear what Lincoln would say in his Second Inaugural. Douglass commented in his diary, "The whole proceeding was wonderfully quiet, earnest, and solemn." Douglass thought he understood why. "The address sounded more like a sermon than a state paper."[25]

> *With malice toward none; with charity for all; with firmness in the right, as God gives us to see the right, let us strive on to finish the work we are in; to bind up the nation's wounds; to care for him who shall have borne the battle, and for his widow, and his orphan—to do all which may achieve and cherish a just, and a lasting peace, among ourselves, and with all nations.*

The partisanship in Lincoln had been emptied out through the experiences of war. He must have wondered, as he moved quickly to his concluding paragraph, whether he could carry his audience and the American people with him beyond their partisanship toward a new spirit of reconciliation.

The *Washington National Intelligencer* would conclude its editorial about the address with acclaim for the words of the final paragraph. "They are equally distinguished for patriotism, statesmanship, and benevolence, and deserve to be printed in gold."[26]

In the final paragraph Lincoln picks up the inclusive language with which he began his address. Instead of "us" and "them," it is *us, we,* and *ourselves.*

> *as God gives us to see the right,*
> *let us strive on to finish the work we are in*
> *among ourselves, and with all nations*

At the beginning of the address Lincoln used inclusive language to underline a common responsibility for the origins of the war. In his conclusion he uses inclusive language to point forward to a reconciled nation. His hope was that the leaders of the nation would meet together in the coming four years under the new iron dome of the Capitol.

He concluded his Second Inaugural with an entreaty of reconciliation:

> *to bind up . . .*
> *to care for . . .*
> *to do all which may achieve and cherish a just, and a lasting peace, among ourselves, and with all nations*

Images of the lash and the sword are to be replaced with acts of healing and restoration.

If this was the sermon that Douglass claimed it to be, Lincoln's final imperative was a plea to live into the future in reconciliation.

AS LINCOLN COMPLETED his Second Inaugural Address, people were even now arriving at the east front of the Capitol. He had been speaking for barely six to seven minutes. The crowd applauded and Lincoln bowed low in recognition of their commendation.

Chief Justice Salmon P. Chase stepped forward. The clerk of the Supreme Court handed him a Bible. (George Washington had brought his own Bible to the first presidential inauguration.) Lincoln placed his right hand on the Bible, open to Isaiah 5. The chief justice invited Lincoln to swear upon the Bible. Lincoln repeated the presidential oath after the chief justice. Lincoln ended with an emphatic "So help me God." He bent down and kissed the Bible.[27]

Lincoln left the platform and went immediately to the basement entrance of the Capitol, where his plain two-horse barouche waited on him. Lincoln and his young son, Tad, were driven back to the White House. One thoughtful admirer, Walt Whitman, watched this scene and noted that the president "look'd very much worn and tired; the lines . . . cut deeper than ever upon his dark brown face." Whitman, as always, looked deeper, to see "yet all the old goodness, tenderness, sadness, and canny shrewdness, underneath the furrows."[28] Surrounding the carriage were numerous men with large yellow scarfs over their shoulders. Sharpshooters were still able to be seen from numerous buildings. John Wilkes Booth ambled back to the center of the capital.

LINCOLN WAS THE BEST commentator on Lincoln. Later on Inauguration Day, Thurlow Weed, New York Republican politician, wrote to Lincoln to commend him.[29] Lincoln answered Weed eleven days later, on March 15. "I expect the latter to wear as well—perhaps better than anything I have produced." Lincoln's evaluation achieves even greater force after we hear and examine the First Inaugural Address, messages to Congress, public letters, and the Gettysburg Address of the previous four years.[30]

Lincoln quickly added, "But I believe it is not immediately popular." Lincoln by then had read the diverse editorials and reviews in the newspapers.

Why was it not immediately popular? Lincoln offered his response. "Men are not flattered by being shown that there has been a difference of purpose between the Almighty and them." He continued, in the same spirit of his address, "To deny it, however, in this case, is to deny that there is a God governing the world." He concluded by telling Weed why he offered a Second Inaugural that both confounded and surprised all expectations. "It is a truth that I thought needed to be told."

EPILOGUE

BARELY A MONTH after Lincoln's second inauguration, on April 9, 1865, Lee surrendered to Grant at Appomattox Court House, in Virginia. Official news of the surrender reached Washington on April 10, setting off pandemonium throughout the capital. Secretary of War Stanton ordered the firing of hundreds of guns, shattering windows on Lafayette Square. Lincoln had breakfast at the White House with Noah Brooks, who everyone said would become his secretary in his second term, and continued his careful planning for reconstruction. That evening thousands marched to the White House, where they cheered the president and called for a speech. Even at this moment of high triumph Lincoln was true to form, excusing himself from speaking, but promising a formal speech the following evening.

The next evening, April 11, thousands came to the White House to hear the president. Lincoln addressed the throng from a second-story window, Brooks holding a candle behind him for illumination. This would be Lincoln's first and only speech in the new, postwar era of peace. He read the speech to avoid any missteps or misunderstandings. The largest part of the speech concerned his plans for a reconstruction government in Louisiana. He defended his policies against many critics, including members of his own Republican Party. The speech failed to catch fire. Lincoln was cautious, not wanting to play his hand too soon after the armistice of April 9. He was not ready to issue a proclamation for the reorganization of the Southern states. It was too early to talk about full political and economic rights for blacks. For many in the audience the speech was disappointing, too cautious and technical, whereas they hungered, again, for something more triumphal.

FOR MANY OTHER LISTENERS, however, the speech was too radical. In the middle of the speech one observer in the crowd heard Lincoln say, "*It is also unsatisfactory to some that the elective franchise is not given to the colored man.*" Lincoln then offered his own opinion: "*I would myself prefer that it were now conferred on the very intelligent, and on those who serve our cause as soldiers.*"[1]

"That means nigger citizenship," muttered the listener. John Wilkes Booth then swore, "That is the last speech he will ever make."[2]

And so it was. Lincoln was assassinated by Booth three nights later at Ford's Theatre. Lincoln died at 7:22 A.M. on Saturday, April 15.

His voice was stilled forever. But not his words.

"IT'S ONLY WORDS." It cannot be denied that the modern shibboleth "It's only words" has sometimes seemed to win the day. This portrait of Lincoln has turned on the axis that words matter.

In an era of speechwriters and ghostwriters, many have become cynical about both the speaker and the speech. This portrait has revealed how Lincoln's speeches are Lincoln's speeches.

Many today might complete the shibboleth by adding, ". . . as opposed to actions." In this account of Lincoln, words are actions. Abraham Lincoln and Winston Churchill led their nations through the great crises of the Civil War and World War II with words that galvanized the faltering courage of each nation.

Lincoln's words in his First Inaugural announced the actions the government would and would not take. He understood, in a way his early critics did not, that his Message to Congress in Special Session on July 4, 1861, was his opportunity to speak not only to Congress but to the American people about the course he intended to pursue now that Fort Sumter had been attacked. He held no press conferences, but he used his public letters to Horace Greeley and Albert G. Hodges in 1862 and 1864 to speak to critics as much as to supporters. He transformed the usually perfunctory annual messages to Congress, even when he knew they would be read by clerks, with conclusions that rise to some of his finest eloquence. When he declared in his annual message for 1862,

> *The fiery trial through which we pass, will light us down, in honor or dishonor, to the latest generation.*

he was writing for the future, and we still marvel at his words.

WHAT, FINALLY, IS ELOQUENCE? In the prologue we recounted three definitions by Aristotle and suggested that Lincoln, not having read the ancient philosopher, nevertheless embodied his principles of rhetoric. Lincoln understood that great speakers do not simply persuade people by their arguments, although he spent a great deal of the capital of his First Inaugural trying to do so. Lincoln's later speeches, especially the speech to the Springfield rally (his letter to Conkling) and the Second Inaugural, represent his greater willingness to use emotion to touch the deepest sentiments of his audience. In the end, Lincoln's eloquence, although it can be described by his deft use of parallel structures, alliteration, and imaginative imagery, is rooted in one compelling reality. People came to trust Lincoln's judgment because, in Aristotle's words, "Persuasion is achieved by means of moral character, when the speech shall have been spoken in such a way as to render the speaker worthy of confidence."[3]

WHATEVER HAPPENED TO ELOQUENCE? Do twenty-first-century Americans not really care about rhetoric? Is rhetoric an old-fashioned word that looks backward to an earlier age? Today's politicians are often attached to a teleprompter, reading a speech instead of speaking a speech. It sometimes feels that we live in a tone-deaf culture. We no longer expect our presidents to be eloquent speakers. We may wish for eloquence but do not trust, in Aristotle's terms, the integrity of the persuasion.

Today, presidents and presidential candidates do quote scripture. The propriety of the use of the Bible and religion in public speech is the subject of vigorous debate. I believe Lincoln would welcome that debate. He spoke a great deal about the misuse of the Bible. His use of the Bible was always informed and inclusive.

THERE IS ONE LAST piece in the puzzle. Why do Lincoln's words still resonate today? In the midst of marvelous modern memorials dedicated both to great leaders and to the heroes and victims of the wars of the twentieth century, why do so many of the world's citizens still climb the steps of the Lincoln Memorial to ponder the Daniel Chester French statue of Lincoln and read the words of the Gettysburg Address and the Second Inaugural? Why does Lincoln continue to enjoy such modern access to people of all walks of life in all nations?

Lincoln's eloquence may prove to be his most lasting legacy. As we take time to ponder Lincoln's words, he becomes strangely contemporary. He is the representative American who is able to paint our highest ideals in word pictures. At the beginning of the twenty-first century his words continue to cross all boundaries of time and location.

The Lincoln that is accessible to us offers his own struggle for reconciliation at the end of his life. His winsome words remind us of the presence of an absence in contemporary political discourse. A man of his time, he encourages us to define America in our time.

APPENDICES

Abraham Lincoln's eloquence is best appreciated when we hear and read the complete texts of his speeches, messages to Congress, and public letters. In five of the chapters, excerpts from longer texts are analyzed—the speeches and remarks on the train trip from Springfield to Washington (chapter 2), the Message to Congress in Special Session (chapter 4), the Annual Message to Congress in 1862 (chapter 7), the letter to the Springfield rally (chapter 8), and the letter to Albert G. Hodges (chapter 10)—but the full text for each is provided in the following appendices. In addition, the appendices provide multiple versions of the Farewell Address at Springfield, the First Inaugural Address, the letter to the Springfield rally, the Gettysburg Address, and the Second Inaugural Address. The multiple versions allow us to see Lincoln as a reviser and editor at work. They are also windows, on two occasions, into suggestions he received from William H. Seward and how he accepted or rejected his counsel.

The staff of the Papers of Abraham Lincoln project at Springfield, Illinois, prepared the transcriptions, with the exception of Appendices 2 and 7. The transcription symbols listed below are employed to indicate changes to the texts, questions, or clarifications.

TRANSCRIPTION SYMBOLS

[...]	unrecoverable text
[~~...~~]	unrecoverable stricken text
^	indicates interlinear or marginal insertion of text
∀	indicates insertion of text from a separate sheet of paper
[roman?]	conjectural transcription of text
[*italics*]	editorial insertion, for clarity, of a word that does not appear in the original text

APPENDIX 1

FAREWELL ADDRESS AT SPRINGFIELD

FEBRUARY 11, 1861

After delivering his farewell remarks at the Great Western station in Springfield and boarding the train for Washington, Lincoln sat down to write out his words from memory. Having to contend with a moving train, he handed the paper to his secretary, John G. Nicolay, at the beginning of the fifth sentence and dictated the remaining words.

The second version is a transcription of the speech printed the next day in the *Illinois State Journal* of Springfield. This version does not have the same rhythmic qualities of the first version. There is a long-running debate about the reasons for the differences in the two texts. Is it because a reporter, not expecting a speech, hurriedly wrote down the sense of the speech but failed to capture the exact wording? Or is it because Lincoln, writing on the train, smoothed out the rough places in his extemporaneous remarks?

The third version is a transcription of the address published in *Harper's Weekly* on February 23, 1861.

Version 1

My friends.

No one, not in my situation, can appreciate my feeling of sadness at this parting. To this place, and the kindness of these people, I owe every thing. Here I have been a quarter of a century, and have passed from a young to an old man. Here my children have been born, and one is buried. I now [leave not?][1] leave, not knowing when, or whether ever, I may return, with a task before me greater than that which rested upon Washington. Without the assistance of that Divine Being, ~~which~~ ^who^ ever attended him, I cannot succeed. With that assistance I cannot fail. Trusting in Him, who can go with me, and remain with you and be every where for good, let us confidently hope that all will yet be well. To His care [~~...~~] commending you, as I hope in your prayers you will commend me, I bid you an affectionate farewell

---

1. Nicolay wrote the remainder of the document, except as noted.

Version 2

Friends, no one who has never been placed in a like position, can understand my feelings at this hour, nor the oppressive sadness I feel at this parting. For more than a quarter of a century I have lived among you, and during all that time I have received nothing but kindness at your hands. Here I have lived from my youth until now I am an old man. Here the most sacred ties of earth were assumed; here all my children were born; and here one of them lies buried. To you, dear friends, I owe all that I have, all that I am. All the strange, chequered past seems to crowd now upon my mind. Today I leave you; I go to assume a task more difficult than that which devolved upon General Washington. Unless the great God who assisted him, shall be with and aid me, I must fail. But if the same omniscient mind, and the same Almighty arm that directed and protected him, shall guide and support me, I shall not fail, I shall succeed. Let us all pray that the God of our fathers may not forsake us now. To him I commend you all—permit me to ask that with equal security[2] and faith, you all will invoke His wisdom and guidance for me. With these few words I must leave you—for how long I know not. Friends, one and all, I must now bid you an affectionate farewell.

Version 3

My Friends,— No one not in my position can appreciate the sadness I feel at this parting. To this people I owe all that I am. Here I have lived more than a quarter of a century, here my children were born, and here one of them lies buried. I know not how soon I shall see you again. A duty devolves upon me which is, perhaps, greater than that which has devolved upon any other man since the days of Washington. He never would have succeeded except for the aid of Divine Providence, upon which he at all times relied. I feel that I can not succeed without the same Divine aid which sustained him; and in the same Almighty Being I place my reliance for support, and I hope you, my friends, will all pray that I may receive that Divine assistance, without which I can not succeed, but with which success is certain. Again I bid you all an affectionate farewell.

---

2. In the newspaper held by the Abraham Lincoln Presidential Library and Museum, "security" is stricken and "sinserity" is handwritten in the column to the right.

APPENDIX 2

SPEECHES AND REMARKS
TRAIN TRIP FROM SPRINGFIELD TO WASHINGTON
FEBRUARY 11–23, 1861

Lincoln's speeches, remarks, and responses on the train trip from Springfield to Washington from February 11 to February 23, 1861, have often been overlooked or undervalued. Before leaving Springfield he had decided to wait until he arrived in Washington to say anything definitive about his policies and plans, yet his speeches and responses reveal glimpses of his ideas. They are sometimes rough antecedents of his polished First Inaugural Address of March 4, 1861. At the same time he struggled with the burden of delivering many extemporaneous speeches and remarks as well as responding to the unpredictable remarks of political hosts in the various cities and towns along the way.

The texts of the speeches from Springfield to Washington are from *The Collected Works of Abraham Lincoln.* Editor Roy P. Basler and his colleagues published a text for each address; in some cases, the text was collated from more than one newspaper version. The major newspapers relied upon for the text, along with variants from other newspapers, are indicated in footnotes.

Speech from the Balcony of the Bates House at Indianapolis, Indiana[1] *February 11, 1861*

It is not possible, in my journey to the national capital, to address assemblies like this which may do me the great honor to meet me as you have done, but very briefly. I should be entirely worn out if I were to attempt it. I appear before you now to thank you for this very magnificent welcome which you have given me, and still more for the very generous support which your State recently gave to the political cause of the whole country, and the whole world. [Applause.] Solomon has said, that there is a time to keep silence. [Renewed and deafening applause.] *********** We know certain that they

1. *Indianapolis Daily Sentinel,* February 12, 1861.

mean the same thing while using the same words now, and it perhaps would be as well if they would keep silence.

The words "coercion" and "invasion" are in great use about these days. Suppose we were simply to try if we can, and ascertain what, is the meaning of these words. Let us get, if we can, the exact definitions of these words—not from the dictionaries, but from the men who constantly repeat them—what things they mean to express by the words. What, then, is "coercion"? What is "invasion"? Would the marching of an army into South Carolina, for instance, without the consent of her people, and in hostility against them, be coercion or invasion? I very frankly say, I think it would be invasion, and it would be coercion too, if the people of that country were forced to submit. But if the Government, for instance, but simply insists upon holding its own forts, or retaking those forts which belong to it,—[cheers,]—or the enforcement of the laws of the United States in the collection of duties upon foreign importations,—[renewed cheers]—or even the withdrawal of the mails from those portions of the country where the mails themselves are habitually violated; would any or all of these things be coercion? Do the lovers of the Union contend that they will resist coercion or invasion of any State, understanding that any or all of these would be coercing or invading a State? If they do, then it occurs to me that the means for the preservation of the Union they so greatly love, in their own estimation, is of a very thin and airy character. [Applause.] If sick, they would consider the little pills of the homeopathist as already too large for them to swallow. In their view, the Union, as a family relation, would not be anything like a regular marriage at all, but only as a sort of free-love arrangement,—[laughter,]—to be maintained on what that sect calls passionate attraction. [Continued laughter.] But, my friends, enough of this.

What is the particular sacredness of a State? I speak not of that position which is given to a State in and by the Constitution of the United States, for that all of us agree to—we abide by; but that position assumed, that a State can carry with it out of the Union that which it holds in sacredness by virtue of its connection with the Union. I am speaking of that assumed right of a State, as a primary principle, that the Constitution should rule all that is less than itself, and ruin all that is bigger than itself. [Laughter.] But, I ask, wherein does consist that right? If a State, in one instance, and a country in another, should be equal in extent of territory, and equal in the number of people, wherein is that State any better than the country? Can a change of name change the right? By what principle of original right is it that one-fiftieth or one-nineteenth of a great nation, by calling themselves a State, have the right to break up and ruin that nation as a matter of original principle? Now, I ask the question—I am not deciding anything—[laughter.]—and with the request that you will think somewhat upon that subject and decide for yourselves, if you choose, when you get ready,—where is the mysterious, original right, from principle, for a certain district of country with inhabitants, by merely being called a State, to play tyrant over all its own citizens, and deny the authority of everything greater than itself. [Laughter.] I say I am deciding nothing, but simply giving something for you to reflect upon; and, with having said this much, and having declared, in the start, that I will make no long speeches, I thank you again for this magnificent welcome, and bid you an affectionate farewell. [Cheers.]

Speech at Cincinnati, Ohio[1]
February 12, 1861

Mr. Mayor, ladies and gentlemen: Twenty-four hours ago, at the Capital of Indiana, I said to myself I have never seen so many people assembled together in winter weather. I am no longer able to say that. But it is what might reasonably have been expected—that this great city of Cincinnati would thus acquit herself on such an occasion. My friends, I am entirely overwhelmed by the magnificence of the reception which has been given, I will not say to me, but to the President elect of the United States of America. [Loud cheering.] Most heartily do I thank you, one and all for it. [Applause.]

I am reminded by the address of your worthy Mayor, that this reception is given not by any one political party, and even if I had not been so reminded by His Honor I could not have failed to know the fact by the extent of the multitude I see before me now. I could not look upon this vast assemblage without being made aware that all parties were united in this reception. [Applause.] This is as it should be. It is as it should have been if Senator Douglas had been elected. It is as it should have been if Mr. Bell had been elected—as it should have been if Mr. Breckinridge had been elected—as it should ever be when any citizen of the United States is constitutionally elected President of the United States. [Great applause.] Allow me to say that I think what has occurred here to-day could not have occurred in any other country on the face of the globe, without the influence of the free institutions which we have unceasingly enjoyed for three-quarters of a century. [Applause.] There is no country where the people can turn out and enjoy this day precisely as they please, save under the benign influence of the free institutions of our land. [Applause.]

I hope that, although we have some threatening National difficulties

1. *Cincinnati Daily Gazette,* February 13, 1866.

now—I hope that while these free institutions shall continue to be in the enjoyment of millions of free people of the United States, we will see repeated every four years what we now witness. [Applause.]

In a few short years, I and every other individual man who is now living will pass away. I hope that our national difficulties will also pass away, and I hope we shall see in the streets of Cincinnati—good old Cincinnati—for centuries to come, once every four years her people give such a reception as this to the constitutionally elected President of the whole United States. [Applause.] I hope you shall all join in that reception, and that you shall also welcome your brethren far across the river to participate in it. We will welcome them in every State of the Union, no matter where they are from. From away South we shall extend them a cordial good will when our present differences shall have been forgotten and blown to the winds forever. [Applause.]

I have spoken but once, before this, in Cincinnati. That was a year previous to the late Presidential election. On that occasion, in a playful manner, but with sincere words, I addressed much of what I said, to the Kentuckians. I gave my opinion that we, as Republicans, would ultimately beat them as democrats; but that they could postpone that result longer by nominating Senator Douglas for the Presidency than they could in any other way. They did not, in any true sense of the word, nominate Douglas, and the result has come certainly as soon as even I expected. I also told them how I expected they would be treated, after they should have been beaten; and I now wish to re-call their attention to what I then said upon that subject. I then said: "When we do, as we say, beat you, you perhaps want to know what we will do with you. I will tell you, so far as I am authorized to speak for the opposition, what we mean to do with you. We mean to treat you, as near as we possibly can, as Washington, Jefferson, and Madison treated you. We mean to leave you alone, and in no way to interfere with your institution; to abide by all and every compromise of the constitution, and, in a word, coming back to the original proposition, to treat you, so far as degenerated men (if we have degenerated) may, according to the examples of those noble fathers—Washington, Jefferson and Madison. We mean to remember that you are as good as we; that there is no difference between us, other than the difference of circumstances. We mean to recognize, and bear in mind always, that you have as good hearts in your bosoms as other people, or as we claim to have, and treat you accordingly."

Fellow citizens of Kentucky—friends—brethren, may I call you—in my new position, I see no occasion, and feel no inclination, to retract a word of this. [Applause.] If it shall not be made good, be assured, the fault shall not be mine. [Applause.]

And now, fellow citizens of Ohio, have you, who agree with him who now addresses you, in political sentiment—have you ever entertained other sentiments towards our brethren of Kentucky than those I have expressed to you. [Loud and continued cries of "No."] If not, then why shall we not, as heretofore, be recognized and acknowledged as brethren again, living in peace and harmony one with another? [Cries of "We will."] I take your response as the most reliable evidence that it may be so, along with other evidence, trusting that the good sense of the American people, on all sides of all rivers in America, under the Providence of God, who has never deserted us, that we shall again be brethren, forgetting all parties—ignoring all parties. My friends I now bid you farewell. [Long continued applause.]

Address to the Ohio Legislature, Columbus[1]
February 13, 1861

MR. PRESIDENT AND MR. SPEAKER AND GENTLEMEN OF THE GENERAL ASSEMBLY:— It is true, as has been said by the President of the Senate, that very great responsibility rests upon me in the position to which the votes of the American people have called me. I am deeply sensible of that weighty responsibility. I cannot but know what you all know, that, without a name, perhaps without a reason why I should have a name, there has fallen upon me a task such as did not rest even upon the Father of his country, and so feeling I cannot but turn and look for the support without which it will be impossible for me to perform that great task. I turn, then, and look to the American people and to that God who has never forsaken them. Allusion has been made to the interest felt in relation to the policy of the new administration. In this I have received from some a degree of credit for having kept silence, and from others some deprecation. I still think that I was right. In the varying and repeatedly shifting scenes of the present, and without a precedent which could enable me to judge by the past, it has seemed fitting that before speaking upon the difficulties of the country, I should have gained a view of the whole field, to be sure, after all, being at liberty to modify and change the course of policy, as future events may make a change necessary. I have not maintained silence from any want of real anxiety. It is a good thing that there is no more than anxiety, for there is nothing going wrong. It is a consoling circumstance that when we look out there is nothing that really hurts anybody. We entertain different views upon political questions, but nobody is suffering anything. This is a most consoling circumstance, and from it we may conclude that all we want is time, patience and a reliance on that God who has never forsaken this people. Fellow citi-

1. *New York Herald,* February 14, 1861.

zens, what I have said, I have said altogether extemporaneously, and I will now come to a close.

Speech from the Steps of the Capitol at Columbus, Ohio[1]
February 13, 1861

LADIES AND GENTLEMEN:— I appear before you only to address you briefly. I shall do little else than to thank you for this very kind reception, to greet you and bid you farewell. I should not find strength, if I were otherwise inclined, to repeat speeches of very great length, upon every occasion similar to this—although few so large—which will occur on my way to the Federal Capitol. The General Assembly of the great State of Ohio has just done me the honor to receive me, and to hear a few broken remarks from myself. Judging from what I see, I infer that that reception was one without party distinction, and one of entire kindness—one that had nothing in it beyond a feeling of the citizenship of the United States of America. Knowing, as I do, that any crowd, drawn together as this has been, is made up of the citizens near about, and that in this country of Franklin there is great difference of political sentiment, and those agreeing with me having a little the shortest row, [laughter,] from this, and the circumstances I have mentioned, I infer that you do me the honor to meet me here without distinction of party. I think this is as it should be. Many of you who were not favorable to the election of myself to the Presidency were favorable to the election of the distinguished Senator from the State in which I reside. If Senator Douglas had been elected to the Presidency in the late contest, I think my friends would have joined heartily in meeting and greeting him on his passage through your Capital, as you have me to-day. If any of the other candidates had been elected, I think it would have been altogether becoming and proper for all to have joined in showing honor, quite as well to the office, and the country, as to the man. The people are themselves honored by such a concentration. I am doubly thankful that you have appeared here to give me this greeting. It is not much to me, for I shall very soon pass away from you; but we have a large country and a large future before us, and the manifestations of good-will towards the government, and affection for the Union which you may exhibit are of immense value to you and your posterity forever. [Applause.] In this point of view it is that I thank you most heartily for the exhibition you have given me, and with this allow me to bid you an affectionate farewell. [Deafening applause and cheers.]

1. *The Crisis* (Columbus), February 21, 1861.

Speech at Steubenville, Ohio[1]
February 14, 1861

Mr. Chairman and Fellow-Citizens:— The subject of the short address which has been made to me, though not an unfamiliar one, involves so many points, that in the short time allotted to me, I shall not be able to make a full and proper response. Though the people have made me by electing me, the instrument to carry out the wishes expressed in the address, I greatly fear that I shall not be the repository of the ability to do so. Indeed I know I shall not, more than in purpose, unless sustained by the great body of the people, and by the Divine Power, without whose aid we can do nothing. We everywhere express devotion to the Constitution. I believe there is no difference in this respect, whether on this or on the other side of this majestic stream. I understand that on the other side, among our dissatisfied brethren, they are satisfied with the Constitution of the United States, if they can have their rights under the Constitution. The question is, as to what the Constitution means—"What are their rights under the Constitution?" That is all. To decide that, who shall be the judge? Can you think of any other, than the voice of the people? If the majority does not control, the minority must—would that be right? Would that be just or generous? Assuredly not! Though the majority may be wrong, and I will not undertake to say that they were not wrong in electing me, yet we must adhere to the principle that the majority shall rule. By your Constitution you have another chance in four years. No great harm can be done by us in that time—in that time there can be nobody hurt. If anything goes wrong, however, and you find you have made a mistake, elect a better man next time. There are plenty of them.

[Here the engine whistled.] These points involve the discussion of many questions which I have not time to consider. I merely give them to you for your reflection. I almost regret that I alluded to it at all.

Ladies, gentlemen and friends, I thank you for this kind and overwhelming reception, and bid you farewell.

Speech at Pittsburgh, Pennsylvania[1]
February 15, 1861

Mayor Wilson and Citizens of Pennsylvania: I most cordially thank his Honor Mayor Wilson, and the citizens of Pittsburg generally for this flatter-

1. *The American Union* (Steubenville), February 20, 1861.
1. *Pittsburgh Dispatch,* February 16, 1861. In some places the *New York Tribune* version is provided in a footnote.

ing reception. It is[2] the more grateful, because I know that, while it is not given to me alone, but to the cause which I represent, yet it is given under circumstances which clearly prove to me that there is good will and sincere feeling at the bottom of it.

And here, fellow citizens, I may remark that in every short address I have made to the people, and in every crowd through which I have passed of late, some allusion has been made to the present distracted condition of the country. It is naturally expected that I should say something upon this subject, but to touch upon it all would involve an elaborate discussion of a great many questions and circumstances, would require more time than I can at present command, and would perhaps unnecessarily commit me upon matters which have not yet fully developed themselves. [Immense cheering, and cries of "Good!" "That's right!"]

The condition of the country, fellow-citizens, is an extraordinary one, and fills the mind of every patriot with anxiety and solicitude. My intention is to give this subject all the consideration which I possibly can before I speak fully and definitely in regard to it—so that, when I do speak, I may be as nearly right as possible. And when I do speak, fellow-citizens, I hope to say nothing in opposition to the spirit of the Constitution, contrary to the integrity of the Union, or which will in any way prove inimical to the liberties of the people or to the peace of the whole country. And, furthermore, when the time arrives for me to speak on this great subject, I hope to say nothing which will disappoint the reasonable expectations of any man, or disappoint the people generally throughout the country, especially if their expectations have been based upon anything which I may have heretofore said.

Notwithstanding the troubles across the river, [the speaker pointing southwardly, and smiling] there is really no crisis, springing from anything in the government itself. In plain words, there is really no crisis except an *artificial one*! What is there now to warrant the condition of affairs presented by our friends "over the river"? Take even their own view of the questions involved, and there is nothing to justify the course which they are pursuing. I repeat it, then—*there is no crisis,* excepting such a one as may be gotten up at any time by designing politicians.[3] My advice, then, under such circumstances, is to keep cool. If the great American people will only keep their temper, on both sides of the line, the troubles will come to an end, and the question which now distracts the country will be settled just as surely as all other difficulties of like character which have originated in this government

2. The *New York Tribune* version reads "I am," probably correctly.
3. The *New York Tribune* version reads, "by turbulent men, aided by designing politicians."

have been adjusted. Let the people on both sides keep their self-possession, and just as other clouds have cleared away in due time, so will this, and this great nation shall continue to prosper as heretofore. But, fellow citizens, I have spoken longer on this subject than I had intended in the outset—and I shall say no more at present.

Fellow citizens, as this is the first opportunity which I have had to address a Pennsylvania assemblage, it seems a fitting time to indulge in a few remarks upon the important question of a tariff—a subject of great magnitude, and one which is attended with many difficulties, owing to the great variety of interests which it involves. So long as direct taxation for the support of government is not resorted to, a tariff is necessary. The tariff is to the government what a meal is to the family; but, while this is admitted, it still becomes necessary to modify and change its operations according to new interests and new circumstances. So far there is little difference of opinion among politicians, but the question as to how far imposts may be adjusted for the protection of home industry, gives rise to various views and objections. I must confess that I do not understand this subject in all its multiform bearings, but I promise you that I will give it my closest attention, and endeavor to comprehend it more fully. And here I may remark that the Chicago platform contains a plank upon this subject, which I think should be regarded as law for the incoming administration. In fact, this question, as well as all other subjects embodied in that platform, should not be varied from what we gave the people to understand would be our policy when we obtained their votes. Permit me, fellow citizens, to read the tariff plank of the Chicago platform, or rather, to have it read in your hearing by one who has younger eyes than I have.

[Mr. Lincoln's private Secretary then read section twelfth of the Chicago platform, as follows:]

That, while providing revenue for the support of the General Government by duties upon imposts, sound policy requires such an adjustment of the imposts as to encourage the development of the industrial interest of the whole country, and we commend that policy of national exchanges which secures to the working men liberal wages, to agriculture remunerating prices, to mechanics and manufacturers an adequate reward for their skill, labor and enterprise, and to the nation commercial prosperity and independence.

[Mr. Lincoln continued—] Now, fellow-citizens, I must confess that there are shades of difference in construing even this plank of the platform. But I am not now intending to discuss these differences, but merely to give you some general ideas upon this subject. I have long thought that if there be any article of necessity which can be produced at home with as little or nearly the same labor as abroad, it would be better to protect that article. Labor is the true standard of value. If a bar of iron, got out of the mines of England, and a bar of iron taken from the mines of Pennsylvania, be produced at the same cost, it follows that if the English bar be shipped from Manchester to Pittsburg, and the American bar from Pittsburg to Manchester, the cost of carriage is appreciably lost. [Laughter.] If we had no iron here, then we should encourage its shipment from foreign countries; but not when we can make it as cheaply in our own country. This brings us back to our first proposition, that if any article can be produced at home with nearly the same cost as abroad, the carriage is lost labor.

The treasury of the nation is in such a low condition at present that this subject now demands the attention of Congress, and will demand the immediate consideration of the new Administration. The tariff bill now before Congress may or may not pass at the present session. I confess I do not understand the precise provisions of this bill, and I do not know whether it can be passed by the present Congress or not. It may or may not become the law of the land—but if it does, that will be an end of the matter until a modification can be effected, should it be deemed necessary. If it does not pass (and the latest advices I have are to the effect that it is still pending) the next Congress will have to give it their earliest attention.

According to my political education, I am inclined to believe that the people in the various sections of the country should have their own views carried out through their representatives in Congress, and if the consideration of the Tariff bill should be postponed until the next session of the National Legislature, no subject should engage your representatives more closely than that of a tariff. And if I have any recommendation to make, it will be that every man who is called upon to serve the people in a representative capacity, should study this whole subject thoroughly, as I intend to do myself, looking to all the varied interests of our common country, so that when the time for action arrives adequate protection can be extended to the coal and iron of Pennsylvania, the corn of Illinois, and the "reapers of Chicago." Permit me to express the hope that this important subject may receive such consideration at the hands of your representatives, that the interests of no part of the country may be overlooked, but that all sections may share in common the benefits of a just and equitable tariff. [Applause.]

But I am trespassing upon your patience—[cries of "no!" "no!" "Go on—we'll listen!"] and must bring my remarks to a close. Thanking you most cordially for the kind reception which you have extended me, I bid you all adieu. [Enthusiastic applause.]

Speech at Cleveland, Ohio[1]
February 15, 1861

MR. CHAIRMAN AND FELLOW CITIZENS OF CLEVELAND:— We have been marching about two miles through snow, rain and deep mud. The large numbers that have turned out under these circumstances testify that you are in earnest about something or other. But do I think so meanly of you as to suppose that that earnestness is about me personally? I would be doing you injustice to suppose you did. You have assembled to testify your respect to the Union, the constitution and the laws, and here let me say that it is with you, the people, to advance the great cause of the Union and the constitution, and not with any one man. It rests with you alone. This fact is strongly impressed on my mind at present. In a community like this, whose appearance testifies to their intelligence, I am convinced that the cause of liberty and the Union can never be in danger. Frequent allusion is made to the excitement at present existing in our national politics, and it is as well that I should also allude to it here. I think that there is no occasion for any excitement. The crisis, as it is called, is altogether an artificial crisis. In all parts of the nation there are differences of opinion and politics. There are differences of opinion even here. You did not all vote for the person who now addresses you. What is happening now will not hurt those who are farther away from here. Have they not all their rights now as they ever have had? Do they not have their fugitive slaves returned now as ever? Have they not the same constitution that they have lived under for seventy odd years? Have they not a position as citizens of this common country, and have we any power to change that position? [Cries of "No."] What then is the matter with them? Why all this excitement? Why all these complaints? As I said before, this crisis is all artificial. It has no foundation in facts. It was not argued up, as the saying is, and cannot, therefore, be argued down. Let it alone and it will go down of itself [Laughter]. Mr. Lincoln said they must be content with but a few words from him. He was very much fatigued, and had spoken so frequently that he was already hoarse. He thanked them for the cordial and magnificent reception they had given him. Not less did he thank them for the votes they gave him last fall, and quite as much he thanked them for the efficient aid they had given the cause which he represented—a cause which he would say was a good one. He had one more word to say. He was given to understand that this reception was not tendered by his own party supporters, but by men of all parties. This is as it should be. If Judge Douglas had been elected and had

---

1. *New York Herald,* February 16, 1861.

been here on his way to Washington, as I am to-night, the republicans should have joined his supporters in welcoming him, just as his friends have joined with mine to-night. If all do not join now to save the good old ship of the Union this voyage nobody will have a chance to pilot her on another voyage. He concluded by thanking all present for the devotion they have shown to the cause of the Union.

Speech at Buffalo, New York[1]
February 16, 1861

Mr. Mayor, and Fellow Citizens of Buffalo and the State of New York:— I am here to thank you briefly for this grand reception given to me, not personally, but as the representative of our great and beloved country. [Cheers.] Your worthy Mayor has been pleased to mention in his address to me, the fortunate and agreeable journey which I have had from home, on my rather circuitous route to the Federal Capital. I am very happy that he was enabled in truth to congratulate myself and companions [company] on that fact. It is true we have had nothing, thus far, to mar the pleasure of the trip. We have not been met alone by those who assisted in giving the election to me—I say not alone—but by the whole population of the country through which we have passed. This is as it should be.

Had the election fallen to any other of the distinguished candidates instead of myself, under the peculiar circumstances, to say the least, it would have been proper for all citizens to have greeted him as you now greet me. It is evidence of the devotion of the whole people to the Constitution, the Union, and the perpetuity of the liberties of this country. [Cheers.] I am unwilling, on any occasion, that I should be so meanly thought of, as to have it supposed for a moment that I regard these demonstrations as tendered to me personally. They should be tendered to no individual man. They are tendered to the country, to the institutions of the country, and to the perpetuity of the [liberties of the] country for which these institutions were made and created.

Your worthy Mayor has thought fit to express the hope that I may be able to relieve the country from its present—or I should say, its threatened difficulties. I am sure I bring a heart true to the work. [Tremendous applause.] For the ability to perform it, I must trust in that Supreme Being who has never forsaken this favored land, through the instrumentality of this

---

1. *Buffalo Morning Express,* February 18, 1861; *New York Herald,* February 17, 1861. The *Express* and *Herald* versions are basically the same. A few variants from the *Herald* are indicated in brackets.

great and intelligent people. Without that assistance I shall surely fail. With it I cannot fail.

When we speak of threatened difficulties to the country, it is natural that there should be expected from me something with regard to particular measures. Upon more mature reflection, however, others will agree with me that when it is considered that these difficulties are without precedent, and have never been acted upon by any individual situated as I am, it is most proper I should wait, see the developments, and get all the light I can, so that when I do speak authoritatively I may be as near right as possible. [Cheers.] When I shall speak authoritatively, I hope to say nothing inconsistent with the Constitution, the Union, the rights of all the States, of each State, and of each section of the country, and not to disappoint the reasonable expectations of those who have confided to me their votes.

In this connection allow me to say that you, as a portion of the great American people, need only to maintain your composure. Stand up to your sober convictions of right, to your obligations to the Constitution, act in accordance with those sober convictions, and the clouds which now arise in the horizon will be dispelled, and we shall have a bright and glorious future; and when this generation has passed away, tens of thousands will inhabit this country where only thousands inhabit [it] now.

I do not propose to address you at length—I have no voice for it. Allow me again to thank you for this magnificent reception, and bid you farewell.

Speech at the Astor House, New York City[1]
February 19, 1861

Mr. CHAIRMAN AND GENTLEMEN:— I am rather an old man to avail myself of such an excuse as I am now about to do, yet the truth is so distinct and presses itself so distinctly upon me that I cannot well avoid it, and that is that I did not understand when I was brought into this room that I was brought here to make a speech. It was not intimated to me that I was brought into the room where Daniel Webster and Henry Clay had made speeches, and where one in my position might be expected to do something like those men, or do something unworthy of myself or my audience. I therefore will beg you to make very great allowance for the circumstances under which I have been by surprise brought before you. Now, I have been in the habit of thinking and speaking for some time upon political questions that have for some years past

1. *New York Herald,* February 20, 1861.

agitated the country, and if I were disposed to do so, and we could take up some one of the issues as the lawyers call them, and I were called upon to make an argument about it to the best of my ability, I could do that without much preparation. But that is not what you desire to be done here to-night. I have been occupying a position, since the Presidential election, of silence, of avoiding public speaking, of avoiding public writing. I have been doing so because I thought, upon full consideration, that was the proper course for me to take. [Great applause.] I am brought before you now and required to make a speech, when you all approve, more than anything else, of the fact that I have been silent—[loud laughter, cries of "Good—good," and applause]—and now it seems to me from the response you give to that remark it ought to justify me in closing just here. [Great laughter.] I have not kept silent since the Presidential election from any party wantonness, or from any indifference to the anxiety that pervades the minds of men about the aspect of the political affairs of this country. I have kept silence for the reason that I supposed it was peculiarly proper that I should do so until the time came when, according to the customs of the country, I should speak officially. [Voice, partially interrogative, partially sarcastic, "Custom of the country?"] I heard some gentleman say, "According to the custom of the country"; I alluded to the custom of the President elect at the time of taking his oath of office. That is what I meant by the custom of the country. I do suppose that while the political drama being enacted in this country at this time is rapidly shifting in its scenes, forbidding an anticipation with any degree of certainty to-day what we shall see to-morrow, that it was peculiarly fitting that I should see it all up to the last minute before I should take ground, that I might be disposed by the shifting of the scenes afterwards again to shift. [Applause.] I said several times upon this journey, and I now repeat it to you, that when the time does come I shall then take the ground that I think is right—[interruption by cries of "Good," "good," and applause]—the ground I think is right for the North, for the South, for the East, for the West, for the whole country—[cries of "Good," "Hurrah for Lincoln," and great applause]. And in doing so I hope to feel no necessity pressing upon me to say anything in conflict with the constitution, in conflict with the continued union of these States—[applause]—in conflict with the perpetuation of the liberties of these people—[cheers]—or anything in conflict with anything whatever that I have ever given you reason to expect from me. [Loud cheers.] And now, my friends, have I said enough. [Cries of "No, no," "Go on," &c.] Now, my friends, there appears to be a difference of opinion between you and me, and I feel called upon to insist upon deciding the question myself. [Enthusiastic cheers.]

Address to the New Jersey Senate at Trenton, New Jersey[1]
February 21, 1861

MR. PRESIDENT AND GENTLEMEN OF THE SENATE OF THE STATE OF NEW-JERSEY: I am very grateful to you for the honorable reception of which I have been the object. I cannot but remember the place that New-Jersey holds in our early history. In the early Revolutionary struggle, few of the States among the old Thirteen had more of the battle-fields of the country within their limits than old New-Jersey. May I be pardoned if, upon this occasion, I mention that away back in my childhood, the earliest days of my being able to read, I got hold of a small book, such a one as few of the younger members have ever seen, "Weem's Life of Washington." I remember all the accounts there given of the battle fields and struggles for the liberties of the country, and none fixed themselves upon my imagination so deeply as the struggle here at Trenton, New-Jersey. The crossing of the river; the contest with the Hessians; the great hardships endured at that time, all fixed themselves on my memory more than any single revolutionary event; and you all know, for you have all been boys, how these early impressions last longer than any others. I recollect thinking then, boy even though I was, that there must have been something more than common that those men struggled for. I am exceedingly anxious that that thing which they struggled for; that something even more than National Independence; that something that held out a great promise to all the people of the world to all time to come; I am exceedingly anxious that this Union, the Constitution, and the liberties of the people shall be perpetuated in accordance with the original idea for which that struggle was made, and I shall be most happy indeed if I shall be an humble instrument in the hands of the Almighty, and of this, his almost chosen people, for perpetuating the object of that great struggle. You give me this reception, as I understand, without distinction of party. I learn that this body is composed of a majority of gentlemen who, in the exercise of their best judgment in the choice of a Chief Magistrate, did not think I was the man. I understand, nevertheless, that they came forward here to greet me as the constitutional President of the United States—as citizens of the United States, to meet the man who, for the time being, is the representative man of the nation, united by a purpose to perpetuate the Union and liberties of the people. As such, I accept this reception more gratefully than I could do did I believe it was tendered to me as an individual.

---

1. *New York Tribune*, February 22, 1861.

Speech in Independence Hall, Philadelphia, Pennsylvania[1] *February 22, 1861*

Mr. CUYLER:— I am filled with deep emotion at finding myself standing here in the place where were collected together the wisdom, the patriotism, the devotion to principle, from which sprang the institutions under which we live. You have kindly suggested to me that in my hands is the task of restoring peace to our distracted country. I can say in return, sir, that all the political sentiments I entertain have been drawn, so far as I have been able to draw them, from the sentiments which originated, and were given to the world from this hall in which we stand. I have never had a feeling politically that did not spring from the sentiments embodied in the Declaration of Independence. [Great cheering.] I have often pondered over the dangers which were incurred by the men who assembled here and adopted[2] that Declaration of Independence—I have pondered over the toils that were endured by the officers and soldiers of the army, who achieved that Independence. [Applause.] I have often inquired of myself, what great principle or idea it was that kept this Confederacy so long together. It was not the mere matter of the separation of the colonies from the mother land; but something in that Declaration giving liberty,[3] not alone to the people of this country, but hope to the world for all future time. [Great applause.] It was that which gave promise that in due time the weights should be lifted from the shoulders of all men, and that *all* should have an equal chance. [Cheers.] This is the sentiment embodied in that Declaration of Independence.

Now, my friends, can this country be saved upon that basis? If it can, I will consider myself one of the happiest men in the world if I can help to save it. If it can't be saved upon that principle, it will be truly awful. But, if this country cannot be saved without giving up that principle—I was about to say I would rather be assassinated on this spot than to surrender it. [Applause.]

Now, in my view of the present aspect of affairs, there is no need of bloodshed and war. There is no necessity for it. I am not in favor of such a course, and I may say in advance, there will be no blood shed unless it be forced upon the Government. The Government will not use force unless force is used against it.[4] [Prolonged applause and cries of "That's the proper sentiment."]

1. *Philadelphia Inquirer*, February 23, 1861. Variants from the *New York Tribune* version of the text are indicated in footnotes.
2. The *New York Tribune* version reads, "and framed and adopted"
3. The *Tribune* version reads, "but that sentiment in the Declaration of Independence which gave liberty"
4. The *Tribune* version reads, in place of this sentence, ". . . , and then it will be compelled to act in self-defense"

My friends, this is a wholly unprepared speech. I did not expect to be called upon to say a word when I came here—I supposed I was merely to do something towards raising a flag. I may, therefore, have said something indiscreet, [cries of "no, no"], but I have said nothing but what I am willing to live by, and, in the pleasure[5] of Almighty God, die by.

Speech at the Flag Raising Before Independence Hall, Philadelphia, Pennsylvania[1]
February 22, 1861

FELLOW CITIZENS:— I am invited and called before you to participate in raising above Independence Hall the flag of our country, with an additional star upon it. [Cheers.] I propose now, in advance of performing this very pleasant and complimentary duty, to say a few words. I propose to say that when that flag was originally raised here it had but thirteen stars. I wish to call your attention to the fact, that, under the blessing of God, each additional star added to that flag has given additional prosperity and happiness to this country until it has advanced to its present condition; and its welfare in the future, as well as in the past, is in your hands. [Cheers.] Cultivating the spirit that animated our fathers, who gave renown and celebrity to this Hall, cherishing that fraternal feeling which has so long characterized us as a nation, excluding passion, ill-temper and precipitate action on all occasions, I think we may promise ourselves that not only the new star placed upon that flag shall be permitted to remain there to our permanent prosperity for years to come, but additional ones shall from time to time be placed there, until we shall number as was anticipated by the great historian, five hundred millions of happy and prosperous people. [Great applause.] With these few remarks, I proceed to the very agreeable duty assigned me.

---

5. The *Tribune* version reads, "and if it be the pleasure"
1. *Philadelphia Inquirer*, February 23, 1861.

APPENDIX 3

FIRST INAUGURAL ADDRESS

MARCH 4, 1861

Abraham Lincoln completed a first draft of his address in Springfield in January. The address was set in type and printed in the offices of the *Illinois State Journal.* Two copies are in the Lincoln Papers at the Library of Congress, marked "First Edition."

The first transcription is of the second printed draft of the address. Lincoln showed it to Orville H. Browning in Indianapolis and William H. Seward in Washington. Seward returned a marked copy as well as six pages of suggestions. Lincoln had ended with the question "With you, and not with me, is the solemn question of 'Shall it be peace, or a sword?' " Seward made two suggestions for a new concluding paragraph. Lincoln chose the shorter one, but changed Seward's ideas into his own prose poetry.

The second text is another copy of the second printed draft with the interlineations and strikeouts that Lincoln made by hand.

Both copies of the second printed edition are in the Robert Todd Lincoln Collection of the Abraham Lincoln Papers at the Library of Congress.

Seward Revisions to Second Draft

In compliance with a custom as old as the government itself, I appear before you to address you briefly, and to take, in your presence, the oath prescribed by the Constitution of the United States, to be taken by the President "before he enters on the execution of his office."

The more modern custom of ~~electing~~ ^nominating^ a Chief Magistrate upon a previously declared ~~platform~~ ^summary^ of principles, supercedes, in a great measure, the necessity of re-stating those principles in an address of this sort. ~~Upon the plainest grounds of good faith, one so elected is not at liberty to shift his position.~~ It is necessarily implied, if not expressed, that, ~~in his judgment, the platform which he thus accepts, binds him~~ ^the summary binds the offices elected^ to nothing either unconstitutional or inexpedient.

~~Having been so elected upon the Chicago Platform, and while I would repeat nothing in it, of aspersion or epithet or question of motive against any man or party, I hold myself bound by duty as well as impelled by inclination to follow, within the executive sphere, the principles therein declared. By no other course could I meet the reasonable expectations of the country.~~ ^With this explanation I deem it my duty as I am disposed in feeling to follow so far as they apply to the Executive sphere the principles on which I was brought before the American People.[1]

I do not consider it necessary at present for me to say more than I have, in relation to those matters of administration, about which there is no special excitement.

☞Apprehension seems to exist among the people of the Southern States, that by the accession of a Republican Administration, their property, and their peace, and personal security, are to be endangered. There has never been any reasonable cause for such apprehension. Indeed, the most ample evidence to the contrary has all the while existed, and been open to their inspection. It is found in nearly all the published speeches of him who now addresses you. I do but quote from one of those speeches when I declare that "I have no purpose, directly or indirectly, to interfere with the institution of slavery in the States where it exists. I believe I have no lawful right to do so, and I have no inclination to do so." Those who nominated and elected me did so with full knowledge that I had made this, and many similar declarations, and had never recanted them. And more than this, they placed in the platform, for my acceptance, and as a law to themselves, and to me, the clear and emphatic resolution which I now read:

"*Resolved*, That the maintenance inviolate of the rights of the States, and especially the right of each State to order and control its own domestic institutions according to its own judgment exclusively, is essential to that balance of power on which the perfection and endurance of our political fabric depend; and we denounce the lawless invasion by armed force of the soil of any State or Territory, no matter under what pretext, as among the gravest of crimes."

[I] now reiterate these sentiments: and in doing so, I only press upon the public at[te]ntion the most conclusive evidence of which the case is susceptible, that the property, [p]eace and security of no section are to be in anywise endangered by the now incoming Administration. I add too, that all the protection which, consistently with the Constitution and the laws, can be given, will be cheerfully given ^in every case and under all circumstances^ to all the States—as cheerfully to one section as to another.

---

1. There is a box around the two previous paragraphs with a notation at the right, "omit the whole."

☞There is much controversy about the delivering up of fugitives from service or labor. The clause I now read is as plainly written in the Constitution as any other of its provisions:

"No person held to service or labor in one State, under the laws thereof, escaping into another, shall, in consequence of any law or regulation therein, be discharged from such service or labor, but shall be delivered up on claim of the party to whom such service or labor may be due."

It is scarcely questioned that this provision was intended by those who made it, for the reclaiming of what we call fugitive slaves; and the intention of the law-giver is the law. All members of Congress swear their support to the whole Constitution—to this provision as much as to any other. To the proposition, then, that slaves whose cases come within the terms of this clause, "shall be delivered up," their oaths are unanimous. Now, if they would make the effort in good temper, could they not, with nearly equal unanimity, frame and pass a law, by means of which to keep good that unanimous oath?

There is some difference of opinion whether this clause should be enforced by national or by state authority; but surely that difference is not a very material one. If the slave is to be surrendered, it can be of but little consequence to him, or to others, by which authority it is done. And should any one, in any case, be content that his oath shall go unkept, on a merely unsubstantial controversy as to *how* it shall be kept?

Again, in any law upon this subject, ought not all the safeguards of liberty known in civilized and humane jurisprudence to be introduced, so that a free man be not, in any case, surrendered as a slave?

☞I take the official oath to-day, with no mental reservations, and with no purpose to construe the Constitution or laws, by any hypercritical rules. And while I do not think proper now to specify particular acts of Congress as proper to be enforced, I do suggest that it will be much safer for all, both in official and private stations, to conform to, and abide by, all those acts which stand unrepealed, than to violate any of them, trusting to find impunity in having them held to be unconstitutional.

☞It is ~~now~~ seventy-two years since the first inauguration of a President under our national Constitution. During that period fifteen different and greatly distinguished citizens, have, in succession, administered the executive branch of the government. They have conducted it through many perils; and, ~~on the whole~~ ^generally^, with great success. Yet, with all this scope for precedent, I now enter upon the same task for the brief constitutional term of four years, under great and peculiar difficulty. A disruption of the Federal Union ^heretofore only menaced is now formidably attempted.^~~is menaced, and, so far as can be on paper, is already effected~~. The particulars of what has been done are so familiar and so fresh, that I need not to waste any time in recounting them.

I hold, that in contemplation of universal law, and of the Constitution, the Union of these States is perpetual. Perpetuity is implied, if not expressed, in the fundamental law of all national governments. It is safe to assert that no government proper, ever had a provision in its organic law for its own termination. Continue to execute all the express provisions of our national Constitution, and the Union will endure forever—it being impossible to destroy it, except by some action not provided for in the instrument itself.

Again, if the United States be not a government proper, but an association of States in the nature of contract merely, can it, as a contract, be peaceably unmade, by less than all the parties who made it? One party to a contract may violate it—break it, so to speak; but does it not require all to lawfully rescind it?

Descending from these general principles, we find the proposition that, in legal contemplation, the Union is perpetual, confirmed by the history of the Union itself. The Union is much older than the Constitution. It was formed in fact, by the Articles of Association in 1774. It was matured and continued by the Declaration of Independence in 1776. It was further matured and expressly declared and pledged, to be perpetual, by the Articles of Confederation in 1778. And finally, in 1787, one of the declared objects for ordaining and establishing the Constitution, was "*to form a more perfect union.*"

But if destruction of the Union, by one, or by a part only, of the States, be lawfully possible, the Union is *less* perfect than before, which contradicts the Constitution,[2] ~~and therefore is absurd~~.

It follows from these views that no State, upon its own mere motion, can lawfully get out of the Union,—that *resolves* and *ordinances* to that effect are legally ~~nothing~~ ^void^; and that acts of violence, within any State or States, against the authority of the United States, are insurrectionary or ~~treasonable~~ ^ revolutionary^, according to circumstances.

I therefore consider that ^in the view of the Constitution and the laws^ the Union is unbroken; and, to the extent of my ability, I shall take care ^as the Constitution itself expressly enjoins upon me^ that the laws of the Union be faithfully executed in all the States. Doing this I deem to be only a simple duty on my part; and I shall perform it, so far as practicable, unless my rightful masters, the American people, shall withhold the requisite means, or, in some ~~tangible way~~ ^authoritative manner^, direct the contrary. I trust this will not be regarded as a menace, but only as the declared purpose of the

2. Period written over a comma.

Union that it ~~*will* have its own, and *defend* itself.~~ ^will constitutionally defend, and maintain itself.^

In doing this there needs to be no bloodshed or violence; and there shall be none, unless it be forced upon the national authority. ~~All the power at my disposal will be used to reclaim the public property and places which have fallen; to hold, occupy and possess these, and all other property and places belonging to the government, and to collect the duties on imposts; but beyond what may be necessary for these objects, there will be no invasion of any State. Where hostility to the United States, in any interior locality, shall be so great and so universal, as to prevent competent resident citizens from holding the Federal offices, there will be no attempt to force obnoxious strangers among the people for that object. While the strict legal right may exist in the government to enforce the exercise of these offices, the attempt to do so would be so irritating, and so nearly impracticable with all, that I deem it better to forego, for the time, the uses of such offices.~~ ^The power confided to me shall be used indeed with efficacy, but also with discretion in every case and exigency according to the circumstances actually existing, and with a view and a hope of a peaceful solution of the national troubles and the restoration of fraternal sympathies and affections. There are in this government as in every other, emergencies when the exercise of power lawful in itself is less certain to secure the just ends of administration than a temporary forbearance from it, with reliance on the voluntary though delayed acquiescence of the people in the laws which have been made by themselves and for their own benefit. I shall not lose sight of this obvious maxim.^

The mails, unless refused, will continue to be furnished in all parts of the Union. So far as possible, the people everywhere shall have that sense of perfect security which is most favorable to calm thought and reflection. This course will be pursued until current experience shall show a modification or change to be proper.

☞That there are persons ^in one section as well as in the other^ who seek to destroy the Union at all events, and are glad of any pretext to do it, I will neither affirm or deny; but if there be such, I need address no word to them ^because I am sure they must be few in number and of little influence when their pernicious principles are fully understood^. To those, however, who really love the Union, may I not speak?

Before entering upon so grave a matter as the destruction of our national Union, would it not be wise to ascertain precisely why we do it? Will you hazard so desperate a step, while there is any possibility that any portion of the ills you fly from have no real existence? Will you, while the certain ills you fly to, are greater than all the real ones you fly from? Will you risk the commission of so fearful a mistake?

All profess to be content in the Union, if all constitutional rights can be maintained. Is it true, then, that any ^distinct^ right, plainly written in the Constitution, has been denied? I think not. Happily the human mind is so constructed, that no party can reach to the audacity of doing this. Think, if you can, of a single instance in which a plainly written provision of the Constitution has ever been denied. If, by the mere force of numbers, a majority should deprive a minority of any clearly written constitutional right, it might, in a moral point of view, justify revolution—certainly would, if such right were a vital one;—but such is not our case. All the vital rights of minorities, and of individuals, are so plainly assured to them, by affirmations and negations ^guarantees and prohibitions^ in the Constitution, that controversies never arise concerning them. But no organic law can ever be framed with a provision specifically applicable to every ^possible^ question which may occur in practical administration. No foresight can anticipate, nor any document of reasonable length contain express provisions for all possible questions. Shall fugitives from labor be surrendered by national or by State authority? The Constitution does not expressly say. *May* Congress prohibit slavery in the territories? The Constitution does not expressly say. *Must* Congress protect slavery in the territories? The Constitution does not expressly say.

From questions of this class spring all our constitutional controversies, and we divide upon them into majorities and minorities. If the minority will not ~~submit~~ ^acquiesce^, the majority must, or the government must cease. There is no other alternative; for continuing the government, is ~~submission~~ ^acquiescence^ on one side or the other. If a minority, in such case, will secede rather than submit, they make a precedent which, in turn, will divide and ruin them; for a minority of their own number will secede from them whenever a majority refuses to be controlled by such minority. For instance, why may not ~~South Carolina~~ ^Alabama or Florida^, a year or two hence, arbitrarily, secede from a new Southern Confederacy, just as she now claims to secede from the present Union? Her people, and, indeed, all secession ~~people~~ ^communities^, are now being educated to the precise temper of doing this. Is there such perfect identity of interests among the States to compose a Southern Union, as to produce harmony only, and prevent renewed secession?

Plainly, the central idea of secession, is the essence of anarchy. A ~~constitutional majority~~ ^majority held in restraint by constitutional checks and limitations and always changing easily with deliberate changes of popular opinions and sentiments^ is the only true sovereign of a free people. Whoever rejects it, does, of necessity, fly to anarchy or to despotism. Unanimity is impossible; the rule of a minority, as a permanent arrangement, is wholly inadmissible; so that, rejecting the majority principle, anarchy or despotism in some form is all that is left.

I do not forget the position assumed by some, that constitutional questions are to be decided by the Supreme Court; nor do I deny that such decisions must be binding in any case, upon the parties to a suit, as to the object of the suit ^while they are entitled to very high respect and consideration in all parallel cases by all the Departments of the government^. And while it is obviously possible that such decision may be erroneous in any given case, still the evil effect following it, being limited to that particular case, with the chance that it may be over-ruled, and never become a precedent for other cases, can better be borne than could the greater evils of a different ~~rule~~ ^practice.^. ~~But~~ ^At the same time the candid citizen must confess that^ if the policy of the government, upon vital questions affecting the whole people, is to be irrevocably fixed by decisions of the Supreme Court, ~~it is plain that~~ ^made in the ordinary course of litigation between parties in personal actions^ the people will have ceased to be their own rulers, having ~~turned their government over to the despotism of the few life-officers composing the Court~~ ^practically resigned their government into the hands of that eminent tribunal^. Nor is there, in this view any assault upon the Court or the judges. It is a duty from which they may not shrink, to decide cases properly brought before them; and it is no fault of theirs if others seek to turn their decisions to political purposes.

~~☞The Republican party, as I understand, have avowed the purpose to prevent, if they can, the extension of slavery, under the national auspices; and upon this arises the only dispute between the sections.~~

One section ^of our country^ believes slavery is *right,* and ought to be extended, while the other believes it is *wrong,* and ought not to be extended. This is the only substantial dispute. The fugitive slave clause of the Constitution, and the law for the suppression of the foreign slave trade, are each as well enforced, ^perhaps^ as any law can ever be in a community where the moral sense of the people ~~is against~~ ^imperfectly supports^ the law itself. The great body of the people abide by the dry legal obligation in both cases, and a few break over in each. This, I think, cannot be perfectly cured; and it would be worse in both cases *after* the separation of the sections, than before. The foreign slave trade, now imperfectly suppressed, would be ^ultimately^ revived without restriction, in one section; while fugitive slaves, now only partially surrendered, would not be surrendered at all, by the other.

Physically speaking, we cannot separate. We cannot remove our respective sections from each other, nor build an impassable wall between them. A husband and wife may be divorced, and go out of the presence, and beyond the reach of each other; but the different parts of our country cannot do this.

They cannot but remain face to face; and intercourse, either amicable or hostile, must continue between them. Is it possible to make that intercourse more advantageous or satisfactory, *after* separation than *before*? Can aliens make treaties easier than friends can make laws? Can treaties be more faithfully enforced between aliens than laws can among friends? Suppose you go to war, you cannot fight always; and when, after much loss on both sides, and no gain on either, you cease fighting, the identical old questions, as to terms of intercourse, are again upon you.

This country, with its institutions, belongs to the people who inhabit it. Whenever they shall grow weary of the existing government, they can exercise their *constitutional* right of amending it, or their *revolutionary* right to dismember or overthrow it. ~~As I am not much impressed with the belief that the present Constitution can be improved, I make no recommendations of amendments~~. ^While so great a diversity of opinion exists on the question what amendments, if indeed any would be effective in restoring peace and safety it would only tend to aggravate the dispute if I were to attempt to give direction to the public mind in that respect.^ I am, rather, for the old ship, and the chart of the old pilots. If, however, the people desire a new, or an altered vessel, the matter is exclusively their own, and they can move in the premises, as well without as with an executive recommendation. I shall place no obstacle in the way of what may appear to be their wishes.

The Chief Magistrate derives all his authority from the people, and they have conferred none upon him to fix terms for the separation of the States. The people themselves can do this if they choose; but the executive, as such, has nothing to do with it. His duty is to administer the present government, as it came to his hands, and to transmit it, ^if possible^ unimpaired by him, to his successor.

Why should there not be a patient confidence in the ultimate justice of the people? Is there any better or equal hope, in the world? In our present differences, is either party without faith in the right? If the Almighty Ruler of nations, with his eternal truth and justice, be ~~on our side, or on yours~~ ^on the side of the North or of the South, of the East or of the West^, that truth and that justice will surely prevail, by the judgment of this great tribunal, the American people.

By the frame of the government under which we live, this same people have wisely given their public servants but little power for mischief; and have, with equal wisdom, provided for the return of that little to their own hands at very short intervals.

While the people ~~remain patient, and true to themselves, no man, even in the presidential chair,~~ ^retain their virtue and vigilance no legislature and no administration can^ by any extreme of wickedness or folly, ~~can~~ very seriously injure the government in the short space of four years.

☞My countrymen, one and all, ~~take *time*~~ ^think calmly^ and think *well,* upon this whole subject. ~~Nothing valuable can be lost by taking time. Nothing worth preserving is either breaking or burning.~~ If there be an object to *hurry* any of you, in hot haste, to a step which you would never take *deliberately,* that object will be frustrated by taking time; but no good object can be frustrated by it. Such of you as are now dissatisfied, still have the old Constitution unimpaired, and, on the sensitive point, the laws of your own framing under it; while the new administration will have no immediate power, if it would, to change either. If it were admitted that you who are dissatisfied, hold the right side in the dispute, there still is no single good reason for precipitate action. Intelligence, patriotism, Christianity, and a firm reliance on Him, who has never yet forsaken this favored land, are still competent to adjust, in the best way, all our present difficulty.

In *your* hands, my dissatisfied fellow countrymen, and not in *mine,* is the momentous issue of civil war. The government will not assail *you,* ~~unless you *first assail it*~~. You can have no conflict, without being yourselves the aggressors. *You* have no oath registered in Heaven to destroy the government, while *I* shall have the most solemn one to "preserve, protect and defend" it. ~~*You* can forbear the *assault* upon it; I can *not* shrink from the *defense* of it. With *you,* and not with *me,* is the solemn question of "Shall it be peace, or a sword?"~~

∀I close. We are not we must not be aliens or enemies but ~~countrym~~ fellow countrymen and brethren. Although passion has strained our bonds of affection too hardly they must not ~~be broken~~ ~~they will not~~, I am sure they will not be broken. The mystic chords which proceeding from ~~every~~ ~~ba~~ so many battle fields and ~~patriot~~ so many patriot graves ~~bind~~ pass through all the hearts and ~~hearths~~ all the hearths in this broad continent of ours will yet ~~harmon~~ again harmonize in their ancient music when ~~touched as they surely~~ breathed upon ~~again~~ by the ~~better angel~~ guardians angel of the nation.∀[3]

∀Suggestions for a closing paragraph.[4]

However unusual it may be at such a time to speak of sections or to sections, yet in view of the misconceptions & agitations which have strained the ties of brotherhood so far, I hope it will not be deemed a departure from propriety, whatever it may be from custom, to say that if in the criminations and misconstructions which too often imbue our political contest, any man south of this capital has been led to believe that I regard with a less friendly eye, his rights, his interests or his domestic safety and happiness or those of his State, than I do those of any other portion of my country or that I would invade or

---

3. This paragraph, written by William H. Seward, was originally located on the back of the fourth page of his handwritten notes of suggested changes.
4. "Suggestions for a closing paragraph" in the handwriting of Frederick W. Seward, William H. Seward's son.

disturb any legal right or domestic institution in the South he mistakes both my principles and feelings and does not know me. I aspire to come in the spirit, however far below the ability and the wisdom, of Washington, of Madison, of Jackson and of Clay. In that spirit I here declare that in my Administration I shall know no rule but the Constitution, no guide but the laws, and no sentiment but that of equal devotion to my whole country, east, west, north and south.∀

Lincoln's Revisions to the Second Draft

In compliance with a custom as old as the government itself, I appear before you to address you briefly, and to take, in your presence, the oath prescribed by the Constitution of the United States, to be taken by the President "before he enters on the execution of his office."

~~The more modern custom of electing a Chief Magistrate upon a previously declared platform of principles, supercedes, in a great measure, the necessity of re-stating those principles in an address of this sort. Upon the plainest grounds of good faith, one so elected is not at liberty to shift his position. It is necessarily implied, if not expressed, that, in his judgment, the platform which he thus accepts, binds him to nothing either unconstitutional or inexpedient.~~

~~Having been so elected upon the Chicago Platform, and while I would repeat nothing in it, of aspersion or epithet or question of motive against any man or party, I hold myself bound by duty, as well as impelled by inclination to follow, within the executive sphere, the principles therein declared. By no other course could I meet the reasonable expectations of the country.~~

~~I do not consider it necessary at present for me to say more than I have, in relation to those matters of administration, about which there is no special excitement.~~

∀I do not consider it necessary, at present, for me to discuss those matters of administration about which there is no special anxiety, or excitement.∀

ΛApprehension seems to exist among the people of the Southern States, that by the accession of a Republican Administration, their property, and their peace, and personal security, are to be endangered. There has never been any reasonable cause for such apprehension. Indeed, the most ample evidence to the contrary has all the while existed, and been open to their inspection. It is found in nearly all the published speeches of him who now addresses you. I do but quote from one of those speeches when I declare that

"I have no purpose, directly or indirectly, to interfere with the institution of slavery in the States where it exists. I believe I have no lawful right to do so, and I have no inclination to do so." Those who nominated and elected me did so with full knowledge that I had made this, and many similar declarations, and had never recanted them. And more than this, they placed in the platform, for my acceptance, and as a law to themselves, and to me, the clear and emphatic resolution which I now read:

"*Resolved*, That the maintenance inviolate of the rights of the States, and especially the right of each State to order and control its own domestic institutions according to its own judgment exclusively, is essential to that balance of power on which the perfection and endurance of our political fabric depend; and we denounce the lawless invasion by armed force of the soil of any State or Territory, no matter under what pretext, as among the gravest of crimes."

I now reiterate these sentiments; and in doing so, I only press upon the public attention the most conclusive evidence of which the case is susceptible, that the property, peace and security of no section are to be in anywise endangered by the now incoming Administration. I add too, that all the protection which, consistently with the Constitution and the laws, can be given, will be cheerfully given to all the States ^when lawfully demanded, for whatever cause—^—as cheerfully to one section^,^ as to another.

☞There is much controversy about the delivering up of fugitives from service or labor. The clause I now read is as plainly written in the Constitution as any other of its provisions:

"No person held to service or labor in one State, under the laws thereof, escaping into another, shall, in consequence of any law or regulation therein, be discharged from such service or labor, but shall be delivered up on claim of the party to whom such service or labor may be due."

It is scarcely questioned that this provision was intended by those who made it, for the reclaiming of what we call fugitive slaves; and the intention of the law-giver is the law. All members of Congress swear their support to the whole Constitution—to this provision as much as to any other. To the proposition, then, that slaves whose cases come within the terms of this clause, "shall be delivered up," their oaths are unanimous. Now, if they would make the effort in good temper, could they not, with nearly equal unanimity, frame and pass a law, by means of which to keep good that unanimous oath?

There is some difference of opinion whether this clause should be enforced by national or by state authority; but surely that difference is not a very material one. If the slave is to be surrendered, it can be of but little consequence to him, or to others, by which authority it is done. And should any one, in any case, be content that his oath shall go unkept, on a merely unsubstantial controversy as to *how* it shall be kept?

Again, in any law upon this subject, ought not all the safeguards of liberty known in civilized and humane jurisprudence to be introduced, so that a free man be not, in any case, surrendered as a slave? ^And might it not be well, at the same time, to provide by law for the enforcement of that clause in the Constitution which guarranties that "The citizens of each State shall be entitled to all privileges and immunities of citizens in the several States"?^

☞I take the official oath to-day, with no mental reservations, and with no purpose to construe the Constitution or laws, by any hypercritical rules. And while I do not ~~think proper now~~ ^choose^ to specify particular acts of Congress as proper to be enforced, I do suggest^,^ that it will be much safer for all, both in official and private stations, to conform to, and abide by, all those acts which stand unrepealed, than to violate any of them, trusting to find impunity in having them held to be unconstitutional.

☞It is ~~now~~ seventy-two years since the first inauguration of a President under our national Constitution. During that period fifteen different and greatly distinguished citizens, have, in succession, administered the executive branch of the government. They have conducted it through many perils; and, ~~on the whole~~ ^generally,^, with great success. Yet, with all this scope for precedent, I now enter upon the same task for the brief constitutional term of four years, under great and peculiar difficulty. A disruption of the Federal Union ^heretofore only menaced, is now formidably attempted.^ ~~is menaced, and so far as can be on paper, is already effected. The particulars of what has been done are so familiar and so fresh, that I need not to waste any time in recounting them.~~

I hold, that in contemplation of universal law, and of the Constitution, the Union of these States is perpetual. Perpetuity is implied, if not expressed, in the fundamental law of all national governments. It is safe to assert that no government proper, ever had a provision in its organic law for its own termination. Continue to execute all the express provisions of our national Constitution, and the Union will endure forever—it being impossible to destroy it, except by some action not provided for in the instrument itself.

Again, if the United States be not a government proper, but an association of States in the nature of contract merely, can it, as a contract, be peaceably unmade, by less than all the parties who made it? One party to a contract may violate it—break it, so to speak; but does it not require all to lawfully rescind it?

Descending from these general principles, we find the proposition that, in legal contemplation, the Union is perpetual, confirmed by the history of the Union itself. The Union is much older than the Constitution. It was formed in fact, by the Articles of Association in 1774. It was matured and continued by the Declaration of Independence in 1776. It was further matured ^and the faith of all the then thirteen States expressly plighted and engaged that it should be^ ~~and expressly declared and pledged, to be~~ perpetual, by the Articles of Confederation in 1778. And finally, in 1787, one of the declared objects for ordaining and establishing the Constitution, was "*to form a more perfect union.*"

But if destruction of the Union, by one, or by a part only, of the States, be lawfully possible, the Union is *less* perfect than before~~, which contradicts~~ the Constitution, ~~and therefore is absurd.~~ ^having lost the vital element of perpetuity.^

It follows from these views that no State, upon its own mere motion, can lawfully get out of the Union,—that *resolves* and *ordinances* to that effect are legally ^void;^ ~~nothing~~; and that acts of violence, within any State or States, against the authority of the United States, are insurrectionary or ~~treasonable~~ ^revolutionary^, according to circumstances.

~~I therefore consider that the Union is unbroken; and, to the extent of my ability, I shall take care that the laws of the Union be faithfully executed in all the States.~~ ∀I therefore consider that, in view of the constitution and the laws, the Union is unbroken; and, to the extent of my ability, I shall take care, as the constitution itself expressly enjoins upon me, that the laws of the Union be faithfully executed in all the states.∀ Doing this I deem to be only a simple duty on my part; and I shall perform it, so far as practicable, unless my rightful masters, the American people, shall withhold the requisite means, or, in some ~~tangible way~~ ^authoritative manner^, direct the contrary. I trust this will not be regarded as a menace, but only as the declared purpose of the Union that it *will* ~~have its own, and *defend* itself~~. ^constitutionally defend, and maintain itself.^

In doing this there needs to be no bloodshed or violence; and there shall be none, unless it be forced upon the national authority. ~~All the power at my disposal will be used to reclaim the public property and places which have fallen; to hold, occupy and possess these, and all other property and places belonging to the government, and to collect the duties on imposts; but beyond what may be necessary for these objects, there will be no invasion of any State.~~

∀The power confided to me, will be used to hold, occupy, and possess the property, and places belonging to the government, and to collect the duties [~~...~~] ^and^ imposts; but beyond what may be necessary for these objects, there will be no invasion—no using of force against, or among the people anywhere.∀ Where hostility to the United States, in any interior locality, shall be so great and so universal, as to prevent competent resident citizens from holding the Federal offices, there will be no attempt to force obnoxious strangers among the people for that object. While the strict legal right may exist in the government to enforce the exercise of these offices, the attempt to do so would be so irritating, and so nearly impracticable with all, that I deem it better to forego, for the time, the uses of such offices.

The mails, unless ~~refused~~ ^repelled^, will continue to be furnished in all parts of the Union. So far as possible, the people everywhere shall have that sense of perfect security which is most favorable to calm thought and reflection. ~~This course will be pursued until current experience shall show a modification or change to be proper.~~ ∀The course here indicated will be followed, unless current events, and experience, shall show a modification, or change, to be proper; and in every case and exigency, my best discretion will be exercised, according to circumstances actually existing, and with a view and a hope of a peaceful solution of the national troubles, and the restoration of fraternal sympathies and affections.∀

☞That there are persons ^in one section, or another^ who seek to destroy the Union at all events, and are glad of any pretext to do it, I will neither affirm or deny; but if there be such, I need address no word to them. To those, however, who really love the Union, may I not speak?

Before entering upon so grave a matter as the destruction of our national ~~Union,~~ ^fabric, with all its benefits, it's memories, and it's hopes,^ would it not be wise to ascertain precisely why we do it? Will you hazard so desperate a step, while there is any possibility that any portion of the ills you fly from^,^ have no real existence? Will you, while the certain ills you fly to, are greater than all the real ones you fly from? Will you risk the commission of so fearful a mistake?

All profess to be content in the Union, if all constitutional rights can be maintained. Is it true, then, that any ^~~distinct~~^ right, plainly written in the Constitution, has been denied? I think not. Happily the human mind is so ~~constructed~~ ^constituted^, that no party can reach to the audacity of doing this. Think, if you can, of a single instance in which a plainly written provision of the Constitution has ever been denied. If, by the mere force of numbers, a majority should deprive a minority of any clearly written constitutional right, it might, in a moral point of view, justify revolution—certainly would, if such right were a vital one.[1] But[2] such is not our case. All the vital rights of minorities, and of individuals, are so plainly assured to them, by affirmations and negations ^guarranties and prohibitions,^ in the Constitution, that controversies never arise concerning them. But no organic

---

1. ";—" changed to "."
2. "but" changed to "But"

law can ever be framed with a provision specifically applicable to every ^~~possible~~^ question which may occur in practical administration. No foresight can anticipate, nor any document of reasonable length contain express provisions for all possible questions. Shall fugitives from labor be surrendered by national or by State authority? The Constitution does not expressly say. *May* Congress prohibit slavery in the territories? The Constitution does not expressly say. *Must* Congress protect slavery in the territories? The Constitution does not expressly say.

From questions of this class spring all our constitutional controversies, and we divide upon them into majorities and minorities. If the minority will not ~~submit~~ ^acquiesce^, the majority must, or the government must cease. There is no other alternative; for continuing the government, is ~~submission~~ ^acquiescence^ on one side or the other. If a minority, in such case, will secede rather than ~~submit~~ ^acquiesce^, they make a precedent which, in turn, will divide and ruin them; for a minority of their own ~~number~~ will secede from them^,^ whenever a majority refuses to be controlled by such minority. ~~For instance, why may not South Carolina, a year or two hence, arbitrarily, secede from a new Southern Confederacy, just as she now claims to secede from the present Union? Her people, and, indeed, all secession people, are now being educated to the precise temper of doing this.~~ ∀For instance, why may not any portion of a new Confederacy, a year or two hence, arbitrarily secede again, precisely as portions of the present Union now claim to secede from it. All who cherish disunion sentiments are now being educated to the exact temper of doing this.∀ Is there such perfect identity of interest among the States to compose a ~~Southern~~ ^new^ Union, as to produce harmony only, and prevent renewed secession?

Plainly, the central idea of secession, is the essence of anarchy. ~~A constitutional majority is the only true sovereign of a free people.~~ ∀A majority, held in restraint by constitutional checks, and limitations, and always changing easily, with deliberate changes of popular opinions and sentiments, is the only true sovereign of a free people.∀ Whoever rejects it, does, of necessity, fly to anarchy or to despotism. Unanimity is impossible; the rule of a minority, as a permanent arrangement, is wholly inadmissible; so that, rejecting the majority principle, anarchy^,^ or despotism in some form^,^ is all that is left.

I do not forget the position assumed by some, that constitutional questions are to be decided by the Supreme Court; nor do I deny that such decisions must be binding in any case, upon the parties to a suit, as to the object of ~~the~~ ^that^ suit~~.~~^,^ ∀while they are also entitled to very high respect and consideration, in all paralel cases, by all other departments of the government.∀ And while it is obviously possible that such decision may be erroneous in any given case, still the evil effect following it, being limited to that particular case, with the chance that it may be over-ruled, and never become a precedent for other cases, can better be borne than ~~could the greater evils of a different rule ^practice.^. But if the policy of the government, upon vital questions affecting the whole people, is to be irrevocably fixed by decisions of the Supreme Court, it is plain that the people will have ceased to be their own rulers, having turned their government over to the despotism of the few life-officers composing the Court. Nor is there, in this view^,^ any assault upon the Court or the judges. It is a duty from which they may not shrink, to decide cases properly brought before them; and it is no fault of theirs if others seek to turn their decisions to political purposes.~~

~~☞The Republican party, as I understand, have avowed the purpose to prevent, if they can, the extension of slavery, under the national auspices; and upon this arises the only dispute between the sections.~~ ∀could the evils of a different practice. At the same time the candid citizen must confess, that if the policy of the government, upon vital questions, affecting the whole people, is to be irrevocably fixed by decisions of the Supreme Court, the instant they are made, in ordinary litigation between parties, in personal actions, ~~it is plain that~~ the people will have ceased, ~~to~~ to be their own rulers, having, to that extent, practically resigned their government, into the hands of that eminent tribunal. Nor is there, in this view, any assault upon the Court, or the judges. It is a duty, from which they may not shrink, to decide cases properly brought before ~~brought before~~ them; and it ^is^ no fault of theirs, if others seek to turn their decisions to political purposes.∀

One section ^of our country^ believes slavery is *right*, and ought to be extended, while the other believes it is *wrong*, and ought not to be extended. This is the only substantial dispute. The fugitive slave clause of the Constitution, and the law for the suppression of the foreign slave trade, are each as well enforced, ^perhaps^ as any law can ever be in a community where the moral sense of the people ~~is against~~ ^imperfectly supports^ the law itself. The great body of the people abide by the dry legal obligation in both cases, and a few break over in each. This, I think, cannot be perfectly cured; and it would be worse in both cases *after* the separation of the sections, than before. The foreign slave trade, now imperfectly suppressed, would be ^ultimately^ revived without restriction, in one section; while fugitive slaves, now only partially surrendered, would not be surrendered at all, by the other.

Physically speaking, we cannot separate. We cannot remove our respective sections from each other, nor build an impassable wall between them. A husband and wife may be divorced, and go out of the presence, and beyond the reach of each other; but the different parts of our country cannot do this. They cannot but remain face to face; and intercourse, either amicable or hostile, must continue between them. Is it possible ^~~possible~~ then^ to make that intercourse more advantageous^,^ or ^more^ satisfactory, *after* separation than *before?* Can aliens make treaties easier than friends can make laws? Can treaties be more faithfully enforced between aliens^,^ than laws can among friends? Suppose you go to war, you cannot fight always; and when, after much loss on both sides, and no gain on either, you cease fighting, the identical old questions, as to terms of intercourse, are again upon you.

^☞^This country, with its institutions, belongs to the people who inhabit it. Whenever they shall grow weary of the existing government, they can exercise their *constitutional* right of amending it, or their *revolutionary* right to dismember^,^ or overthrow [it.] ~~As I am not much impressed with the belief that the present Constitution can be improved, I make no recommendations of amendments. I am, rather, for the old ship, and the chart of the old pilots. If, however, the people desire a new, or an altered vessel, the matter is exclusively their own, and they can move in the premises, as well without as with an executive recommendation. I shall place no obstacle in the way of what may appear to be their wishes.~~ ∀I can not be ignorant of the fact that many worthy, and patriotic citizens are desirous ~~that~~ ^of having^ the national Constitution ~~shall be~~ amended. While I make no recommendation of amendments, I fully recognize the rightful authority of the people over the ^whole^ subject, to be exercised in either of the modes prescribed in the instrument itself; and I should, under existing circumstances, favor, rather than oppose, a fair oppertunity being afforded the people to act upon it.∀ ∀I will venture to add that, to me, the Convention mode seems preferable, in that it allows amendments to originate with the people themselves, instead of ^only permitting^ ~~allowing~~ them ~~merely~~ to take, or reject, propositions, originated by others, not especially chosen for the purpose, and which might not be precisely such, as they would wish to either accept or ~~reject~~ ^refuse^.∀ ∀I understand a proposed amendment to the constitution ^which amendment, however, I have not seen,^ has passed ~~the House of Representatives~~ ^Congress^, to the effect that the federal government, shall never interfere with the domestic institutions of the States, including that of persons held to service. To avoid misconstruction of what I have said, I depart from my purpose not to speak of particular amendments, so far as to say that, holding such a provision to now be implied Constitutional law, I have no objection to it's being made express, and irrevocable.∀

The Chief Magistrate derives all his authority from the people, and they have conferred none upon him to fix terms for the separation of the States. The people themselves can do this ^also^ if they choose; but the executive, as such, has nothing to do with it. His duty is to administer the present government, as it came to his hands, and to transmit it, unimpaired by him, to his successor.

Why should there not be a patient confidence in the ultimate justice of the people? Is there any better or equal hope, in the world? In our present differences, is either party without faith ^of being^ in the right? If the

Almighty Ruler of nations, with his eternal truth and justice, be on ^on your side of the North, or on yours of the South,^ ~~our side, or on yours~~, that truth^,^ and that justice^,^ will surely prevail, by the judgment of this great tribunal, the American people.

By the frame of the government under which we live, this same people have wisely given their public servants but little power for mischief; and have, with equal wisdom, provided for the return of that little^,^ to their own hands^,^ at very short intervals.

While the people ^retain their virtue, and vigilence, no administration^ ~~remain patient, and true to themselves, no man, even in the presidential chair~~ ^~~can~~^, by any extreme of wickedness or folly, can very seriously injure the government^,^ in the short space of four years.

☞My countrymen, one and all, ^think calmly and^ ~~take *time* and think~~ *well*, upon this whole subject. Nothing valuable can be lost by taking time. ~~Nothing worth preserving is either breaking or burning.~~ If there be an object to *hurry* any of you, in hot haste, to a step which you would never take *deliberately*, that object will be frustrated by taking time; but no good object can be frustrated by it. Such of you as are now dissatisfied, still have the old Constitution unimpaired, and, on the sensitive point, the laws of your own framing under it; while the new administration will have no immediate power, if it would, to change either. If it were admitted that you who are dissatisfied, hold the right side in the dispute, there still is no single good reason for precipitate action. Intelligence, patriotism, Christianity, and a firm reliance on Him, who has never yet forsaken this favored land, are still competent to adjust, in the best way, all our present difficulty.

In *your* hands, my dissatisfied fellow countrymen, and not in *mine*, is the momentous issue of civil war. The government will not assail *you*^.^ ~~, unless you *first* assail *it*.~~ You can have no conflict, without being yourselves the aggressors. *You* have no oath registered in Heaven to destroy the government, while *I* shall have the most solemn one to "preserve, protect and defend" it. ~~*You* can forbear the *assault* upon it; *I* can *not* shrink from the *defense* of it. With *you*, and not with *me*, is the solemn question of "Shall it be peace, or a sword?"~~

^☞I am loth to close. We are not enemies, but friends. We must not be enemies. Though passion may have strained, it must not break our bonds of affection. The mystic chords of memory,[3] streching from every battlefield, and patriot grave, to every living heart and hearthstone, all over this broad land, will yet swell the chorus of the Union, when again touched, as surely they will be, by the better angels of our nature.

---

3. "memories" changed to "memory"

APPENDIX 4

MESSAGE TO CONGRESS IN SPECIAL SESSION

JULY 4, 1861

Several draft copies of Abraham Lincoln's Message to Congress in Special Session exist. The first version is a handwritten draft with numerous changes. The second version is a printed draft with handwritten insertions and deletions. The third version is two copies of a second printed draft. One copy has changes suggested by Secretary of State William Seward. The other copy has changes made by Lincoln. The transcription that follows is of Lincoln's copy of the second printed draft, with changes suggested by Seward indicated in notes. All four documents are part of the Robert Todd Lincoln Collection of Abraham Lincoln Papers at the Library of Congress.

MESSAGE.

Fellow-citizens of the Senate and House of Representatives:

Having been convened on an extraordinary occasion, as authorized by the Constitution, your attention is not called to any ordinary subject of legislation.

At the beginning of the present presidential term, four months ago, ~~all~~[1] the functions of the federal government were found to be ~~entirely~~ ^generally^[2] suspended within the several States of South Carolina, Georgia, Alabama, Mississippi, Louisiana, and Florida, excepting only those of the Post Office Department.

Within these States all the forts, arsenals, dock-yards, custom-houses, and the like, including the movable and stationary property in and about them, had been seized, and were held in open hostility to this government, excepting only Forts Pickens, Taylor, and Jefferson, on and near the Florida coast, and Fort Sumter, in Charleston harbor, South Carolina. The forts thus seized had been put in improved condition; new ones had been built, and

1. Deletion suggested by Seward.
2. Deletion and addition suggested by Seward.

armed forces had been organized, and were organizing, all avowedly with the same hostile purpose.

The forts remaining in the possession of the federal government in and near these States were ^either besieged or^[3] menaced by warlike preparations, and especially Fort Sumter was nearly surrounded by well-protected hostile batteries, with guns equal in quality to the best of its own, and outnumbering the latter as ^perhaps ten^ to one. A disproportionate share, ~~both in number and quality,~~ of the federal ^muskets and rifles,^ ~~arms and ammunition~~, had somehow found their way into these States, and had been seized to be used against the government. Accumulations of the public revenue, lying within ~~these States~~ ^them^[4], had been seized for the same object. The navy was scattered~~; and~~[5] in distant seas;[6] leaving but a very small part of it within the immediate reach of the government. ~~The~~ Officers[7] of the federal army and navy^,^ had resigned in great numbers;[8] and of those resigning^,^ a large proportion had taken up arms against the government. Simultaneously, and in connexion with all this, the purpose to sever the Federal Union was openly avowed. In accordance with this purpose, an ordinance had been adopted in each of these States, declaring the States, respectively, to be separated from the National Union. ~~Also the forms of establishing a federal government of these States, with departments^,^ and provisions^,^ similar to our own, had been gone through; and this supposed federal government, under the name and style of "The Confederate States of America," had assumed national independence, and was suing for its recognition^,^ by the powers of the earth.~~ ^A formula for instituting a combined government of these states had been promulgated; and this illegal organization, in the character of Confederate states was already invoking recognition, aid, and intervention, from Foreign Powers.^[9]

Finding this condition of things, and believing it to be an imperative duty upon the incoming Executive^,^ to prevent, if possible, the consummation of such attempt to destroy the Federal Union, a choice of means to that

---

3. Insertion suggested by Seward.
4. Deletion and addition suggested by Seward.
5. Deletion suggested by Seward.
6. "," changed to ";"
7. "officers" changed to "Officers"; deletion suggested by Seward.
8. "," changed to ";"
9. Seward suggested the following changes to this passage: "~~Also the~~ ^A formula^ forms of establishing a ~~federal~~ ^combined^ government of these States, ~~with departments and provisions similar to our own,~~ had been ~~gone through~~ ^promulgated^; and this ~~supposed federal government~~ ^illegal organization^, under the name ~~and style~~ of "The Confederate States of America," ~~had assumed national independence, and was suing for its recognition by the powers of the earth.~~ ^invoking recognition aid and intervention ~~by Fore~~ from Foreign Powers;^"

end became indispensable. This choice was made, and was declared in the inaugural address. The policy chosen looked to the exhaustion of all peaceful measures, before a resort to any stronger ones. It sought only to hold the public places and property not already wrested from the government, and to collect the revenue; relying for the rest, on time, discussion, and the ballot-box. It promised a continuance of the mails, at government expense, to the very people who were resisting the government; and it gave repeated pledges against any disturbance to any of the people, or any of their rights. Of all that which a President might constitutionally^,^ and justifiably^,^ do in such a case^,^ —[10] everything was forborne, without which, it was believed possible to keep the government on foot.

On the 5th of March, (the present incumbent's first full day in office,) a letter of Major Anderson, commanding at Fort Sumter, written on the 28th of February, and received at the War Department on the 4th of March, was, by that department, placed in his hands. This letter expressed the professional opinion of the writer, that re-enforcements could not be thrown into that fort within the time for his relief, rendered necessary by the limited supply of provisions, and with a view of holding possession of the same, with a force of less than twenty thousand good and well-disciplined men. This opinion was concurred in by all the officers of his command, and their *memoranda* on the subject, were made enclosures of Major Anderson's letter. The whole was immediately laid before Lieutenant General Scott, who at once concurred with Major Anderson in opinion. On reflection, however, he took full time, consulting with other officers, both of the army and the navy, and, at the end of four days, came reluctantly, but decidedly, to the same conclusion as before. He also stated at the same time that no such sufficient force was then at the control of the government, or could be raised and brought to the ground within the time when the provisions in the fort would be exhausted. In a purely military point of view, this reduced the duty of the administration^,^ in the case, to the mere matter of getting the garrison safely out of the fort.

It was believed, however, that to so abandon that position^, under the circumstances,^[11] would be utterly ruinous; that the *necessity* under which it was to be done would not be fully understood; that by many, it would be construed as a part of a *voluntary* policy; that at home, it would discourage the friends of the Union, [12]embolden its adversaries, and go far to insure to the latter, a recognition ~~of independence~~[13] abroad; that, in fact, it would be

10. Em dash stricken out.
11. Insertion suggested by Seward; commas inserted by an unknown person.
12. Insertion of "and" here suggested by Seward.
13. Deletion suggested by Seward.

our national destruction consummated. This could not be allowed. Starvation was not yet upon the garrison; and ere it would be reached, Fort Pickens[14] might be re-enforced. This last^,^ would be a clear indication of *policy*, and would better enable the country to accept the evacuation of Fort Sumter, as a military *necessity*. An order was at once directed to be sent for the landing of the troops from the steamship Brooklyn, into Fort Pickens. This order could not go by land, but must take the longer and slower route by sea. The first return news from the order was received just one week before the fall of Fort Sumter. The news itself was, that the officer commanding the Sabine, to which vessel the troops had been transferred from the Brooklyn, acting upon some *quasi* armistice of the late administration, (and of the existence of which the present administration, up to the time the order was despatched, had only too vague and uncertain rumors to fix attention,) had refused to land the troops. To now re-enforce Fort Pickens, before a crisis would be reached at Fort Sumter, was impossible—rendered so by the near exhaustion of provisions in the latter-named fort. In precaution against such a conjuncture, the government had, a few days before, commenced preparing an expedition, as well adapted as might be, to relieve Fort Sumter, which expedition was intended to be ultimately used, or not, according to circumstances. The strongest anticipated case for using it^,^ was now presented; and it was resolved to send it forward. As had been intended, in this contingency, it was also resolved to notify the governor of South Carolina, that he might expect an attempt would be made to provision the fort; and that, if the attempt should not be resisted, there would be no effort to throw in men, arms, or ammunition, without further notice, or in case of an attack upon the fort. This notice was accordingly given; whereupon the fort was attacked, and bombarded to its fall, without even awaiting the arrival of the provisioning expedition.

It is thus seen that the assault upon, and reduction of, Fort Sumter, was, in no sense, a matter of self defence on the part of the assailants. They well knew that the garrison in the fort could, by no possibility, commit aggression upon them. They knew—they were expressly notified—that the giving of bread to the few brave and hungry men of the garrison, was all which would ^on that occasion^[15] be attempted, unless themselves, by resisting so much, should provoke more. They knew that this government desired to keep the garrison in the fort, not to assail them, but merely to maintain visible possession, and thus to preserve the Union from actual and immediate dissolution—trusting, as herein before stated, to time, discussion, and the

14. "Fort Pickens" is underlined, and "Ital." is written in the margin.
15. Insertion suggested by Seward.

ballot-box^,^ for final adjustment; and they assailed, and reduced the fort, for precisely the reverse object—to drive out the visible anthority [*authority*] of the federal Union, and thus force it to immediate dissolution. That this was their object^,^ the Executive well understood; and having said to them, in the inaugural address, "You can have no conflict without being yourselves the aggressors," he took pains, not only to keep this declaration good, but also to keep the case so free from the power of ingenious sophistry, as that the world should not be able to misunderstand it. By the affair at Fort Sumter, with its surrounding circumstances, that point was reached. Then, and thereby, the assailants of the government, began the conflict of arms, without a gun in sight, or in expectancy to return their fire, save only the few in the fort, sent to that harbor, years before, for their own protection, and still ready to give that protection in whatever was lawful. In this act, discarding all else, they have forced upon the country, the distinct issue: "Immediate dissolution or blood."

And this issue embraces more than the fate of these United States. It presents to the whole family of man the question, whether a ^Constitutional republic, or a^ democracy—a government of the people, by the same people—can, or cannot, maintain its territorial integrity against its own domestic foes. It presents the question, whether discontented individuals, too few in numbers to control administration, according to organic law, in any case, can always, upon the pretences made in this case, or on any other pretences, or arbitrarily, without any pretence, break up their government, and thus practically put an end to free government upon the earth. It forces us to ask: "Is there, in all republics, this inherent and fatal weakness?" "Must a government, of necessity, be too *strong* for the liberties of its own people, or too *weak* to maintain its own existence?"

So viewing the issue, no choice was left but to call out the war power of the government; and so to resist force, employed for its destruction, by force, for its preservation.

The call was made, and the response of the country was most gratifying;[16] surpassing in unanimity, and spirit, the most sanguine expectation. Yet,[17] none of the States commonly called slave States^,^ ^except Delaware,^ gave a regiment through regular State organization. A few regiments have been organized within some ^others^ of those States by individual enterprise, and received into the government service. Of course, the seceded States, so called, (and to which Texas had been joined about the time of the inauguration,) gave no troops to the cause of the Union. The border States,

16. "," changed to ";"
17. Insertion of "except patriotic Delaware" suggested by Seward.

so called, were not uniform in their action; some of them being almost *for* the Union, while ^in^ others—as Virginia, North Carolina, Tennessee, and Arkansas—^the Union sentiment was nearly ~~silenced, and~~ repressed, and silenced.^ ~~were apparently *quite* against it.~~ The course taken in Virginia was the most remarkable—perhaps the most important. A convention, elected by the people of that State to consider this very question of disrupting the Federal Union, was in session at the capital of Virginia when Fort Sumter fell. To this body the people had chosen a large majority of *professed* Union men. Almost immediately after the fall of Sumter, many members of that majority went over to the original disunion minority, and, with them, adopted an ordinance for withdrawing the State from the Union. Whether this change was wrought by their great approval of the assault upon Sumter, or their great resentment at the government's resistance to that assault, is not definitely known. Although they submitted the ordinance, for ratification, to a vote of the people, to be taken on a day ^then^ somewhat more than a month distant, the convention, and the legislature, (which was also in session at the same time and place,) with leading men of the State, not members of either, immediately commenced acting as if the State ^were^ ~~was~~ already out of the Union. They pushed military preparations vigorously forward all over the State. They seized the United States armory at Harper's Ferry, and the navy yard at Gosport, near Norfolk. They received—perhaps invited—into their State large bodies of troops, with their warlike appointments, from the so-called seceded States. They formally entered into a treaty of temporary alliance, and co-operation with the so-called "Confederate States^"^ ~~of America,~~"[18] and sent members to their Congress at Montgomery. And, finally, they permitted the insurrectionary government to be transferred to their capital at Richmond.

The people of Virginia have thus allowed this giant insurrection to make its nest within her borders; and this government has no choice left but to deal with it *where* it finds it. And it has the less regret, as the loyal citizens have, in due form, claimed its protection. Those loyal citizens^,^ this government is bound to recognize, and protect, as being Virginia.

In the border States, so called—in fact, the middle States—there are those who favor a policy which they call "armed neutrality:" that is, an arming of those States to prevent the Union forces passing one way, or the disunion the other, over their soil. This would be disunion ~~consummated.~~ ^completed.^ Figuratively speaking, it would be the building of an impassable wall along the line of separation—and yet, not quite an impassable one; for, under the guise of neutrality, it would tie the hands of the Union men,

18. Deletion suggested by Seward.

and freely pass supplies from among them to the insurrectionists, which it could not do as an open enemy. At a stroke, it would take all the trouble off the hands of secession, except only what proceeds from the external blockade. It would do for the disunionists that which, of all things, they most desire—feed them well, and give them disunion without a struggle of their own. It recognizes no fidelity to the Constitution, no obligation to maintain the Union; and while ~~they may not all be traitors who have favored it, the thing is, in fact, treason in disguise.~~ ^very many who have favored ^it^ are, doubtless, loyal citizens, it is, nevertheless, treason in effect,^[19]

Recurring to the action of the government, it may be stated that, at first, a call was made for seventy-five thousand militia; and rapidly following this, a proclamation was issued for closing the ports of the insurrectionary districts by proceedings in the nature of blockade. So far all was believed to be strictly legal. At this point the insurrectionists announced their purpose to enter upon the practice of privateering. ~~On more mature reflection, with observation on current events, it was concluded that the measures adopted, were inadequate to the occasion;~~[20] ~~both by reason of the very limited time the militia would be held to serve, and the general insufficiency of numbers, in the regular land and naval forces. Accordingly another call was made for ——— vol-~~

~~^Other calls for vol^~~

∀Other calls were made for vol-∀[21] unteers^,^ to serve three years, unless sooner discharged; and also for large additions to the regular army and navy. These measures, whether strictly legal or not, were ventured upon, under what appeared to be a popular demand, and a public necessity; trusting, then as now, that Congress would readily ratify them. It is believed that nothing has been done beyond the constitutional competency of Congress.

~~Whether the proceedings in the nature of blockade, be technically a blockade, scarcely needs to be considered; since foreign nations only claim what we concede, that, as between them and us, the strict law of blockade shall apply.~~

~~The attention of Congress is sought in aid of this means for suppressing the insurrection, as the one affording at once the greatest efficiency, and least danger to life, of any at the control of the government.~~[22]

Soon after the first call for militia, it was considered a duty to authorize the commanding general, in proper cases, according to his discretion, to sus-

---

19. Deletion and insertion of "very many who have favored it are loyal citizens it is nevertheless treason in effect" suggested by Seward.
20. "," changed to ";"
21. Deletion and insertion suggested by Seward.
22. Deletions of two paragraphs suggested by Seward.

pend the privilege of the writ of habeas corpus;[23] or, in other words, to arrest and detain, without resort to the ordinary processes and forms of law, such individuals as he might deem dangerous to the public safety. This authority has purposely been exercised but very sparingly. Nevertheless, the legality and propriety of what has been done under it are questioned, and the attention of the country has been called to the proposition that one who is sworn to "take care that the laws be faithfully executed," should not himself violate them. Of course some consideration was given to the questions of power^,^ and propriety^,^ before this matter was acted upon. The whole of the laws which were required to be faithfully executed^,^ were being resisted, and failing of execution in nearly one-third of the States.[24] ~~must~~ ^Must^ they be allowed to finally fail of execution, even had it been perfectly clear^,^ that by the use of the means necessary to their execution, some single law, made in such extreme tenderness of the citizen's liberty, that practically^,^ it relieves more of the guilty^,^ than of the innocent, should, to a very limited extent, be violated?[25] To state the question more directly, are all the laws *but one* to go unexecuted, and the government itself go to pieces, lest that one be violated? Even in such a case^,^ would not the official oath be broken, if the government should be overthrown, when it was believed that disregarding the single law, would tend to preserve it? But it was not believed that this question was presented. It was not believed that any law was violated. The provision of the Constitution that "the privilege of the writ of habeas corpus shall not be suspended unless when, in cases of rebellion or invasion, the public safety may require it," is equivalent to a provision—is a provision—that such privilege may be suspended when, in cases of rebellion or invasion, the public safety *does* require it. It was decided that we have a case of rebellion, and that the public safety does require the qualified suspension of the privilege of the writ ~~of habeas corpus~~ which was authorized to be made. Now it is insisted that Congress, and not the Executive, is vested with this power. But the Constitution itself is silent as to which^,^ or who^,^ is to exercise the power; and as the provision was plainly made for a dangerous emergency, it cannot be believed ~~that~~ the framers of the instrument intended^,^ that in every case, the danger should run its course^,^ until Congress could be called together; the very assembling of which might be prevented, as was intended in this case, by the rebellion.

No more extended argument is now offered;[26] as an opinion, at some length, will probably be presented by the Attorney General. Whether there

23. "," changed to ";"
24. "," changed to "."
25. Seward suggested "broken" in place of "violated"
26. "," changed to ";"

shall be any legislation upon the subject, and if any, what, is submitted entirely to the better judgment of Congress.

The forbearance of this government had been so extraordinary, and so long continued, as to lead some foreign nations to shape their action as if they supposed the early destruction of our National Union was probable. While this, on discovery, gave the Executive some concern, he is now happy to say ~~he finds no cause of complaint against the present course, of any foreign power, upon this ^the^ subject^s of our domestic difficulty.^~~ ∀that the sovereignty, and rights of the United States, are now everywhere practically respected by foreign powers; and a general sympaply with the country is manifested throughout the world.∀[27]

The reports of the Secretaries of the Treasury, War, and the Navy, will give the information in detail deemed necessary, and convenient for your deliberation, and action; while the Executive, and all the departments, will stand ready to supply omissions, or to communicate new facts, considered important for you to know.

It is now recommended that you give the legal means for making this contest a short^,^ and ^a^ decisive one; that you ~~authorize to be applied to the work~~[28] ~~at least —~~[29] ~~hundred thousand~~ ~~men; and three hundred~~ ^place at the control of the government, for the work, at least four hundred thousand men, and four[30] hundred^ millions of dollars. That number of men is ~~less than one-twelfth~~ ^about one tenth^ of those of proper ages within the regions where, apparently, *all* are willing to engage; and the sum is less than a ~~thirtieth~~ ^twentythird^ part of the money value owned by the men who seem ready to devote the whole. A debt of six hundred millions of dollars *now,* is a less sum per head, than was the debt of our revolution when we came out of that struggle; and the money value in the country now, bears even a greater proportion to what it was *then,* than does the population. Surely each man has as strong a motive *now,* to *preserve* our liberties, as each had *then,* to *establish* them.

A right result, at this time, will be worth more to the world than ten times the men, and ten times the money^.^ ~~it will cost.~~ The evidence reaching us from the country^,^ leaves no doubt^,^ that the material for the work is abundant; and that it needs only the hand of legislation to give it legal sanction, and the hand of the Executive to give it practical shape and efficiency.

---

27. Deletion and insertion of "that the sovereignty and rights of the United States are now everywhere practically respected by foreign powers, and a general sympathy with the country is manifested throughout the world." suggested by Seward.
28. Seward suggested the insertion of "if necessary" here.
29. Seward suggested the insertion of "4" in this blank space.
30. "four" written over line.

One of the greatest perplexities of the government is to avoid receiving troops faster than it can provide for them. In a word, the people will save their government, if the government itself, will do its part, only indifferently well.

It might seem, at first thought, to be of little difference whether the present movement at the South be called "secession" or "rebellion." The movers, however, well understand the difference. At the beginning^,^ they knew they could never raise their treason to any respectable magnitude by any name which implies *violation* of law. They knew their people possessed as much of moral sense, as much of devotion to law and order, and as much pride in, and reverence for, the history and government of their common country^,^ as any other civilized and patriotic people. They knew they could make no advancement directly in the teeth of these strong and noble sentiments. Accordingly they commenced by an insidious debauching of the public mind. They invented an ingenious sophism, which, if conceded, was followed by perfectly logical steps, through all the incidents, to the complete destruction of the Union. The sophism itself ~~was, and~~ is, that any State of the Union may, *consistently* with the national Constitution, and therefore *lawfully,* and *peacefully,* withdraw from the Union, without the consent of the Union, or of any other State. The little disguise that the supposed right is to be exercised only for just cause, themselves to be the sole judge of its justice, is too thin to merit any notice.

With rebellion thus sugar-coated, they have been drugging the public mind of their section for more than thirty years; and until at length they have brought many good men to a willingness to take up arms against the government the day *after* some assemblage of men have enacted the farcical pretence of taking their State out of the Union, who could have been brought to no such thing the day *before.*

This sophism derives much, perhaps the whole, of its currency from the assumption that there is some omnipotent and sacred supremacy pertaining to a *State*—to each State of our Federal Union. Our States have neither more, nor less power, than that reserved to them, in the Union, by the Constitution—no one of them ever having been a State *out* of the Union. The original ones passed into the Union even *before* they cast off their British colonial dependence; and the new ones each came into the Union directly from a condition of dependence, excepting Texas. And even Texas, in its temporary independence, was never designated a State. The new ones only took the designation of States, on coming into the Union, while that name was first adopted for the old ones, in and by the Declaration of Independence. Therein the "United Colonies" were declared to be "free and independent States;" but, even then, the object plainly was not to declare their independence of *one another,* or of the *Union;*[31] but directly the contrary, as their mutual pledge, and their mutual action, before, at the time, and afterwards, abundantly show. The express plighting of faith, by each and all of the original thirteen, in the Articles of Confederation, two years later, that the Union shall be perpetual, is most conclusive. Having never been States, either in substance or in name, *outside* of the Union, whence this magical omnipotence of "State rights," asserting a claim of power to lawfully destroy the Union itself? Much is said about the "sovereignty" of the States; but the word, even, is not in the national Constitution;[32] nor, as is believed, in any of the State constitutions. What is a "sovereignty," in the political sense of the term? Would it be far wrong to define it, "A political community^,^ without a political superior?" Tested by this, no one of our States, except Texas, ever was a sovereignty. And even Texas gave up the character on coming into the Union;[33] by which act^,^ she acknowledged the Constitution of the United States, and the laws and treaties of the United States made in pursuance of the Constitution, to be, for her, the supreme law of the land. The States have their *status* IN the Union, and they have no other legal *status.* If they break from this, they can only do so against law, and by revolution. The Union, and not themselves separately, procured their independence and their liberty. By conquest^,^ or purchase^,^ the Union gave each of them^,^ whatever of independence aud [*and*] liberty it has. The Union is older than any of the States, and, in fact, it created them as States. ~~As States, the Union gave birth to them.~~[34] Originally some dependent colonies made the Union, and, in turn, the Union threw off their old dependence^,^ ^for them,^ and made them States, such as they are. Not one of them ever had a State constitution independent of the Union. Of course, it is not forgotten that all the new States framed their constitutions before they entered the Union; nevertheless, dependent upon, and preparatory to, coming into the Union.

Unquestionably the States have the powers and rights reserved to them in and by the national Constitution; but among ~~those~~ ^these,^, surely, are not included all conceivable powers, however mischievous or destructive; but, at most, such only as were known in the world^,^ at the time^,^ as governmental powers; and certainly a power to destroy the government itself had never been known as a governmental—as a merely administrative power. This relative matter of national power^,^ and State rights, as a principle, is no other than the principle of *generality* and *locality.* Whatever concerns the

---

31. "," changed to ";"
32. "," changed to ";"
33. "," changed to ";"
34. "run on" written in left margin to connect sentences before and after stricken sentence.

whole^,^ should be confided to the whole—to the general government; while whatever concerns *only* the State^,^ should be left exclusively to the State. This is all there is of original principle about it. Whether the national Constitution, in defining boundaries between the two, has applied the principle with exact accuracy, is not to be questioned. We are all bound by that defining, without question.

What is now combatted, is the position that secession is *consistent* with the Constitution—is *lawful,* and *peaceful.* It is not contended that there is any express law for it; and nothing should ever be implied as law, which leads to unjust or absurd consequences. The nation purchased, with money, the countries out of which several of these States were formed. Is it just that they shall go off without leave, and without refunding? The nation paid very large sums, (in the aggregate, I believe nearly a hundred millions,) to relieve Florida of the aboriginal tribes. Is it just that she shall now be off without consent, or without making any return? The nation is now in debt for money applied to the benefit of these so-called seceding States, in common with the rest. Is it just, either that ~~the~~ creditors shall go unpaid, or the remaining States pay the whole? A part of the present national debt was contracted to pay the old debts of Texas. Is it just that she shall leave, and pay no part of this herself?

Again, if one State may secede, so may another; and when all shall have seceded, none is left to pay the debts. Is this quite just to creditors? Did we notify them of this sage view of ours^,^ when we borrowed their money? If we now recognize this doctrine^,^ by allowing the seceders to go in peace, it is difficult to see what we can do^,^ if others choose to go, or to extort terms upon which they will promise to remain.

The seceders insist that our Constitution admits of secession. They have assumed to make a national constitution of their own, in which, of necessity, they have either *discarded* or *retained* the right of secession, as, they insist, it exists in ours. If they have discarded it, they thereby admit that, on principle, it ought not to be in ours. If they have retained it, by their own construction of ours they show that ^to be consistent they must^ ~~they will~~ secede from one another, whenever they shall find it the easiest way of settling their debts, or effecting any other selfish or unjust object. The principle itself is one of disintegration, and upon which no government can possibly endure.

If all the States, save one, should assert the power to *drive* that one out of the Union, it is presumed the whole class of seceder politicians would at once deny the power, and denounce the act as the greatest outrage upon State rights. But suppose that precisely the same act, instead of being called "driving the one out," should be called "the seceding of the others from that one," it would be exactly what the seceders claim to do; unless, indeed, they make the point, that the one, because it is a minority, may rightfully do what the others, because they are a majority, may not rightfully do. These politicians are subtle^,^ and profound^,^ on the rights of minorities. ~~The dread of their existence is~~ ^They are not partial to^ that power which made the Constitution, and speaks from the preamble, calling itself "We, the People."

It may well be questioned whether there is, to-day, a majority of the legally qualified voters of any State, except ^perhaps^[35] South Carolina, in favor of disunion. There is much reason to believe that the Union men are the majority in many, if not in every other one, of the so-called seceded States. The contrary has not been demonstrated in any one of them. It is ventured to affirm this, even of Virginia and Tennessee; for the result of an election, held in military camps, where the bayonets are all on one side of the question voted upon, can scarcely be considered as demonstrating popular sentiment. At such an election^,^ all that large class who are, at once, *for* the Union, and *against* coercion, would be coerced to vote against the Union.

It may be affirmed, without extravagance, that the free institutions we enjoy have developed the powers, and improved the condition, of our whole people, beyond any example in the world. Of this we now have a striking^,^ and an impressive illustration. So large an army as the government has now on foot, was never before known, without a soldier in it, but who had taken his place there, of his own free choice. But more than this: there are many single regiments whose members, one and another, possess full practical knowledge of all the arts, sciences, professions, and whatever else, whether useful or elegant, is known in the world; and there is scarcely one^,^ from which there could not be selected, a President, a Cabinet, a Congress, and perhaps a Court, abundantly competent to administer the government itself! Nor do I ~~know that~~ ^say^[36] this is not true, also, in the army of our late friends, now adversaries^,^ in this contest; but if it is, so much better the reason why the government, which has conferred such benefits on both them and us, should not be broken up. Whoever, in any section, proposes to abandon such a government, would do well to consider, in deference to what principle it is that he does it—what better he is likely to get in its stead—whether the substitute will give, or be intended to give, so much of good to the people. There are some foreshadowings on this subject. Our adversaries have adopted some declaration^s^ of independence;[37] in which, unlike the good old one, penned

---

35. Insertion suggested by Seward.
36. Deletion of "Nor do I know" and insertion of "I do not say ~~that this~~" suggested by Seward.
37. "," changed to ";"

by Jefferson, they omit the words "all men are created equal." Why? They have adopted a temporary national constitution, in the preamble of which, unlike our good old one, signed by Washington, they omit "We, the people," and substitute "We, the deputies of the sovereign and independent States." Why? Why this deliberate pressing out of view, the rights of men, and the authority of the people?

This is essentially a People's contest. On the side of the Union, it is a struggle for maintaining in the world, that form and substance of government, whose leading object is, to elevate the condition of men—to lift artificial weights from all shoulders; to clear the paths of laudable pursuit for all; to afford all^,^ an unfettered start, and a fair chance^,^ in the race of life. Yielding to partial and temporary departures, from necessity, this is the leading object of the government for whose existence we contend.

I am most happy to believe that the plain people understand and appreciate this. It is worthy of note, that while in this, the government's hour of trial, large numbers of those in the army and navy who have been favored with the offices, have resigned, and ~~played~~ ^proved^ false to the ~~very~~ hand which had pampered them, not one common soldier, or common sailor, ^is known to have^ ~~has~~ deserted his flag.

Great~~er~~ honor is due to those officers who remained true, despite the example of their treacherous associates; but the greatest honor, and most important fact of all, is the unanimous firmness of the common soldiers, and common sailors. To the last man, ^so far ^as^ known,^ they have successfully resisted the traitorous efforts of those whose commands, but an hour before, they obeyed as absolute law. This is the patriotic instinct of plain people. They understand, without an argument, that ~~the~~ destroying the government^,^ which was made by Washington^,^ means no good to them.

Our popular government has often been called an experiment. Two points in it our people have already settled—the successful *establishing* and the successful *administering* of it. One still remains—~~the~~ ^it's^ successful *maintenance* ~~of it~~, against a formidable attempt to overthrow it. It is now for them to demonstrate to the world, that those who can fairly carry an election, can also suppress a rebellion; that ballots are the rightful^,^ and peaceful^,^ successors of bullets; and that when ballots have fairly^,^ and constitutionally decided, there can be no successful appeal back to bullets; that there can be no successful appeal^,^ except to ballots themselves, at succeeding elections. Such will be a great lesson of peace; teaching men that what they cannot take by an election, neither can they take it by a war; teaching all^,^ the folly of being the beginners of a war.

Lest there be some uneasiness in the minds of candid men^,^ as to what is to be the course of the government^,^ towards the southern States^,^ *after* the rebellion shall have been suppressed, the Executive deems it proper to say^,^ it will be his purpose then, as ever, to be guided by the Constitution and the laws;[38] and that he probably will have no different understanding of the powers and duties of the federal government ~~relative~~ ^relatively^ to the rights of the States^,^ and the people, under the Constitution, than that expressed in the inaugural address:

He desires to preserve the government, that it may be administered for all, as it was administered by the men who made it. Loyal citizens everywhere, have the right to claim this of their government; and the government has no right to withhold, or neglect it. It is not perceived that, in giving it, there is any coercion, any conquest, or any subjugation, ^in any just sense of those terms.^~~which any honest man should regret.~~[39] ^The Constitution provides, and all the States have accepted the provision, that "The United States shall guarantee to every State in this Union a republican form of government." But, if a State may lawfully go out of the Union, having done so, it may also discard the republican form of government; so that to prevent it's going out, is an indispensable <u>means</u>, to the <u>end</u>, of maintaining the guaranty mentioned; and when an end is lawful and obligatory, the indispensable means to it, are also lawful, and obligatory.^

It was with the deepest regret that the Executive found the duty of employing the war-power, in defence of the government, forced upon him. He could but perform this duty, or surrender the existence of the government. No compromise, by public servants, could, in this case, be a cure; not that compromises are not often proper, but that no popular government can long survive a marked precedent, that those who carry an election^,^ can only save the government from immediate destruction^,^ by giving up the main point^,^ upon which^,^ the people gave the election. The people themselves, and not their servants, can safely reverse their own deliberate decisions.

As a private citizen, ~~he~~ ^the Executive^ could not have consented that these institutions shall perish; much less could he, in betrayal of so vast^,^ and so sacred a trust^,^ as these free people had confided to him. He felt that he had no moral right to shrink;[40] nor even to count the chances of his own life, in what might follow. In full view of his great responsibility, he has, so far, done what he has deemed his duty. You will now, according to your own judgment, perform yours. He sincerely hopes that your views, and your ac-

---

38. "," changed to ";"
39. Deletion and insertion of "or any defamation of any citizen of any right of life liberty or pursuit of happiness granted to him by the Constitution or the laws of the land." suggested by Seward.
40. "," changed to ";"

tion, may so accord with his^,^ as to assure all faithful citizens, who have been disturbed in their rights, of a certain^,^ and speedy restoration to them, under the Constitution and the laws.

And having thus chosen our course, without guile, and with pure purpose, let us renew our trust in God, and go forward without fear, and with manly hearts.

^ABRAHAM LINCOLN
JULY 4, 1861^

APPENDIX 5

ABRAHAM LINCOLN TO HORACE GREELEY

AUGUST 22, 1862

Lincoln's handwritten letter to Horace Greeley is at the Wadsworth Atheneum (a gift of Elizabeth L. Dixon), in Hartford, Connecticut. Greeley published the letter in his *New York Tribune* on August 22, 1862. This transcription is of the handwritten letter, with changes other than typeface in the published version indicated in notes.

EXECUTIVE MANSION,
WASHINGTON, AUGUST 22,, 1862.[1]

Hon. Horace Greely[2]:
Dear Sir:

I have just read yours of the 19th[3] addressed to myself through the New-York[4] Tribune. If there be in it any statements,[5] or assumptions of fact,[6] which I may know to be erroneous, I do not,[7] now and here,[8] controvert them. If there be in it any inferences which I may believe to be falsely drawn, I do not now and here,[9] argue against them. If there be perceptable[10] in it an impatient and dictatorial tone, I waive it in deference to an old friend, whose heart I have always supposed to be right.

As to the policy I "seem to be pursuing[11]" as you say, I have not meant to leave any one in doubt.

---

1. "Executive Mansion, Washington," and ", 186" are printed. The inserts and underscores are handwritten. The printed version has one "," after "22"
2. "Greeley" in printed version.
3. "," here in printed version.
4. "N.Y." in printed version.
5. No "," here in printed version.
6. No "," here in printed version.
7. No "," here in printed version.
8. No "," here in printed version.
9. No "," here in printed version.
10. "perceptible" in printed version.
11. "," her in printed version.

I would save the Union. I would save it the shortest way under the Constitution. The sooner the national[12] authority can be restored, the nearer the Union will be "the Union as it was." ~~Broken eggs can never be mended, and the longer the breaking proceeds the more will be broken.~~ If there be ^those^ ~~any~~ who would not save the Union,[13] unless they could at the same time save slavery,[14] I do not agree with them. If there be ~~any~~ ^those^ who would not save the Union unless they could at the same time destroy slavery,[15] I do not agree with them. My paramount object in this struggle is to save the Union, and is not either to save or to destroy[16] slavery.[17] If I could save the Union without freeing any slave[18] I would do,[19] it,[20] and if I could save it by freeing all the slaves[21] I would do it; and if I could save[22] it by freeing some and leaving others alone[23] I would also do that. What I do about slavery,[24] and the colored race, I do because I believe it helps to save the[25] Union; and what I forbear, I forbear because I do not believe it would help to save the Union. I shall do less whenever I shall believe what I am doing hurts the cause, and I shall do more whenever I shall believe doing more will help the cause. I shall try to correct errors when shown to be errors; and I shall adopt new views so fast as they shall appear to be true views.[26]

I have here stated my purpose according to my view of official duty;[27] and I intend no modification of my oft-expressed personal wish that all men everywhere could[28] be free.

Yours,
A. Lincoln[29]

---

12. "National" in printed version.
13. No "," in printed version.
14. "Slavery" in printed version.
15. "Slavery" in printed version.
16. "to save or to destroy" changed to "to save or destroy" in printed version.
17. "Slavery" in printed version.
18. "," here in printed version.
19. No "," here in printed version.
20. ";" here in printed version.
21. "," here in printed version.
22. "save" changed to "do" in printed version.
23. "," here in printed version.
24. "Slavery" in printed version.
25. "the" changed to "this" in printed version.
26. No new paragraph here in printed version.
27. "," here in printed version.
28. "all men everywhere could" changed to "all men, everywhere, could" in printed version.
29. "." here in printed version.

APPENDIX 6

MEDITATION ON THE DIVINE WILL

SEPTEMBER 2(?), 1862

Lincoln wrote this private reflection in September 1862. His secretary John Hay discovered the text after Lincoln's death. Hay furnished the title "Meditation on the Divine Will." Lincoln's musing was undated. Lincoln's secretaries, Hay and Nicolay, provided a date of September 30, 1862, in their *Complete Works,* which was published in 1894 (volume VIII, page 52). They associated the meditation with Lincoln's struggles over the questions related to the Emancipation Proclamation. Roy P. Basler and the other editors of *The Collected Works of Abraham Lincoln* suggest that the meditation was written earlier, on September 2, 1862, after Lincoln learned of the disastrous Union defeat in the Second Battle of Bull Run.

This document is in the Lincoln Collection in the John Hay Library at Brown University, Providence, Rhode Island.

The will of God prevails. In great contests each party claims to act in accordance with the will of God. Both may be, and one must be wrong. God can not be for, and against the same thing at the same time. In the present civil war it is quite possible that God's purpose is something different from the purpose of either party—and yet the human instrumentalities, working just as they do, are of the best adaptation to effect ~~his~~ ^His^ purpose. I am almost ready to say this is probably true—that God wills this contest, and wills that it shall not end yet. By his mere quet [*quiet*] power, on the minds of the now contestants, He could have either saved or destroyed the Union without a human contest. Yet the contest began. And having begun He could give the final victory to either side any day. Yet the contest proceeds.

APPENDIX 7

ANNUAL MESSAGE TO CONGRESS

DECEMBER 1, 1862

Clerks in the House of Representatives and Senate read Lincoln's Annual Message to Congress on December 1, 1862. The annual message was the State of the Union address of its day.

Lincoln's four annual messages to Congress ascended beyond the limits of the event. Almost always, when the annual message of 1862 has been used in collections of Lincoln documents, only the last paragraph and a half are printed. His annual messages, as was the custom, included whole sections that had been given to him by cabinet officers. Heard and contrasted against the larger whole, Lincoln's ability to move from reporting of the ordinary to extraordinary rhetoric can be appreciated in greater measure.

The text is from *The Collected Works of Abraham Lincoln,* edited by Roy P. Basler.

Fellow-citizens of the Senate and House of Representatives:

Since your last annual assembling another year of health and bountiful harvests has passed. And while it has not pleased the Almighty to bless us with a return of peace, we can but press on, guided by the best light He gives us, trusting that in His own good time, and wise way, all will yet be well.

The correspondence touching foreign affairs which has taken place during the last year is herewith submitted, in virtual compliance with a request to that effect, made by the House of Representatives near the close of the last session of Congress.

If the condition of our relations with other nations is less gratifying than it has usually been at former periods, it is certainly more satisfactory than a nation so unhappily distracted as we are, might reasonably have apprehended. In the month of June last there were some grounds to expect that the maritime powers which, at the beginning of our domestic difficulties, so unwisely and unnecessarily, as we think, recognized the insurgents as a belligerent, would soon recede from that position, which has proved only less injurious to themselves, than to our own country. But the temporary reverses which afterwards befell the national arms, and which were exaggerated by our own disloyal citizens abroad have hitherto delayed that act of simple justice.

The civil war, which has so radically changed for the moment, the occupations and habits of the American people, has necessarily disturbed the social condition, and affected very deeply the prosperity of the nations with which we have carried on a commerce that has been steadily increasing throughout a period of half a century. It has, at the same time, excited political ambitions and apprehensions which have produced a profound agitation throughout the civilized world. In this unusual agitation we have forborne from taking part in any controversy between foreign states, and between parties or factions in such states. We have attempted no propagandism, and acknowledged no revolution. But we have left to every nation the exclusive conduct and management of its own affairs. Our struggle has been, of course, contemplated by foreign nations with reference less to its own merits, than to its supposed, and often exaggerated effects and consequences resulting to those nations themselves. Nevertheless, complaint on the part of this government, even if it were just, would certainly be unwise.

The treaty with Great Britain for the suppression of the slave trade has been put into operation with a good prospect of complete success. It is an occasion of special pleasure to acknowledge that the execution of it, on the part of Her Majesty's government, has been marked with a jealous respect for the authority of the United States, and the rights of their moral and loyal citizens.

The convention with Hanover for the abolition of the state dues has been carried into full effect, under the act of Congress for that purpose.

A blockade of three thousand miles of sea-coast could not be established, and vigorously enforced, in a season of great commercial activity like the present, without committing occasional mistakes, and inflicting unintentional injuries upon foreign nations and their subjects.

A civil war occurring in a country where foreigners reside and carry on trade under treaty stipulations is necessarily fruitful of complaints of the violation of neutral rights. All such collisions tend to excite misapprehensions, and possibly to produce mutual reclamations between nations which have a common interest in preserving peace and friendship. In clear cases of these kinds I have, so far as possible, heard and redressed complaints which have been presented by friendly powers. There is still, however, a large and an augmenting number of doubtful cases upon which the government is unable to agree with the governments whose protection is demanded by the claimants. There are, moreover, many cases in which the United States, or their citizens, suffer wrongs from the naval or military authorities of foreign nations, which the governments of those states are not at once prepared to redress. I have proposed to some of the foreign states, thus interested, mutual conventions to examine and adjust such complaints. This proposition has been made especially to Great Britain, to France, to Spain, and to Prussia. In each case it has been kindly received, but has not yet been formally adopted.

I deem it my duty to recommend an appropriation in behalf of the owners of the Norwegian bark Admiral P. Tordenskiold, which vessel was, in May, 1861, prevented by the commander of the blockading force off Charleston from leaving that port with cargo, notwithstanding a similar privilege had, shortly before, been granted to an English vessel. I have directed the Secretary of State to cause the papers in the case to be communicated to the proper committees.

Applications have been made to me by many free Americans of African descent to favor their emigration, with a view to such colonization as was contemplated in recent acts of Congress. Other parties, at home and abroad—some from interested motives, others upon patriotic considerations, and still others influenced by philanthropic sentiments—have suggested similar measures; while, on the other hand, several of the Spanish-American republics have protested against the sending of such colonies to their respective territories. Under these circumstances, I have declined to move any such colony to any state, without first obtaining the consent of its government, with an agreement on its part to receive and protect such emigrants in all the rights of freemen; and I have, at the same time, offered to the several states situated within the tropics, or having colonies there, to negotiate with them, subject to the advice and consent of the Senate, to favor the voluntary emigration of persons of that class to their respective territories, upon conditions which shall be equal, just, and humane. Liberia and Hayti are, as yet, the only countries to which colonists of African descent from here, could go with certainty of being received and adopted as citizens; and I regret to say such persons, contemplating colonization, do not seem so willing to migrate to those countries, as to some others, nor so willing as I think their interest demands. I believe, however, opinion among them, in this respect, is improving; and that, ere long, there will be an augmented, and considerable migration to both these countries, from the United States.

The new commercial treaty between the United States and the Sultan of Turkey has been carried into execution.

A commercial and consular treaty has been negotiated, subject to the Senate's consent, with Liberia; and a similar negotiation is now pending with the republic of Hayti. A considerable improvement of the national commerce is expected to result from these measures.

Our relations with Great Britain, France, Spain, Portugal, Russia, Prussia, Denmark, Sweden, Austria, the Netherlands, Italy, Rome, and the other European states, remain undisturbed. Very favorable relations also continue to be maintained with Turkey, Morocco, China and Japan.

During the last year there has not only been no change of our previous relations with the independent states of our own continent, but, more friendly sentiments than have heretofore existed, are believed to be entertained by these neighbors, whose safety and progress, are so intimately connected with our own. This statement especially applies to Mexico, Nicaragua, Costa Rica, Honduras, Peru, and Chile.

The commission under the convention with the republic of New Granada closed its session, without having audited and passed upon, all the claims which were submitted to it. A proposition is pending to revive the convention, that it may be able to do more complete justice. The joint commission between the United States and the republic of Costa Rica has completed its labors and submitted its report.

I have favored the project for connecting the United States with Europe by an Atlantic telegraph, and a similar project to extend the telegraph from San Francisco, to connect by a Pacific telegraph with the line which is being extended across the Russian empire.

The Territories of the United States, with unimportant exceptions, have remained undisturbed by the civil war, and they are exhibiting such evidence of prosperity as justifies an expectation that some of them will soon be in a condition to be organized as States, and be constitutionally admitted into the federal Union.

The immense mineral resources of some of those Territories ought to be developed as rapidly as possible. Every step in that direction would have a tendency to improve the revenues of the government, and diminish the burdens of the people. It is worthy of your serious consideration whether some extraordinary measures to promote that end cannot be adopted. The means which suggests itself as most likely to be effective, is a scientific exploration of the mineral regions in those Territories, with a view to the publication of its results at home and in foreign countries—results which cannot fail to be auspicious.

The condition of the finances will claim your most diligent consideration. The vast expenditures incident to the military and naval operations required for the suppression of the rebellion have hitherto been met with a promptitude, and certainty, unusual in similar circumstances and the public credit has been fully maintained. The continuance of the war, however, and the increased disbursements made necessary by the augmented forces now in the field, demand your best reflections as to the best modes of providing the necessary revenue, without injury to business and with the least possible burdens upon labor.

The suspension of specie payments by the banks, soon after the commencement of your last session, made large issues of United States notes unavoidable. In no other way could the payment of the troops, and the satisfaction of other just demands, be so economically, or so well provided for. The judicious legislation of Congress, securing the receivability of these notes for loans and internal duties, and making them a legal tender for other debts, has made them an universal currency; and has satisfied, partially, at least, and for the time, the long felt want of an uniform circulating medium, saving thereby to the people, immense sums in discounts and exchanges.

A return to specie payments, however, at the earliest period compatible with due regard to all interests concerned, should ever be kept in view. Fluctuations in the value of currency are always injurious, and to reduce these fluctuations to the lowest possible point will always be a leading purpose in wise legislation. Convertibility, prompt and certain convertibility into coin, is generally acknowledged to be the best and surest safeguard against them; and it is extremely doubtful whether a circulation of United States notes, payable in coin, and sufficiently large for the wants of the people, can be permanently, usefully and safely maintained.

Is there, then, any other mode in which the necessary provision for the public wants can be made, and the great advantages of a safe and uniform currency secured?

I know of none which promises so certain results, and is, at the same time, so unobjectionable, as the organization of banking associations, under a general act of Congress, well guarded in its provisions.

To such associations the government might furnish circulating notes, on the security of United States bonds deposited in the treasury. These notes, prepared under the supervision of proper officers, being uniform in appearance and security, and convertible always into coin, would at once protect labor against the evils of a vicious currency, and facilitate commerce by cheap and safe exchanges.

A moderate reservation from the interest on the bonds would compensate the United States for the preparation and distribution of the notes and a general supervision of the system, and would lighten the burden of that part of the public debt employed as securities. The public credit, moreover, would be greatly improved, and the negotiation of new loans greatly facilitated by the steady market demand for government bonds which the adoption of the proposed system would create.

It is an additional recommendation of the measure, of considerable weight, in my judgment, that it would reconcile, as far as possible, all existing interests, by the opportunity offered to existing institutions to reorganize under the act, substituting only the secured uniform national circulation for the local and various circulation, secured and unsecured, now issued by them.

The receipts into the treasury from all sources, including loans and balance from the preceding year, for the fiscal year ending on the 30th June, 1862, were $583,885,247 06, of which sum $49,056,397 62 were derived from customs; $1,795,331,73 from the direct tax; from public lands $152,203,77; from miscellaneous sources, $931,787 64; from loans in all forms, $529,692,460 50. The remainder, $2,257,065 80, was the balance from last year.

The disbursements during the same period were for congressional, executive, and judicial purposes, $5,939,009 29; for foreign intercourse, $1,339,710,35; for miscellaneous expenses, including the mints, loans, post office deficiencies, collection of revenue, and other like charges, $14,129,771 50; for expenses under the Interior Department, $3,102,985 52; under the War Department, $394,368,407,36; under the Navy Department, $42,674,569 69; for interest on public debt, $13,190,324 45; and for payment of public debt, including reimbursement of temporary loan, and redemptions, $96,096,922 09; making an aggregate of $570,841,700 25; and leaving a balance in the treasury on the first day of July, 1862, of $13,043,546,81.

It should be observed that the sum of $96,096,922 09, expended for reimbursements and redemption of public debt, being included also in the loans made, may be properly deducted, both from receipts and expenditures, leaving the actual receipts for the year $487,788,324 97; and the expenditures, $474,744,778 16.

Other information on the subject of the finances will be found in the report of the Secretary of the Treasury, to whose statements and views I invite your most candid and considerate attention.

The reports of the Secretaries of War, and of the Navy, are herewith transmitted. These reports, though lengthy, are scarcely more than brief abstracts of the very numerous and extensive transactions and operations conducted through those departments. Nor could I give a summary of them here, upon any principle, which would admit of its being much shorter than the reports themselves. I therefore content myself with laying the reports before you, and asking your attention to them.

[Report of the Post Office Department.]

The Secretary of the Interior reports as follows in regard to the public lands. . . .

The Indian tribes upon our frontiers have, during the past year, manifested a spirit of insubordination, and, at several points, have engaged in open hostilities against the white settlements in their vicinity. The tribes occupying the Indian country south of Kansas, renounced their allegiance to the United States, and entered into treaties with the insurgents. Those who remained loyal to the United States were driven from the country. The chief of the Cherokees has visited this city for the purpose of restoring the former relations of the tribe with the United States. He alleges that they were constrained, by superior force, to enter into treaties with the insurgents, and that the United States neglected to furnish the protection which their treaty stipulations required.

In the month of August last the Sioux Indians, in Minnesota, attacked the settlements in their vicinity with extreme ferocity, killing, indiscriminately, men, women, and children. This attack was wholly unexpected, and, therefore, no means of defence had been provided. It is estimated that not less than eight hundred persons were killed by the Indians, and a large amount of property was destroyed. How this outbreak was induced is not definitely known, and suspicions, which may be unjust, need not to be stated. Information was received by the Indian bureau, from different sources, about the time hostilities were commenced, that a simultaneous attack was to be made upon the white settlements by all the tribes between the Mississippi river and the Rocky mountains. The State of Minnesota has suffered great injury from this Indian war. A large portion of her territory has been depopulated, and a severe loss has been sustained by the destruction of property. The people of that State manifest much anxiety for the removal of the tribes beyond the limits of the State as a guarantee against future hostilities. The Commissioner of Indian Affairs will furnish full details. I submit for your especial consideration whether our Indian system shall not be remodelled. Many wise and good men have impressed me with the belief that this can be profitably done.

I submit a statement of the proceedings of commissioners, which shows the progress that has been made in the enterprise of constructing the Pacific railroad. And this suggests the earliest completion of this road, and also the favorable action of Congress upon the projects now pending before them for enlarging the capacities of the great canals in New York and Illinois, as being of vital, and rapidly increasing importance to the whole nation, and especially to the vast interior region hereinafter to be noticed at some greater length. I purpose having prepared and laid before you at an early day some interesting and valuable statistical information upon this subject. The military and commercial importance of enlarging the Illinois and Michigan canal, and improving the Illinois River, is presented in the report of Colonel Webster to the Secretary of War, and now transmitted to Congress. I respectfully ask attention to it.

To carry out the provisions of the act of Congress of the 15th of May last, I have caused the Department of Agriculture of the United States to be organized.

The Commissioner informs me that within the period of a few months this department has established an extensive system of correspondence and exchanges, both at home and abroad, which promises to effect highly beneficial results in the development of a correct knowledge of recent improvements in agriculture, in the introduction of new products, and in the collection of the agricultural statistics of the different States.

Also that it will soon be prepared to distribute largely seeds, cereals, plants and cuttings, and has already published, and liberally diffused, much valuable information in anticipation of a more elaborate report, which will in due time be furnished, embracing some valuable tests in chemical science now in progress in the laboratory.

The creation of this department was for the more immediate benefit of a large class of our most valuable citizens; and I trust that the liberal basis upon which it has been organized will not only meet your approbation, but that it will realize, at no distant day, all the fondest anticipations of its most sanguine friends, and become the fruitful source of advantage to all our people.

On the twenty-second day of September last a proclamation was issued by the Executive, a copy of which is herewith submitted.

In accordance with the purpose expressed in the second paragraph of that paper, I now respectfully recall your attention to what may be called "compensated emancipation."

A nation may be said to consist of its territory, its people, and its laws. The territory is the only part which is of certain durability. "One generation passeth away, and another generation cometh, but the earth abideth forever." It is of the first importance to duly consider, and estimate, this ever-enduring part. That portion of the earth's surface which is owned and inhabited by the people of the United States, is well adapted to be the home of one national family; and it is not well adapted for two, or more. Its vast extent, and its variety of climate and productions, are of advantage, in this age, for one people, whatever they might have been in former ages. Steam, telegraphs, and intelligence, have brought these, to be an advantageous combination, for one united people.

In the inaugural address I briefly pointed out the total inadequacy of disunion, as a remedy for the differences between the people of the two sections. I did so in language which I cannot improve, and which, therefore, I beg to repeat:

"One section of our country believes slavery is *right,* and ought to be extended, while the other believes it is *wrong,* and ought not to be extended.

This is the only substantial dispute. The fugitive slave clause of the Constitution, and the law for the suppression of the foreign slave trade, are each as well enforced, perhaps, as any law can ever be in a community where the moral sense of the people imperfectly supports the law itself. The great body of the people abide by the dry legal obligation in both cases, and a few break over in each. This, I think, cannot be perfectly cured; and it would be worse in both cases *after* the separation of the sections, than before. The foreign slave trade, now imperfectly suppressed, would be ultimately revived without restriction in one section; while fugitive slaves, now only partially surrendered, would not be surrendered at all by the other.

"Physically speaking, we cannot separate. We cannot remove our respective sections from each other, nor build an impassable wall between them. A husband and wife may be divorced, and go out of the presence, and beyond the reach of each other; but the different parts of our country cannot do this. They cannot but remain face to face; and intercourse, either amicable or hostile, must continue between them. Is it possible, then, to make that intercourse more advantageous, or more satisfactory, *after* separation than *before*? Can aliens make treaties, easier than friends can make laws? Can treaties be more faithfully enforced between aliens, than laws can among friends? Suppose you go to war, you cannot fight always; and when, after much loss on both sides, and no gain on either, you cease fighting, the identical old questions, as to terms of intercourse, are again upon you."

There is no line, straight or crooked, suitable for a national boundary, upon which to divide. Trace through, from east to west, upon the line between the free and slave country, and we shall find a little more than one-third of its length are rivers, easy to be crossed, and populated, or soon to be populated, thickly upon both sides; while nearly all its remaining length, are merely surveyor's lines, over which people may walk back and forth without any consciousness of their presence. No part of this line can be made any more difficult to pass, by writing it down on paper, or parchment, as a national boundary. The fact of separation, if it comes, gives up, on the part of the seceding section, the fugitive slave clause, along with all other constitutional obligations upon the section seceded from, while I should expect no treaty stipulation would ever be made to take its place.

But there is another difficulty. The great interior region, bounded east by the Alleghanies, north by the British dominions, west by the Rocky mountains, and south by the line along which the culture of corn and cotton meets, and which includes part of Virginia, part of Tennessee, all of Kentucky, Ohio, Indiana, Michigan, Wisconsin, Illinois, Missouri, Kansas, Iowa, Minnesota and the Territories of Dakota, Nebraska, and part of Colorado, already has above ten millions of people, and will have fifty millions within fifty years, if not prevented by any political folly or mistake. It contains more than one-third of the country owned by the United States—certainly more than one million of square miles. Once half as populous as Massachusetts already is, it would have more than seventy-five millions of people. A glance at the map shows that, territorially speaking, it is the great body of the republic. The other parts are but marginal borders to it, the magnificent region sloping west from the Rocky Mountains to the Pacific, being the deepest, and also the richest, in undeveloped resources. In the production of provisions, grains, grasses, and all which proceed from them, this great interior region is naturally one of the most important in the world. Ascertain from the statistics the small proportion of the region which has, as yet, been brought into cultivation and also the large and rapidly increasing amount of its products, and we shall be overwhelmed with the magnitude of the prospect presented. An [*And*] yet this region has no sea-coast, touches no ocean anywhere. As part of one nation, its people now find, and may forever find, their way to Europe by New York, to South America and Africa by New Orleans, and to Asia by San Francisco. But separate our common country into two nations, as designed by the present rebellion, and every man of this great interior region is thereby cut off from some one or more of these outlets, not, perhaps, by a physical barrier, but by embarrassing and onerous trade regulations.

And this is true, *wherever* a dividing, or boundary line, may be fixed. Place it between the now free and slave country, or place it south of Kentucky, or north of Ohio, and still the truth remains, that none south of it, can trade to any port or place north of it, and none north of it, can trade to any port or place south of it, except upon terms dictated by a government foreign to them. These outlets, east, west, and south, are indispensable to the well-being of the people inhabiting, and to inhabit, this vast interior region. *Which* of the three may be the best, is no proper question. All, are better than either, and all, of right, belong to that people, and to their successors forever. True to themselves, they will not ask *where* a line of separation shall be, but will vow, rather, that there shall be no such line. Nor are the marginal regions less interested in these communications to, and through them, to the great outside world. They too, and each of them, must have access to this Egypt of the West, without paying toll at the crossing of any national boundary.

Our national strife springs not from our permanent part; not from the land we inhabit; not from our national homestead. There is no possible severing of this, but would multiply, and not mitigate, evils among us. In all its adaptations and aptitudes, it demands union, and abhors separation. In fact, it would, ere long, force re-union, however much of blood and treasure the separation might have cost.

Our strife pertains to ourselves—to the passing generations of men; and it can, without convulsion, be hushed forever with the passing of one generation.

In this view, I recommend the adoption of the following resolution and articles amendatory to the Constitution of the United States:

"*Resolved by the Senate and House of Representatives of the United States of America in Congress assembled,* (two thirds of both houses concurring,) That the following articles be proposed to the legislatures (or conventions) of the several States as amendments to the Constitution of the United States, all or any of which articles when ratified by three-fourths of the said legislatures (or conventions) to be valid as part or parts of the said Constitution, viz:

"Article ——.

"Every State, wherein slavery now exists, which shall abolish the same therein, at any time, or times, before the first day of January, in the year of our Lord one thousand and nine hundred, shall receive compensation from the United States as follows, to wit:

"The President of the United States shall deliver to every such State, bonds of the United States, bearing interest at the rate of —— per cent, per annum, to an amount equal to the aggregate sum of for each slave shown to have been therein, by the eighth census of the United States, said bonds to be delivered to such State by installments, or in one parcel, at the completion of the abolishment, accordingly as the same shall have been gradual, or at one time, within such State; and interest shall begin to run upon any such bond, only from the proper time of its delivery as aforesaid. Any State having received bonds as aforesaid, and afterwards reintroducing or tolerating slavery therein, shall refund to the United States the bonds so received, or the value thereof, and all interest paid thereon.

"Article ——.

"All slaves who shall have enjoyed actual freedom by the chances of the war, at any time before the end of the rebellion, shall be forever free; but all owners of such, who shall not have been disloyal, shall be compensated for them, at the same rates as is provided for States adopting abolishment of slavery, but in such way, that no slave shall be twice accounted for.

"Article ——.

"Congress may appropriate money, and otherwise provide, for colonizing free colored persons, with their own consent, at any place or places without the United States."

I beg indulgence to discuss these proposed articles at some length. Without slavery the rebellion could never have existed; without slavery it could not continue.

Among the friends of the Union there is great diversity, of sentiment, and of policy, in regard to slavery, and the African race amongst us. Some would perpetuate slavery; some would abolish it suddenly, and without compensation; some would abolish it gradually, and with compensation; some would remove the freed people from us, and some would retain them with us; and there are yet other minor diversities. Because of these diversities, we waste much strength in struggles among ourselves. By mutual concession we should harmonize, and act together. This would be compromise; but it would be compromise among the friends, and not with the enemies of the Union. These articles are intended to embody a plan of such mutual concessions. If the plan shall be adopted, it is assumed that emancipation will follow, at least, in several of the States.

As to the first article, the main points are: first, the emancipation; secondly, the length of time for consummating it—thirty-seven years; and thirdly, the compensation.

The emancipation will be unsatisfactory to the advocates of perpetual slavery; but the length of time should greatly mitigate their dissatisfaction. The time spares both races from the evils of sudden derangement—in fact, from the necessity of any derangement—while most of those whose habitual course of thought will be disturbed by the measure will have passed away before its consummation. They will never see it. Another class will hail the prospect of emancipation, but will deprecate the length of time. They will feel that it gives too little to the now living slaves. But it really gives them much. It saves them from the vagrant destitution which must largely attend immediate emancipation in localities where their numbers are very great; and it gives the inspiring assurance that their posterity shall be free forever. The plan leaves to each State, choosing to act under it, to abolish slavery now, or at the end of the century, or at any intermediate time, or by degrees, extending over the whole or any part of the period; and it obliges no two states to proceed alike. It also provides for compensation, and generally the mode of making it. This, it would seem, must further mitigate the dissatisfaction of those who favor perpetual slavery, and especially of those who are to receive the compensation. Doubtless some of those who are to pay, and not to receive will object. Yet the measure is both just and economical. In a certain sense the liberation of slaves is the destruction of property—property acquired by descent, or by purchase, the same as any other property. It is no less true for having been often said, that the people of the south are not more responsible for the original introduction of this property, than are the people of the north; and when it is remembered how unhesitatingly we all use cotton and sugar, and share the profits of dealing in them, it may not be quite safe to say, that the south has been more responsible than the north for its continuance. If then, for a common object, this property is to be sacrificed is it not just that it be done at a common charge?

And if, with less money, or money more easily paid, we can preserve the benefits of the Union by this means, than we can by the war alone, is it not also economical to do it? Let us consider it then. Let us ascertain the sum we have expended in the war since compensated emancipation was proposed last March, and consider whether, if that measure had been promptly accepted, by even some of the slave States, the same sum would not have done more to close the war, than has been otherwise done. If so the measure would save money, and, in that view, would be a prudent and economical measure. Certainly it is not so easy to pay *something* as it is to pay *nothing;* but it is easier to pay a *large* sum than it is to pay a larger one. And it is easier to pay any sum *when* we are able, than it is to pay it *before* we are able. The war requires large sums, and requires them at once. The aggregate sum necessary for compensated emancipation, of course, would be large. But it would require no ready cash; nor the bonds even, any faster than the emancipation progresses. This might not, and probably would not, close before the end of the thirty-seven years. At that time we shall probably have a hundred millions of people to share the burden, instead of thirty one millions, as now. And not only so, but the increase of our population may be expected to continue for a long time after that period, as rapidly as before; because our territory will not have become full. I do not state this inconsiderately. At the same ratio of increase which we have maintained, on an average, from our first national census, in 1790, until that of 1860, we should, in 1900, have a population of 103,208,415. And why may we not continue that ratio far beyond that period? Our abundant room—our broad national homestead—is our ample resource. Were our territory as limited as are the British Isles, very certainly our population could not expand as stated. Instead of receiving the foreign born, as now, we should be compelled to send part of the native born away. But such is not our condition. We have two millions nine hundred and sixty-three thousand square miles. Europe has three millions and eight hundred thousand, with a population averaging seventy-three and one-third persons to the square mile. Why may not our country, at some time, average as many? Is it less fertile? Has it more waste surface, by mountains, rivers, lakes, deserts, or other causes? Is it inferior to Europe in any natural advantage?

If, then, we are, at some time, to be as populous as Europe, how soon? As to when this *may* be, we can judge by the past and the present; as to when it *will* be, if ever, depends much on whether we maintain the Union. Several of our States are already above the average of Europe—seventy three and a third to the square mile. Massachusetts has 157; Rhode Island, 133; Connecticut, 99; New York and New Jersey, each, 80; also two other great States, Pennsylvania and Ohio, are not far below, the former having 63, and the latter 59. The States already above the European average, except New York, have increased in as rapid a ratio, since passing that point, as ever before; while no one of them is equal to some other parts of our country, in natural capacity for sustaining a dense population.

Taking the nation in the aggregate and we find its population and ratio of increase, for the several decennial periods, to be as follows:—

1790	3,929,827		
1800	5,305,937	35.02 per cent.	{ratio of increase
1810	7,239,814	36.45	"
1820	9,638,131	33.13	"
1830	12,866,020	33.49	"
1840	17,069,453	32.67	"
1850	23,191,876	35.87	"
1860	31,443,790	35.58	"

This shows an average decennial increase of 34.60 per cent. in population through the seventy years from our first, to our last census yet taken. It is seen that the ratio of increase, at no one of these seven periods, is either two per cent. below, or two per cent. above, the average; thus showing how inflexible, and, consequently, how reliable, the law of increase, in our case, is. Assuming that it will continue, gives the following results:—

1870	42,323,341	1910	138,918,526
1880	56,967,216	1920	186,984,335
1890	76,677,872	1930	251,680,914
1900	103,208,415		

These figures show that our country *may* be as populous as Europe now is, at some point between 1920 and 1930—say about 1925—our territory, at seventy-three and a third persons to the square mile, being of capacity to contain 217,186,000.

And we *will* reach this, too, if we do not ourselves relinquish the chance, by the folly and evils of disunion, or by long and exhausting war springing from the only great element of national discord among us. While it cannot be foreseen exactly how much one huge example of secession, breeding lesser ones indefinitely, would retard population, civilization, and prosperity, no one can doubt that the extent of it would be very great and injurious.

The proposed emancipation would shorten the war, perpetuate peace, insure this increase of population, and proportionately the wealth of the country. With these, we should pay all the emancipation would cost, together with our other debt, easier than we should pay our other debt, without it. If we had allowed our old national debt to run at six per cent. per annum, simple interest, from the end of our revolutionary struggle until to day, without paying anything on either principal or interest, each man of us would owe less upon that debt now, than each man owed upon it then; and this because our increase of men, through the whole period, has been greater than six per cent.; has run faster than the interest upon the debt. Thus, time alone relieves a debtor nation, so long as its population increases faster than unpaid interest accumulates on its debt.

This fact would be no excuse for delaying payment of what is justly due; but it shows the great importance of time in this connexion—the great advantage of a policy by which we shall not have to pay until we number a hundred millions, what, by a different policy, we would have to pay now, when we number but thirty one millions. In a word, it shows that a dollar will be much harder to pay for the war, than will be a dollar for emancipation on the proposed plan. And then the latter will cost no blood, no precious life. It will be a saving of both.

As to the second article, I think it would be impracticable to return to bondage the class of persons therein contemplated. Some of them, doubtless, in the property sense, belong to loyal owners; and hence, provision is made in this article for compensating such.

The third article relates to the future of the freed people. It does not oblige, but merely authorizes, Congress to aid in colonizing such as may consent. This ought not to be regarded as objectionable, on the one hand, or on the other, in so much as it comes to nothing, unless by the mutual consent of the people to be deported, and the American voters, through their representatives in Congress.

I cannot make it better known than it already is, that I strongly favor colonization. And yet I wish to say there is an objection urged against free colored persons remaining in the country, which is largely imaginary, if not sometimes malicious.

It is insisted that their presence would injure, and displace white labor and white laborers. If there ever could be a proper time for mere catch arguments, that time surely is not now. In times like the present, men should utter nothing for which they would not willingly be responsible through time and in eternity. Is it true, then, that colored people can displace any more white labor, by being free, than by remaining slaves? If they stay in their old places, they jostle no white laborers; if they leave their old places, they leave them open to white laborers. Logically, there is neither more nor less of it. Emancipation, even without deportation, would probably enhance the wages of white labor, and, very surely, would not reduce them. Thus, the customary amount of labor would still have to be performed; the freed people would surely not do more than their old proportion of it, and very probably, for a time, would do less, leaving an increased part to white laborers, bringing their labor into greater demand, and, consequently, enhancing the wages of it. With deportation, even to a limited extent, enhanced wages to white labor is mathematically certain. Labor is like any other commodity in the market—increase the demand for it, and you increase the price of it. Reduce the supply of black labor, by colonizing the black laborer out of the country, and, by precisely so much, you increase the demand for, and wages of, white labor.

But it is dreaded that the freed people will swarm forth, and cover the whole land? Are they not already in the land? Will liberation make them any more numerous? Equally distributed among the whites of the whole country, and there would be but one colored to seven whites. Could the one, in any way, greatly disturb the seven? There are many communities now, having more than one free colored person, to seven whites; and this, without any apparent consciousness of evil from it. The District of Columbia, and the States of Maryland and Delaware, are all in this condition. The District has more than one free colored to six whites; and yet, in its frequent petitions to Congress, I believe it has never presented the presence of free colored persons as one of its grievances. But why should emancipation south, send the free people north? People, of any color, seldom run, unless there be something to run from. *Heretofore* colored people, to some extent, have fled north from bondage; and *now,* perhaps, from both bondage and destitution. But if gradual emancipation and deportation be adopted, they will have neither to flee from. Their old masters will give them wages at least until new laborers can be procured; and the freed men, in turn, will gladly give their labor for the wages, till new homes can be found for them, in congenial climes, and with people of their own blood and race. This proposition can be trusted on the mutual interests involved. And, in any event, cannot the north decide for itself, whether to receive them?

Again, as practice proves more than theory, in any case, has there been any irruption of colored people northward, because of the abolishment of slavery in this District last spring?

What I have said of the proportion of free colored persons to the whites, in the District, is from the census of 1860, having no reference to persons called contrabands, nor to those made free by the act of Congress abolishing slavery here.

The plan consisting of these articles is recommended, not but that a restoration of the national authority would be accepted without its adoption.

Nor will the war, nor proceedings under the proclamation of September 22, 1862, be stayed because of the *recommendation* of this plan. Its timely *adoption,* I doubt not, would bring restoration and thereby stay both.

And, notwithstanding this plan, the recommendation that Congress provide by law for compensating any State which may adopt emancipation, before this plan shall have been acted upon, is hereby earnestly renewed. Such would be only an advance part of the plan, and the same arguments apply to both.

This plan is recommended as a means, not in exclusion of, but additional to, all others for restoring and preserving the national authority throughout the Union. The subject is presented exclusively in its economical aspect. The plan would, I am confident, secure peace more speedily, and maintain it more permanently, than can be done by force alone; while all it would cost, considering amounts, and manner of payment, and times of payment, would be easier paid than will be the additional cost of the war, if we rely solely upon force. It is much—very much—that it would cost no blood at all.

The plan is proposed as permanent constitutional law. It cannot become such without the concurrence of, first, two-thirds of Congress, and, afterwards, three-fourths of the States. The requisite three-fourths of the States will necessarily include seven of the Slave states. Their concurrence, if obtained, will give assurance of their severally adopting emancipation, at no very distant day, upon the new constitutional terms. This assurance would end the struggle now, and save the Union forever.

I do not forget the gravity which should characterize a paper addressed to the Congress of the nation by the Chief Magistrate of the nation. Nor do I forget that some of you are my seniors, nor that many of you have more experience than I, in the conduct of public affairs. Yet I trust that in view of the great responsibility resting upon me, you will perceive no want of respect to yourselves, in any undue earnestness I may seem to display.

Is it doubted, then, that the plan I propose, if adopted, would shorten the war, and thus lessen its expenditure of money and of blood? Is it doubted that it would restore the national authority and national prosperity, and perpetuate both indefinitely? Is it doubted that we here—Congress and Executive—can secure its adoption? Will not the good people respond to a united, and earnest appeal from us? Can we, can they, by any other means, so certainly, or so speedily, assure these vital objects? We can succeed only by concert. It is not "can *any* of us *imagine* better?" but "can we *all* do better?" Object whatsoever is possible, still the question recurs "can we do better?" The dogmas of the quiet past, are inadequate to the stormy present. The occasion is piled high with difficulty, and we must rise with the occasion. As our case is new, so we must think anew, and act anew. We must disenthrall our selves, and then we shall save our country.

Fellow-citizens, *we* cannot escape history. We of this Congress and this administration, will be remembered in spite of ourselves. No personal significance, or insignificance, can spare one or another of us. The fiery trial through which we pass, will light us down, in honor or dishonor, to the latest generation. We *say* we are for the Union. The world will not forget that we say this. We know how to save the Union. The world knows we do know how to save it. We—even *we here*—hold the power, and bear the responsibility. In *giving* freedom to the *slave,* we *assure* freedom to the *free*—honorable alike in what we give, and what we preserve. We shall nobly save, or meanly lose, the last best, hope of earth. Other means may succeed; this could not fail. The way is plain, peaceful, generous, just—a way which, if followed, the world will forever applaud, and God must forever bless.

December 1, 1862. ABRAHAM LINCOLN

APPENDIX 8

ABRAHAM LINCOLN TO JAMES C. CONKLING

LETTER TO THE SPRINGFIELD RALLY

AUGUST 26, 1863

Although the letter appears in *The Collected Works of Abraham Lincoln* as the letter to James C. Conkling, I have taken the liberty of changing the title to "Letter to the Springfield Rally," believing that this designation represents the purpose for which the letter was intended. Lincoln wrote this public letter as a speech, which he wanted Conkling to read "slowly."

There are three manuscript versions of this public letter. The first two versions were written by Abraham Lincoln, who made changes to the text. The final version was written by a clerk or secretary, and Lincoln made a few changes and signed it. After he sent the letter to Conkling, he telegraphed two additional paragraphs with instructions on where Conkling should insert them. The first two versions and the telegraphed addition to the final version are part of the Robert Todd Lincoln Collection of Abraham Lincoln Papers at the Library of Congress. The final version is in the Abraham Lincoln Presidential Library and Museum.

First Version

~~^Grand^fathers employed to establish it? and our own fathers have already employed ones to maintain it? Are we degenerate? unworthy sons of noblest sires?~~

But say some of you, we know for what our sires fought; what fight we for now? ^So far as it is for me to answer^ I have told you many times. I will ~~try again~~ ^repeat in another form.^. You desire peace; and you blame me that we do not have it. I desire it also. But how can we attain it? There are but three conceivable ways. First, to suppress the rebellion by arms. This I am trying to do. Are you for it? If you are, so far we are agreed. If you are not for it, a second way is, to give up the union. I am against this. Are you for it? If you are, you should say so plainly. If you are not for force, nor yet for dissolution, there only remains some immagineable compromise. I do not believe any compromise, embracing the maintainance of the Union, is ^now^

possible. All I learn leads to a [~~directly opposite~~?] ^directly opposite^ belief. The strength of the rebellion is it's military—its army—which ^army,^ completely dominates all the country, and ^all the^ people within it's range. Any offer of terms from any man, or men, within that range, in opposition to that army, is simply nothing ^for the present;^ because such man, or men have no ~~particle of~~ power ^whatever^ to enforce their side of a compromise, if one were made with them. A compromise, to be enforced, must be either made with that army—that is, with the men ^who^ ~~that~~ control the army—or with the people ^first^ liberated from it's domination, by ~~its first having been, vanquished by~~ ^the success of^ our armies. Now, let me assure you, that no word, or intimation, from that army, or any of the men controlling it, in relation to any ^peace^ compromise ~~for peace~~ has ever come to my knowledge. All charges or insinuations, to the contrary, are utter humbuggery, and falsehood. And I promise you that if any such proposition shall hereafter come, it shall not be rejected, and kept a secret from you. I freely acknowledge myself your servant, according to the bond of service—the United States' Constitution, and ^that^ as such ^I am^ responsible to you.

But, to be plain, some of you are dissatisfied with me about the colored man. Quite likely there is a difference of opinion between ^some of^ you and ^myself^ ~~me~~ upon that subject. I certainly wish that all men, [~~everywhere~~?], could be free; while I suppose many of you do not. Yet, I have neither adopted, or proposed, any measure, which is not consistent with even your view, provided you are for the Union. I had suggested compensated emancipation, to which you replied you wished not to be taxed to ~~by~~ buy negroes. But I had not asked you to be taxed to buy negroes, unless in such way, as to save you from greater taxation, to preserve the Union ^exclusively^ by other means.

You dislike the emancipation proclamation; and, perhaps, would have it retracted. You say it is unconstitutional. I think differently. I think the constitution invests it's commander-in-Chief, with the laws of war, in time of war. The most that can be said, ~~is~~ if so much, is that slaves are property. Is there—has there ever been—any question that, by the law of war, property both of enemies and friends, may be taken when needed? And it is needed whenever taking it helps us, or hurts the enemy. Armies, the world over, destroy enemies property when they ^can reach it and^ can not use it; and even destroy their own, to keep it from the enemy. Civilized beligerents do ~~every thing~~ ^all^ in their power to help themselves, or hurt the enemy, except a few things regarded as barborous and cruel. Among these exceptions, are the massacre of vanquished foes, and of non-combatants, male and female.

But the proclamation ^as law,^ either is valid, ~~as law~~, or ~~it~~ is not ^valid.^. If it is not so valid, the courts will ~~so~~ hold ^accordingly,^ and men of your views will not be hurt by it. If it is valid, it can no more be effectually retracted, than a judge can retract a judgment after it's final rendering. Some of you profess to think it's retraction would work ~~wonders~~ ^favorably^ for the Union. Why better after the retraction, than before the issue? There was more than a year and a half of trial upon ~~your~~ ^that^ plan, before the proclamation issued, the last one hundred days of which passed under a^n^ ~~distinct~~ ^explicit^ notice that the proclamation was coming ^unless averted^ by those in rebellion, returning to their allegiance. The war has certainly proceeded as favorably since its issue, as before. Some generals in the field, not originally partial to to the proclamation, now think it has been of ~~assistance~~ ^service^ to them.

You say you will not fight to free negroes. Very well, fight exclusively to save the Union. I issued the proclamation, on purpose to aid you in the task of saving the Union. Whenever you shall have conquered all resistance to the Union, if I shall ask you to still fight on, it will then be an apt time to declare you will not fight to free negroes. I thought that, in your struggle for the Union, to whatever extent the negroes should cease helping your enemy, to that extent, it weakened the enemy in their resistance to you. Do you think differently? I thought that whatever negroes can be got to do as soldiers, leaves just so much less for white soldiers to do, in saving the Union. Does it appear otherwise to you? But negroes, like other people, are creatures of motives. Why shall they do any thing for us; if we will do nothing for them? If they ~~take~~ stake their lives for us, they must be prompted by the strongest motive—even the promise of freedom. And the promise being made, must be kept.

Final Version

Executive Mansion,
Washington, August 26, 1863.

Hon. James C. Conkling
My Dear Sir,

Your letter inviting me to attend a mass-meeting of unconditional Union-men, to be held at the Capitol of Illinois on the 3^{d} day of September, has been received.

It would be very agreeable to me, to thus meet my old friends, at my own home; but I can not, just now, be absent from here, so long as a visit there, would require.

The meeting is to be of all those who maintain unconditional devotion to the Union; and I am sure my old political friends will thank me for tendering, as I do, the nation's gratitude to those other noble men, whom no partizan malice, or partizan hope, can make false to the nation's life.

There are those who are dissatisfied with me. To such I would say: You desire peace; and you blame me that we do not have it. But how can we attain it? There are but three conceivable ways. First, to suppress the rebellion by force of arms. This, I am trying to do. Are you for it? If you are, so far we are agreed. If you are not for it, a second way is, to give up the Union. I am against this. Are you for it? If you are, you should say so plainly. If you are not for <u>force</u>, nor yet for <u>dissolution</u>, there only remains some imaginable <u>compromise</u>. I do not believe any compromise, Embracing the maintenance of the Union, is now possible. All I learn, leads to a directly opposite belief. The strength of the rebellion, is its military—its army. That army dominates all the country, and all the people, within its range. Any offer of terms made by any man or men within that range, in opposition to that army, is simply nothing for the present; because such man or men, have no power whatever to enforce their side of a compromise, if one were made with them. To illustrate—Suppose refugees from the South, and peace men of the North, get together in convention, and frame and proclaim a compromise embracing a restoration of the Union; in what way can that compromise be used to keep Lee's army out of Pennsylvania? Meade's army can keep Lee's army out of Pennsylvania; and, I think, can ultimately drive it out of existence. But no paper compromise, to which the controllers of Lee's army are not agreed, can, at all, affect that army. In an effort at such compromise we should waste time, which the enemy would improve to our disadvantage; and that would be all. A compromise, to be effective, must be made either with those who control the rebel army, or with the people first liberated from the domination of that army, by the success of our ^own^ army. Now allow me to assure you, that no word or intimation, from that rebel army, or from any of the men controlling it, in relation to any peace compromise, has ever come to my knowledge or belief. All charges and insinuations to the contrary, are deceptive and groundless. And I promise you, that if any such proposition shall hereafter come, it shall not be rejected, and kept a secret from you. I freely acknowledge myself the servant of the people, according to the bond of service—the United States Constitution; and that, as such, I am responsible to them.

But, to be plain, you are dissatisfied with me about the negro. Quite likely there is a difference of opinion between you and myself upon that subject. I certainly wish that all men could be free, while I suppose you do not. Yet I have neither adopted, nor proposed any measure, which is not consistent with even your view, provided you are for the Union. I suggested compensated emancipation; to which you replied you wished not to be taxed to buy negroes. But I had not asked you to be taxed to buy negroes, except in such way, as to save you from greater taxation to save the Union exclusively by other means.

You dislike the emancipation proclamation; and, perhaps, would have it retracted. You say it is unconstitutional—I think differently. I think the constitution invests its Commander-in-Chief, with the law of war, in time of war. The most that can be said, if so much, is, that slaves are property. Is there—has there ever been—any question that by the law of war, property, both of enemies and friends, may be taken when needed? And is it not needed whenever taking it, helps us, or hurts the enemy? Armies, the world over, destroy enemie's property when they can not use it; and even destroy their own to keep it from the enemy. Civilized belligerents do all in their power to help themselves, or hurt the enemy, except a few things regarded as barbarous or cruel. Among the exceptions are the massacre of vanquished foes, and non-combatants, male and female.

But the proclamation, as law, either is valid, or is not valid. If it is not valid, it needs no retraction. If it is valid, it can not be retracted, any more than the dead can be brought to life. Some of you profess to think its retraction would operate favorably for the Union. Why better after the retraction, than before the issue? There was more than a year and a half of trial to suppress the rebellion before the proclamation issued, the last one hundred days of which passed under an explicit notice that it was coming, unless averted by those in revolt, returning to their allegiance. The war has certainly progressed as favorably for us, since the issue of the proclamation as before.[1]

∀"I know, as fully as one can know the opinions of others, that some of the commanders of our armies in the field, who have given us our most important successes, believe the emancipation policy, and the use of colored troops constitute the heaviest blow yet dealt to the rebellion; and that at least one of those important successes could not have been achieved when it was, but for the aid of black soldiers. Among the commanders holding these views are some who have never had any affinity with what is called abolitionism, or with Republican party politics, but who hold them purely as military opinions.

I submit these opinions as being entitled to some weight against the objections, often urged, that emancipation, and arming the blacks, are unwise as military measures, and were not adopted, as such, in good faith.∀[2]

You say you will not fight to free negroes. Some of them seem willing to fight for you; but, no matter. Fight you, then, exclusively to save the Union. I issued the proclamation on purpose to aid you in saving the Union. When-

---

1. James C. Conkling wrote "(Here insert Telegram" here in the text he received from Lincoln.

2. Insertion from Abraham Lincoln to James C. Conkling, August 31, 1863, Robert Todd Lincoln Collection of Abraham Lincoln Papers, Library of Congress.

ever you shall have conquered all resistance to the Union, if I shall urge you to continue fighting, it will be an apt time, then, for you to declare you will not fight to free negroes.

I thought that in your struggle for the Union, to whatever extent the negroes should cease helping the enemy, to that extent it weakened the enemy in his resistance to you. Do you think differently? I thought that whatever negroes can be got to do as soldiers, leaves just so much less for white soldiers to do, in saving the Union. Does it appear otherwise to you?

But negroes, like other people, act upon motives. Why should they do any thing for us, if we will do nothing for them? If they stake their lives for us, they must be prompted by the strongest motive—even the promise of freedom. And the promise being made, must be kept.

The signs look better. The Father of Waters again goes unvexed to the sea. Thanks to the great North-West for it. Nor yet wholly to them. Three hundred miles up, they met New England, Empire, Key-Stone, and Jersey, hewing their way right and left. The Suny South too, in more colors than one, also lent a hand. On the spot, their part of the history was jotted down in black and white. The job was a great national one: and let none be banned who bore an honorable part in it. And while those who have cleared the great river may well be proud, even that is not all. It is hard to say ^that^ anything has been more bravely, and well done, than at Antietam, Murfreesboro, Gettysburg, and on many fields of lesser note. Nor must Uncle Sam[s] web-feet be forgotten. At all the watery margins they have been present. Not only on the deep sea, the broad bay, and the rapid river, but also up the narrow muddy bayou, and wherever the ground was a little damp, they have been, and made their tracks. Thanks to all. For the great republic—for the principle it lives by, and keeps alive—for man's vast future,—thanks to all.

Peace does not appear so distant as it did. I hope it will come soon, and come to stay; and so come as to be worth the keeping in all future time. It will then have been proved that, among free men, there can be no successful appeal from the ballot to the bullet; and that they who take such appeal are sure to lose their case, and pay the cost. And then, there will be some black men who can remember that, with silent tongue, and clenched teeth, and steady eye, and well-~~borne~~^poised^ bayonet, they have helped mankind on to this great consummation; while, I fear, there will be some white ones, unable to forget that, with malignant hearts, and deceitful speech, they have strove to hinder it.

Still let us not be over-sanguine of a speedy final triumph. Let us be quite sober. Let us diligently apply the means, never doubting that a just God, in his own good time, will give us the rightful result.

Yours very truly
A. Lincoln

APPENDIX 9

GETTYSBURG ADDRESS

NOVEMBER 19, 1863

There are five known copies of the address—the John G. Nicolay copy and the John Hay copy, both at the Library of Congress; the Alexander Bliss copy, at the White House; the Edward Everett copy, at the Abraham Lincoln Presidential Library and Museum; and the George Bancroft copy, at Cornell University in Ithaca, New York. The first transcription that follows is of the Nicolay copy, Lincoln's first draft of the speech. The second transcription is of the Hay copy, Lincoln's second draft. The third transcription is of the Bliss copy, which Lincoln made in March 1864, with notations marking differences between it and the Everett and Bancroft copies, both of which Lincoln wrote in February 1864.

John G. Nicolay Copy (First Draft)

EXECUTIVE MANSION,
WASHINGTON,________, 186 .[1]

Four score and seven years ago our fathers brought forth, upon this continent, a new nation, conceived in liberty, and dedicated to the proposition that "all men are created equal"

Now we are engaged in a great civil war, testing whether that nation, or any nation so conceived, and so dedicated, can long endure. We are met on a great battle field of that war. We have come to dedicate a portion of it, as a final resting place for those who died here, that the nation might live. This we may, in all propriety do. But, in a larger sense, we can not dedicate—we can not consecrate—we can not hallow, this ground. The brave men, living and

1. Preceding text is the printed portion of the Executive Mansion stationery.

dead, who struggled here, have hallowed it, far above our poor power to add or detract. The world will little note, nor long remember what we say here; while it can never forget what they did here.

It is rather for us, the living, ~~to stand here~~, ^we here be dedica^ted to the great task remaining before us—that, from these honored dead we take increased devotion to that cause for which they here, gave the last full measure of devotion—that we here highly resolve these dead shall not have died in vain; that this nation, shall have a new birth of freedom, and that government of the people by the people for the people, shall not perish from the earth.

John Hay Copy (Second Draft)

Four score and seven years ago our fathers brought forth, upon this continent, a new nation, conceived in Liberty, and dedicated to the proposition that all men are created equal.

Now we are engaged in a great civil war, testing whether that nation, or any nation, so conceived, and so dedicated, can long endure. We are met here on a great battle-field of that war. We ~~are met~~ ^have come^ to dedicate a portion of it as ~~the~~ ^a^ final resting place ~~of~~ ^for^ those who here gave their lives that that nation might live. It is altogether fitting and proper that we should do this.

But in a larger sense we can not dedicate—we can not consecrate—we can not hallow this ground. The brave men, living and dead, who struggled here, have consecrated it far above our ^poor^ power to add or detract. The world will little note, nor long remember, what we say here, but can never forget what they did here. It is for us, the living, rather to be dedicated here to the unfinished ^work^ which they have, thus far, so nobly carried on. It is rather for us to be here dedicated to the great task remaining before ^us—^—that from these honored dead we take increased devotion to ~~the~~ ^that^ cause for which they here gave ~~gave~~ the last full measure of devotion—that we here highly resolve that these dead shall not have died in vain; that this nation shall have a new birth of freedom; and that this government of the people, by the people, for the people, shall not perish from the earth.

Alexander Bliss Copy
(as Compared to the Edward Everett and George Bancroft Copies)

Address delivered at the dedication of the Cemetery at Gettysburg.[1]

Four score and seven years ago our fathers brought forth[2] on[3] this continent, a new nation, conceived in Liberty, and dedicated to the proposition that all men are created equal.[4]

Now we are engaged in a great civil war, testing whether that nation, or any nation so conceived[5] and so dedicated, can long endure. We are met on a great battle-field of that war. We have come to dedicate a portion of that field, as a final resting place[6] for those who here gave their lives[7] that that nation might live. It is altogether fitting and proper that we should do this.

But, in a larger sense, we can not dedicate—we can not consecrate—we can not hallow—this ground. The brave men, living and dead, who struggled here, have consecrated it,[8] far above our poor power to add or detract. The world will little note, nor long remember[9] what we say here, but it can never forget what they did here. It is for us[10] the living, rather, to be dedicated here to the unfinished work which they who fought here[11] have[12] thus far[13] so nobly advanced. It is rather for us to be here dedicated to the great task remaining before us—that from these honored dead we take increased devotion to that cause for which they[14] gave the last full measure of devotion—that we here highly resolve that these dead shall not have died in vain—that this nation, under God, shall have a new birth of freedom—and that[15] government of the people, by the people, for the people, shall not perish from the earth.

Abraham Lincoln.
November 19. 1863.[16]

---

1. The preceding phrase is not in the Everett and Bancroft copies.
2. The Bancroft copy has a "," here.
3. The Everett copy has "upon" here.
4. The Everett and Bancroft copies indent this paragraph.
5. The Everett copy has a "," here.
6. The Bancroft copy changed "resting place" to "resting-place"
7. The Everett and Bancroft copies have a "," here.
8. The Bancroft copy does not have a "," here.
9. The Everett copy has a "," here.
10. The Everett copy has a "," here.
11. The Everett copy has a "," here.
12. The Everett copy has a "," here.
13. The Everett copy has a "," here.
14. The Everett and Bancroft copies have "here" here.
15. The Everett copy has a "," here.
16. The Everett and Bancroft copies are not signed and dated.

APPENDIX 10

"LITTLE SPEECH" TO ALBERT G. HODGES

APRIL 4, 1864

Lincoln's handwritten copy of his letter to Hodges is in the Robert Todd Lincoln Collection of Abraham Lincoln Papers at the Library of Congress. Hodges published the letter in his Frankfort, Kentucky, newspaper, *The Commonwealth,* on April 25, 1865. This transcription is of Lincoln's copy, with differences other than typeface in the published version indicated in notes.

EXECUTIVE MANSION,
WASHINGTON, APRIL 4, 1864.[1]

A. G. Hodges, Esq
Frankfort, Ky.
My dear Sir:

You ask me to put in writing the substance of what I verbally said[2] the other day, in yours[3] presence, to Governor Bramlette and Senator Dixon. It was about as follows:

"I am naturally anti-slavery. If slavery is not wrong, nothing is wrong. I can not remember when I did not so think,[4] and feel. And yet[5] I have never understood that the Presidency conferred upon me an unrestricted right to act officially upon this judgment and feeling. It was in the oath I took[6] that I would,[7] to the best of my ability, preserve, protect, and defend the constitution of the United States. I could not take the office without taking the oath.

---

1. "Executive Mansion, Washington," and ", 186 ." are printed on manuscript version.
2. "," here in printed version.
3. "yours" changed to "your" in printed version.
4. No "," here in printed version.
5. "," here in printed version.
6. "," here in printed version.
7. No "," here in printed version.

Nor was it my view[8] that I might take an oath to get power, and break the oath[9] in using the power. I understood, too, that[10] in ordinary civil administration[11] this oath even forbade me[12] to practically indulge my primary[13] abstract judgment on the moral question of slavery. I have publicly declared this many times, and in many ways. And I aver that, to this day, I have done no official act in mere deference to my abstract judgment and feeling on slavery.[14] I did understand ~~hower~~, ^however,^ that my oath to preserve the constitution[15] ^to^ the best of my ability, imposed upon me the duty of preserving, by every indispensable means, that government[16]—that nation[17]—of which that constitution[18] was the organic law. Was it possible to lose the nation,[19] and ^yet^ preserve the constitution?[20] By general law[21] life and[22] limb must be protected; yet often a limb must be amputated to save a life; but a life is never wisely given to save a limb. I felt that measures, otherwise unconstitutional, might become lawful, by becoming indispensable[23] to the preservation of the constitution,[24] through the preservation of the nation.[25] Right or wrong, I assumed this ground, and now avow it. I could not feel[26] that,[27] to the best of my ability, I had even tried to preserve the constitution, if,[28] to save slavery, or any minor matter, I should permit the wreck of government,[29] country,[30] and ~~constution~~ ^constitution^[31] all together. When,[32] early in the war, Gen. Fremont[33] attempted military emancipation,[34] I forbade it, because

8. "," here in printed version.
9. "," here in printed version.
10. "," here in printed version.
11. "," here in printed version.
12. "," here in printed version.
13. "," here in printed version.
14. New paragraph begins here in printed version.
15. "constitution" changed to "Constitution" in printed version.
16. "government" changed to "Government" in printed version.
17. "nation" changed to "Nation" in printed version.
18. "constitution" changed to "Constitution" in printed version.
19. "nation" changed to "Nation" in printed version.
20. "constitution" changed to "Constitution" and new paragraph begins here in printed version.
21. "," here in printed version.
22. "and" not italicized in printed version.
23. "indispensable" italicized in printed version.
24. "constitution" changed to "Constitution" in printed version.
25. "nation" changed to "Nation" in printed version.
26. "," here in printed version.
27. No "," here in printed version.
28. No "," here in printed version.
29. "government" changed to "Government" in printed version.
30. "country" changed to "Country" in printed version.
31. "constitution" changed to "Constitution" in printed version.
32. No "," here in printed version.
33. "When early in the war, Gen. Fremont" italicized in printed version.
34. ";" here in printed version.

I did not then think it an indispensable necessity. When a little later, Gen. Cameron, then Secretary of War, suggested the arming of the blacks, I objected,[35] because I did not yet think it an indispensable necessity. When, still later, Gen. Hunter attempted military emancipation, I again forbade it,[36] because I did not yet think the indispensable necessity had come.[37] When, in March, and May, and July 1862[38] I made earnest,[39] and successive appeals to the border states[40] to favor compensated emancipation, I believed the indispensable necessity for military emancipation, and arming the blacks would come, unless averted by that measure,[41] They declined the proposition; and I was, in my best judgment, driven to the alternative[42] of either surrendering the Union, and with it, the Constitution, or of laying strong hand upon the colored element. I chose the latter. In choosing it, I hoped for greater gain than loss; but of this,[43] I was not entirely confident. More than a year of trial now shows no loss by it[44] in our foreign relations,[45] none in our home popular sentiment,[46] none in our white military force,[47]—no loss by it[48] any how, or ^any^ where. On the contrary, it shows a gain of quite a hundred and thirty thousand soldiers, seamen, and laborers. These are palpable facts, about which, as facts, there can be no cavilling. We have the men; and we could not have had them without the measure.

And now[49] let any Union man[50] who complains of the measure, test himself[51] by writing down in one line[52] that he is for subduing the rebellion by force of arms;[53] and in the next, that he is for taking these hundred and thirty thousand men from the Union side, and placing them where they would be but for the measure he condemns. If he can not face his case[54] so stated, it is only because he can not face the truth.[55]

---

35. ";" here in printed version.
36. ";" here in printed version.
37. New paragraph begins here in printed version.
38. "July 1862" changed to "July, 1862," in printed version.
39. No "," here in printed version.
40. "," here in printed version.
41. "." here in printed version.
42. "," here in printed version.
43. ";" here in printed version.
44. "," here in printed version.
45. ";" here in printed version.
46. ";" here in printed version.
47. ";" here in printed version.
48. "," here in printed version.
49. "," here in printed version.
50. "," here in printed version.
51. "," here in printed version.
52. "," here in printed version.
53. "," here in printed version.
54. "case" changed to "cause" in printed version.
55. Closing quotation marks here in printed version.

I add a word[56] which was not in the verbal conversation. In telling ^this^ tale[57] I attempt no compliment to my own sagacity. I claim not to have controlled events, but confess plainly that events have controlled me. Now, at the end of three years[58] struggle[59] the nation's[60] condition is not what either party,[61] or any man devised,[62] or expected. God alone can claim it. Whither it is tending seems plain. If God now wills the removal of a great wrong, and wills also that we of the North[63] as well as you of the South, shall pay fairly for our complicity in that wrong, impartial history will find therein ~~no~~ ^new^ cause to ~~question~~ ^~~applaud~~^ ^attest[64] and revere^ the justice [~~...~~] ^and^ goodness of God.

Yours truly[65]
A. LINCOLN

56. "," here in printed version.
57. "," here in printed version.
58. " ' " here in printed version.
59. "," here in printed version.
60. "nation's" changed to "Nation's" in printed version.
61. No "," here in printed version.
62. No "," here in printed version.
63. "," here in printed version.
64. "," here in printed version.
65. "," here in printed version.

APPENDIX 11

SECOND INAUGURAL ADDRESS
MARCH 4, 1865

The first text is a transcription of the only known manuscript of the Second Inaugural Address. The address is only 701 words, the second-shortest inaugural address. The words "Fellow Countrymen," written in pencil at the beginning of the address, are not in Lincoln's hand. They may be the addition of a typesetter. The manuscript was given to John Hay on April 10, 1865.

The second text is Lincoln's reading text.[1] A determination may have been made to print the address, perhaps for distribution to the press. Lincoln fashioned a speaking text from uncorrected galleys. In doing so he changed the four paragraphs of his written manuscript into twenty-four sections arranged in two columns. Lincoln also underlined certain key words for emphasis. The reading copy shows many punctuation changes. The new structure, the underlining, and the punctuation were cues to Lincoln the speaker.

Version 1

Fellow Countrymen[2]

At this second appearing, to take the oath of the presidential office, there is less occasion for an extended address than there was at the first. Then a statement, somewhat in detail, of a course to be pursued, seemed fitting and proper. Now, at the expiration of four years, during which public declarations have been constantly called forth on every point and phase of the great contest which still absorbs the attention, and engrosses the enerergies of the nation, little that is new could be presented. The progress of our arms, upon which all else chiefly depends, is as well known to the public as to myself; and it is, I trust, reasonably satisfactory and encouraging to all. With high hope for the future, no prediction in regard to it is ventured.

---

1. Douglas L. Wilson, "A Note on the Text of Lincoln's Second Inaugural," *Documentary Editing* 24 (June 2002): 37–41.
2. "Fellow Countrymen" and also "Flynn" in the margin written by an unknown author.

On the occasion corresponding to this four years ago, all thoughts were anxiously directed to an impending civil war. All dreaded it—all sought to avert it. While the inaugeral address was being delivered from this place, devoted altogether to <u>saving</u> the Union without war, insurgent agents were in the city seeking to <u>destroy</u> it without war–seeking to dissole the Union, and—divide effects, by negotiation. Both parties deprecated war; but one of them would <u>make</u> war rather than let the nation survive; and the other would <u>accept</u> war rather than let it perish. And the war came.

One eighth of the whole population were colored slaves, not distributed generally over the Union, but localized in the Southern ^part^ ~~half~~ of it. These slaves constituted a peculiar and powerful interest. All knew that this interest was, somehow, the cause of the war. To strengthen, perpetuate, and extend this interest was the object for which the insurgents would rend the Union, even by war; while the government claimed no right to do more than to restrict the territorial enlargement of it. Neither party expected for the war, the magnitude, or the duration, which it has already attained. Neither anticipated that the <u>cause</u> of the conflict might cease with, or even before, the conflict itself should cease. Each looked for an easier triumph, and a result less fundamental and astounding. Both read the same Bible, and pray to the same God; and each invokes His aid against the other. It may seem strange that any men should dare to ask a just God's assistance in wringing their bread from the sweat of other men's faces; but let us judge not that we be not judged. The prayers of both could not be answered; that of neither has been answered fully. The Almighty has His own purposes. "Woe unto the world because of offences! for it must needs be that offences come; but woe to that man by whom the offence cometh!" If we shall suppose that American Slavery is one of those offences which, in the providence of God, must needs come, but which, having continued through His appointed time, He now wills to remove, and that He gives to both North and South, this terrible war, as the woe due to those by whom the offence came, shall we discern therein any departure from those divine attributes which the believers in a Living God always ascribe to Him? Fondly do we hope—fervently do we pray—that this mighty scourge of war may speedily pass away. Yet, if God wills that it continue, until all the wealth piled by the bond-man's two hundred and fifty years of unrequited toil shall be sunk, and until every drop ^of^ blood drawn with the lash, shall be paid by another drawn with the sword, as was said three thousand years ago, so still it must be said "the judgments of the Lord, are true and righteous altogether"

With malice toward none; with charity for all; with firmness in the right, as God gives us to see the right, let us strive on to finish the work we are in; to bind up the nation's wounds; to care for him who shall ^have^ borne the battle, and for his widow, and his orphan—to do all which may achieve and cherish a just, and a lasting peace, among ourselves, and with ^all nations.^ ~~the world.~~

Version 2

FELLOW COUNTRYMEN:

At this second appearing to take the oath of the presidential office, there is less occasion for an extended address than there was at the first.

Then, a statement, somewhat in detail, of a course to be pursued, seemed fitting and proper.

Now, at the expiration of four years, during which public declarations have been constantly called forth^,^ on every point and phase of the great contest which still absorbs the attention^,^ and engrosses the energies of the nation, little that is new could be presented.

The progress of our arms, upon which all else chiefly depends, is as well known to the public as to myself; and it is, I trust, reasonably satisfactory and encouraging to all. With high hope for the future, no prediction in regard to it is ventured.

On the occasion corresponding to this four years ago, all thoughts were anxiously directed to an impending civil war.

All dreaded it—all sought to avert it.

While the inaugural address was being delivered from this place, devoted altogether to <u>saving</u> the Union without war, insurgent agents were in the city seeking to <u>destroy</u> it without war—seeking to dissolve the Union, and divide effects, by negotiation.

Both parties deprecated war; but one of them would <u>make</u> war rather than let the nation survive; and the other would <u>accept</u> war rather than let it perish.

And the war came.

One-eighth of the whole population were colored slaves, not distributed generally over the Union, but localized in the Southern ~~half~~ ^part^ of it.

These slaves constituted a peculiar^,^ and powerful interest.

All knew that this interest was, somehow, the cause of the war.
To strengthen, perpetuate and extend this interest^,^ was the object for which the insurgents would rend the Union, even by war;[1] while the government claimed no right to do more^,^ than to restrict the territorial enlargement of it.

Neither party expected for the war^,^ the magnitude^,^ or the duration^,^ which it has already attained.

Neither anticipated that the *cause* of the conflict might cease with, or even before, the conflict itself should cease.

Each looked for an easier triumph^,^ and a result less fundamental and astounding.

Both read the same Bible^,^ and pray to the same God;[2] and each invokes His aid against the other.

It may seem strange that any men should dare to ask a just God's assistance in wringing their bread from the sweat of other men's faces; but let us judge not, that we be not judged.

The prayers of both could not be answered—that of neither^,^ has been answered fully.

The Almighty has His own purposes.

"Woe unto the world because of offences! for it must needs be that offences come; but woe to that man by whom the offence cometh."

If we shall suppose that American slavery is one of those offences which, in the providence of God, must needs come, but which, having continued through His appointed time, He now wills to remove and that He gives to both north and south this terrible war as the woe due to those by whom the offence came, shall we discern therein any departure from those divine attributes which the believers in a living God always ascribe to Him?

---

1. "," changed to ";"
2. "," changed to ";"

Fondly do we hope—fervently do we pray—that this mighty scourge of war may speedily pass away.

Yet, if God wills that it continue until all the wealth piled by the bondman's two hundred and fifty years of unrequited toil shall be sunk, and until every drop of blood drawn with the lash^,^ shall be paid by another drawn with the sword, as was said three thousand years ago, so still it must be said, "the judgments of the Lord are true and righteous altogether."

With malice toward none; with charity for all; with firmness in the right, as God gives us to see the right, let us strive on to finish the work we are in; to bind up the nation's wounds; to care for him who shall have borne the battle, and for his widow, and his orphan—to do all which may achieve and cherish^,^ a just and a lasting peace^,^ among ourselves, and with ~~the world.~~ ^all nations.^

NOTES

KEY TO ABBREVIATIONS

AL	Abraham Lincoln
ALP	Abraham Lincoln Papers at the Library of Congress
CW	*The Collected Works of Abraham Lincoln,* ed. Roy P. Basler (New Brunswick, N.J.: Rutgers University Press, 1953–55) and *Supplement, 1832–1865* (Westport, Conn.: Greenwood Press, 1974)
Donald	David H. Donald, *Lincoln* (New York: Simon & Schuster, 1995)
HI	*Herndon's Informants: Letters, Interviews, and Statements About Abraham Lincoln,* ed. Douglas L. Wilson and Rodney O. Davis (Urbana, Ill.: University of Illinois Press, 1998)
N&H	John G. Nicolay and John Hay, *Abraham Lincoln: A History* (New York: Century, 1890)
Strong	*The Diary of George Templeton Strong,* ed. Allan Nevins and Milton Halsey Thomas, vol. III, *The Civil War, 1860–1865* (New York: Macmillan Co., 1952)

PROLOGUE

1. N&H X, 351; Waldo W. Braden makes this point in his introduction to *Abraham Lincoln, Public Speaker* (Baton Rouge: Louisiana State University Press, 1988), 1–3.
2. J. G. Randall, *Lincoln the President: Springfield to Gettysburg,* vol. I (New York: Dodd, Mead, and Co., 1945), 95.
3. Aristotle, *Treatise on Rhetoric,* trans. Theodore Buckley (London: Bell and Daldy, 1872), 11–13.
4. Multiple observers commented on how slowly Lincoln spoke. Some newspaper reports noted the time of delivery of Lincoln's most important addresses as president. I have estimated the figure at 105 to 110 words per minute by divid-

ing the number of words in two of his most important addresses, the Gettysburg Address (272 words) and the Second Inaugural (701 words), by the time it took to deliver them (2½ to 3 minutes and 6 to 7 minutes).

CHAPTER I
"WITH A TASK BEFORE ME GREATER THAN . . . WASHINGTON"

1. *New York Tribune*, Feb. 11, 1861; Henry Villard, *Memoirs of Henry Villard: Journalist and Financier, 1835–1900*, vol. I (Boston: Houghton Mifflin, 1904), 149.
2. William E. Barton, *The Life of Abraham Lincoln*, vol. I (New York: Bobbs-Merrill, 1925), 463.
3. Sarah Bush Lincoln elaborated on these sentiments in her interview with William Herndon on September 8, 1865: "I did not want Abe to run for Presdt—did not want him Elected—was afraid Somehow or other—felt it in my heart that Something would happen to him and when he came down to see me after he was Elected Presdt I still felt that Something told me that Something would befall Abe and that I should see him no more." *HI*, 108.
4. *Illinois State Journal*, Feb. 4 and 5, 1861.
5. Amy Louise Sutton, "Lincoln and Son Borrow Books," *Illinois Libraries* (June 1966), 443–44.
6. Harry E. Pratt, *Lincoln's Springfield* (Springfield, Ill.: Illinois State Historical Society, 1955), 12; Harry B. Rankin, *Intimate Character Sketches of Abraham Lincoln* (Philadelphia: J. B. Lippincott, 1924), 146–47.
7. William H. Herndon and Jesse W. Weik, *Abraham Lincoln: The True Story of a Great Life*, vol. I (New York: D. Appleton, 1889), 211; AL, eulogy on Henry Clay, July 6, 1852, *CW* II, 126; Robert V. Remini, *Henry Clay: Statesman for the Union* (New York: W. W. Norton, 1993), 733–38.
8. Wayne C. Temple, *Abraham Lincoln and Others at St. Nicholas* (Springfield, Ill.: St. Nicholas Corporation, 1968), 14–154; Wayne C. Temple, "Lincoln as Seen by T. D. Jones," *Illinois Libraries* LVIII (June 1976), 447–56. This article includes reprints of Jones's "Recollections of Mr. Lincoln," originally published in the *Cincinnati Commercial*, Oct. 18, 1871, and three Jones letters.
9. Temple, *Abraham Lincoln and Others*, 24.
10. *Illinois State Journal*, Feb. 5 and 6, 1861.
11. Anna Ridgely, Diary, entry for Nov. 11, 1860, Abraham Lincoln Presidential Library.
12. Ibid., Feb. 10, 1861.
13. Herndon and Weik, *Abraham Lincoln*, vol. I, 193–94.
14. Ibid., 194.
15. Joshua F. Speed, *Reminiscences of Abraham Lincoln and Notes of a Visit to California: Two Lectures* (Louisville, Ky.: John P. Morton & Co., 1884), 21–22.
16. *Illinois State Journal*, Apr. 15, 1837.
17. This speech has fascinated scholars in their search to understand the ideas of the young Lincoln. See Thomas F. Schwartz, "The Springfield Lyceums and Lin-

coln's 1838 Speech," *Illinois Historical Journal* 83 (1990), 45–49, and Mark E. Neeley, Jr., "Lincoln's Lyceum Speech and the Origins of a Modern Myth," *Lincoln Lore,* nos. 1776–77 (1987).

18. AL, address before the Young Men's Lyceum of Springfield, Ill., Jan. 27, 1838, *CW* I, 108.
19. Ibid.
20. Ibid.
21. Ibid., 108–9.
22. Ibid., 115.
23. *New York Tribune,* Feb. 12, 1861; *Harper's Weekly,* Feb. 23, 1861.
24. *Illinois State Journal,* Feb. 12, 1861.
25. Villard, *Memoirs,* vol. I, 149.
26. James C. Conkling to Clinton Conkling, Feb. 12, 1861, in Pratt, *Lincoln's Springfield,* 50.
27. *Illinois State Journal,* Feb. 12, 1861.

CHAPTER 2
"THIS, HIS ALMOST CHOSEN PEOPLE"

1. Much of the detail of the journey to Washington is taken from local newspapers. The newspapers of this period were intensely political. They often served as the political voice for parties in their communities. Some of the reports of Henry Villard for the *New York Herald,* which were also distributed through the Associated Press to many newspapers, can be found in Henry Villard, *Lincoln on the Eve of '61,* ed. Harold G. Villard and Oswald Garrison Villard (New York: Alfred A. Knopf, 1941). The standard account of the train trip to Washington is Victor Searcher, *Lincoln's Journey to Greatness: A Factual Account of the Twelve-Day Inaugural Trip* (Philadelphia: John C. Winston, 1960). The difficulty with Searcher's account is that it contains no footnotes. See also Daniel Elizor, "The Constitution, the Union, and the Liberties of the People," *Publius: The Journal of Federalism* 8, no. 3 (summer 1978), 141–75.
2. *New York Times,* Feb. 13, 1861.
3. *Illinois State Journal,* June 19, July 24, and Aug. 29, 1860; Harold Holzer, *Lincoln Seen and Heard* (Lawrence: University Press of Kansas, 2000), 169.
4. AL, remarks at a Republican rally, Springfield, Ill., Aug. 8, 1860, *CW* IV, 91.
5. Robert W. Johannsen, *Stephen A. Douglas* (New York: Oxford University Press, 1973), 640–41.
6. William H. Seward to AL, Dec. 29, 1860, *CW* IV, 170 n. 1. The letter, highly secret, was unsigned.
7. N&H III, 289.
8. Descriptions of Jefferson Davis's train trip can be found in William Cooper, *Jefferson Davis, American* (New York: Alfred A. Knopf, 2000), 328–29; William C. Davis, *Jefferson Davis: The Man and His Hour* (New York: HarperCollins, 1991), 304–6; *New York Times,* Feb. 11, 1861; and Brian R. Dirck, *Lincoln &*

Davis: Imagining America, 1809–1865 (Lawrence: University Press of Kansas, 2001), 179–81.

9. AL, reply to Oliver P. Morton at Indianapolis, Ind., Feb. 11, 1861, *CW* IV, 193.
10. Matthew 16:18. All quotations from the Bible used by Lincoln are from the King James Version, which was the Protestant version of the Bible in Lincoln's day.
11. AL, reply to Morton, *CW* IV, 193.
12. Ibid.
13. Rutherford B. Hayes to Laura Plant, Feb. 13, 1861, Hayes MSS, Hayes Presidential Center, cited in Donald, 274, 642.
14. AL, remarks from the balcony at Bates House, Indianapolis, Ind., Feb. 11, 1861, *CW* IV, 195.
15. Ibid.
16. Ibid.
17. Ibid.
18. Searcher, *Lincoln's Journey,* 29–31.
19. Newspaper clipping, "Mr. Lincoln's Speeches at Indianapolis, as Revised by Himself," from John Hay's scrapbook, private collection, as cited in Holzer, *Lincoln Seen and Heard,* 212, n. 15.
20. *Chicago Tribune,* Feb. 12, 1861; *New York Times,* Feb. 12, 1861.
21. "Lincoln Has Spoken!" *Cleveland Plain Dealer,* Feb. 12, 1861.
22. *New Orleans Daily Delta,* Feb. 14 and 17, 1861; *Papers of Jefferson Davis,* ed. Lynda Lasswell Crist and Mary Seaton Dix, vol. VII (1861) (Baton Rouge, La.: Louisiana State University Press, 1992), 38, 41; Davis, *Jefferson Davis,* 304–5.
23. *Chicago Tribune,* Feb. 13, 1861.
24. Ibid.
25. Ibid.
26. AL, fragment of speech intended for Kentuckians, *CW* IV, 200–201.
27. AL, speech at Cincinnati, Ohio, Feb. 12, 1861, *CW* IV, 199.
28. Ibid.
29. AL to William H. Seward, Jan. 3, 1861, *CW* IV, 170.
30. Lucius E. Chittenden, *Recollections of President Lincoln and His Administration* (New York: Harper & Brothers, 1891), 38.
31. AL, address to the Ohio legislature, Columbus, Ohio, Feb. 13, 1861, *CW* IV, 204.
32. AL, speech from the steps of the Capitol at Columbus, Ohio, Feb. 13, 1861, *CW* IV, 205.
33. Searcher, *Lincoln's Journey,* 68–69.
34. AL, speech at Steubenville, Ohio, Feb. 14, 1861, *CW* IV, 206.
35. Ibid.
36. *Memphis Daily Appeal,* Feb. 19, 1861, in *Papers of Jefferson Davis,* vol. VII (1861), 42–43; Dirck, *Lincoln & Davis,* 178–79.
37. *Pittsburgh Gazette,* Feb. 15, 1861; *Cincinnati Commercial,* Feb. 15, 1861.
38. Villard, *Memoirs,* vol. I, 152.
39. AL, speech at Pittsburgh, Penn., Feb. 15, 1861, *CW* IV, 211–12.
40. Villard, *Memoirs,* vol. I, 152.
41. AL, speech at Cleveland, Ohio, Feb. 15, 1861, *CW* IV, 215.
42. AL, remarks at Westfield, N.Y., Feb. 16, 1861, *CW* IV, 219.

43. AL, remarks at Dunkirk, N.Y., Feb. 16, 1861, *CW* IV, 220.
44. Searcher, *Lincoln's Journey,* 129.
45. *Atlanta Intelligencer,* Feb. 18, 1861; *Papers of Jefferson Davis,* vol. VII (1861), 44–45.
46. *New York Tribune,* Mar. 5, 1861.
47. *Charleston Mercury,* Feb. 19, 1861, in *Jefferson Davis Constitutionalist: His Letters, Papers, and Speeches,* vol. V, ed. Dunbar Rowland (Jackson, Miss.: Mississippi Department of Archives and History, 1923), 47.
48. *New York Tribune,* Feb. 17 or 18, 1861.
49. Jefferson Davis, inaugural address, Feb. 18, 1861, *Papers of Jefferson Davis,* vol. VII (1861), 45–50.
50. Dirck, *Lincoln & Davis,* 181.
51. AL, reply to Gov. Edwin D. Morgan at Albany, N.Y., Feb. 18, 1861, *CW* IV, 225.
52. *The Complete Writings of Walt Whitman,* ed. Richard Maurice Bucke, Thomas B. Harned, and Horace L. Traubel, vol. V (New York: G. P. Putnam's Sons, 1902), 243–44.
53. Ibid.
54. AL, speech at Astor House, New York City, Feb. 19, 1861, *CW* IV, 230.
55. Strong, entry for Feb. 18, 1861, 100.
56. Ibid., 101.
57. *New York Herald,* Feb. 22, 1861; Robert S. Harper, *Lincoln and the Press* (New York: McGraw-Hill, 1951), 319.
58. *New York Herald,* Feb. 22, 1861.
59. Villard, *Memoirs,* vol. I, 152.
60. AL, address to the New Jersey Senate at Trenton, N.J., Feb. 21, 1861, *CW* IV, 235.
61. Ibid., 236.
62. AL, reply to Mayor Alexander Henry at Philadelphia, Penn., Feb. 21, 1861, *CW* IV, xxx.
63. AL, speech in Independence Hall, Philadelphia, Penn., Feb. 22, 1861, *CW* IV, 240.
64. Ibid.
65. Ibid.
66. Ibid.
67. Donald, 278.
68. "Lincoln and His Wayside Speeches," *Baltimore Sun,* reprinted in the *Crisis* (Columbus, Ohio), Feb. 21, 1861.
69. *Chicago Tribune,* Feb. 21, 1861.
70. Stephen G. Weisner, *Embattled Editor: The Life of Samuel Bowles* (Lanham, Md.: University Press of America, 1986), 27; George Merriam, *The Life and Times of Samuel Bowles,* vol. I (New York: Century Co., 1885), 318.
71. Charles Francis Adams, Diary, Feb. 20, 1861, cited in Martin B. Duberman, *Charles Francis Adams, 1807–1886* (Boston: Houghton Mifflin, 1961), 253–54.
72. Paul Revere Frothingham, *Edward Everett, Orator and Statesman* (Port Washington, N.Y.: Kennikat Press, 1925), 415.
73. *Chicago Tribune,* Feb. 21, 1861.

CHAPTER 3
"THE MYSTIC CHORDS OF MEMORY"

1. For biographies of William H. Seward, see Glyndon G. Van Deusen, *William Henry Seward* (New York: Oxford University Press, 1967), and John M. Taylor, *William Henry Seward: Lincoln's Right Hand* (New York: HarperCollins, 1991).
2. Van Deusen, *Seward,* 121–23; Taylor, *Seward,* 84–85.
3. Van Deusen, *Seward,* 193–94; Taylor, *Seward,* 106–8.
4. Francis B. Carpenter, "A Day with Governor Seward at Auburn," July 1870, William Henry Seward Papers, University of Rochester, cited in Taylor, *Seward,* 73–74; Frederick Seward, *Seward at Washington as Senator and Secretary of State: A Memoir of His Life, with Selections from His Letters, 1846–1861* (New York: Derby and Miller, 1891), 79–80.
5. *Charles Francis Adams, 1835–1915: An Autobiography* (Boston: Houghton Mifflin Company, 1916), 64.
6. William H. Seward to Frances Seward, Feb. 23, 1861, in Seward, *Seward at Washington,* 511.
7. Wilhemus Bogart Bryan, *A History of the National Capital,* vol. II, *1815–1878* (New York: MacMillan, 1916), 420.
8. Ibid., 445.
9. Allan Johnston, *Surviving Freedom: The Black Community of Washington, D.C., 1860–1880* (New York: Garland, 1993), 76–77; Richard C. Wade, *Slavery in the Cities: The South 1820–1860* (New York: Oxford University Press, 1964), 325–27. See also Constance McLaughlin Green, *The Secret City: A History of Race Relations in the Nation's Capital* (Princeton, N.J.: Princeton University Press, 1967).
10. Johnson, *Surviving Freedom,* 88–89; Green, *The Secret City,* 49; Donald, 133–37.
11. Villard, *Memoirs,* vol. I, 156.
12. *The Diary of Orville Hickman Browning,* vol. II, ed. Theodore Calvin Pease and James G. Randall, Collections of the Illinois State Historical Library, vol. XX (1925), 455–56.
13. AL, "First Inaugural Address—First Edition and Revisions," *CW* IV, 254. This copy, with Browning's comments in his handwriting, is in the Henry E. Huntington Library, San Marino, Calif. See also Maurice G. Baxter, *Orville H. Browning: Lincoln's Friend and Critic* (Bloomington, Ind.: Indiana University Press, 1957), 108–9.
14. Donald, 283.
15. William H. Seward to AL, Feb. 24, 1861, in N&H III, 319–20. All of these suggestions are included in the footnotes of the text of the First Inaugural in *CW* IV, 249–71, and in N&H III, 327–44. Nicolay and Hay include the alternative last paragraph that Lincoln decided not to use. A new edition of the Abraham Lincoln Papers at the Library of Congress is being transcribed and annotated by the Lincoln Studies Center, Knox College, Galesburg, Ill. Available online, the annotation of the final version of the First Inaugural allows the researcher and reader to trace more clearly the process of Lincoln's revising.

16. N&H III, 319–20.
17. AL to George D. Prentice, Feb. 2, 1861, *CW* IV, 184.
18. Charles Aldrich, "At Lincoln's First Inauguration," *Annals of Iowa* 8, third series (1907–8), 43–45.
19. Ibid., 45.
20. *New York Times,* Mar. 4, 1861.
21. Aldrich, "At Lincoln's First Inauguration," 45.
22. *New York World,* Mar. 4, 1861.
23. *Philadelphia Morning Pennsylvanian,* Mar. 4, 1861; Kenneth M. Stampp, *And the War Came: The North and the Secession Crisis, 1860–1861* (Baton Rouge: Louisiana State University Press, 1950), 197.
24. *Chicago Tribune,* Mar. 9, 1861; *New York Daily Tribune,* Mar. 5, 1861.
25. Aldrich, "At Lincoln's First Inauguration," 46.
26. *New York Times,* Mar. 5, 1861.
27. Bryan, *History,* vol. II, 469.
28. *Washington National Intelligencer,* Mar. ?, 1861.
29. AL, "First Inaugural Address—Final Text," *CW* IV, 262.
30. *New York Tribune,* Mar. 5, 1861.
31. William H. Herndon, *Herndon's Lincoln: The True Story of a Great Life,* vol. II (New York: D. Appleton, 1892), 234.
32. Horace White, "Abraham Lincoln in 1854," *Transactions of the Illinois State Historical Society, 1908,* no. 13, 32; White, "Lincoln and Douglas Debates: An Address Before the Chicago Historical Society, February 7, 1914," 20.
33. *New York Herald,* Feb. 28, 1860.
34. *Washington National Intelligencer,* Mar. 5, 1861; *Cincinnati Commercial,* quoted in the *Chicago Tribune,* Mar. 8, 1861.
35. This is a place where the online edition at the Library of Congress describes Lincoln's process of editing more fully than the older Basler edition of *The Collected Works of Abraham Lincoln.*
36. AL, speech at Columbus, Ohio, Sept. 16, 1859, *CW* III, 402; AL, first debate with Stephen A. Douglas, at Ottawa, Ill., Aug. 21, 1858, *CW* III, 16; AL, sixth debate with Stephen A. Douglas, at Quincy, Ill., Oct. 13, 1858, *CW* III, 249.
37. Constitution of the United States, Article IV, Section 2.
38. Patricia A. Chantrill offers helpful analysis about Lincoln's treatment of the Fugitive Slave Law in what she argues has been an overlooked element in Lincoln's inaugural. See "Reclaiming the Fugitive in Lincoln's First Inaugural Address," Ph.D. dissertation, Washington State University, 1997.
39. *New York Tribune,* Mar. 6, 1861.
40. *Boston Transcript,* Mar. 5, 1861.
41. William H. Seward to AL, in N&H III, 321.
42. The Washington diary of Horatio Nelson Taft, which he kept from 1861 to 1865, was presented to the Library of Congress in 2000. The three-volume diary, unknown outside the immediate family, is a newly discovered source of information about daily life in Washington as well as attitudes toward Lincoln. *Washington During the Civil War: The Diary of Horatio Nelson Taft, 1861–1865,* entry for Mar. 4, 1861, Library of Congress.

43. Strong, entry for Mar. 4, 1861, 105–6.
44. Ibid., 106.
45. *Illinois State Journal,* Mar. 6, 1861; *Chicago Tribune,* Mar. 5, 1861.
46. *New York Times,* Mar. 5, 1861; *New York Tribune,* Mar. 6, 1861. The *Indianapolis Daily Journal* is quoted in the *New York Tribune,* Mar. 7, 1861.
47. *Chicago Times,* Mar. 6, 1861; *New York Herald,* Mar. 6 or 7, 1861; *Philadelphia Evening Journal,* in *New York Tribune,* Mar. 7, 1861.
48. *New York Tribune,* Mar. 5, 1861.
49. John G. Nicolay, *A Short Life of Abraham Lincoln* (New York: Century, 1902), 38; Noah Brooks, *Life of Lincoln* (New York: G. P. Putnam's Sons, 1888), 129.
50. *Charleston Mercury,* Mar. 5, 1861; *Richmond Enquirer,* Mar. 5, 1861.
51. *New York Times,* Mar. 6, 1861.
52. Frothingham, *Edward Everett,* 414–15.

CHAPTER 4
"THIS IS . . . A PEOPLE'S CONTEST"

1. Browning, *Diary,* vol. I, entry for July 3, 1861, 476. Browning, after his visit to Lincoln at the White House on the evening of July 3, 1861, recorded in his diary, "He told me that the very first thing placed in his hands after his inauguration was a letter from Major Anderson announcing the impossibility of defending or relieving Sumner."
2. William Howard Russell, *My Diary North and South,* ed. Eugene H. Berwanger (1863; repr. New York: Alfred A. Knopf, 1988), 44–45.
3. John Hay, *Addresses of John Hay* (New York: Century Co., 1906), 323–24.
4. Robert L. Wilson to William H. Herndon, Feb. 10, 1866, *HI,* 207. The "Long Nine" led the successful campaign in 1836 to move the Illinois capital from Vandalia to Springfield.
5. AL, brief autobiography, June [15?], 1858, *CW* II, 459; John G. Nicolay and John Hay, editors of the *Complete Works of Abraham Lincoln* (New York: Century, 1894), include Lincoln's reply with his answer, "defective," vol. II, 368. Charles Lanman, compiler of the *Dictionary of the United States Congress Containing Biographical Sketches of Its Members from the Foundation of the Government* (Philadelphia: J. B. Lippincott, 1859), 298, evidently edited Lincoln's original answer, to read "received a limited education."
6. AL to Jesse W. Fell, "Enclosing Autobiography," Dec. 20, 1859, *CW* III, 511.
7. AL, autobiography written for John L. Scripps, June 1860, *CW* IV, 60–67.
8. William Scott, *Lessons in Elocution, or, A Selection of Pieces in Prose and Verse, for the Improvement of Youth in Reading and Speaking* (Baltimore: Warner and Hanna, 1806), 43–53; Louis A. Warren, *Lincoln's Youth: Indiana Years, Seven to Twenty-one, 1816–1830* (Indianapolis: Indiana Historical Society, 1959), 76–79.
9. Warren, *Lincoln's Youth,* 78.
10. Herndon and Weik, *Abraham Lincoln,* vol. I, 75.

11. Samuel Kirkham, *English Grammar in Familiar Lectures* (Rochester, N.Y.: Marshall & Dan, 1829), 8. A Kirkham grammar, one Lincoln owned and gave to Ann Rutledge, is now in the Library of Congress. This copy was handed down through the Ann Rutledge family; she was a young woman Lincoln had courted in New Salem. There is no evidence that this is the grammar Lincoln acquired from farmer Vance.
12. Herndon and Weik, *Abraham Lincoln,* vol. I, 75–76.
13. Mentor Graham to William H. Herndon, *HI,* 10. Douglas Wilson, in *Honor's Voice: The Transformation of Abraham Lincoln* (New York: Alfred A. Knopf, 1998), 64, believes that the details of Graham's reminiscence "lend it an air of reality."
14. AL, autobiography written for John L. Scripps, June 1860, *CW* IV, 62.
15. Seward's letter, "Some thoughts for the President's consideration," Apr. 1, 1861, is in *CW* IV, 317; Taylor, *Seward,* 150–54.
16. *CW* IV, 318.
17. Ibid., 316.
18. *New York Times,* Apr. 3, 1861.
19. Ibid., 447.
20. I am indebted to Tom Schwartz for encouraging attention to Lincoln's silence and to Harold Holzer for his insights in *Lincoln Seen and Heard,* 163–78. See also Braden, *Abraham Lincoln, Public Speaker,* 41–42.
21. Holzer, *Lincoln Seen and Heard,* 171.
22. Helen Nicolay, *Lincoln's Secretary: A Biography of John Nicolay* (New York: Longmans, Green, and Co., 1949), 106–7.
23. Quoted in Taylor, *Seward,* 181.
24. Herndon and Weik, *Abraham Lincoln,* vol. I, 317–18.
25. Ibid., vol. II, 66.
26. Noah Brooks, "Personal Reminiscences of Lincoln," *Scribner's Monthly,* Feb. 1878, 565–66.
27. Strong, entry for July 15, 1861, 164.
28. Seward, *Seward at Washington,* 592; *CW* IV, 421 n. 1.
29. In *CW* IV, 421–41, Basler has 119 footnotes to the Message to Congress in Special Session detailing the changes suggested by Seward that were made by Lincoln as well as Lincoln's changes. In the online Abraham Lincoln Papers at the Library of Congress, check the version titled "Second Printed Draft, with Suggested Changes by William H. Seward" to see both the image of the document with Seward's changes written by his son Frederick and a transcription of the complete document with the changes.
30. Browning, *Diary,* vol. I, entry for July 3, 1861, 475.
31. H. Nicolay, *Lincoln's Secretary,* 107.
32. AL to Winfield Scott, April 27, 1861, *CW* IV, 347.
33. Donald, 299.
34. AL to Winfield Scott, July 2, 1861, *CW* IV, 419.
35. N&H IV, 176–78; James G. Randall, *Constitutional Problems Under Lincoln* (New York: D. Appleton, 1926), 121–23.

36. United States Constitution, article I, section 9, paragraph 2.
37. Mark E. Neely, Jr., *The Fate of Liberty: Abraham Lincoln and Civil Liberties* (New York: Oxford University Press, 1991), 11–13.
38. Donald, 302.
39. Paul M. Angle, "Lincoln's Power with Words," *Abraham Lincoln Association Papers* (Springfield, Ill.: Abraham Lincoln Association, 1935), 80; Roy Basler, "Lincoln's Development as a Writer," *A Touchstone for Greatness* (Westport, Conn.: Greenwood Press, 1973), 90.
40. Edward Cary, *George William Curtis* (Boston: Houghton Mifflin, 1894), 147.

CHAPTER 5
"MY PARAMOUNT OBJECT IN THIS STRUGGLE"

1. Biographies of Horace Greeley include Glyndon G. Van Deusen, *Horace Greeley: Nineteenth-Century Crusader* (New York; Hill and Wang, 1953) and Don C. Seitz, *Horace Greeley, Founder of the New York Tribune* (Indianapolis: Bobbs-Merrill, 1926). Excellent chapters on Greeley are to be found in Daniel Walker Howe, *The Political Culture of the American Whigs* (Chicago: University of Chicago Press, 1979), 184–197, and Constance M. Rourke, *Trumpets of Jubilee* (New York: Harcourt, Brace, 1927), 241–365.
2. *New York Tribune,* Feb. 18, 1862.
3. Strong, entries for July 11 and Aug. 4, 1862, 244.
4. Ralph Waldo Emerson to Thomas Carlyle, March 1854, in *The Correspondence of Emerson and Carlyle,* ed. Joseph Slater (New York: Columbia University Press, 1964), 499; Henry Luther Stoddard, *Horace Greeley: Printer, Editor, Crusader* (New York: G. P. Putnam's Sons, 1946), 92–93.
5. *New York Times,* May 16, 1860.
6. Harper, *Lincoln and the Press,* 100–101; Ralph Ray Fahrney, *Horace Greeley and the Tribune in the Civil War* (Cedar Rapids, Iowa: Torch Press, 1936), 1–2.
7. *New York Tribune,* Dec. 3, 1845; Glyndon G. Van Deusen, *Horace Greeley: Nineteenth-Century Crusader* (Philadelphia: University of Pennsylvania Press, 1953), 51.
8. Seitz, *Greeley,* 226.
9. AL, second lecture on discoveries and inventions, Feb. 11, 1859, *CW* III, 362.
10. Francis B. Carpenter, *The Inner Life of Abraham Lincoln: Six Months at the White House* (New York: Hurd and Houghton, 1866), 154.
11. Harper, *Lincoln and the Press,* 97.
12. *New York Tribune,* July 14, 1847.
13. Ibid., Feb. 28, 1860.
14. Joseph Medill to AL, Jan. 15, 1865, ALP.
15. AL to Henry J. Raymond, Mar. 9, 1862, *CW* V, 152–53.
16. Van Deusen, *Greeley,* 276–78; Stoddard, *Greeley,* 213–14.
17. Van Deusen, *Greeley,* 278; Stoddard, *Greeley,* 214.
18. Stoddard, *Greeley,* 219–20.

19. Seitz, *Greeley*, 240.
20. For a discussion of the Confiscation Act, see Allen C. Guelzo, *Lincoln's Emancipation Proclamation: The End of Slavery in America* (New York: Simon & Schuster, 2004), 37–42.
21. *New York Times*, Aug. 25, 1862.
22. James Clark Welling, "The Emancipation Proclamation," *North American Review* 130 (Feb. 1860), 163–85; *Addresses, Lectures, and Other Papers* (Cambridge, Mass.: Riverside Press, 1904), ix. In 1870 Princeton would call Welling to become professor of belles lettres.
23. James C. Welling, in *Reminiscences of Abraham Lincoln*, ed. Allen Thorndike Rice (New York: North American Publishing, 1886), 525–26 n; AL to Horace Greeley, Aug. 22, 1862, *CW* V, 388–89 n. 2.
24. Welling, *Reminiscences*, ibid.
25. AL to John A. McClernand, Jan. 8, 1863, *CW* VI, 48–49.
26. Welling, *Reminiscences*, 523.
27. James C. Conkling, "The Early Branch and Bar of Central Illinois," delivered before the Chicago Bar Association, Jan. 12, 1881, reprinted in part in Rufus Rockwell Wilson, *Lincoln Among His Friends* (Caldwell, Idaho: Caxton Printers, 1942), 107.
28. *Washington National Intelligencer*, Aug. 22, 1862.
29. William Harlan Hale, *Horace Greeley: Voice of the People* (New York: Harper & Brothers, 1950), 263.
30. Noah Brooks, *Sacramento Daily Union*, May 17, 1865 (published June 14, 1865), in *Lincoln Observed: Civil War Dispatches of Noah Brooks*, ed. Michael Burlingame (Baltimore: Johns Hopkins University Press, 1998), 197–98.

CHAPTER 6
"GOD WILLS THIS CONTEST"

1. *CW* V, 404 n. 1.
2. AL, "Meditation on the Divine Will," Sept. 2?, 1862, *CW* V, 404. Lincoln's reflection is undated. Basler calculates the date as Sept. 2, after the defeat at the Second Battle of Bull Run, but places a question mark after the date.
3. The text of the Meditation is in the John Hay Library at Brown University.
4. N&H VI, 342.
5. AL, address to the New Jersey Senate at Trenton, N.J., Feb. 21, 1861, *CW* IV, 235.
6. AL, handbill replying to charges of infidelity, July 31, 1846, *CW* I, 382.
7. The preference for fatalism as the rubric under which to understand Lincoln's later theological thinking is seen in the biographies by Stephen B. Oates and David H. Donald. For a critique of this older approach, with his own insightful suggestions of an alternative point of view, see Stewart Winger, *Lincoln, Religion, and Romantic Cultural Politics* (Dekalb, Ill.: Northern Illinois University Press, 2003), especially chapters 6 and 7.

8. Francis Wharton, *A Treatise on Theism, and on the Modern Skeptical Theories* (Philadelphia: J. B. Lippincott, 1859), 147, 152.
9. Wayne C. Temple, *Abraham Lincoln: From Skeptic to Prophet* (Mahomet, Ill.: Mayhaven, 1995), 140–42.
10. William E. Schenck, *A Memorial Sermon on the Life, Labours and Christian Character of Phineas Densmore Gurley* (Washington, D.C.: William Ballentyne, 1869), 16–18.
11. Charles Hodge, *Systematic Theology,* vol. 1 (New York: Scribner, 1871), 583, 616.
12. The theme of providence is present in a collection of Gurley sermons at the Presbyterian Historical Society. Unfortunately, the sermons are undated, so it is not possible to say whether any were preached at New York Avenue Presbyterian Church.
13. Schenck, *A Memorial Sermon,* 42.
14. Leonard W. Volk, "The Lincoln Life Mask and How It Was Made," *Century Magazine,* Dec. 1881, 226; Schenck, *A Memorial Sermon,* 29.
15. Phineas D. Gurley, "Funeral Address on the Occasion of the Death of William Wallace Lincoln," Washington, D.C., n.p., 1862, 3.
16. Ibid., 3–4.
17. Reinhold Niebuhr, "The Religion of Abraham Lincoln," *Christian Century,* Feb. 10, 1965.
18. Ibid.
19. Ibid.
20. Ibid.
21. *Chicago Tribune,* Sept. 5 and 8, 1862.
22. AL, reply to emancipation memorial presented by Chicago Christians of all denominations, Sept. 13, 1862, *CW* V, 419–20; *Chicago Tribune,* Sept. 15, 1862.
23. *Inside Lincoln's Cabinet: The Civil War Diaries of Salmon P. Chase,* ed. David Donald (New York: Longmans, Green, 1954), entry for Sept. 22, 1862, 150.
24. *Diary of Gideon Welles: Secretary of the Navy Under Lincoln and Johnson,* vol. I (Boston: Houghton Mifflin Company, 1911), entry for Sept. 22, 1862, 143.

CHAPTER 7
"*WE* CANNOT ESCAPE HISTORY"

1. *Washington National Intelligencer,* Dec. 2, 1862.
2. AL, "Emancipation Proclamation—First Draft," July 22, 1862, *CW* V, 336–38.
3. Mark E. Neeley, Jr., *The Union Divided: Party Conflict in the Civil War North* (Cambridge: Harvard University Press, 2002), 37–38.
4. *New York Times,* Nov. 7, 1862. The traditional viewpoint has been that the 1862 elections, at both the national and state levels, were a disaster for the Republicans. James M. McPherson argues, "But a closer look at the results challenges the conclusion." Republicans did maintain a twenty-five-seat majority in the House, experiencing the smallest net loss in twenty years. See *Battle Cry*

of Freedom: The Civil War Era (New York: Oxford University Press, 1988), 561–62.

5. David Homer Bates, *Lincoln in the Telegraph Office* (New York: Century Co., 1907), 9.
6. Ibid., 38–39.
7. Albert Chandler, "Lincoln and the Telegrapher," *American Heritage* 12 (Apr. 1961), 33.
8. Ibid.
9. Browning, *Diary,* vol. II, entry for Oct. 14, 578; Baxter, *Browning,* 152.
10. Browning, *Diary,* vol. II, entry for Nov. 29, 1862, 588.
11. *Springfield (Mass.) Republican,* Nov. 29, 1862.
12. Lawrence A. Gobright to John G. Nicolay, Dec. 1, 1862, ALP.
13. John W. Forney to John G. Nicolay, Dec. 1, 1862, ALP.
14. Gabor S. Boritt shows the linkage between Lincoln's economic dream and his opposition to slavery in "Lincoln and the Economics of the American Dream," in *The Historian's Lincoln: Pseudohistory, Psychohistory, and History,* ed. Gabor S. Boritt (Urbana: University of Illinois Press, 1988), 87–106. See also Boritt, *Lincoln and the Economics of the American Dream* (Memphis, Tenn.: Memphis State University Press, 1978).
15. AL, reply to Eliza P. Gurney, Oct. 26, 1862, *CW* V, 478 n. 1.
16. Ibid.
17. David Zarefsky, "Lincoln's 1862 Annual Message: A Paradigm of Rhetorical Leadership," *Rhetoric and Public Affairs* 3, no. 1, 5.
18. Ibid., 12–13.

CHAPTER 8
"YOU SAY YOU WILL NOT FIGHT TO FREE NEGROES"

1. The request from James C. Conkling of Aug. 14, 1863, is contained in note 1, AL to James C. Conkling, Aug. 20, 1863, *CW* VI, 399.
2. Ibid. At the lower left-hand corner of the telegram was a note, "Mr. C—Mr. Wilson got this in cipher." Mr. Wilson was the superintendent of the Eastern Division of the Illinois and Mississippi Telegraph Company. The note was signed simply "Operator." This notation suggested the desire to keep the movements of the president secret.
3. N&H. VII, 379–80.
4. James C. Conkling to AL, Aug. 21, 1863, ALP.
5. AL to James C. Conkling, Aug. 26, 1863, *CW* VI, 406.
6. AL to James C. Conkling, Aug. 27, 1863, *CW* VI, 414. An excellent essay on the letter to Conkling is Allen C. Guelzo's "Defending Emancipation: Abraham Lincoln and the Conkling Letter, 1863," *Civil War History* 48 (Dec. 2002), 313–37. Word of the Conkling invitation triggered a similar invitation from New York. Benjamin Field, secretary of the Union State Committee of New York, telegraphed Lincoln on Aug. 26 telling him of plans to hold "a mass con-

vention" in Syracuse, also on Sept. 3. Field asked that Lincoln send the New York convention "the same address" that he was sending to Illinois. Lincoln wrote to Field on Aug. 29 telling him that he was sending by mail a copy of "the Springfield letter"; *CW* VI, 420.

7. William H. Herndon to AL, Aug. 29, 1863, ALP. Herndon asserted that he wrote many letters to Lincoln during his presidency, but this is the only one that is in the Lincoln papers.
8. *Inside Lincoln's White House: The Complete Civil War Diary of John Hay,* ed. Michael Burlingame and John R. Turner Ettlinger (Carbondale, Ill.: Southern Illinois University Press, 1997), entry for Aug. 23, 1863, 76.
9. William O. Stoddard, *Inside the White House in War Times: Memoirs and Reports of Lincoln's Secretary,* ed. Michael Burlingame (Lincoln: University of Nebraska Press, 2000), 129–30.
10. See the editorial notes to the letter to Conkling, Aug. 26, 1863, in the online Abraham Lincoln Papers cooperative project of Knox College and the Library of Congress.
11. Victor Hicken, *Illinois in the Civil War* (Urbana: University of Illinois Press, 1966), 128–29.
12. N&H. VII, 378.
13. *Illinois State Journal,* Aug. 14, 1863; Paul Selby, "Light on a Famous Lincoln Letter," *Chicago Tribune,* June 23, 1895.
14. *Illinois State Journal,* Sept. 3, 1863.
15. Octavia Roberts Corneau and Georgia L. Osborne, "A Girl in the Sixties: Excerpts from the Journal of Anna Ridgley (Mrs. James L. Hudson), *Journal of the Illinois State Historical Society* 23 (Oct. 1929), 429; *Chicago Tribune,* Sept. 4, 1863; Camilla A. Quinn, *Lincoln's Springfield in the Civil War,* Western Illinois Monograph Series no. 8 (Macomb, Ill.: Western Illinois University, 1991), 51.
16. *Illinois State Journal,* Sept. 4, 1863; *Springfield Register,* Sept. 4, 1863.
17. Donald, 391; H. Nicolay, *Lincoln's Secretary,* 118; Hay, *Addresses,* 324.
18. Kenneth J. Winkle, *The Young Eagle: The Rise of Abraham Lincoln* (Dallas, Tex.: Taylor, 2001), 24–26.
19. David W. Blight, *Frederick Douglass' Civil War: Keeping Faith in Jubilee* (Baton Rouge: Louisiana State University Press, 1989), 156–57.
20. AL to Ulysses S. Grant, Aug. 9, 1863, *CW* VI, 374.
21. Frederick Douglass, "Emancipation, Racism, and the Work Before Us," address delivered in Philadelphia, Penn., Dec. 4, 1863, in *The Frederick Douglass Papers,* ed. John W. Blasingame, series I, vol. III, 1855–1863 (New Haven: Yale University Press, 1992), 606–7.
22. AL to Ulysses S. Grant, Aug. 9, 1863, *CW* VI, 374; Grant to AL, Aug. 23, 1863, ALP.
23. AL to James C. Conkling, Aug. 31, 1863, *CW* VI, 423.
24. AL to James C. Conkling, Aug. 27, 1863, *CW* VI, 414.
25. Ibid.
26. This book is focusing on Lincoln's presidential rhetoric. On the Cooper Union address, see Harold Holzer, *Lincoln at Cooper Union: The Speech That Made Abraham Lincoln President* (New York: Simon & Schuster, 2004).

27. Henry S. Commager, "Lincoln and the Whole Nation," in *Lincoln for the Ages*, ed. Ralph G. Newman (Garden City, N.Y.: Doubleday, 1960), 363–64.
28. Stoddard, *Inside the White House*, 173.
29. James C. Conkling to AL, Sept. 4, 1863, ALP.
30. Strong, entry for Sept. 3, 1863, 355.
31. AL to James C. Conkling, Sept. 3, 1863, *CW* VI, 430.
32. James C. Conkling to AL, Sept. 4, 1863, ibid., n. 1.
33. James W. Forney to AL, ibid.
34. *New York Tribune*, Sept. 3, 1863.
35. John Z. Goodrich to AL, Sept. 3, 1863, ALP.
36. Charles Sumner to AL, Sept. 7, 1863, ALP; Donald, 321.
37. Henry Wilson to AL, Sept. 3, 1863, ALP.
38. J. M. Forbes to AL, Sept. 8, 1863, in *Letters and Recollections of John Murray Forbes*, ed. Sarah Forbes Hughes, vol. II (Boston: Houghton Mifflin, 1890), 73.
39. Josiah Quincy to AL, Sept. 7, 1863, ALP; see also Lincoln's response to Quincy, Sept. 12, 1863, *CW* VI, 443.
40. Hay, *Inside Lincoln's White House*, diary entry for Sept. 10, 1863, 81.
41. John Hay to John G. Nicolay, Sept. 11, 1863, in *Letters of John Hay and Extracts from Diary*, ed. Clara Louise Hay, vol. I, 102.
42. *Times* (London), Sept. 17, 1863.
43. Strong, entry for Sept. 3, 1863, 355.
44. N&H VII, 384.
45. Ibid., 130.

CHAPTER 9
"THIS NATION, UNDER GOD, SHALL HAVE A NEW BIRTH OF FREEDOM"

1. AL, remarks at Jersey City, N.J., June 24, 1862, *CW* V, 284.
2. AL, speech at Frederick, Md.; second speech at Frederick, Md., Oct. 4, 1862, *CW* V, 450.
3. J. M. Forbes to AL, Sept. 8, 1863, in *Letters and Recollections of John Murray Forbes*, vol. II, 76.
4. Benjamin P. Thomas, *Abraham Lincoln: A Biography* (New York: Alfred A. Knopf, 1952), 400.
5. Benjamin P. Thomas, *Autobiographical Sketch*, ca. 1953, Benjamin P. Thomas Papers, Abraham Lincoln Presidential Library, see John Hay, *At Lincoln's Side: John Hay's Civil War Correspondence and Selected Writings*, ed. Michael Burlingame (Carbondale, Ill.: Southern Illinois University Press, 2000), 237 n. 119.
6. Kathleen R. Georg, "This Grand National Enterprise: The Origins of Gettysburg's Soldiers National Cemetery & Gettysburg Battlefield Memorial Association" (1982), on file at the library at the National Military Park at Gettysburg, 82.
7. Frothingham, Edward *Everett*, 82.
8. David Wills to AL, Nov. 2, 1863, in Louis A. Warren, *Lincoln's Gettysburg*

Declaration: "A New Birth of Freedom" (Fort Wayne, Ind.: Lincoln National Life Foundation, 1964), 45–46.

9. Warren, *Lincoln's Gettysburg Declaration,* 42.
10. *Indianapolis Daily Journal,* Nov. 23, 1863.
11. AL, remarks to citizens of Gettysburg, Penn., Nov. 18, 1863, *CW* VII, 16; *New York Tribune,* Nov. 20, 1863.
12. Hay, *Inside Lincoln's White House,* Nov. 18, 1863, 112.
13. Isaac N. Arnold, *The History of Abraham Lincoln and the Overthrow of Slavery* (Chicago: Clarke & Co., 1866), 422–23.
14. Frank L. Klement, *The Gettysburg Soldiers' Cemetery and Lincoln's Address* (Shippensburg, Penn.: White Mane Publishing, 1993), 86.
15. Mary Raymond Shipman Andrews, *The Perfect Tribute* (New York: Charles Scribner's Sons, 1906). I found the letter from Andrews to Judd Stewart tucked into a copy of *The Perfect Tribute* at the Huntington Library. The Judd Stewart Collection forms a central part of the Huntington's Lincoln collection.
16. Ward Hill Lamon, *Recollections of Abraham Lincoln, 1847–1865,* ed. Dorothy Lamon Teillard (Chicago: A. C. McClurg, 1895), 172–73.
17. Noah Brooks, *Washington in Lincoln's Time,* ed. Herbert Mitgang (New York: Rinehart & Co., 1958), 253.
18. John G. Nicolay, "Lincoln's Gettysburg Address," *Century Magazine* 47, (Feb. 1894), 601.
19. AL, response to a serenade, July 7, 1863, *CW* VI, 319–20; *New York Tribune, Herald, Times,* July 8, 1863.
20. Nicolay, "Lincoln's Gettysburg Address," 601–2.
21. A long-running debate continues as to the site of the platform and Lincoln's address. The traditional site, where the tall column of the Soldiers' National Monument, dedicated on July 4, 1869, now stands, has been challenged. For a discussion of the contending views, see Garry Wills, *Lincoln at Gettysburg: The Words That Remade America* (New York: Simon & Schuster, 1992), Appendix II, 205–10.
22. Hay, *Inside Lincoln's White House,* 113.
23. Psalm 90:10, King James Version.
24. See White, *Lincoln's Greatest Speech,* 108–12; Matthew Pinsker, *Lincoln's Sanctuary: Abraham Lincoln and the Soldiers' Home* (New York: Oxford University Press, 2003), 5.
25. James Hurt, "All the Living and the Dead," *American Literature* 52 (1980), 377–79.
26. Warren, *Lincoln's Gettysburg Declaration,* 106.
27. AL, Message to Congress in Special Session, July 4, 1861, *CW* IV, 439.
28. Sarah Joan Ankeney, "Parallel Construction in Abraham Lincoln's Gettysburg Address—Not So Parallel," *Lincoln Herald,* summer 2000, 82–84.
29. *The Papers of Daniel Webster: Speeches and Formal Writings,* vol. I, 1800–1833, ed. Charles M. Wiltse and Alan R. Berolzheimer (Dartmouth, N.H.: Dartmouth University Press, 1986), 339–40; Merrill D. Peterson, *The Great Triumvirate: Webster, Clay, and Calhoun* (New York: Oxford University Press, 1987), 179–80.

30. Garry Wills offers a trenchant analysis of Parker and his influence on Lincoln in *Lincoln at Gettysburg*, 105–18.
31. *CW* IV, 426.
32. Donald, 462.
33. I am indebted to the insights of Kenneth Cmiel on Lincoln's use of Saxon language. See Cmiel, *Democratic Eloquence: The Fight over Popular Speech in Nineteenth-Century America* (Berkeley: University of California Press, 1990), 95–97, 116–17.
34. Ibid., 117; James Russell Lowell, "Abraham Lincoln" (1864), in *My Study Windows* (London: George Routledge & Sons, n.d.), 164.
35. James C. Conkling, "The Early Branch and Bar of Central Illinois," 107–8.
36. Edwin Black, "Gettysburg and Silence," *Quarterly Journal of Speech* 80 (1994), 27; William E. Barton, *Lincoln at Gettysburg: What He Intended to Say; What He Said; What He Was Reported to Have Said; What He Wished He Had Said* (Indianapolis: Bobbs-Merrill, 1930), 149.
37. Edwin Black, "The Ultimate Voice of Lincoln," *Rhetoric and Public Affairs*, 3, no. 1 (2000), 49–50.
38. Ibid., 51.
39. *Chicago Tribune*, Nov. 20, 1863.
40. *Springfield (Mass.) Republican*, Nov. 20, 1863.
41. *Providence Daily Journal*, Nov. 20, 1863.
42. *Chicago Times*, Nov. 20, 1863.
43. *Harrisburg Patriot and Union*, Nov. 20, 1863.
44. *Times* (London), Dec. 4, 1863.
45. *Harper's Weekly*, Dec. 5, 1863.
46. Frothingham, Edward *Everett*, 458.
47. AL to Edward Everett, Nov. 20, 1863, *CW* VII, 24.
48. Taylor, *Seward*, 224.

CHAPTER 10
"I CLAIM NOT TO HAVE CONTROLLED EVENTS"

1. *The Diary of Edward Bates, 1859–1866*, ed. Howard K. Beale (Washington: Government Army Office, 1933), entry for Mar. 26, 352. *CW* V, 404n.
2. Lowell H. Harrison, *Lincoln of Kentucky* (Lexington: University of Kentucky Press, 2000), 236–37.
3. Thomas E. Bramlette to AL, Jan. 5, 1864, ALP.
4. AL to Bramlette, Jan. 6, 1864, *CW* VII, 109.
5. Bramlette to AL, Jan. 8, 1864, *CW* VII, 134–35; AL to Bramlette, Jan. 17, 1864, *CW* VII, 134.
6. Quoted in Harrison, *Lincoln of Kentucky*, 184.
7. Ibid.
8. *The Diary of Edward Bates*, entry for Mar. 28, 1864, 352.
9. *The Diary of Orville Hickman Browning*, vol. I, entry for Apr. 3, 1864, 665.
10. Winkle, *Young Eagle*, 12, 250–51; Warren, *Lincoln's Youth*, 12–14.

11. Guelzo, *Lincoln's Emancipation Proclamation,* 44–47, 70–73.
12. Donald, 10, 14.
13. *Frankfort Commonwealth,* Apr. 25, 1854; Albert G. Hodges to AL, Apr. 22, 1864, ALP; Hodges also wrote to Lincoln on Apr. 25, May 27, July 19, Aug. 11, Sept. 15, Sept. 29, Oct. 24, Nov. 1, Nov. 12, Dec. 1, and Dec. 9, 1864, and Mar. 1 and Apr. 1, 1865. ALP.

CHAPTER 11
"WITH MALICE TOWARD NONE; WITH CHARITY FOR ALL"

1. Lathrop C. Keith to Fannie Keith, Mar. 5, 1865. I am grateful to Don McCue, curator of the Lincoln Shrine in Redlands, California, for making available to me the Keith letter, which he had recently acquired for the Shrine's library.
2. Ibid.
3. Francis B. Carpenter, *The Inner Life of Abraham Lincoln: Six Months at the White House* (New York: Hurd and Houghton, 1874), 234. Carpenter had become well known for his painting *First Reading of the Emancipation Proclamation.*
4. Raymond's letter is quoted in *CW* VII, 517–18.
5. AL, memorandum concerning his probable failure of reelection, Aug. 23, 1864, *CW* VII, 514–15.
6. George Washington, Second Inaugural Address, Mar. 4, 1793, in *Inaugural Addresses of the Presidents of the United States from George Washington 1789 to John F. Kennedy 1961* (Washington, D.C.: U.S. Government Printing Office, 1961), 5.
7. Thomas Jefferson, Second Inaugural Address, ibid., 17.
8. James Madison, Second Inaugural Address, ibid., 26.
9. James Monroe, Second Inaugural Address, ibid., 34.
10. Andrew Jackson, Second Inaugural Address, ibid., 58.
11. Philip S. Paludan, *"A People's Contest": The Union and the Civil War, 1861–1865* (New York: Harper & Row, 1988), 316–17, allows us to see the war through the lives of individuals and communities.
12. David V. Derickson, "The President's Guard," typescript recollection courtesy of Jane Westerfield, Ida M. Tarbell Papers, Allegheny College, Meadville, Penn., quoted in Pinsker, *Lincoln's Sanctuary,* 5, 57, 202–3, 205 n. 10.
13. James M. McPherson, *For Cause and Comrade: Why Men Fought in the Civil War* (New York: Oxford University Press, 1997), 63. See also, Steven E. Woodworth, *While God Is Marching On: The Religious World of Civil War Soldiers* (Lawrence, Kans.: University Press of Kansas, 2001).
14. AL, Meditation on the Divine Will, Sept. [2?,] 1862, *CW* V, 404 n. 1.
15. Ibid.
16. AL, letter to Albert G. Hodges, Apr. 4, 1864, *CW* VII, 281–83.
17. Lerone Bennett, in *Forced into Glory: Abraham Lincoln's White Dream* (Chicago: Johnson Publishing, 2000), is silent about the Second Inaugural Address in his criticism of Lincoln's views on slavery.

18. A fine treatment of the story of the passage of the Thirteenth Amendment is Michael Vorenberg, *Final Freedom: The Civil War, the Abolition of Slavery, and the Thirteenth Amendment* (Cambridge: Cambridge University Press, 2001).
19. Isaac N. Arnold, *The Life of Abraham Lincoln* (Chicago: Jansen, McClurg, 1885), 357–58; Vorenberg, *Final Freedom,* 123.
20. Vorenberg, *Final Freedom,* 180.
21. Charles R. Douglass to Frederick Douglass, Feb. 9, 1865, quoted in Vorenberg, *Final Freedom,* 207–8.
22. AL, response to a serenade, Feb. 1, 1865, *CW* VIII, 254–55.
23. Rebecca R. Pomeroy, "What His Nurse Knew," *Magazine of History* 32, no. 1 (extra no. 125; 1926), 47.
24. *New York Herald,* Mar. 6, 1865.
25. Frederick Douglass, *Autobiographies* (New York: Library of America, 1994 [reprint of 1893 edition]), 801.
26. *Washington National Intelligencer,* Mar. 6, 1865.
27. *New York World,* Mar. 6, 1865.
28. Walt Whitman, *Specimen Days,* in *The Complete Writings of Walt Whitman,* ed. Richard Maurice Bucke, Thomas B. Harned, and Horace L. Traubel (New York: G. Putnam's Sons, 1902), 109.
29. Abraham Lincoln to Thurlow Weed, Mar. 15, 1865, *CW,* vol. VIII, 356. No letter from Weed mentioning the Second Inaugural has been found. Weed had written to commend Lincoln's reply on March 2 to the committee of Congress informing the president of his reelection. Weed also mentioned the second inauguration earlier that day. Lincoln evidently misconstrued Weed's commendation as kind words about both "my little notification speech" and his inaugural address.
30. Ibid.

EPILOGUE

1. AL, last public address, Apr. 11, 1865, *CW* VIII, 403.
2. Francis Wilson, *John Wilkes Booth* (New York: Houghton Mifflin, 1929), 50–54.
3. Aristotle, *Treatise on Rhetoric,* trans. Theodore Buckley (London: Bell and Daldy, 1872), 11.

BIBLIOGRAPHICAL ESSAY

The major resource for this book was Lincoln's words, their creation and delivery and the response to them. The other main resources were contemporary newspapers, letters, and diaries. This bibliographical essay will focus on a selected list of books and articles for those who want to continue the exploration of Lincoln's eloquence.

The place to begin is collections of Lincoln's words. *The Collected Works of Abraham Lincoln,* edited by Roy P. Basler (New Brunswick, N.J.: Rutgers University Press, 1953–55) and *Supplement, 1832–1865* (Westport, Conn.: Greenwood Press, 1974), is a basic source. A second collection is a new online edition of the Abraham Lincoln Papers at the Library of Congress being prepared by the Lincoln Studies Center at Knox College, Illinois, and directed by Douglas L. Wilson and Rodney O. Davis. The advantage of this edition, in addition to its accessibility on the Internet, is the increased ability for the reader to trace the evolution of the various versions of Lincoln's speeches. The texts are accompanied by an annotation that allows one to see, more clearly than in the Basler edition, the various drafts of Lincoln's writings and speeches. Because this is a work in progress, readers need to be cautioned that the annotations and even the transcriptions continue to change. Finally, the Abraham Lincoln Association in Springfield, which commissioned the original Basler edition, is beginning work on a new edition of the papers of Abraham Lincoln. This project, under the editorship of Daniel W. Stowell, promises to be thorough and will take at least ten years to complete.

Although the focus of this book is on the evolution of Lincoln's eloquence during the four years of his presidency, his entire life and career are always in view. Each generation produces biographies that lift up different aspects of Lincoln's life and career. The most valuable one-volume biographies are Benjamin P. Thomas, *Abraham Lincoln: A Biography* (New York: Alfred A. Knopf, 1952); Stephen Oates, *With Malice Toward None: A Life of Abraham Lincoln* (New York: Harper & Row, 1977); David H. Donald, *Lincoln* (New

York: Simon & Schuster, 1995); Allen Guelzo, *Abraham Lincoln: Redeemer President* (Grand Rapids: Wm. B. Eerdman, 1999); and Richard Carwardine, *Lincoln* (New York: Longmans, 2003). Lincoln's speeches, messages, and public letters, even in these fine biographies, receive too little attention. William E. Gienapp helps remedy this persistent problem by pairing his fine brief biography, *Abraham Lincoln and Civil War America* (New York: Oxford University Press, 2002), with *This Fiery Trial: The Speeches and Writings of Abraham Lincoln* (New York: Oxford University Press, 2002).

The unsurpassed book on the Civil War is James M. McPherson's *Battle Cry of Freedom: The Civil War Era* (New York: Oxford University Press, 1988).

The meaning and impact of the Emancipation Proclamation, although not treated as a separate chapter in this book, stands behind several of the speeches that are examined. See Allen C. Guelzo's excellent *Lincoln's Emancipation Proclamation: The End of Slavery in America* (New York: Simon & Schuster, 2004). Margaret Leech, *Reveille in Washington: 1860–1865* (New York: Harper & Brothers, 1941), remains a classic for its treatment of the people and pulse of wartime Washington.

I have made extensive use of newspapers in order to understand the context of and chart the responses to Lincoln's speeches. Nineteenth-century newspapers were extremely political, representing the interests of political parties in their cities and towns, and sometimes led by publishers or editors who were themselves politicians. Robert S. Harper, *Lincoln and the Press* (New York: McGraw-Hill, 1951), is an older book, but still helpful in descriptions both of editors and of the changing trajectories of newspapers in the volatile Civil War era. Herbert S. Mitgang, ed., *Abraham Lincoln: A Press Portrait* (New York: Fordham University Press, 2000), includes selections from a wide variety of newspapers and their responses to Lincoln's speeches.

A central dilemma in the study of Lincoln is how to weigh the many reminiscences about him, some offered years later. An invaluable resource is, *Herndon's Informants: Letters, Interviews, and Statements About Abraham Lincoln*, edited by Douglas L. Wilson and Rodney O. Davis (Urbana, Ill.: University of Illinois Press, 1998). A second resource is *Recollected Words of Abraham Lincoln*, compiled and edited by Don E. and Virginia Fehrenbacher (Stanford: Stanford University Press, 1996), where the remembered words of Lincoln are evaluated for their authenticity.

An appreciation of Lincoln's rhetoric needs to be set in the very different world of nineteenth-century rhetoric. Kenneth Cmiel, *Democratic Eloquence: The Fight over Popular Speech in Nineteenth-Century America*

(Berkeley: University of California Press, 1990), places Lincoln in the struggle between elite and popular speech. See also Nan Johnson, *Nineteenth-Century Rhetoric in North America* (Carbondale, Ill.: Southern Illinois University Press, 1991), and *Rhetorical and Political Culture in Nineteenth-Century America,* edited by Thomas W. Benson (East Lansing: Michigan State University Press, 1997).

There are two places to begin in understanding Lincoln as public speaker. Waldo Braden's *Abraham Lincoln: Public Speaker* (Baton Rouge: Louisiana State University Press, 1988) is a small but valuable study. A second place is to listen to David Zarefsky, a dean of teachers of speech communications, who offers a twenty-four-lecture audio series, *Abraham Lincoln: In His Own Words* (Springfield, Va.: The Teaching Company, 1999). In addition, Harold Holzer, in his marvelous *Lincoln at Cooper Union: The Speech That Made Abraham Lincoln President* (New York: Simon & Schuster, 2004), although focused on one prepresidential address, shines a bright light on Lincoln's whole career as an orator.

Some excellent studies of Lincoln's rhetoric, usually focusing on specific speeches, have been offered by professors of speech communication. These contributions have too seldom been utilized by biographers and historians of Lincoln. Two articles that have proved valuable have been James Arnt Aune, "Lincoln and the American Sublime," *Communication Reports* (winter 1988), 70–75, and Edwin Black, "The Ultimate Voice of Lincoln," *Rhetoric and Public Affairs* 3, no. 1 (2000), 49–57.

Far more books and articles have been written about Lincoln as a writer than as a speaker. Two older gems are Roy P. Basler, *A Touchstone for Greatness: Essays, Addresses, and Occasional Pieces About Abraham Lincoln* (Westport, Conn.: Greenwood Press, 1973), and Paul M. Angle, "Lincoln's Power with Words," *Abraham Lincoln Association Papers* (1935), 59–87. See also James Hurt's incisive "All the Living and the Dead: Lincoln's Imagery," *American Literature* 52 (1980), 351–80, and Herbert Joseph Edwards and John Erskine Hankins, "Lincoln the Writer: The Development of His Literary Style," in *Studies in English and American Literature* (Orono, Me.: University of Maine Press, 1962).

Appraisals from contemporaries about Lincoln the public speaker are to be found tucked away in sentences about other subjects in diaries and letters. Michael Burlingame has provided Lincoln researchers and readers invaluable resources by his careful editing of the diaries and writings of Lincoln's secretaries. See *An Oral History of Abraham Lincoln: John G. Nicolay's Interviews and Essays* (Carbondale, Ill.: Southern Illinois University Press, 1996);

Inside Lincoln's White House: The Complete Civil War Diary of John Hay, edited by Michael Burlingame and John R. Turner Ettlinger (Carbondale, Ill.: Southern Illinois University Press, 1997); and William O. Stoddard, *Inside the White House in War Times: Memoirs and Reports of Lincoln's Secretary,* edited by Michael Burlingame (Lincoln: University of Nebraska Press, 2000).

Noah Brooks, correspondent for the *Sacramento Daily Union,* became a close friend of Lincoln and was probably to become his secretary in a second term. See *Lincoln Observed: Civil War Dispatches of Noah Brooks,* edited by Michael Burlingame (Baltimore: Johns Hopkins University Press, 1998). See also Noah Brooks, *Washington in Lincoln's Time,* edited by Herbert Mitgang (New York: Rinehart & Co., 1958). Lincoln's Illinois friend Sen. Orville Hickman Browning includes references to Lincoln's habits of preparing speeches in *The Diary of Orville Hickman Browning,* vol. II, edited by Theodore Calvin Pease and James G. Randall (Collections of the Illinois Historical Library, vol. XX, 1925).

For the oratory of Edward Everett, see Paul Revere Frothingham, *Edward Everett, Orator and Statesman* (Port Washington, N.Y.: Kennikat Press, 1925), and Paul A. Varg, *The Intellectual in the Turmoil of Politics* (Selinsgrove, Penn.: Susquehanna University Press, 1992).

As for individual speeches, Henry Villard wrote about Lincoln's Farewell Address at Springfield as well as his speeches from Springfield to Washington for the *New York Herald* and the Associated Press. See Henry Villard, *Memoirs of Henry Villard: Journalist and Financier, 1835–1900,* vol. I (Boston: Houghton Mifflin, 1904), and *Lincoln on the Eve of '61,* edited by Harold G. and Oswald Garrison Villard (New York: Alfred A. Knopf, 1941).

Victor Searcher's *Lincoln's Journey to Greatness: A Factual Account of the Twelve-Day Inaugural Trip* (Philadelphia: John C. Winston, 1960) is a fast-moving account of the journey from Springfield to Washington, but marred by the absence of footnotes. For a more analytical vantage point, see Daniel Elizor, "The Constitution, the Union, and the Liberties of the People," *Publius: The Journal of Federalism* 8, no. 3 (summer 1978), 141–75.

In attempting to understand the composition of the First Inaugural, one encounters William S. Seward as a fascinating figure in terms of his contributions to and assessments of Lincoln the speaker. The best biographies of Seward are Glyndon G. Van Deusen, *William Henry Seward* (New York: Oxford University Press, 1967), and John M. Taylor, *William Henry Seward: Lincoln's Right Hand* (New York: HarperCollins, 1991). Marie Hochmuth Nichols's "Lincoln's First Inaugural," in *Methods of Rhetorical Criticism: A Twentieth Century Perspective,* edited by Robert L. Scott and Bernard L.

Brock (New York: Harper & Row, 1972), is a splendid example of the contributions of rhetorical criticism.

To understand Lincoln's reply to Horace Greeley, one must appreciate the many-sided personality of Horace Greeley. The most helpful biographies for the focus of this book have been Luther Stoddard, *Horace Greeley: Printer, Editor, Crusader* (New York: G. P. Putnam's Sons, 1946), and Glyndon G. Van Deusen, *Horace Greeley: Nineteenth-Century Crusader* (Philadelphia: University of Pennsylvania Press, 1953). See also Harlan Hoyt Horner, *Lincoln and Greeley* (Urbana: University of Illinois Press, 1953).

The Meditation on the Divine Will focuses the large subject of Lincoln's deepening religious interests in the Civil War. Richard Carwardine argues persuasively for the central role of evangelical Protestantism in the years leading up to Lincoln's presidency in *Evangelicals and Politics in Antebellum America* (New Haven: Yale University Press, 1993). For other angles of vision on this same territory, see the fine collection of essays in *Religion and the American Civil War,* edited by Randall M. Miller, Harry S. Stout, and Charles Reagan Wilson (New York: Oxford University Press, 1998). For studies of Lincoln's religion, especially as it relates to his politics, see two recent books: Stewart Lance Winger, *Lincoln, Religion, and Romantic Cultural Politics* (DeKalb: Northern Illinois University Press, 2002), and Joseph R. Fornieri, *Abraham Lincoln's Political Faith* (DeKalb: Northern Illinois University Press, 2003).

Lincoln's annual message to Congress in December 1862 is admirably analyzed by David Zarefsky in "Lincoln's 1862 Annual Message: A Paradigm of Rhetorical Leadership," *Rhetoric and Public Affairs* 3, no. 1, 5–15.

The Gettysburg Address has attracted the most attention of any of Lincoln's speeches. Garry Wills, *Lincoln at Gettysburg: The Words That Remade America* (New York: Simon & Schuster, 1992), is an intriguing and powerful analysis set within a larger convergence of ideas. Louis A. Warren offered an able treatment in *Lincoln's Gettysburg Declaration: "A New Birth of Freedom"* (Fort Wayne, Ind.: Lincoln National Life Foundation, 1964). See also Frank L. Klement, *The Gettysburg Soldiers' Cemetery and Lincoln's Address* (Shippensburg, Penn.: White Maine Publishing, 1993).

For the Second Inaugural Address, another admirable example of the approach of speech communication studies is Amy R. Schlegel, "Anatomy of a Masterpiece: A Close Textual Analysis of Abraham Lincoln's Second Inaugural Address," *Communication Studies* 42, no. 2 (summer 1991), 155–71. James Tackach, in *Lincoln's Moral Vision: The Second Inaugural Address* (Jackson: University of Mississippi Press, 2002), analyzes the address thematically. Also see Ronald C. White, Jr., *Lincoln's Greatest Speech: The Second Inaugural* (New York: Simon & Schuster, 2002).

ACKNOWLEDGMENTS

Abraham Lincoln, upon returning to Illinois in 1849 from a single term in Congress, where he had taken an unpopular stand against a popular war with Mexico, was grateful to those friends who had stood by him. He wrote to his friend from southern Illinois Joseph Gillespie, and observed that "the better part of life is friendship."

In writing on Abraham Lincoln I have been introduced to an ever widening circle of friends of Mr. Lincoln who have become my friends. That so many persons would gather in Washington and Gettysburg, Galesburg and Redlands to talk and ask questions about Lincoln has been an increasingly enriching experience. More than endnotes can ever say, I have benefited from the wisdom of countless people who have been thinking about all things Lincoln for a much longer time than I have.

I begin by acknowledging my gratitude to libraries. I am grateful to my home base, the Huntington Library, Art Collections, and Botanical Gardens. The staff, and a seasonal coming and going of "readers," have fashioned a space and ethos for research and writing that is unparalleled in my experience. I thank Steven Koblik, president; Robert C. Ritchie, W. M. Keck director of research; David S. Zeidberg, Avery director of the library; and John Rhodehamel, Norris Foundation curator, American historical manuscripts. My special thanks go to the people who helped me on a regular basis: Romaine Ahlstrom, head of readers' services; Jill Cogan, reference librarian; Christopher J. S. Adde, stacks supervisor; and Susie Krasnoo and Mona Noureldin, library assistants. I also thank Barbara Quinn, library associate, and Bert Rinderle, library assistant, for their regular helpfulness in copying and interlibrary loan.

At the Library of Congress I have called upon John Sellers, historical specialist for the Civil War and Reconstruction, whose wide knowledge of Lincoln, the Civil War, and the resources of the Library of Congress has been invaluable. I also wish to thank Clark Evans, director, Rare Book Division; Mary Ison, head of the Photography and Prints Division; and Maria Nugent, head of the Book and Paper Treatment Section.

The Abraham Lincoln Presidential Library (formerly the Illinois State

Historical Library), in Springfield, Illinois, both people and collections, was important at various seasons in my research and writing. Tom Schwartz, Illinois state historian, has become a friend whose generosity in sharing both insights and hospitality is unbounded. Kim Bauer, director of the Henry Horner Lincoln Collection, has always been ready to offer his expertise and assistance. I thank Daniel W. Stowell, director and editor of the Lincoln Legal Papers, and now the director and editor of the new Abraham Lincoln Presidential Papers project, for his encouragement of my writing and his wisdom about what goes into the careful editing of texts. I also thank Cheryl Schnirring of the Manuscripts Division.

I wish to thank Mary Jo Kline, curator of the Brown University Libraries; John Heiser, at the library of the National Military Park at Gettysburg; Lonnie Bunch, president of the Chicago Historical Society; and Don McCue, curator of the Lincoln Shrine, Redlands, California.

The research and writing of this book began during a sabbatical granted by San Francisco Theological Seminary in the spring semester of 2002. I want to thank interim president James G. Emerson, Jr., president Philip Butin, dean Jana Childers, vice-president David Tomlinson, and the faculty and trustees of the seminary for their encouragement and support throughout the writing of the book.

In the process of writing this book I received invitations that allowed me to receive helpful responses to chapters in progress. I accepted an invitation from Kent Gramm to deliver a version of Lincoln's letter to the Springfield rally at the Seminary Ridge Foundation conference in Gettysburg on November 1, 2003. I offered a different version of this same letter for the Lincoln Fellowship of Pennsylvania at their luncheon in Gettysburg on November 19, 2003, the 140th anniversary of Lincoln's Gettysburg Address. I spoke on Lincoln's private Meditation on the Divine Will at the National Presbyterian Church in Washington, D.C., on January 11, 2004. Finally, I thank Tom Schwartz and the Abraham Lincoln Association for the invitation to present a lecture on Lincoln's letter to James Conkling in Decatur, Illinois, on April 29, 2004.

I want to thank a cadre of old and new friends who generously read the entire manuscript. Jack Rogers, professor of theology at San Francisco Theological Seminary, has been my first reader, and rereader. His encouragement and insight over many Huntington lunches are deeply appreciated. Paul Zall, a Huntington colleague whose interest in my work is unflagging, offered wise counsel, especially about the literary and rhetorical side of Lincoln, from his great reservoir of knowledge of Lincoln on Lincoln.

Thomas W. Schwartz, state historian of Illinois, offered his knowledge of Lincoln in a careful reading of the text. Daniel W. Howe, historian at UCLA and Oxford, and Avery fellow at the Huntington, asked important questions that helped strengthen the manuscript. Harold Holzer, vice president for communications and marketing at the New York Metropolitan Museum of Art, and co-chair of the Abraham Lincoln Bicentennial Commission, whose long list of Lincoln books is known throughout the Lincoln community, helped me place Lincoln's rhetoric on a wider canvas. Peter Baugher, lawyer and new Lincoln friend, made many helpful suggestions that stimulated my rethinking a number of themes. Daniel W. Stowell, director and editor of the Papers of Abraham Lincoln, read the full manuscript through the eyes of his special understanding of texts. Stowell also generously offered the expertise of the staff of the Papers of Abraham Lincoln in Springfield to transcribe and proof nine of the appendices. I wish to thank Kelley Boston, Susan Krause, John A. Lupton, Stacy Pratt McDermott, Christopher A. Schnell, and Dennis E. Suttles for their thorough work.

Finally, Jim McPherson, in the semester of his retirement from Princeton, generously found time to give my efforts his close reading based on his unparalleled understanding of the Civil War.

I have been assisted by three research assistants. Jan Opdyke helped with newspapers in the earliest stages of the work. Annie Russell, Ph.D. candidate at the Graduate Theological Union in Berkeley, brought her great skills to assist both in research and as a reader. She has been a conversation partner throughout.

Karen Needles, a history teacher, has assisted me in countless searches at the Library of Congress and the National Archives. Her enthusiasm for history, her digital camera, and her knowledge of technology allowed us to work together in cyberspace as well as in person.

I am pleased to have entered into partnership with many talented people at Random House. I wish to thank Katie Hall, who acquired the book in September 2002. She understood the concept and narrative. I express thanks to Elena Schneider, who worked with me at the beginning stages of writing. I thank Julia Cheiffitz, who steadfastly helped to keep the project on time and answered innumerable questions. I am grateful to Tom Perry, director of publicity, a Civil War buff, who was eager to offer the resources of his staff to promote the book. I also thank Steve Messina, Pei Loi Koay, Chuck Antony, and Gretchen Achilles.

Especially do I thank my editor at Random House, David Ebershoff. David is a gifted and award-winning writer whose counsel on the structure and writing of this book was always perceptive. I have benefited from my collaboration with David, whether across cyberspace or in timely meetings in New York and Pasadena.

Mary Evans, my literary agent, who championed the concept for this book from the beginning, worked with me on the proposal and read drafts at various stages. Mary's upbeat affirmation, her belief in my abilities, and her energy are deeply appreciated.

Finally, I thank my wife, Cynthia. As an associate dean at the University of Southern California, her life and career are very full without Mr. Lincoln entering our conversation on a regular basis. She is also a talented photographer. Cynthia is a voracious reader who always managed to ask helpful questions and offer thoughtful insights for a book aimed at the thoughtful general reader. Most of all I thank her for her support and love.

INDEX

Page numbers in *italics* refer to illustrations and maps.

ABOUT THE AUTHOR

RONALD C. WHITE, JR., is the author or editor of seven books, most recently *Lincoln's Greatest Speech,* which was a *Washington Post* bestseller, a *San Francisco Chronicle* bestseller, and a *New York Times* Notable Book. White earned his Ph.D. at Princeton and has taught at UCLA, Princeton Theological Seminary, Whitworth College, and Colorado College. He is currently Professor of American Intellectual and Religious History at San Francisco Theological Seminary and a Fellow at the Huntington Library in San Marino, California. He has lectured on Lincoln's eloquence at the White House, the Library of Congress, and Gettysburg. He lives with his wife, Cynthia, in La Cañada, California.

ABOUT THE TYPE

This book was set in Garamond, a typeface originally designed by the Parisian typecutter Claude Garamond (1480–1561). This version of Garamond was modeled on a 1592 specimen sheet from the Egenolff-Berner foundry, which was produced from type assumed to have been brought to Frankfurt by the punchcutter Jacques Sabon.

Claude Garamond's distinguished romans and italics first appeared in *Opera Ciceronis* in 1543–44. The Garamond types are clear, open, and elegant.